Books are to be returned on or before
the last date below.

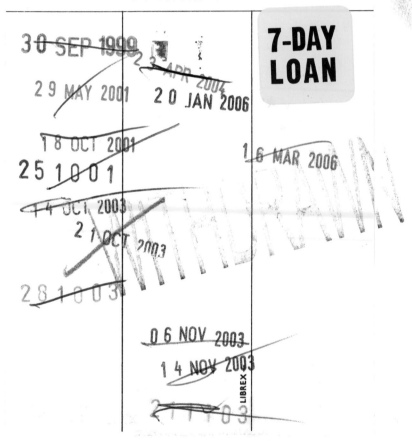

FIFA and the Contest for World Football

Who Rules the Peoples' Game?

JOHN SUGDEN AND ALAN TOMLINSON

Polity Press

First published in 1998 by Polity Press in association
with Blackwell Publishers Ltd.

Editorial office:
Polity Press
65 Bridge Street
Cambridge CB2 1UR, UK

Marketing and production:
Blackwell Publishers Ltd
108 Cowley Road
Oxford OX4 1JF, UK

Published in the USA by
Blackwell Publishers Inc.
Commerce Place
350 Main Street
Malden, MA 02148, USA

A CIP catalogue record for this book is available from the British Library.

Library of Congress Cataloging-in-Publication Data

Sugden, John.
    FIFA and the contest for world football : who rules the peoples'
game? / John Sugden and Alan Tomlinson.
      p. cm.
    Includes bibliographical references and index.
    ISBN 0–7456–1660–7 (hb : alk. paper). — ISBN 0–7456–1661–5 (pbk)
    1. Fédération internationale de football association. 2. Soccer—
Social aspects.   3. Soccer—Political aspects. I. Tomlinson,
Alan. II. Fédération internationale de football association.
III. Title.
GV943.9.S64S84   1998
796.334'66—dc21   97–51453
                                                               CIP

Typeset in 10 on 12 pt Palatino
by Ace Filmsetting Ltd, Frome, Somerset
Printed in Great Britain by T. J. International Ltd.
This book is printed on acid-free paper.

Contents

Preface

This book is the product of a sustained period of collaborative and complementary work by the authors on the politics and sociology of sport. Published in 1986, *Off the Ball: the football World Cup* – a collection of essays on world football edited by Tomlinson and Whannel and published by Pluto Press – contained the first academic assessment of FIFA's contribution to the development of world football. That collection, and responses to it, suggested that the politics of world football was under-researched and warranted further investigation. In 1990 both authors attended the International Sociological Association's World Congress in Madrid. This event coincided with the football World Cup Finals in Italy. We were intrigued to observe that many delegates from all corners of the world were as interested in events unfolding in stadia throughout Italy as they were with conference proceedings in Spain. This reinforced our view that football was a subject which could be taken seriously in an academic setting, and during the Madrid event we outlined our proposal for an edited collection of essays on football cultures and national identity which, under the title *Hosts and Champions: soccer cultures, national identities and the USA World Cup*, was published by Arena/Ashgate in 1994.

Inspired by the interest which this book generated we determined to undertake a full-scale investigation of the politics of world football. The most appropriate organizing focus for such a study was the sport's world governing body FIFA – as the following pages will reveal, a highly complex global organization. The fulfilment of this project demanded a correspondingly adventurous research strategy and investigative trail which many, including prominent research agencies, thought to be unrealistic if not impossible. Fortunately, our employers in the Universities of Brighton and Ulster showed more faith and were able to offer a measure of support in both time and resources which, supplemented by our personal investments, made the study possible. On a 'shoe-string' budget, this trail has taken us from 'Brechin to Buenos Aires', that is, from our base in the UK to North and South America, mainland and Eastern Europe, southern Africa and North Africa, the Middle East, the Far East and South-East Asia.

En route, we have amassed a significant collection of archive materials and documents, including transcripts from interviews with more than seventy of the most prominent figures in the politics of world football. Our major language for the research we have conducted has been English. Though not the only official language of FIFA, it is the primary language in which the politics of world football are conducted. The grammar of some of our interviewees is therefore distinctive and at times eccentric. It has been decided to report responses verbatim, to preserve the immediacy and the authentic idiosyncrasies of the original exchanges, but with some cuts of repetitious phrases. All sources are indicated in footnotes, though anonymity has been guaranteed whenever requested. In the footnotes, published references are cited in abbreviated form. The full details of the reference appear in the Bibliography at the end of the book.

This book is investigative and interpretative. As such we are aware that some commentators may not share our observations and conclusions. We encourage informed scepticism, and we hope that this study challenges critics and others to engage in their own research and increase the body of knowledge in this fascinating area.

John Sugden and Alan Tomlinson
Brighton, September 1997

Acknowledgements

For support which made fieldwork and writing up possible we would like to thank: the University of Ulster for funding trips to South Africa and Canada; the University of Brighton's research support fund for funding trips to Egypt, France and the USA; the University of Brighton's Chelsea School for funding fieldwork in South Africa, the USA and mainland and Eastern Europe; the British Council for fares to Argentina, Uruguay and Brazil; the University of Buenos Aires for accommodation and hospitality; and the Japan Society for the Sociology of Sport for travel costs to Malaysia, Singapore and Japan.

Many individuals and agencies have helped in this study, and we are grateful for all their inputs. We would like to give special thanks to: Andrew Jennings and Vyv Simson for stimulation and encouragement throughout the project; Nick Lord, Yorkshire TV for generously donating his collection of documents and materials on world football; the English FA, particularly Rose-Marie Breitenstein for invaluable access to Sir Stanley Rous's papers and David Barber for the use of the FA library; Ted van Leeuwen of Votbal International for early directions; FIFA and the continental confederations for supportive responses to our numerous enquiries. We are grateful to our copy editor, Helen Rappaport, for her professional and scholarly diligence.

Finally, we would like to thank our families and friends for their support and forbearance over the period of the project. Most of all, thanks to Chris, Alex and Jack Sugden; to Rowan and Alys Tomlinson; and to Yvonne Bishop.

The authors and publisher gratefully acknowledge the following:

E. Maradas for an extract from 'The Long Road to South Africa', from *African Soccer* magazine (January/February 1996), reprinted by permission of the publisher; Bryon Butler and Stanley Rous for extracts from 'Sir Stanley Rous', reproduced by kind permission of the BBC, Bryon Butler and Rose-Marie Breitenstein; FIFA Communications Department, Zurich, Switzerland for permission to use FIFA material; J. Burns and P. Harverson for 'Rivals Jostle for FIFA Presidency', *Financial Times* (6 June 1997), reprinted by permission of *Financial Times*; T. Weir for an extract from 'Column' in *USA TODAY* (17 December 1993), reproduced by permission of *Los Angeles Times* Syndication International; Erskine McCullough of Agence France-Presse for permission to be cited in notes 27 and 71, chapter 7; *The Independent*, for an extract from 'A Game of Two Bureaucracies' (4 February 1997), by permission of Newspaper Publishing Plc; Professor James Riordan for an extract from 'Sport and Nationalism in the CCCP: Socialist Internationalism Versus a Strong Russian State' (unpublished paper presented at the BSA Annual Conference, 1996) reprinted by kind permission of the author; TEAM, Lucerne, Switzerland for table 4.1, 'Worldwide live TV coverage of the UEFA Champions League', reprinted with permission; Guido Tognoni for permission to use extracts from an interview with the authors in Zurich, Switzerland, 21 May 1996.

Every effort has been made to trace all copyright holders whose material is included in this book, but if any have been inadvertently overlooked, the publishers will be pleased to make the necessary arrangement at the first opportunity.

1

Introduction: FIFA and the contest for world football – an interpretive and conceptual framework

The most powerful men in the world never walk alone. So it was when Dr João Havelange, FIFA president, swept through the lobby of Cairo's elite Marriot hotel on the banks of the Nile. Flanked by body guards and pulling in his wake an entourage of factotums, courtiers and assorted FIFA bureaucrats, belying his eighty-one years he strode athletically towards the hotel exit. In town to open the Under-17 World Championship Finals and to chair one of the few remaining FIFA Executive Committee meetings before stepping down after twenty-four years at FIFA's helm, Havelange, in his long-standing role as IOC member, would, within a few days, be jetting back to Switzerland to take part in the critical vote that was to award the Greek city of Athens the 2004 summer Olympic Games.

FIFA's executive brings together the heads of FIFA's worldwide family – the leading figures in the global football industry, a business estimated to have grown to be worth more than $250 billion dollars a year during Havelange's reign. As he took the chair in the main committee room of Cairo's modern exhibition centre, within the gaze of Havelange's piercing, steel-blue eyes were men such as Sepp Blatter, FIFA general secretary, Havelange's one-time apprentice, long-standing confidant and, now, perhaps, rival; Mong Joon Chung of South Korea, member of parliament and head of Hyundai heavy industries, a man who sees within his football mission a greater prize – the unification of Korea, perhaps under his own political stewardship; Cameroonian, Issa Hayatou, boss of the African Confederation and with more than fifty FIFA congress votes within his gift, one of the most powerful players at the table; Abdulah-al-dabal, Saudi Arabian football supremo, bringing with him the power and influence of the oil-rich Gulf States; David Will, the little-known Scottish lawyer, but one of the Committee's longest standing and most influential members; flamboyant entrepreneur Chuck Blazer, general secretary of the North and Central American Confederation, and controversial successor to deceased veteran executive member and senior FIFA vice president, Mexican media baron, Guillermo Cañedo; Viacheslav Koloskov, one-time head of the mighty Soviet Football Federation and now the representative of Russia; Julio Grondona, arbiter of South American interests, defender of Argentinian football during that country's recently turbulent political history and one of those Havelange has been said to favour as his successor; New Zealander and expatriate Scot, Charlie Dempsey CBE, tireless champion of football in the peripheral South Pacific region.

Perhaps Havelange's gaze rested longest on the man who would be king, his bitter rival, the burly transportation businessman from Sweden, Lennart Johansson, current UEFA president and front-runner to succeed to the FIFA presidency when Havelange steps down in June 1998. What is the nature of the organization over which Johansson seeks to preside and what motives drive such ambitions? What is the cultural and political significance of football in the regions which the men sitting around this table represent? How, through understanding the development of FIFA, can we come to know more of global change in the twentieth century? These are the questions at the core of this book.

In the year 2004 FIFA, the organization which is charged with the task of administering the game of professional football world-wide, will be 100 years old. During its existence, this body has overseen a massive, global expansion in the popularity of a sport which the historian James Walvin, with simplicity and powerful accuracy, labelled in 1975 as 'the people's game'.[1] When it was established in 1904, FIFA had only seven members, all of them European. By the time the World Cup Finals took place in the USA in 1994, it could boast 170 members from all corners of the globe and it was anticipated that before the next millennium this figure would be in excess of 200 countries.

\ The FIFA story is more than a tale of successful sporting development, however. While the increase from seven to 200 member countries signifies the game's growing global appeal, more significantly international football is now influenced by the constant fluctuations in international relations, the growth of nations and nationalism, and the emergence of trans-national organizations through which powerful individuals seek to manage the pace and direction of global, economic, political and cultural development. For this reason, the book will also discuss the political and economic dimensions of world football by presenting a critical overview of the workings of FIFA, since in many respects the story of the organization's rise to prominence can be read as a commentary on the international dynamics of the twentieth century itself.

This chapter sets out to summarize and describe in the context of the FIFA story, some of the key theoretical arguments which are the basis for the interpretations and analyses presented throughout the book as a whole. The approach adopted embraces several disciplines, in that any adequate overview of world football, must – in addressing questions of political economy and cultural analysis – be both social historical and sociological in its approach. It must also take account of the dimensions of power employed by those who run the game, and the forms of expression to which these ambitions give rise. To this end the narrative incorporates both personal observation by those involved in the game of football, together with documentary analysis, archive searches and in-depth interviews with some of the most experienced and influential personnel within FIFA and other football-related organizations. MacAloon has argued convincingly for the importance of fieldwork methods – 'face-to-face observation and extended "listening-in"' – for the discovery of what the world is really like.[2] This study employs such methods, in an awareness too of the 'perils' of ethnography and its unpredictability.[3] The study is also framed as an investigative enquiry, in which the road to understanding and truth involves probing beyond the official and formal surface of social phenomena.[4] An approach is therefore offered for the development of a grounded and contextualized interpretation of global football politics and cultures, in which the conditions of production, the discourses and formal properties of, and the modes of interpretation of, the game are scrutinized from a world perspective.[5] The book is not conceived as a comprehensive overview and summary of the growth of football world-wide. Such a task has already been accomplished, in world terms, by Murray, and in South American continental terms by Mason,[6] though the comprehensive sweep of such works has been achieved, in part, at the expense of any binding focusing theme, and in the absence of any overall theory. It is the organizational base of world football development, as manifest in FIFA's contribution, and the theoretical debate about how best to make sense of this, that binds together and coheres the relatively self-contained themes and analyses covered within this book.

Football is the world's most popular game. This popularity goes beyond a mere fondness for the thing itself – like having a favourite rock band or preferred variety of wine. Football is peerless in its capacity to generate passionate and rooted feelings of local and national pride or shame. In the latter part of the century, there are few, if any, other social gathering points like football.\People congregate around football, either interpersonally, at the game itself or related events, or intellectually, through the media and other forms of popular communication, to make strong public declarations of who they are, what groups they identify with, what they stand for and who and what they stand against.\Football is an emotive form of popular theatre which has proven to be open to the expression of distinct sets of values and ideologies, transcending any intrinsic meaning which the game itself has. Whether we like it or not, in this regard, football can be conceived of as a cultural milieu for the working up of quasi-political formulations. 'Quasi-political' refers to the way in which clusters of ideas about communities of power inform and are informed by relationships of domination and oppression in the wider society and which, under certain circumstances, can lead to more formal expression of political will.

\ Football, because it means so much to so many people, is also a vehicle for the acquisition of power and the expression of status in the international community. Those who control international football exert an authority over the hopes and passions of billions of people. They share top billing in the theatre of the great, being fêted by presidents, monarchs and the leaders of global industry.\Moreover, the fact that the modern game is at the centre of a massive global industry introduces another and equally significant economic dimension to any analysis of the politics of world football. Yet there has been little scrutiny of the game's global economy. Where there are riches on this scale, it is inevitable that questions concerning who rules international football will lead the inquisitive into a world of power, politics, deal-making and corruption. For the analysis presented in this study, power – in the terms defined above – nationalism and money are the three engines of FIFA's socio-political persona. FIFA's socio-political character is both extremely complex and fluid, and can be discerned on several levels: the intra-organizational, involving the relations between national football associations, continental confederations and the FIFA hierarchy; the inter-

4

organizational, in which FIFA personnel interact with representatives of other sports bodies such as the International Olympic Committee, financial partners in the sports industry, and political bodies such as the European Commission; the interpersonal, manifest in struggles for power within FIFA; and the level of world politics and international relations.

It would be possible, but inappropriate and potentially misleading, to treat these different levels as analytically distinct. For one of the intriguing features of FIFA is its capacity to impact on a number of coterminous levels, to represent the defining features of its time in all of the spheres of the commercial, the political, the organizational and the cultural. Although the balance of consideration of these levels will vary from chapter to chapter, the guiding principle has been to achieve an integrated analysis of how FIFA has operated according to particular principles, strategies, pragmatics and imperatives, across all of the levels.

■ FIFA's Status and its Place in the World Order

As a way into the question of who rules the peoples' game and how, it is useful to view FIFA as a particular example of the growth in number and scope of INGOs (International Non-Government Organizations). These are bodies which have global remits but which are not accountable to any particular national government or governments.[7] Examples of INGOs would include environmental pressure groups, such as Greenpeace or Friends of the Earth, religious forums, such as the CWR (Council of World Religions), academic bodies, like the ISA (International Sociological Association) and world sport governing bodies, such as the ICC (International Cricket Conference) or the IOC (International Olympic Committee). INGOs can be contrasted with IGOS (International Government Organizations) which likewise are regional and or global in scope, but which, as exemplified by the United Nations or the European Union, are controlled via the vested authority of their constituent member nation-states. We attribute to FIFA what Waters observes of INGOs in general:

> INGOs may be regarded as more important than IGOs because they outflank nation states and threaten borders. They are unruly because complexity defies command and their capacity to link diverse people in relation to common causes and interests undermines the saliency of the state.[8]

Furthermore, because of FIFA's considerable economic leverage, it is useful to blend the notion of the INGO with that of the OFC (Offshore Financial Centre) which has been defined as 'a centre that hosts financial activities that are separated from major regulating units (states) by geography and / or by legislation'.[9] FIFA's political and fiscal autonomy (and unaccountability) is underlined by the location of FIFA headquarters in Switzerland, the international centre of OFC dealing. Sklair has outlined the major levels of impact of transnational practices: the economic, the political, and the cultural-ideological.[10] The impact of FIFA, as a strongly established INGO with an OFC base, can be distinguished at all of these levels.

In 1996, the FIFA 'family' – as those at its centre consistently refer to FIFA – consisted of 191 full-member nations, two countries with provisional status and eight associate members. So long as it took part in a FIFA-sponsored competition, each full member was entitled to vote at FIFA's congresses. Regardless of size, longevity of membership or playing status, one member's vote is equal to that of every other FIFA member. For instance, Brazil's or Germany's votes carry no more weight than those from Mali or Armenia. This has had great significance in the internal politics of FIFA.

The interesting situation of the confederations warrants clarification. International football is organized within the embrace of six regional confederations. These are:

- UEFA: Union des Associations Européennes de Football – formed 1954; in 1996 fifty members.
- CONMEBOL: Confederación Sudamericana de Fútbol – formed 1916; in 1996 ten members.
- CONCACAF: Confederación Norte-/Centroamericana y del Caribe de Fútbol – formed 1961; in 1996 thirty members.
- CAF: Confédération Africaine de Football – formed 1957; in 1996 fifty-one members.
- AFC: Asian Football Confederation formed 1954; in 1996 forty-two members.
- OFC: Oceania Football Confederation – formed 1966; in 1996 ten members.[11]

The dynamics of power involved in the relations between FIFA and the confederations have shaped the face of world football for most of the century. One of the most heated debates in FIFA's history climaxed in 1995, over UEFA's suggestion (in the *Visions* proposals discussing reform of the administration of the game, and of World Cup finances) (see Appendix), that more authority for the running of the game globally should be ceded from FIFA to the confederations. The languages of the confederations' titles demonstrate the early Spanish, French and English influences across world football's organizational origins, and examination of the tensions between these dominant early influences and emergent powers in the world game is a recurrent focus in the book.

At one level, the outer circle of FIFA can be represented, in terms of organizational power, as a particularly advanced case of progressive global bureaucratization and rationalization, albeit with a democratic facade. At another, deeper level, FIFA's inner circle is best viewed as an hierarchical organization, so steeped in oligarchic and corporate patronage, that its organizational coherence has bordered on a form of total power often conveyed in European social thought as 'oriental despotism'.[12] The juxtaposition of these two articulations of power has made a major contribution to a crisis growing within the heart of FIFA which threatens to undermine the organization's global mission.

In the 1990s the crisis borne of the clash between an accountable, democratic form of organization, and one of oligarchic control, was personified in the power struggle taking place between the incumbent FIFA President and his counterpart at the helm of UEFA, the Swede, Lennart Johansson. Such interpersonal and intra-institutional political dimensions of FIFA only make sense in the broader and historically located context of world economic and political relations. FIFA has overseen a massive expansion in the competitive structure of international football. FIFA claims this expansion, in its own internal publication celebrating its ninetieth anniversary *90 Years of FIFA*, not only in terms of sports development, but also in the language of universalism and international diplomacy:

> football embraces such a gigantic family, creating spontaneous human bonds and reconciling peoples all around the globe. In the words of FIFA's President, Dr João Havelange: 'Wherever people can find an outlet for communication and – especially – play, you will always find peace and harmony.'[13]

Internationalism then, through the expansion of the FIFA family and the promotion of harmony among nations and power blocs, is fundamental to FIFA's sense of mission. At one level, this mission can be interpreted as part of a broader twentieth-century project to move towards a world order which, in the wake of two world wars, was more co-ordinated, regulated and 'civilized'. [14] And in this respect

FIFA can be revealed as a body with supra-national or modernist aspirations.

The missions of more formally politically constituted internationalist organizations, such as the League of Nations between the two world wars, and the United Nations since, have been undone by the pervasive persistence of forms of nationalism. One of FIFA's main problems has been balancing its global ideals with the fact that international football *per se* tends to stimulate and promote parochial forms of nationalism. Sport in general, and football in particular, have proven to be significant theatres for the working-up and expression of national identity, and, in its mobilized form, nationalism. Jim Farry, chief executive of the Scottish Football Association, recognizes the central paradox of football as this capacity to create bonds between peoples of differing backgrounds, whilst fuelling potentially extremist forms of nationalist sentiment, describing this latter form of football nationalism as 'the antithesis of the dogma of the European Union'.[15] Football and sport create special socio-cultural spaces for this. High-profile sports events provide occasions at which sporting nationalism can also resonate with wider currents of national sentiment. When, four days after the funeral of Diana, Princess of Wales, the English football side played Moldova in a World Cup qualifying game at Wembley Stadium, the sense of national loss was echoed in the playing of Elton John's tribute to Diana, 'Candle in the Wind '97', in place of the national anthem. The crowd also jeered the British government's sports minister, Tony Banks, who had a few days before expressed the view that England was not really good enough to win the World Cup. Here, national loss and national restoration were fused in a reaffirmation of national identity rooted in the popular cultural forms of football and song. Two days after the Princess's death in Paris, FIFA president Havelange had been asked, at a press conference in Cairo, whether FIFA had a response to the death of Princess Diana. He answered that naturally FIFA was sympathetic, but expressed surprise that the question was raised at all, as the princess had no connection with football, and the schedules of the world game must be met and could not be affected by personal tragedies. For Havelange, the business of world football could not be interrupted for any single tragic loss. But at Wembley, the English spectators demonstrated an interconnectedness of expressions of national identity and sentiment that belied bullish notions of the separateness and autonomy of sport. Jim Farry, too, failed initially to recognize these realities when planning to stage Scotland's World Cup tie on the afternoon of the day of the Princess's funeral. A tidal wave of public opinion and popular disapproval forced him to back d and move the Scotland game to the Sunday after the funeral. Neve-theless, as John Tomlinson has argued, 'for most people, most of the time, their national identity is not at the forefront of their lived experience'.[16] We do not routinely spend time wondering or worrying about what nation we belong to, unless there is widely felt loss, or a perceived threat to that identity, such as in times of war (international or civil). It is during such times of jingoistic political rhetoric, emblematic mass rallies and national flag-waving that erstwhile passive notions of national identity become mobilized as nationalism.

International football is not war,[17] but because football has been so implicated in the processes through which modern nation-states have been made and proclaimed, international football can act as a surrogate theatre for the working-up of 'passionate nationalism'.[18] An international football match involving 'our' team, intrudes into our daily routine, reminding us of with whom we stand with regard to our fellow nationals, and whom we stand against in the international sphere. Sometimes, simply taking part in FIFA competitions can create the conditions for exaggerated displays of nationalism which have meaning beyond the games themselves, and which, under certain circumstances, are fed by and can feed into more central and turbulent currents of international relations. For instance, in one of the Asian qualifying series for the 1994 World Cup Finals, not long after two Gulf wars, Saudi Arabia found itself in a qualifying group with Iran and Iraq. Included in the same group were North and South Korea and Japan, presenting a mind-boggling series of opportunities through which ancient and contemporary national enmities could be flagged.

Other than being admitted as a member of the United Nations, membership of FIFA (and of a comparable body such as the International Olympic Committee) is the clearest signal that a country's status as a nation state has been recognized by the international community. FIFA claims that when adjudicating the sovereign status of new membership applicants it is guided by decisions already taken by the United Nations. However, this is not always the case. Take the cases of Palestine and Bosnia-Herzegovina, two countries which were given provisional membership of FIFA (and as such permission to organize and play international 'friendlies') before their official status as nation states had been formally recognized by the UN. In the 1990s the whole issue of football, nations and nationalism was thrown into stark relief by events in the Balkans and in the former republics of the Soviet Union. The evidence is convincing that, as

9

Edelman also observes,[19] new football federations have not simply grown up as a consequence of national fragmentation, but that football has been very significant in the working-up and communication of ideas of nationalism.

■ FIFA and the Legacy of Imperialism

At the heart of these and many other related issues is the role which football and FIFA have played in nation building in the post-colonial era. In many respects, until World War II, there was considerable ambiguity over precisely who ruled world football. When FIFA came into being in 1904 its seven founder members were France, Sweden, Belgium, Denmark, Switzerland, Spain and the Netherlands. England joined in 1905 (an Englishman holding the presidency from 1906 to 1918), but withdrew in 1920, affronted by the idea that other nations might not share its view on cutting off 'football relations with former Central Powers' – these being Germany and its allies.[20]

Almost twenty years before FIFA's formation, in 1886, the four 'home' associations of England, Ireland, Scotland and Wales got together to form the International Board, the remit of which was: 'to discuss and decide proposed alterations in the laws of the game and generally any matters affecting association football and its international relations'.[21] The sub-text to this was: 'Britain invented the game, gave it to the world and was going to damn well control it!' The British view was that world football was too weak to be bothered with and, outside of Europe, in most respects in the very early years of the century this was probably true. So long as this remained the case and the International Board stood, why should Britain endorse FIFA? When the English FA did join, it was to accept the proffered leadership role, motivated by its sense of superiority. As stated by the FA's delegation to an international conference in Berne in 1905:

> Therefore it is important to the F.A. and other European Associations that a properly constituted Federation should be established, and the Football Association should use its influence to regulate football on the Continent as a pure sport and give all Continental Associations the full benefit of the many years' experience of the F.A.[22]

When FIFA was formed at the beginning of the twentieth century the world's political geography was significantly different than in the century's final decade. The majority of the two hundred or so countries by then affiliated to FIFA did not exist as independent nation states when the organization was established.

The years before World War I were the watershed of imperialism through which the governance of most of the world had been carved up among a small number of European states. Chief among these was Britain, and the Union Jack flew over approximately one third of the earth's territory. It is well established that organized sport spread around the world on the coat-tails of the British Empire. It is interesting to note that, while football was a part of this global dissemination, it was relatively unique in the way that it became so firmly established in regions which were not colonized by the British.

This may seem to undermine the British claim to have invented football and 'given' it to the world. In fact, what happened was that football spread on the industrial and commercial wings of the British Empire. First in Europe and then in South America, British engineers, traders, commercial travellers, military personnel and diplomats introduced football to countries outside of the formal embrace of the Empire. Here, where the preferred team sports of upper class colonial administrators – most notably, rugby and cricket – had not become established as 'the' games to play, as they had in places like South Africa and Australia, there was social and cultural 'space' for football to develop as the national game. Beyond the 'informal empire', as Perkin refers to sport's place in British colonial and imperial history, football could flourish. This occurred in countries such as Germany, Russia, Italy, Brazil, Argentina, and Korea.

While the idea of FIFA was born in Europe, its post-imperial political persona was developed in Latin America. The Americas, north, south and central, were among the first regions to break free from direct colonial rule from Europe. In the USA there was an ambivalence towards embracing the cultural products of the former colonial master and consequently football failed to develop a strong foothold there. On the other hand, because they had not been colonized by the British, football could more easily develop as the national game in countries such as Mexico, Chile and Colombia. In football, the newly independent countries of Latin America discovered a vehicle through which to express national self-determination, firstly within the sub-continent, but eventually on a world stage.

A major step was taken in 1928 when the International Board admitted four FIFA members with equal voting powers to the four representatives of the home nations. This move was the first formal recognition by the British that 'their game' had become global property,[23] and that FIFA had a say in how it should be run. However, if FIFA were to be allowed a say in the affairs of the International Board it was considered of paramount importance that Europe and particularly Britain should have a strong voice within FIFA itself. This they achieved under the guiding hands of Arthur Drewry and Stanley Rous, who between them held the presidency of FIFA from 1955 until 1974.

Particular attention is paid to the Drewry and Rous years in chapters 2 and 6. The general point to be made here is that while they oversaw FIFA during a period of dramatic, post-imperial, national fragmentation, they failed to appreciate fully what this would mean in terms of the balance of power within world football, for, at least in part, the deep structure of FIFA was forged through the politics of post-colonialism in Latin America (see chapter 2). Similar processes were at work as imperial flags descended in Africa and in Asia after World War II. In post-colonial Africa football was adopted as a symbol of liberation, something over which to drape a new flag of self-rule (see chapter 6). In important ways, football in the Soviet Union was part of a 'mass vernacular' helping to articulate broader struggles for independence (see chapter 8). In ways largely unseen by the Europeans, for many emergent nations participation in international football, and membership of FIFA, were important political statements. As such, football has contributed to national redefinition in Eastern Europe (see chapter 8), the African continent (see chapter 6), and Korea during the period of Japanese colonization and occupation.[24]

Rous and his contemporaries revealed a lack of understanding of how rapidly colonialism was to collapse and what the implications of this were likely to be for what they considered to be their game. In FIFA's regional committee structure, countries which were otherwise politically invisible, discovered a political platform for focusing and asserting often newly acquired independence and national identities. However, in considering the reform of FIFA from the mid-1970s onwards, while there was a degree of 'push' from these new national and regional governing bodies, in equal measure there was the 'pull' of those with vested interests in diminishing European influence – that is, the South Americans – and it was a combination of both forces which was to lead to the election of the first non-European president of FIFA in 1974. This outcome also generated a new financial infrastructure for world football, as media and cultural industries were alerted to the commercial potential of FIFA's product (particularly the World Cup), and UEFA's top-class European products (the European Champions League, and the European Football Championship) in emerging global markets.[25]

■ FIFA? For the Good of the Game?

The benefits provided and penalties incurred by FIFA's, and its powerbrokers', stakes in the contest for world football are reviewed in chapter 10, in general response to the question 'Who rules the peoples' game?' In order to provide a basis for answering this question, the study is structured around different ways of assessing FIFA's transnational practices and impacts, through its economic OFC status and its INGO profile. Chapters 2–5 analyze the historical emergence of FIFA and its leaders, the lived-out institutional nature of the organization, the importance of political, media and commercial partnerships for its growth, and the process whereby World Cup Finals tournaments have been awarded to individual national associations. Chapters 6–9, generally conceived as a means of understanding football's development world-wide through appropriate angles on the confederational structure, also proritize the theme of the (variously unfolded) collapse of empire. FIFA's impact upon regional developments, and the dynamics of power and interest involved in those developments, are considered in the context of the two main emergent confederations (in Africa and Asia), and in the special cases of the collapse of the Soviet Union, and the attempts to establish the USA as a major player on the world stage.

No simple chronological or geo-political rationale shapes the study. Rather, as in Burke's application of the method of the French historian, Marc Bloch – 'his aim was not to jump millennia but to work his way back, step by step, a century or two'[26] – the study frequently moves backwards and forwards between the more modern and the distant in FIFA's history, and lights upon intervening moments and examples for the purposes of comparative understanding. This allows the distinctiveness of the most modern to be understood in terms of the seismic cultural and political changes characteristic of its emergence; and affords the possibility of assessing the contributions and interventions of key agents. As appropriate, further major issues of social and cultural theory also inform the analysis: for instance, issues of agency and structure in chapter 2; theories of liberalization and corruption in chapter 6; globalization theory in chapter 9; corporatist theory in chapter 7; theories of nationalism and *ressentiment* in chapter 8. An integrated application of these within the body of the study has been preferred to an overview of concepts and theories in introductory or appended form.

These approaches mean that, rather than trying to locate one individual or a single development in a self-contained analysis and chapter, such prevailing themes or topics are covered, in complementary ways, throughout the book. To the reader of the whole study, or the discerning user of the index, this offers not repetition, rather a more developed overall understanding, and reaffirmation. Nevertheless, the chapters have been written so that they can stand alone for the scholar or reader interested in the particular theme, topic or emphasis. This permits different approaches to understanding and theorizing the remarkable story of FIFA and its contribution to the politics of the popular in the modern age.

■ PART I

FIFA AND ITS EXPANDING FOOTBALL FAMILY: BACKGROUND AND CONTEXT

■ 2

FIFA, Europe and South America: foundations and contradictions in the football family

In the last quarter of the twentieth century, FIFA has not been slow to celebrate its eightieth and ninetieth birthdays with a self-confident ring of modernity. Hailing the achievements of its president, João Havelange, the organization chose to stress the direction FIFA had taken during his decade at the helm. With Havelange, FIFA has followed 'another direction, that of universality . . . the Brazilian president . . . applied methods in football which were long known in social, economic and political life'.[1] FIFA presented its current president as an uncompromising man of action, who offered a then-uncertain organization a 'necessary dynamism'. Ten years later, marking the ninetieth anniversary of the federation's formation, Havelange was again the focus of the celebratory publication from FIFA. Senior vice-president Guillermo Cañedo provided a gushing encomium to Havelange, 'a dynamic president' and 'the world's leading footballer' who has turned 'what was once a conservative football administration . . . into a dynamic sports institution'.[2]

Havelange was also hailed as 'a football magnate . . . who combines the qualities of far-sightedness and open-mindedness', and as 'an entrepreneur in body and soul' who, on assuming the presidency, 'in no time . . . transformed an administration-oriented institution into a dynamic enterprise brimming with new ideas and the will to see them through'.[3] FIFA's self-image on these anniversaries projected a cosmopolitan and confident universality. Pointing to its new,

modern headquarters located in an upmarket district of Zurich, over-
looking the lake, the organization presented itself as businesslike and
efficient: 'The administration is managed in the form of a modern
firm', claimed one 1984 statement. Former FIFA press officer Guido
Tognoni offers another view on Havelange's style:

TOGNONI: People say that he was leading FIFA like an industry – but he was
        leading FIFA like a private enterprise . . . like a proprietor.
QUESTION: As if he owned it?
TOGNONI: Yes, exactly.[4]

Who, then, really runs the body that runs the peoples' game? An
historical perspective on the leadership of FIFA and its early organizational rivals illuminates the values and the ideologies – expressed
in both institutional and individual fashion – that have shaped FIFA
and, in turn, global football culture.

■ FIFA's Founders and Figureheads

The Fédération Internationale de Football Association (FIFA) was
founded by seven European footballing nations in 1904. In its early
years the organization expanded gradually, but unevenly and
amidst many tensions. An arrogant British isolationism, and the
British associations' dominance of the International Football
Association Board, the rule-making body, meant that the four British associations had a tempestuous relationship with the fledgling
world body. This incorporated disputes over contact with Germany
and its allies after World War I, controversies over the nature of
amateurism and FIFA's admission of the Football Association of the
Irish Free State in 1923. The outcome of this was that the British associations, slow to join FIFA in the first place, left FIFA in 1928, rejoin-
ing only in the years after World War II.[5] The British experience was
not unique. The Bohemian Football Association was accepted into
FIFA in 1907, but expelled the following year. For a while, an international union of amateur football associations also contested FIFA's
authority, staging a European Championship in 1911,[6] in which Bo-
hemia won against England. Throughout this tempestous period of
its formation, though, FIFA was dominated by the European found-
ers.

    A list of FIFA's presidents shows this European dominance, prior
to 1974:

Robert Guérin	France	1904–6
Daniel Woolfall	England	1906–18
Jules Rimet	France	1921–54
Rodolfe Seeldrayers	Belgium	1954–5
Arthur Drewry	England	1956–61
Sir Stanley Rous	England	1961–74
Dr João Havelange	Brazil	1974–98

List compiled by Alan Tomlinson

Guérin, an engineer and newspaper editor, was succeeded by Woolfall, an English civil servant from Blackburn, steeped in Blackburn Rovers' domination of the English cup in the 1880s. When FIFA emerged in the 1920s as the dominant body, it was the French lawyer Jules Rimet, a keen sportsman in his youth, who took the helm, and led the organization for virtually a third of a century. The association had twenty members when he took over, and eighty-five on his retirement. Holt links the inauguration of FIFA by the French to France's diplomatic pedigree.[7] In truth, this pedigree was as much a consequence of the intransigence, insularity and parochialism of the British. But the French stepped into the breach again when, after World War I, Rimet took on the position of president. Rimet viewed FIFA from the position of the patrician head of the family, cautious and traditional, but, as Rous recalled, clever in committee:

> He was conservative by nature wanting to preserve the 'family' of football from worrying change. Of a committee too full of elderly and inert members he commented once to me, 'The "dead" committee man has his use. He prevents unnecessary change.'[8]

Rous thought it essential to divide an expanding FIFA into Confederations, as a way to avoid the organization becoming a 'vast central bureaucracy' based on and in Europe and which would be out of touch with Asia and the Americas. Rimet was reluctant to embrace such radical change, and argued for the preservation of the FIFA 'family' as a unit, objecting that 'decentralisation will destroy FIFA, only direct membership will retain FIFA as one family'.[9] At the FIFA Congress in Rio in 1950 Rimet's opening address prioritized the 'finest human qualities' which football should impart: discipline required for the achievement of the common goal; loyalty to the spirit of the game; moderation in competition and sporting rivalry; and solidarity in clubs and matches. Rimet proposed that the aim of FIFA should be 'to transfer these idealistic qualities of the game to our everyday life', and claimed that the first meeting of the 'conclave of world football . . . held on South American soil' repre-

19

sented 'the perfect unity that holds us together, the spiritual community to which we all adhere with one heart and one will'. Since FIFA's 1948 Congress, he declared:

> world unity of football, the essential goal of FIFA, has been an accomplished fact: unity both moral and material . . . These results are not a matter of chance; they are the pursuit of voluntary action resolutely pursued, the consequence of the magnificent enthusiasm displayed by an elite of directing minds in all the national Associations, of the work, often obscure but always persistent, of the devoted moving spirits of large and small clubs, of the referees who put up with abuse because they have faith, and finally of the patient plodding of all, apostles and disciples, towards a common ideal that fully deserves to be held aloft.[10]

Here, Rimet espouses a messianic philosophy of commonality and unity that has been recurrently restated in FIFA's history. His metaphor of the family was to be powerfully – if differently – applied by his successors in the presidency. Under Rimet, FIFA had spread its wings world-wide. He had built up good working relations with Rous, and the British celebrated their re-entry by hosting a Great Britain vs. FIFA match at Hampden Park, Scotland, at the end of the 1947 season. A crowd of 135,000 saw the British rout this world side 6–1. The receipts of £30,000 were gifted to FIFA. Rous, of England's Football Association, negotiated important rights of membership and representation for the British associations, and those associations retained their dominant position on the International Football Association Board, the rule-making body. The Belgian lawyer Seeldrayers, who succeeded Rimet, was an all-rounder of the classic tradition: a founder member of a prominent football club, national champion in the 110 metres hurdles, hockey international, president of the Belgian Olympic Committee and the Belgian Football Association, and a keen enthusiast for British athleticism.[11] Drewry was in many respects a front-man for the active European football leaders of his time, an ideal predecessor for the Rous succession.

The initially steady, then escalating and dramatic growth of FIFA meant that in the second half of the century it assumed a truly international profile, with post-colonial developments in Africa and Asia increasing the number of eligible nations. By 1974 the politics of international sport began to work against the established Eurocentric domination of the administration of the international game. Havelange's victory against Sir Stanley Rous was a power change of seismic significance not just for soccer, but for the global political economy of sport. At the International Olympic Committee, the Anglo-Irish peer Lord Killanin was to be succeeded as president by Spain/Catalonia's Juan Antonio Samaranch in 1980, and the Italian Primo Nebiolo gained control of the International Amateur Athletic Federation, supported by Adidas's Horst Dassler, in 1981.

The saga of Havelange's ousting of Rous is revealing, and the nature of such challenges and contests in FIFA's history warrants further attention – not from any 'great man' theory of history, but from the recognition that, in Marx's classic formulation 'men make their own history, but they do not make it just as they please; they do not make it under circumstances chosen by themselves, but under circumstances directly encountered, given and transmitted from the past'.[12] The founding fathers of FIFA and their successors in the presidency, and the social and political relationships in which they have been embedded, are indicative of the globalizing forces which have driven the world game as the twentieth century progressed. It is illuminating to look at the two major figures in FIFA's history in the second half of the century, to gauge the circumstances of their history-making and the impact of their particular values and ideologies upon the development of world football. Prior to this, in order to locate these individuals within the context of the constituencies which they represented, the formal organization and mobilization of South American and European football is summarized.

■ South American Football and the Formation of CONMEBOL

The South American confederation (CONMEBOL) was founded in 1916, and in the mid-1990s had ten members. It was the 'Big Three' of South American football, though, that dominated. Uruguay and Argentina fought out early rivalries, and Brazil increased in playing strength towards the middle of the century, becoming the first nation to win the World Cup three times, and so keeeping the orginal Jules Rimet trophy on its third victory in 1970. Twenty four years later Brazil became the only side to win the championship for a fourth time. The early prominence of Uruguay, and the emergent strengths of Argentina and Brazil, ensured the central role of South America in world football politics. It was from such a base of confidence and achievement that Havelange was to emerge as a challenger to Rous.

The official date of formation of the South American federation, 1916, records its existence almost fifty years before the establishment of UEFA. Football was introduced to South America as early as the

1860s, via 'the kit bags of British sailors, the leisure pursuits of British businessmen, and the peculiarities of British expatriates'.[13] Local social elites took up the game, and it spread in popularity among the poorer classes. Organized football had been developed in South America around the River Plate, when British residents of Buenos Aires and Montevideo (honouring the birthday of Queen Victoria in 1888) launched a series of matches. Regular internationals between Argentina and Uruguay were established by the beginning of the twentieth century, and from 1905 an annual competition between the countries took place for a silver challenge cup donated by Sir Thomas Lipton, the British entrepreneur and sports enthusiast.[14] With Brazil and Chile joining in matches and tournaments, and difficult organizational splits in the administration of Argentine football, the need was recognized for some form of international, intra-continental organization. Associations and leagues had discussed by 1912 the possibility of forming a confederation of the River Plate, and FIFA's existence since 1904 (on its exclusively European base) offered a model. A Uruguayan educationalist and politician, Hector R. Gómez, argued the case for 'a powerful governing centre which would reduce the danger of the kind of breakaway currently seen in Argentina'.[15] In 1916, on the centenary of its independence from Spain, the Argentine Football Association staged a tournament involving Uruguay (the winners), Chile and Brazil. Gómez took this as an opportunity to establish the South American Football Confederation as the 'one common authority' for the sub-continent's (amateur) football associations. CONMEBOL expanded the South American Cup, and organized it in a regular (initially annual) slot, hosted by alternating host nations, and played on a league system within a specific time-frame. Paraguay, Peru and Bolivia participated in the 1920s. Wars and conflicts over amateur/professional status meant that not all teams participated regularly in the cup. Ecuador joined CONMEBOL in 1927, but did not participate until twelve years later. Colombia joined the confederation in 1940, but first competed in the cup in 1945. Nevertheless, it is rightly observed that through its organization of the South American nations' championship, CONMEBOL's role in the development of the game in South America was crucial: 'Aside from the big three of Argentina, Brazil and Uruguay, until the last twenty years or so, almost all of the matches played by the other seven countries were in CONMEBOL-sponsored tournaments.'[16] The confederation also formed the club championship, the Copa Libertadores, from 1960 onwards.

The strong development of the South American game was dramatically embodied in Uruguay's progress, 'which was to place South America firmly on the map of world football when, in 1924, like a wolf on the fold, its team swept down on the Paris Olympics and devoured all opponents, astonishing the Europeans'.[17] Uruguay achieved a further Olympic triumph in Amsterdam (1928), defeating Switzerland and Argentina respectively, the latter encounter providing what Mason calls 'one of the key moments in the process by which football became the people's passion'.[18] During the game, the crowds in the squares and the streets of Montevideo and Buenos Aires were hungry for and passionate in response to the cables from Europe relaying the news of the two games that decided the title.

On the basis of such successes in the Olympics (albeit against European amateur sides), an enthusiasm for the game was established that led (along with an indifference from most European footballing powers) to the first World Cup Finals being held in South America. In 1930, in front of 93,000 spectators, on home soil in Montevideo, Uruguay beat Argentina in the first World Cup Final. Uruguayan diplomats are said to have lobbied the FIFA President, Jules Rimet, in Geneva as early as 1925, in the first bidding process for a World Cup hosting role; and July 1930 was 'the centenary celebrations of the adoption of Uruguay's first constitution'.[19] Crucially, the Uruguayan authorities pledged to pay travel and hotel costs of all the participating teams, and to construct the new Centenario Stadium, hailed by Rimet as a 'temple of football'.[20] Fifteen countries took part, including four countries from Europe: France, Belgium, Yugoslavia and Romania. Only Yugoslavia reached the semi-finals, where 80,000 people saw them humiliated 6–1 by the eventual winners.[21] The undeniable popularity of the tournament and the quality of the South Americans in it – and in subsequent tournaments in Italy (1934) and in France (1938) – alerted the British to the fact that the game they had invented now had a credible global presence and that, one way or another, they would have to come to terms with FIFA.

But despite such a pedigree of organization and achievement, in the middle of the century CONMEBOL was viewed by FIFA as little more than a token body, inefficiently and in part dubiously organized, and implicated in a football culture of frequent violence and institutionalized corruption. When the European Federation was formed in the mid-1950s, Rous recalled, 'UEFA became reality as the first genuine confederation'.[22] Addressing a congress of CONMEBOL in Barranquilla in January 1964, Rous, parrying questions concerning South American representation on World Cup committees, spoke out against strategic groupings or 'blocks' being formed within and by confederations. The notes of his address reveal his faith in his own traditional values and philosophy:

> This will not be for the ultimate good of football: if improvements are to be made; if the strong are to help the weak; if rich the poor; if through sport we help to make partners and not enemies – then we have fulfilled our mission. That Gentlemen is my aim and will continue to be 'To help and not to hinder'.
> Until such time as you who form FIFA find a man better able to direct its affairs
>
> > Four things a man must learn to do:
> > if he would make his record true.
> > To think without confusion, clearly
> > To love his fellow men sincerely
> > To act from honest motives purely
> > To trust in God and Heaven securely.[23]

In this remarkable manuscript Rous demonstrated his vain hope that the confederations – very much his own post-World War II initiative, as restated at the beginning of his address, alongside a belief that presidents of the confederations should all be vice-presidents of FIFA, and 'form a Committee of Directors to direct' – would not generate a cabbalistic and conspiratorial power politics in world football. Vain, because to conclude with this kind of Sunday School homily revealed how potentially out of touch with South American football politicians Rous's style and philosophy was. His longhand notes on the manuscript of his address included reminders that 'harmony and goodwill is essential', that a 'far seeing and forward looking role' would be vital; and, alongside the pledge that a member of the 1970 World Cup host's national association should be 'co-opted for the benefit of his association', Rous wrote 'Cañedo'. Cañedo was to rise to Senior FIFA vice-president under Havelange, with organizational and deal-making powers of the like of which Rous could never have dreamt. The respect that CONMEBOL no doubt had for Rous, as dedicated football missionary and effective diplomat and administrator, could scarcely have outweighed the irritation and offence which his paternalistic but patronising tone and approach generated and provoked.

Rous's plea that 'block' interests be avoided had litttle effect, and he soon encountered difficulties in monitoring CONMEBOL activities and claims. In November 1969 his general secretary sent him, from Zurich to his London address, a full briefing letter for a forthcoming CONMEBOL congress. This correspondence catalogued a long list of backstage manoeuvrings which were read as threatening to FIFA's central (but European-based) authority. Two such issues concerned the administration of the confederation, and the process by which referees were appointed for international matches, in World Cup qualifying rounds as well as the finals. First, the FIFA general secretary Dr Helmut Käser expressed surprise that CONMEBOL wished to change completely the administration at the end of a presidential term of office: 'there will be no continuity in administrative business . . . Possibly this is the South American way of thinking'. Second, he noted that: 'As usual South America is pretending that F.I.F.A. is giving preference to European referees and that South American referees are neglected'; and that 'a very delicate matter' could arise concerning referees for World Cup preliminary matches. The delicacy arose from the recommendation from a South American referees' committee member:

> You will remember that he said that in future the referees for World Cup preliminary matches ought to be appointed only at the very last minute to prevent representatives of the countries involved travelling to the countries of the referee. According to information received, it is customary in South America *to make 'pilgrimages' to the referees' countries*.[24]

These issues highlighted FIFA–CONMEBOL tensions that were to be played upon with brilliance by the Brazilian Havelange, as a representative of a Second World experience and sophistication, and on behalf of the Third World's emerging pleas and demands, within the context of business elites and cross-federational 'blocks', as Rous saw them. FIFA in the 1960s clearly had doubts about the practice and the probity of the organizational and administrative dimensions of CONMEBOL's contribution to world football.

There is no doubt that CONMEBOL, with its small numbers and powerful footballing nations, could work for its own interests in well-organized and effective ways: it could operate, as appropriate, in liaison with the Central and North American confederation, in which Mexico was the dominant power and presence. It was CONMEBOL which was to provide Havelange with his campaigning platform. Although, intriguingly, there was no mention of his CONMEBOL experience in his campaign's curriculum vitae, he was described as unanimous candidate of the confederation, beneath a reproduction of the cover of the confederation's Official Bulletin of April 1974, which carried nothing but a portrait of Havelange, and a declaration of his candidature for the FIFA presidency. The cover of the following Bulletin featured Havelange presenting Rous with a present, and hailed the Brazilian as 'FIFA's first American President'. A tribute within the Bulletin claimed Havelange's election as the culmination of a process 'which was initiated and sustained by the unanimous support' of the federation, and 'the work of each and every one of its members'. The text celebrated Havelange's achievement on behalf of 'America, and all the sport of the world', and lauded the qualities that the new president could now apply within FIFA's remit: impeccable organizational and management credentials, 'a spirit of fertile and positive renovation' and 'a richness of soul', an inspiration by actions and example:

> Modern in his conceptions, with the rhythm of the time which more than ever looks towards youth, which is his prime concern, he will bring together without egoism the challenges opened up by his predecessors, ennobling the spiritual legacy of . . . football . . . a true religion which impassions the masses, and unifies in one language of noble effort, all the people of the world.[25]

Havelange's first World Cup as FIFA president was in Argentina in 1978, and it cannot be denied that the biggest controversy of that tournament bore out some of FIFA's concerns over practices in South American football administration. This controversy centred around the victorious Argentinian team, which, though finishing level on points with Brazil in a second round group, played its deciding game after Brazil's last game of the group. This meant that the host nation knew that it must win by four clear goals, having to score five if a goal was conceded, to secure its place in the final. The Peruvian side collapsed, after a lively start, to a 6–0 defeat. World football recorder Oliver has concluded that, with accusations of foul play added to Brazilian cries of 'cheat' over the timing of the matches, 'Brazilian claims that the Peruvians had been bribed were totally unfounded'.[26] In 1986, though, on the day of the Argentina–England match that was to become famous for Maradona's 'Hand of God' goal and his unforgettably brilliant solo effort for a second goal, the *Sunday Times* ran its lead front page story on the 1978 match.[27] Peru was reported to have received its bribe in two ways: 35,000 tons of grain shipped to a Peruvian port over the following two months; and the unfreezing by the Argentine central bank of a $50 million credit account. Avignolo, citing two football officials and one senior civil servant who worked for the Argentinian junta (all of whom, understandably, claimed anonymity) alleged that the match was fixed through direct negotiations between the two country's governments, and through the mediation of Argentina's FIFA representatives.[28] The *Sunday Times* also commented on Peru's eccentric team selection, and carried a complementary report on the extensive use of powerful amphetamines by the Argentine players, citing one Argentine official: 'The urine samples for all 11 players were provided by the team waterboy, Ocampo, who naturally was clean of drugs.'[29] Sir Walter Winterbottom was at the game, and has recalled how in 'an extraordinary game', for the first quarter of an hour the Peruvian side 'overran the Argentinians, they played marvellous, now they wouldn't have done that if there was a fix-up'. Early on in the game a Peruvian missed what Sir Walter called 'the best chance of goal-scoring I had ever seen in my life . . . the bloke miskicked it and he was only about four yards out of goal and he had an open goal.' Sir Walter, as football man and technical purist, found it difficult to conceive how any player could have contrived to miss such an easy chance at the end of a flowing movement. As a world football administrator, a more realistic recollection recognized a pragmatic diplomacy which, applied in world football politics, surely borders on the collusive:

SIR WALTER: Well now, all that background of the choice of this and the background of saying that somebody had paid them, and all this sort of thing, I couldn't say a thing about it. I mean it seemed to me to be a very ridiculous thing to do, because if it was once found out, you know the whole world would turn against Argentine and Peru, they would both have been banned from football for a very long time. But knowing the way things work down in those countries one had to give at least half belief to it.

QUESTION: Do you think FIFA would investigate something like that thoroughly?

SIR WALTER: I don't think they would. Well, I mean, the rumpus it would create in South American football, that these two were being charged or looked into by FIFA and so on, would give credence that there is something there, wouldn't it, I mean, something wrong anyway? And even if nothing happened, they would then say that FIFA is covering it up because Havelange is South American, you know there is that kind of political . . . er . . . It went on behind the scenes, a lot of this talking and so on, but of course it looked as though it had been specially cooked, this thing, this match.[30]

In the first World Cup Finals of Havelange's presidential reign, the South American achievements began to level out. If Brazil had progressed to the final and defeated the unlucky Dutch, it would have won its fourth World Cup, and the military regime in Argentina would have doubtless made a scapegoat of its football team and administration for failing to break the country's duck at world level. In some ways it was the perfect outcome for FIFA and its new president: a first-time World Cup win for a host-nation. It is difficult to avoid the conclusion that the dynamics and conventions of CONMEBOL practice that had so worried Rous and his FIFA administration were not important influences upon this outcome. For the sake of harmony in the world football family, no doubt it was best to keep questions as and where they were at the time – speculative, and behind-the-scenes. Certainly, throughout volatile political events and international tensions, the South American football fraternity has sustained a relatively united front.

After its 55th Ordinary Congress in 1996 the CONMEBOL president, Dr Nicolas Leoz, could reiterate the main goals of the confederation: 'to get on with our work enlarging and improving our sport, and the pursuit of excellence in the managerial area and the harmony reigning among our member Associations, FIFA and all the other continental Confederations'.[31] The record of the Congress confirmed the continuities in South American football's hierarchy. In a revealing shot of the 'opening ceremony' of the Congress, 'Dr. Joao Havelange addresses the audience . . . His mere attendance lent prestige to the Congress. On arrival, he offered a press conference and marvelled everyone for his intelligence.'[32] In other photographs, Havelange is pictured with the CONMEBOL president, flanked on his other side by Cañedo of Mexico and the FIFA Secretary General Joseph S. Blatter; and with a fellow Brazilian, Abilio D'Almeida: 'Havelange remembered "when 40 years ago we attended with Abilio a CONMEBOL Congress for the first time".'[33] With the CONCACAF president also pictured, and the magazine hailing the re-election of Havelange's son-in-law Ricardo Teixeira as president of the Brazilian Football Federation, it was clear that the CONMEBOL organization and networks had lent consistent support to Havelange throughout the period of South American ascendancy in world football politics and development.

■ UEFA and the European Counter-attack

Jules Rimet, then FIFA President, was against the idea of continental federations because it ran contrary to his notion of FIFA as a single 'family'. However, his contemporaries in the European federations, who were concerned that they were being politically out-manoeuvred by the Latin Americans, were all for it. As early as 1952, José Crahay, the Belgian FA's delegate, was warning his European colleagues of the threat posed by what he viewed as a growing Latin American cabal. His recollections of the FIFA Congress in Helsinki that year are worth quoting at some length:

> One of the South American delegates had something general to say on each and every item on the agenda. We saw very clearly that each point had been carefully studied in advance and that the South American delegates had apparently been nominated to defend a certain standpoint which seldom corresponded with that of the FIFA executive Committee (then dominated by Europeans). The FIFA General Secretary of the time, Kurt Gassmann, fought back as well as he could, and all the major issues were deferred until the next Congress. But when it came to voting the European Associations each went their own way with no preconceived policy: the result was that we came close to committing a number of errors which would have done irreparable damage. May it be emphasised that our aim never was, and never shall be, to override anyone else; Europe's only aim was to defend its own interests.[34]

Here, prior to the actual formation of UEFA, can be seen the classic themes which were to dominate UEFA strategy throughout the second half of the twentieth century. On the eve of the birth of the organization those who were to form UEFA expressed concerns of a practical and tactical type, and of a strategic and ideological type:

- a concern, expressed as an impatience, that the FIFA executive no longer assured European interests – coming over as a sense of betrayal, for of course the founding pioneers of the world body had all been Europeans;
- a concomitant perception that Europe now needed a collective voice, to defend its interests and keep its influential role in world footballing affairs;
- *polite* perception of the emerging threat to European dominance;
- a kind of 'reasonable' disquiet concerning the actions of scheming non-Europeans and Latins – whatever the response, though, the civilized Europeans would 'never . . . override anyone else'.

The mounting awareness, within the European associations, of the emerging threat to their privileged position within world football's power structures, was the motivating factor behind UEFA's formation. In terms of the organization of national football associations, Europe had been particularly fragmented prior to the 1950s. There had always been small, insular regional groupings within Europe, such as the separate British, Scandinavian and former Eastern Bloc Associations. In the 1950s when Europe began to take seriously the notion of association football as a world game, this was in many respects a response to a growing concern that a South American consortium of national associations had been formed, giving that continent a uniform and collective voice within FIFA.

Thus, the distribution of power in world football was the inspiration behind UEFA's formation in 1954. The establishment of UEFA gave Europe a collective voice within the world governing body and eased the emergence of two Englishmen, Arthur Drewry and Stanley Rous, who held the reins of FIFA from 1956 until the mid-1970s. These related developments ensured that Europe would have a leading say in the pace and direction of world soccer development in the immediate post-war period. In general terms, however, the patronising, Eurocentric and neo-imperialistic style which characterized FIFA's relations with its constituents at this time became undermined by the successful spread of the game into the Third World. One of FIFA's long-standing objectives has been to develop soccer world-wide and this has had important political consequences. The more successful this policy became the more pressure the organization felt to adopt more and more national associations into the 'FIFA family'. However, FIFA's electoral franchise operated on the principle of one nation one vote, and this meant that, irrespective of their soccer tradition and playing ability, as each new member was admitted the Third World's power base grew. Alarm bells began to ring in the established football nations, particularly in Europe. Thus spoke the UEFA President, Dr Artemio Franchi:

> With ever more states gaining their independence, and with existing countries splitting up into separate states – processes which are to be observed above all in the so called third world – the number of national football associations inevitably continues to grow. And there is nothing to stop these emerging football countries from joining the enlarged FIFA family. This is the uncomfortable truth.[35]

Rous had shown similar concerns eighteen years earlier. In 1961, in his capacity as vice-president of UEFA, he warned of the political consequences for established football nations of the successful spread of the game:

> Many people are convinced that it is unrealistic, for example, that a country like England, where the game started and was first organized, or that experienced countries like Italy or France who have been pillars of FIFA and influential in its problems and world football affairs for so many years, should have no more than equal voting rights with any of the newly created countries of Africa or Asia.[36]

This issue dominated behind-the-scenes debates and discussions of organizational strategies throughout Rous's tenure as FIFA president from 1961 to 1974. Rous was being squeezed by the twin pressures of smaller central European nations, and the campaigning of Third World (primarily African) nations for a fuller recognition of their potential – a recognition which would be most appropriately manifest in the award of some automatic African places among the then sixteen finalists in the World Cup. As early as September 1962, Hans Walch, president of the Austrian Football Association, followed up a UEFA Congress in Sofia with a letter which argued for a united Europe as a bulwark for FIFA, against the threat of newly emerging global influences:

> FIFA needs the support of a strong UEFA who is in harmony, all the more so as the new states in Asia and Africa create new problems on which settlement the big and important European associations of Great Britain, Germany, Italy, France, USSR and Spain must have their good, constructive and sporting influence. I am often thinking of the injustice that each member of FIFA without consideration of his importance has the same number of votes at the Congress. There are now numerous examples to make this fact ridiculous . . . I would like to remind you of the demand of a small Association at the last FIFA Congress to let Asia have another Vice President in the FIFA and I am convinced that the geographically large but in importance small Association cannot even compare its sporting values with Austria.
>
> I would ask you, dear Sir Stanley, not to misunderstand me; neither do I want a special position for myself nor for the Austrian F.A. but I want to see FIFA and UEFA strengthened, political, national and confessional tendencies avoided and give those National Associations more rights who can guarantee a clean and correct guidance of FIFA and UEFA.[37]

Here the threat to Europe's dominance is clearly articulated, with UEFA and FIFA conceived as a single dominant entity, and with ethnocentric suspicions expressed concerning the qualities of associations from Africa and Asia.

Walch's was a far from isolated position, and the perceived threat was far from imagined. The African Confederation's Executive Committee, in July 1964, passed a resolution which was motivated by 'the cause of making of the World Championship a real world manifestation far from any exclusivism',[38] as the General Secretary Mourad Fahmy put it. This resolution states the African case for at least some recognition of their developing levels of performance. FIFA's intransigence on the issue was to lead to the mass African boycott of the 1966 Championship/World Cup.

Football had been a significant cultural and political focus for the resistance to and the eventual break away from colonial rule, particularly in Africa. As such, many of FIFA's new members were more attuned to the political dimension of the game than were longer established football nations, particularly those from Europe. In FIFA's regional committee structure, countries which were otherwise politically invisible, discovered a political platform for focusing and asserting often newly acquired independence and national identities. However, in considering the reform of FIFA from the mid-1970s onwards, while there was a degree of 'push' from these new national and regional governing bodies, in equal measure there was the 'pull' of those with vested interests in diminishing European influence and it was a combination of both forces which had lead to the election of the first non-European president of FIFA in 1974 (see chapter 1).

The emergence of the Third World as an effective political force within FIFA had been making things uncomfortable for the Europeans for some time, driving a wedge between UEFA and South American soccer. At the 1970 FIFA Congress in Mexico the new member nations of Africa and Asia and the South Americans voted together, resulting in Europe losing its majority representation on the World Cup and Olympic Tournament committees.[39] UEFA officials were outraged and the association called its members together for an Extraordinary Congress in Monte Carlo, in June 1971. Louis Wouters, the Belgian delegate, voiced the concerns of all:

> It is not the competence of the European representatives in the FIFA Executive which is at stake but rather the future of Europe in world football ... at the FIFA Congress in Mexico, political questions were given precedence over questions of sport and a clearly anti-European attitude had been exhibited there.[40]

UEFA was particularly worried that its diminished influence on FIFA's most important committees would adversely affect its member's chances of hosting and qualifying for future World Cup Finals. Gustav Wiederkehr, the president of UEFA, at that time, thought that the situation 'had become critical'[41] and was quick to seek assurances from FIFA that the views of European nations on these matters would continue to be respected:

> The European Associations expect the competent committees of FIFA, when taking any decisions but particularly when deciding the distribution of finalist places in the World Cup in 1974 in the Federal Republic of Germany, to take into consideration the various aspects of European football, both from the view of quantity and quality.[42]

Nevertheless, as these tensions stirred and recurred throughout the first two decades of UEFA's existence, so long as the Englishman, Rous, remained as president of FIFA, Europe felt that its interests would be protected. At the Monte Carlo UEFA meeting, Wiederkehr saw trouble coming when he said that he, 'feared a further blow for Europe when Sir Stanley Rous would one day withdraw from the Presidency'.[43] The fact that within three years of the Monte Carlo meeting, Rous had not withdrawn but had been forced out of office – through a power-play led by Brazilian, João Havelange, and involving the under-developed world – spelled even more trouble for UEFA.

■ Sir Stanley Rous: Football Missionary

Secretary of the English Football Association from 1934 to 1962, Rous had led the British Associations back into FIFA in 1946. Rous took over at FIFA in his mid-sixties, the retiring age for male workers. He grasped this new challenge with typical energy and commitment. Walter Winterbottom, England's first manager, commented on BBC Radio that 'in our own country he took us out of being an insular Association Football League and got us back into world football and this was tremendous'; and that his diplomatic, negotiating and interpersonal skills were exceptional.[44]

Rous was a highly influential figure in the English game. He had been a referee of international repute after playing as an amateur. A son of the middle classes (his two elder sisters were school teachers), his 'intention was to go to Emmanuel College, Cambridge',[45] but his father died as arrangements for this were in process. Instead, after service in Africa during World War I, he studied at St Luke's College, Exeter, and then taught at Watford Grammar School. He was part of a socially mobile and developing service profession, no inheritor of established privileges. He played football at college, then in the army during the War, but his major impact on the game, initially, was as a top-class referee. In many respects he went on to modernize the English game, establishing a more efficient bureaucratic base, introducing teaching schemes for all levels of the game – coaching, playing, refereeing. But this mission was not an innocent one. Britain itself was in crisis after World War II, losing an Empire and looking for a role. The educating of football players as coaches – of practitioners as educators – was one way of restoring British prominence in the world game. Rous believed that English and British football could draw upon the examples of international co-operation established during the war (at least with the Allies!) and became more involved in the international dimensions of the game. In a major paper which he presented to the Football Association, first drafted in May 1943, he recognized how the activities of the FA's War Emergency Committee had boosted football's international profile, by fostering relations with government departments, and by establishing links with influential persons through co-operation with the armed forces/ services. Most important, though, was 'the unparallelled opportunity which the war years have given the Association of being of service to countries other than our own', which 'has laid an excellent foundation for post-war international development'.[46] Rous is a key transitional figure in the FIFA story. Arguing for this sort of expansion from his home base, he could hardly dispute the right of the other nations to take up the challenge. Yet despite his innovations he remained trapped in an anachronistic set of values. On the occasion of his ninetieth birthday in April 1985, the BBC honoured him in a radio documentary tribute. Rous recalls his own playing and spectating days of up to eighty years ago:

> We used to look upon it as a sport, as a recreation, we had little regard of points and league position and cup competitions. We used to play friendly matches mostly. There was always such a sporting attitude and the winners always clapped the others off the field and so on . . . that's all changed of course.[47]

And despite his commitment to worldwide expansion, as early as the 1962 World Cup in Chile, in the first years of his presidency, the former English FA secretary mourned the loss of the 1930s when international tours were 'free and easy affairs'.

A set of crucially revealing tensions is expressed here: the old world versus the new; the quiet life versus a global cosmopolitanism; a character-building participation versus win-at-all costs attitudes. Rous could be both innovative and traditional, adventurous yet crabbily cautious; resonant of modernity yet steeped in traditional values. A world figure in sport, he carried into the sporting arena the inherent contradictions of a Britain in the middle period of a very uncertain remaking.

Harry Cavan, senior vice-president of FIFA at the time (or, in Brian Glanville's view, 'the premier apologist for the President, the man who delivered that glutinous address in Zürich on the occasion Havelange celebrated [if that is the word] his tenth anniversary as boss of FIFA' recalled how well prepared Rous's entry on to the world stage was: he was 'probably the most travelled man in football in the world in those days. He had the right connections, he had the right influence and above all he had the ability and the skill to do the job. And of course he was clever. He was generally one or two moves ahead of most of the others.'[48] Havelange's ruthless and ambitious pursuit of the presidency changed things, for without doubt in 1974 Rous was clearly a great many moves behind his challenger. When he stood for re-election as FIFA President, claiming that he wanted just a couple of years in which to push through some important schemes, he either had a confidence which was misplaced, or he miscalculated the institutional politics of FIFA. Ten years on Rous claimed not to have been surprised, 'because I know what activity was being practised by my successor, the appeals that he'd made to countries'. Harry Cavan recalls how Rous seemed to make little real effort to get support; somehow or other he'd lost his momentum. Havelange won in a second ballot. Bryon Butler, the sports journalist, recalled the moment of defeat:

> I remember just before the second ballot was taken you sat down and had an orange squash, quietly in one corner. João Havelange did so much lobbying – he was really such a blur – and that's where you lost.[49]

Sir Stanley's response to this memory combined a sense of almost betrayal, even twenty years on, with his realistic perception of what was happening in the politics of world football:

> Yes, I think an Indian spoke against and I was surprised at that. People like Indonesia voted against me but I don't think they . . . their officers have changed so much in those countries, you know. There were quite a few then who didn't really know me and they were persuaded to vote for Havelange.[50]

Rous wrote, four years after Havelange's victory, that he was most disappointed at the Africans shifting support to Havelange. He found it 'hurtful' that having done a great deal for the development of football in Africa, so much so that he was criticized by European associations, African nations could desert him in his hour of electoral need:

> I could not expect that to be remembered, however, since the Associations are in many cases subject to government direction and when their officials change so frequently. Many of the delegates representing African and Asian Associations were indeed new to me, and when I checked the list afterwards some were members of embassies and it was a surprise to me that they had been properly accredited in time for the Congress. And they were to hold the key to a close contest.[51]

Clearly, Havelange's worldwide campaigning had involved some reshaping of the electoral body, and secured him the support from new representatives with no loyalties to Rous. Who was it who actually emerged from the Third World to assume power in FIFA?

■ Dr João Havelange: Football Entrepreneur

Havelange's parental, family roots were Belgian,[52] and he trained as a lawyer before making several fortunes in ventures in the chemical, insurance and transport industries. As an amateur sportsman – a double Olympian, swimming for Brazil in the 1936 Berlin Olympics, and a member of the water-polo team at the 1952 Helsinki Games – he gained a high profile in the Brazilian sports establishment. Moving into sports administration he became president of the Brazilian sports federation, and supremo of Brazilian football, reshaping the game by the 1970s and forming a national championship out of the various regional and inter-regional championships. This initiative – at times involving up to nearly a hundred clubs travelling across a country of 8.5 million square kilometres – was based, in World Cup fashion, upon groups playing each other. Big clubs had to play small ones, and all clubs had to travel all over the vast country. Not surprisingly, crowds were small, and the travel expenses for the clubs were punitive. Not a few Brazilian commentators have seen this initiative, in tandem with the movement abroad of many players, as an undermining of the Brazilian domestic game. But ironically it was the claiming of credit for Brazil's international success that provided a basis for Havelange's candidature for the FIFA presidency. He had got onto the Brazilian Olympic Committee in 1955, and in 1963 he was elected to the International Olympic Committee. But it was Brazil's international soccer success, whilst Havelange was at the helm of Brazilian sport, that allowed him to promote himself as suited to the top job in world football administration. In his promotional literature for the 1974 election he is described as:

> a great Brazilian sports leader, that is, the man who took over the direction of the CBD and conducted the Brazilian football team to the triple conquest and definite possession of the world's most coveted trophy, the Jules Rimet Cup. Three championships won in a short period under the same direction, sometimes overcoming a lot of unfavourable incomprehensions in his own country, represent a performance, which is not easy to match, by any other sports leader in the world.[53]

There are several Brazilian coaches and team managers – maybe some players too – who would no doubt dispute this inflection in the Havelange curriculum vitae. The Havelange manifesto comprised an eight-point programme:

1 the increase in numbers of participants in the World Cup finals, to 24 in 1982;
2 the creation of a junior, under-20 World Championship;
3 the construction of a new FIFA headquarters for the 'approaching XXI century';
4 to provide materials to underdeveloped associations;
5 to help underdeveloped associations construct and improve stadia;
6 to intensify courses for sports professionals;
7 to provide technical and medical teaching to underdeveloped countries;
8 to introduce an inter-continental club championship.[54]

Lobbying effectively, and pledging these commitments, Havelange – 'a very clever man, a very skilled politician', in Cavan's words – became FIFA's first non-European president. Football officials in Argentina and Uruguay had proposed that Havelange become the South American candidate for the FIFA presidency. Accepting this, the dynamic businessman then moved fast. With the backing of most of the South American countries, he spent the years 1971–3 in worldwide canvassing. Preparing for the 1974 FIFA election, he visited eighty-six FIFA countries, concentrating most of all on Africa and Asia.[55] His candidature was a widely representative one, harnessing simultaneously the resentments and aspirations of South American, southern European, African and Asian footballing nations. Patrick Nally, former business intimate of the late Horst Dassler of Adidas, captures the flavour of Havelange's wooing of the world of international soccer:

> There had never been an election campaign like it for a sports presidency
> . . . Sir Stanley Rous hadn't travelled to all the countries throughout Asia
> and Africa and certainly not to all the little islands. It was such a radical
> change to suddenly have this dynamic, glamorous South American char-
> acter, brimming with *bonhomie*, travelling the world with his wife, meet-
> ing people, pressing the flesh, bringing over the Brazilian team, travelling
> with the likes of Pelé. It was Brazilian carnival time . . . Havelange had
> spent a fortune going round the world with the Brazilian team and had
> canvassed every single member of FIFA. It was unheard of. No sports

president had ever gone round the world glad handing and campaigning.[56]

On his election, to achieve his programme, funding on an unprecedentedly large scale was needed. Under Havelange FIFA strode into the modern world of sponsorship, in ways considered in detail in chapter 4.

Parallels between Havelange's operations in Brazil and in the wider world are undeniable. An indiscriminately expanded Brazilian championship undermined the fabric of the game there. Critics have pointed out that this is precisely what is happening in the World Cup itself. In the 1980s in Brazil the Brazilian Football Federation recognized no difference between amateurs and professionals; unlike in, say, England, there is no football league separate from the Football Association. In the Brazilian Federation each constituent unit had one vote. This means, to take an English analogy, that an amateur league club in Sussex would have the same voting power as Liverpool, Tottenham Hotspur or Manchester United. Control of the federation will go to those who divert resources to the poor and weak countries – buying their support, in effect. Havelange clearly learned his lesson well in his own country. A democracy based upon a premise of inequality of resources was a sound means of gaining unassailable power and, repeated effectively on the international scale in a system conveniently inherited in FIFA, this gave Havelange *carte blanche* in the world federation.

Havelange's success represents a superb irony in the FIFA story. The challenge of the developing world to the advanced world was led by a glamorous figure resonant of the modern, and consolidated economically by money from the capitalist centres of middle Europe and North America. The Third World had been aroused and in footballing terms was on the ascendancy; in power terms, the alliances within FIFA combined the political and cultural interests of emergent nations with the market aspirations of multi-national and trans-national economic interests still based firmly in the first world of capitalism. Leaders such as Havelange have been resented, and the effects of his administration are highly disputed. Tommy Keller, from Switzerland, and president of the International Rowing Federation, spoke out against the new order in world sport, alleging that it was dominated by a Latin American and Latino-European cartel.[57] Artemio Franchi, a former president of UEFA, the European Football Union, was scathing about FIFA's new administrative building when it opened at the end of the 1970s: 'It's ostentation . . . and *South*

American ostentation.'[58] Brian Glanville, the English football journalist to whom Franchi expressed this view, has been outspoken in his criticisms of Havelange and his regime: 'I very much . . . believe that Havelange has ruined the World Cup, has sold it down the river to the Afro-Asians and their ilk'[59]; 'I deeply dislike what FIFA has become under the ineffable Havelange and . . . I as deeply despise the European countries which have truckled to him.'[60] These brazenly Eurocentric criticisms romanticize the earlier history of FIFA, and assume a superiority in an old order which feels itself unaccountable to the rest of the world. But the nations which Glanville appears to be so contemptuous of have, for many, enriched the flavour of the World Cup Finals, helping justify the grandiose label, 'World'.

■ Family Fortunes

FIFA's official history notes the restricted financial base upon which Rous operated during his period as President, with funds coming from just the one main source of profits from the World Cup, and modest levels of subscription from the member associations. So though Rous presided over an expanding family of FIFA members, and ushered the world game into the age of television transmission, Rous's FIFA could be seen, in retrospect, as 'rather conservative . . . and reserved in its decisions . . . It hardly seemed possible to accomplish more without taking risks.'[61] Thus, in the making and writing of its own history, FIFA sets the stage for the entry of Havelange into the FIFA story. He is hailed as a risk-taking entrepreneur rather than a necessarily cautious patrician. Under him, FIFA is said to have followed 'another direction, that of universality', applying 'methods in football which were long known in social, economic and political life'.[62] The implication here is clear. Honourable though Rous may have been, he was out of touch with the modern, unable to exploit the potential of 'long known' methods for the good and development of the game.

The ambitious Havelange moved quickly, noted the body's official history, giving 'FIFA truly international and universal dimensions. His first concern was a comprehensive, worldwide football development programme, which was pursued with the International Academies. As FIFA did not have the necessary financial means, the FIFA President implemented his vast experience and fantasy as a businessman, in order to materialize these ambitious plans. With their great involvement in sports and their worldwide business interests, the Coca-Cola Company were very positive towards this idea and assumed the sponsorship of these projects.'[63] As in all patriarchal families, the telling of the family history reaffirms the status of the incumbent patriarch. But with new members of the family hostile to the ideals of earlier generations, earlier patriarchal figures can be re-evaluated unsympathetically, in the light of more modern developments.

In the glossy internal history of FIFA, the new-found wealth and fortunes of the world footballing family made possible the development of a truly global base to the game. Havelange could accomplish this in style, running up expenses of £100,000 a year by 1979, and annual running costs for his Rio office of £250,000 in 1986. When 'FIFA officials flew into Spain for the World Cup in 1982 their expenses were nearly £2 million – almost as much as it cost to transport and accommodate the twenty-four teams. Their new-found wealth was dazzling. In the next two years FIFA splashed out £650,000 on international travel and gifts.'[64] FIFA had travelled a long way since the British soccer federations could withdraw, just over half a century earlier, in the purity of protest at 'broken-time' payments to amateurs. Havelange achieved much on behalf of Africa, Asia and South America. It is a great irony – yet at the same time a truism of a globalizing world based upon the driving forces of a capitalist political economy and the search for new world-wide consumer markets – that the increased representation of Third World nations will have been celebrated in the heart of the First World capitalist system, in North America and France. But this is hardly an accident. FIFA's deal with Coca-Cola was hammered out in the mid-1970s at the company's headquarters in Atlanta, Georgia. That deal can be seen as a pivotal moment in the history of modern soccer, and from the moment that deal was struck it became likely – regardless of the state of the game within its own sports culture – that the USA would host the biggest soccer event in the world. With the World Soccer Cup in the USA in 1994, and the centenary Summer Olympic Games in Atlanta in 1996, modern sport's, and soccer's, impact and appeal beyond their Western European roots can be seen to be premised upon the patronage of the trans-national political economy.

■ Family Feuds

The construction, expression and maintenance of forms of national identity is a complex process, and identities can be fragile, the reactions to the expression of them unpredictable.[65] Global forces marginalize more culturally distinctive sports: Guttmann concludes an erudite review of the diffusion of sports with the comment that 'the international dominance of Western sports continues and resistance to this form of cultural imperialism remains weak'.[66] But in the case of soccer a different process is at work – not merely the either/or of the domination of the imperialist, or the resistance of the oppressed. Rather, in the FIFA story and the way in which nations have expressed the imaginings of their own community and national identities, the story has been one of appropriation. The form of soccer has been taken and remoulded into the style and the culture of the recipient; soccer has been appropriated and remade in these ways, to the extent that the traditional centres of power in the world game have lost their 'natural' dominance. This has guaranteed that, as in any extended family, disputes and rows have raged over the importance of different traditions and competing values.

When no British side qualified for the 1994 finals in the USA, Sepp Blatter, general secretary of FIFA, launched an attack on British soccer as '30 years behind the times', and on the continued British 'domination of the world game's law-making body, the International Football Association Board', suggesting that 'football's mother country . . . exerts an influence out of all proportion to its current standing in the game'.[67] Harmony-inducing rhetoric of the world football family does not preclude the possibility of intra-familial tensions and rivalries. The legendary Brazilian player Pelé – certainly the biggest star of the USA's own soccer initiatives in the 1970s – was not present on stage at the Las Vegas World Cup draw in December 1993. Embroiled in a row with Havelange's son-in-law Ricardo Teixeira (president of Brazil's Football Federation), Pelé held his own press conference in Las Vegas. 'Already facing a law suit for defamation, he was not prepared to be specific, but said: "I cannot accept corruption, and football has a big problem with that in Brazil . . . ." For speaking out, he had been given no part in the draw.'[68] Guido Tognoni, FIFA's press boss at the time, recalls the incident, and relates how the FIFA general secretary, right up to five minutes before the televised draw, tried to convince Havelange that Pelé should be allowed to be on the stage:

> Havelange said 'only if Pelé apologises'. I went to Pelé immediately you know because we wanted to save the whole procedure . . . we wanted to make American people happy. He was the only one they knew in America, so I went to Pelé and I said 'Listen Pelé, the President says that you can go

on stage if you apologize, if you withdraw all your blames', and then he said 'No way, no way.' So I went back to Sepp, he took the risk to ask the president again, to resolve this problem. But the president didn't want and Pelé, he insisted, he says he has no reason to apologize. It was a family loyalty and Havelange took it very personal – if you attack the son-in-law you attack, it's like his son, he took it very personal. Pelé was smart enough not to attack Havelange as such, he only attacked the son-in-law and that was it.

He was kind of untouchable, the Grand Seigneur of the world sports. Havelange and every person who is in such a position is challenged sometimes, but he made a crucial mistake. This was a crucial mistake. It was a crucial mistake because – I tell you something as a press officer, as PR officer, I was always able to keep negative headlines away from him. I knew that many people were critical of him but I could keep him untouchable. He was, until Las Vegas '93, he was more or less untouchable. The crucial mistake was Pelé, because from then on people were banging personal on him and the hide was broken . . . if on one side is Pelé, who didn't do anything wrong, and on the other side is the president, who boycotted Pelé in a very important event, then you cannot stop the criticism anymore. It is hopeless.[69]

Clearly, the structure of Brazilian football, and Havelange's 'means of gaining unassailable power' in the game,[70] might have left some legacy of resentment in his own country. It has even been said that Pelé accepted injury willingly during the 1966 World Cup Finals, with the intent that Brazil would not retain the World Cup title, so that Havelange could be blamed for this and deposed from his position as president of the Brazilian sports federation.[71] After almost two decades in power at FIFA, though, at the Las Vegas draw Havelange clearly felt little dependence upon a former player, of whatever stature. The loyalties of the Havelange family, in this incident at least, triumphed over the harmony of the FIFA family.

■ Agency and Power in World Football

The leaders of FIFA have been active and effective agents in the development and expansion of world football, of the FIFA football family, to paraphrase the imagery of the major presidents. This is not to say that, without the single human individual Havelange at the helm, FIFA would not have developed as it has done in the last quarter of the century. Tognoni – albeit as slighted erstwhile FIFA insider – is emphatic that the cult of the charismatic leader can obscure the specifics of a situation and context: 'in the 60s it started to explode . . . the money . . . and this is not the merit of Havelange, it is the merit of the circumstances of the time. He didn't do a magical miracle, he did what everybody would have done during this time. For a certain time everybody was praising Havelange as the magic man who made money to FIFA and who made FIFA the modern enterprise and so on and so forth . . . TV made it.'[72] Tognoni is both right and wrong here – right to emphasize the context, but wrong to underplay Havelange's astuteness in seeking the appropriate partners for his development plans. Giddens observes that 'agency' refers most importantly to the capability which people have of acting, of doing things in the first place:

> Agency concerns events of which an individual is the perpetrator, in the sense that the individual could, at any phase in a given sequence of conduct, have acted differently. Whatever happened would not have happened if that individual had not intervened.[73]

There is no doubt that, by this definition, Rimet, Rous and – especially – Havelange were powerful agents in the promotion and governance of world football. It is hard to imagine the narrative of twentieth-century world football stripped of their protagonists' roles: Rimet protected a traditional model of Eurocentric domination; Rous sought to achieve a balancing act of control and delegation in what he was fully aware was a changing post-colonial world; and Havelange proposed a programme for commercial expansion and development, which he makes forceful claims to having delivered. It is testimony to the impact of these figures that it would be a merely partial understanding of world football history and politics that did not recognize the seminal nature of their respective interventions. There are always 'unintended consequences of intentional conduct',[74] and Rimet provoked hostility in the furthest corners of his football family; Rous, acting with unwitting insensitivity on key political issues, drove former allies into the arms of Havelange; and Havelange could hardly have foreseen the extreme forms of influence that marketing and media would have on aspects of football, or quite how the confederations would come to challenge him. But this is not to deny the importance of the agent in historical process and social structure. Tognoni's warning is well-taken. Transnational practices such as world football administration could only impact in the context of prevailing social, economic and political realities. But the capacity of agents to recognize, grasp and act upon the nature of those processes is the very stuff of effective social action and intervention. Giddens observes that 'action logically involves power in the sense of transformative capacity',[75] and it is in this sense that FIFA's founding fathers can be understood as powerful social actors or effective human agents. They made interventions which in their own way – and according to their own particular priorities and ideologies – structured the football world. In turn their own agency structured FIFA and their confederations in ways which would be challenged by other actors. Analysing the respective impact of FIFA's leaders is therefore to understand, in the football system, what Giddens calls the dialectic of control:

> Power within social systems which enjoy some continuity over time and space presumes regularized relations of autonomy and dependence between actors or collectivities in contexts of social interaction. But all forms of dependence offer some resources whereby those who are subordinate can influence the activities of their superiors. This is what I call the *dialectic of control* in social systems.[76]

The immeasurably important wider, supra-national context in which these powerful social actors in FIFA's leadership operated and sought to impact, was that of nationalism and the inherently competing nationalisms of its member associations. All nations, as Benedict Anderson has so eloquently argued,[77] have at some stage to indulge in some form of imagining. The nation, he suggests, is imagined on three levels: as limited, as having boundaries; as free, under the sovereign state; and as a community, 'conceived as deep, horizontal comradeship'. In this final level of imagining – that of the fraternal (*sic*) community – it is forms of symbolic action which state the case for the country itself. FIFA may have expressed, at various stages in its development, principles of world citizenship, or international understanding, and its rhetoric from Rimet to Rous to Havelange has reiterated, in varied ways, such ideals; but one major function has remained unchanged throughout different presidential regimes. It has offered, on the level of popular consciousness, a forum for the expression of different forms of national belonging and superiority.

Havelange emerged from the Second World, speaking too in the interests of an emerging Third World, to give FIFA a ring of modernity, and he accomplished this as a skilled manipulator of others. Tributes to Rous emphasized service; as Bryon Butler put it, service to football, to sport, to youth and to charity. FIFA offered Rous a sizeable pension, but he considered it 'inappropriate for an unpaid job like the presidency then to be pensioned. It is hardly right that you aren't paid when you are working and are when you aren't!.'[78] After Brazil had won the Jules Rimet Trophy outright in 1970, that nation (prompted by Havelange himself) asked Rous to lend his name to a new gold cup to be called the 'Stanley Rous Cup'. Rous refused the honour, believing that major trophies should not bear an individual's name. Any tribute to Havelange would be unlikely to stress service. Dynamism, yes, but not service. And a Rous-like modesty has not been expressed by Havelange when nominated for the Nobel Peace Prize. The president of the Swiss Football Association, Heinrich Röthlisberger, made a nomination in July 1988, praising Havelange for his achievement in turning FIFA into 'a world power binding all nations'.[79] This proposal generated a standing ovation from delegates at the FIFA Congress (in Zurich) at which it was announced. A report from the *Sunday Times* noted that during 1988 Havelange had enjoyed 'the great joy' of an audience with President Reagan in The White House, and had received the Grand Cordon Alaouite from King Hassan of Morocco. Morocco and the USA were candidates to stage what became USA '94. Havelange had also been cited by Jacques Chirac, during the Frenchman's successful presidential campaign, as having negotiated with him the 1998 World Cup, before this had even been considered by FIFA. Havelange, with Chirac in Paris, stated that 'I would be happy to see the committee look favourably on France's candidature', knowing that Morocco would run again, as well as Switzerland. The report concluded, tongue firmly in cheek, that: 'It is probably sheer coincidence that only this month Heinrich Rothlisberger, president of Switzerland's football federation, put forward Dr Havelange for the Nobel Peace prize.'[80]

Rous recalled having a cold bath every morning of his life – Havelange's style would much more likely be, after his early morning swim, to favour a plunge into the jacuzzi. Rous was a teacher, with a mission to educate the world; Havelange has been much more the smooth-talking and ruthless international wheeler-dealer. And this remains a central irony in the FIFA story. The challenge of the new world to the old has been led by a cosmopolitan figure resonant of the modern. The story of FIFA's expanded football family is one of alliances between emerging cultural and political interests in the developing world, and entrenched economic interests in the developed capitalist world. Yet throughout the turbulent family rows and break-ups in this story, soccer has continued to provide gripping drama and sporting spectacle. Havelange's FIFA made much of this possible, in ways and initiatives, and by means, that would not have been undertaken or embraced by the traditional old guard of the Eurocentric founding fathers. When Havelange announced, in December 1996, that he would not be standing for re-election in June 1998, there was a resounding unanimity across the football world that the Brazilian octogenarian would be a hard act to follow.

The *Financial Times* drew up, a year in advance, a job description for the FIFA presidency:

SITUATION VACANT:

President of FIFA. The most powerful post in world sport, with overall responsibility for football's governing body and the 200m people who play the game regularly.

Your first task will be to attend the world's most popular and lucrative sporting event: the World Cup to be held in France in June 1998. The outgoing president will preside over the tournament in a figurehead role, but you may be called upon to hand the cup jointly to the winners.

Thereafter, and with the assistance of committees, sub-committees, sponsors, marketing companies, and government officials, you will seek to build on the universal appeal of the game and the growing resources of one of the world's fastest expanding multinational institutions.

A big part of your role will be to increase revenue from marketing and broadcasting rights, which in the next World Cup in 2,002 will be worth an estimated Sfr1.5bn (£640m).

TERMS OF EMPLOYMENT: Minimum four years, 365 days a year.

SALARY: None. However, substantial expenses covering extensive travel, use of car, personal staff, daily allowances, entertainment and gifts. Perks could amount to anything up to $500,000 (£306,748).[81]

A year ahead of the denouement, the Swede Lennart Johansson, embodying what Sudan's Dr Halim (87 year-old veteran of African, Sudanese, IOC and FIFA politics) referred to as Africa's new close relationship with Europe,[82] was the favourite to succeed Havelange. Such an outcome – if secured in a non-contested single candidature – had the potential to achieve a smooth transition of power, though marginalizing the South American forces which had initially challenged FIFA's Eurocentrism. It is the processes, initiatives and means, promoted and adopted by powerful social agents within the context of such contests for power and influence in world football, with which this study is concerned.

■ 3

FIFA: an organizational and institutional analysis

FIFA, as an international non-government organization, operates as the overarching body for the control of world football. Much of its organizational history, as recorded in congresses, internal publications and minutes, has been concerned with apparently technical matters of institutional precedent and practice, and dull-sounding administrative detail. This has often taken the form of debates concerning, and disputes over, the federation's Statutes. To the superficial observer this may seem to be a combination of the mundane, the trivial and the arcane. In fact, the constitution of the Statutes is critical to the organization's mode of functioning. Interpreting, implementing, and sometimes changing, the Statutes is at the heart of the federation's business – for the Statutes affect the dynamics of power of FIFA, and so influence the way football develops world-wide, throughout the different parts of the world represented by the six continental federations. In that members act – either voluntarily or by constraint – according to the Statutes, the organizational power of FIFA is channelled or filtered through the Statutes. In this chapter, therefore, the major aspects of the Statutes, as they affect FIFA's transnational practices, are presented, discussed and illustrated with selected examples of FIFA's organizational practice. This is accomplished by summary, as appropriate, and critique, of the main articles of the Statutes;[1] by selective reference to the Statutes of the confederations; by drawing upon documentary sources which illuminate the mode of operation of FIFA within its committee and sub-committee structure; and by illustrative citation from exclusive interviews with very senior personnel in both FIFA and the confederations, and experienced insiders around and observers of FIFA dealings and organizational style. Whilst at first sight this might seem to be a dry descriptive task, it is far from that. It is a way of focusing a critical magnifying lens upon the organization itself, and the ways in which decisions are made and power is wielded in both it and associated organizations. For whilst the constitution, the Statutes, the objectives, and the organizational and committee structures of FIFA appear rational and coherent, as in any large organization it is the interpersonal dynamics that really define its way of working. As the formal side of the organization is reviewed and considered it is vital, therefore, to keep in mind Weber's classic perceptions on the inherent anomaly of large-scale organizational life – that organizations can come all too easily to serve not the objectives for which they were purportedly established (and which are often regurgitated in continuing outpourings of self-justifying rhetoric), but rather the self-referential aspirations of the organizational members. To comprehend this process, it is useful to view the formal Statutes of the organization, and its official institutional identity, as a front-stage sphere and public profile, a presentation of the organizational self to the world; and the minutiae of lived organizational life and interpersonal dynamics as the back-stage on the basis of which FIFA's social construction of reality is really accomplished.[2]

■ Organizational Status

The Swiss Government offers a special status to organizations such as FIFA, providing that they meet the criterion whereby they can be defined as an association in terms of the Swiss Civil Code. This is a broad criterion:

> Associations which have a political, religious, scientific, artistic, charitable, social or any other than an industrial object, acquire the status of a person as soon as they show by their constitution their intention to have corporate existence. (Article 60)

The main implication of this status is, in the words of FIFA Deputy General Secretary Michel Zen-Ruffinen, 'that an association shall only pursue ideal purposes and it is deemed to be non-commercial in definition'.[3] It seems too that an organization having 'the status of a person' will be less vulnerable to constraints upon companies or industrial enterprises.

■ Objectives, Membership and Sanctions

FIFA's four stated objectives cover:

1 the promotion of football 'in every way it deems fit';
2 the fostering of 'friendly relations' among member national associations and their officials, by organizing matches and forms of
   support for the game 'by all other means which it deems appropriate';
3 the 'control of every type of association football', by protecting it
   from 'abuses', and 'from improper methods or practices', whilst
   abiding by FIFA's Statutes and the International Football Association Board's Laws of the Game, and upholding a principle of
   no discrimination upon grounds of 'race, religion, or politics'; and
4 the provision for resolving disputes between national associations.

Membership of FIFA covers national football associations, and individuals who are members of a FIFA committee. The continental federations are not members, as such, of FIFA, but are described as
groups of 'national associations affiliated to FIFA and belonging to
the same continent (or assimilable geographic entity).' Membership
comes with strict clauses and constraints. Applicant associations must
submit their own statutes and regulations, which must contain a
'mandatory clause stipulating the restraints and obligations contained
in Art. 58 of the FIFA Statutes'. This Article seeks to place FIFA beyond the reach of any 'court of law' or 'law of a country', reserving
for the Executive Committee the right to decide upon the composition of any internally constituted 'arbitration tribunal'. The Article
declares:

> National associations, clubs or club members shall not be permitted to
> refer disputes with the Federation or other associations, clubs or club
> members to a court of law and they shall agree to submit each one of such
> disputes to an arbitration tribunal appointed by common consent. (Arti-
> cle 58/1)

Any breach of this 'obligation' results in the sanction of suspension,
for the national association, from international activity or fixture
schedules. A separate clause in the Statutes covers issues of player
registration. FIFA could be at times pompous, and myopic, in the
implementation of this 'obligation'. As the famous Bosman Case was

moving towards its climax in the European Union court during 1995,[4] FIFA was announcing its view that its own status as a global body placed it above the merely regional status of the European Union. The following press releases featured on FIFA's World Wide Web/ Internet site:

> In FIFA's view, it is clear that a small group of countries cannot be granted an exemption from sports regulations which are effective in all parts of the world and which operate successfully and efficiently and for the benefit of football at all levels.
> FIFA feels that an international sports organisation simply cannot operate properly unless regulations are universally applied, and any other approach would lead to very serious problems. Such circumstances could even jeopardise the independent status of the 18 FIFA Member associations concerned.[5]

There is a critique here of the right of the European Parliament to pass judgements affecting the practices of the international federation, a naive claim to be above the legal niceties of the European Union. Even when the decision of the European Court went in favour of Bosman, FIFA persisted in its supra-national perspective, claiming that its representative status enabled it to speak for the world beyond Europe:

> FIFA has noted with disappointment the decision taken by the European Court of Justice regarding the case of Jean-Marc Bosman. FIFA points out that the decision affects only 18 of the 193 national associations affiliated to the world body. The current transfer system is based upon the Statutes and Regulations which have been duly approved by all the FIFA member associations and has proved to be effective, and is therefore not cast into doubt by today's decision.[6]

This was an unconvincing response, given the import, profile and potential implications of the Bosman decision: FIFA looked merely obstinate and foolish. Guido Tognoni, FIFA PR boss for more than ten years up until the beginning of 1995, is scathing about such an announcement: 'Blatter was extremely naive in this case, he says "Well, we are responsible for the whole world and we cannot care about what is happening within 18 nations . . ." But it is stupid, this is not realistic. "And we will go to the government and we will speak with the government and so on." I mean this is arrogant, and naive and not living in the real world.'[7] Yet in some ways the response was understandable, for such a case represented a major challenge to the credentials of the Federation's Statutes. That this kind of proselytizing of its global responsibility had such little effect also exposed the vulnerability of its Statutes, which on a closer look are revealed to be far from watertight. In the Statutes of UEFA, for instance,[8] Article 2 on 'objects and duties' includes 'to observe the Statutes and Regulations of FIFA'; and in its Article 28 – 'Unforeseen Circumstances' – it is stated that: 'For all matters not provided for in these Statutes, the Statutes, Regulations and Congress Regulations of FIFA shall be applicable if they cover such an occurrence. Otherwise the Executive Committee of UEFA shall take a decision.' Yet in the previous Article – 'Seat of Decision' – it is clear that 'Swiss law shall be deemed to be applicable in all matters of dispute, and Berne shall be the seat of decision'. This does not fit at all consistently with the FIFA obligation that 'courts of law' and 'laws of countries' should not be brought to bear upon the business of world football. The Bosman case revealed the fragility of FIFA's claim to be above national and international law. Tognoni also pointed out that FIFA's claim to control players' agents is equally fragile:

> FIFA is a monopoly organization, this monopoly maybe some will challenge one day. FIFA for example has issued regulations for players' agents, that you only can be a players' agent and an adviser if you have a FIFA licence. This is basically illegal, if one agent goes to challenge it then it is over.[9]

Also interesting on this issue was the saga of the formation, by the Football Association of Wales (FAW), of the League of Wales. This initiative was instituted in the season 1992–3, following on from demands from African countries that the four British Associations be amalgamated into a single UK Association, with the right to field just the single national UK side. [10] Several clubs refused to play in this new league, and played in exile in England:

> In May 1994 the dispute escalated with the three clubs taking joint legal action against the FAW alleging unreasonable restraint of trade by preventing them playing at home in Wales. To take legal action is to break FIFA statute 57 . . . Caernarfon Town, Colwyn Bay and Newport AFC now had the threat of suspension from world football hanging over them.[11]

In April 1995 the High Court ruled that the FAW's prevention of clubs from playing in Wales was illegal, a restraint of trade. Yet within weeks FIFA's Executive Committee announced that in 1997 it would withdraw its permission for the clubs to play in England. Caernarfon Town soon left England's Northern Premier League and joined the League of Wales for the 1995–6 season. With the full weight of a

High Court judgement against it, FIFA could still threaten sanctions, announcing the conclusions of the Bureau of the FIFA Committee for Legal Matters:

> the Football Association will not be able to include these two clubs in their competitions after 30 June 1997. FIFA's permission for Newport AFC and Colwyn Bay FC to play in the English pyramid until 30 June 1997 has been reconfirmed.
>
> It was noted that the problem impeding the immediate resolution of the situation appeared to be the implementation of the sanctions imposed on the club officials. FIFA will therefore impose the suspensions directly and has requested the F.A. of Wales to provide FIFA with names of officials concerned by 31 August 1995. FIFA will then suspend the relevant persons from all football activity until 15 June 1997 through its own channels.[12]

The FAW's position, under new leadership, was becoming more conciliatory than this. The costs of the High Court case had seriously undermined the finances of the Association, as its secretary general D.G. Collins has confirmed.[13] Its response to FIFA's request was to withhold the details asked for, and to ask that the deadline for the return of the two clubs to Welsh jurisdiction be rescinded. The saga concluded with the two clubs continuing to play, from their home bases in Wales, in the appropriate English league. Clearly, whatever principle of FIFA jurisdiction or quasi-autonomy might have been at stake, the FAW recognized the appropriateness of abiding by the law of the land rather than according to the Statutes of the international federation.

Both the Bosman and the Welsh cases reveal the vulnerability of FIFA's Statutes, and the limits upon some of the controls that it might seek to impose upon its members. National football associations remain politically neutral in such situations, at the mercy of FIFA, whose Statutes have a degree of flexibility which can be used to great effect by people in power, regardless of the membership's involvement or the committee structure. Whereas, for instance, in the Statutes of UEFA 'the legal authorities of UEFA' are the Control and Disciplinary Committee, and the Board of Appeal – members of which are appointed by the Executive Committee but cannot come from that Committee – in FIFA's Statutes Article 21 this is unambiguous: 'The President shall represent the Federation legally.' And whenever items arise or business has to be dealt with between scheduled meetings, the Emergency Committee can deal with the matter (Article 22), comprising the president, the chair of finance committee and an executive committee representative from one of each of the confederations.

Obviously, such busy people, dispersed world-wide, may not be able to gather at short notice for Emergency Committee meetings. The Statutes cater for this sort of emergency:

> if in exceptional circumstances the Committee is unable to convene a meeting, decisions may be reached by means of written communication, in which case the Executive Committee shall be notified immediately.
>
> All decisions taken by the Emergency Committee shall be implemented immediately and ratified by the Executive Committee at its next meeting.

Finally, Article 29 of the Statutes offers limitless possibilities for procedural flexibility: 'Any matters not provided for in these Regulations shall be decided by the Executive Committee.' In various ways, then, FIFA's Statutes allow the central powerholders to exercise legitimated forms of direct and unaccountable power and influence. This might look relatively inconsequential when directly confronting national and international legal systems, but it can be highly effective for internal organizational practice and procedure; and leaves the door open for rule by decree.

■ Secretariat, Committees and Standing Committees

The FIFA Secretariat is defined as 'a permanent administrative body ... called upon to carry out administrative, publicity and technical work', the general secretary fulfilling the role of chief executive. The responsibilities of the general secretary are defined as wide-ranging, covering accounts, implementation of decisions, production of the minutes of *all* levels of committee, correspondence, inter-organizational relations, and appointment and organization of staff in the secretariat. This all-encompassing brief makes the post of general secretary an extremely powerful one.

The FIFA committee structure comprises the executive committee, the emergency committee and fourteen standing committees. In the words of David Will of Scotland, a vice-president from 1990, 'the Executive Committee is all controlling. It controls policy. The chairmen, certainly, of all the major committees are members of the Executive Committee, so there is the Executive Committee as the policy-making body above all ... the committees are all subservient to the Executive Committee. If the Executive Committee says we want you to study that then they are obliged to do that.'[14] The committee structure has been conducive to a combined impact of the president and the general secretary that could be all pervasive and dominating. David Will and Guido Tognoni describe how such a bureaucracy was typically operated by Havelange and Blatter:

WILL: . . . it would have to be said that the General Secretary, Sepp Blatter, is a very strong personality and has created a very strong, you would almost say a decision-making, base for himself . . . he's the power behind the throne if the throne were not as strong, the president is a very very strong character.

They are very different personalities, but they are fiercely protective of the power of FIFA and the importance of FIFA as leading football on a worldwide basis, and they almost go too far. The major criticism of them, which you no doubt have heard in your other interviews and will hear again, the major criticism is the two – either together or one of them – take far too many in-house decisions without it going through a committee. There are no doubts that there are decisions taken which we, you know, you virtually read about it in the *FIFA News*, and you sort of look at one another and say 'Well who took . . . ? That's my committee!' Or 'That's a committee I sit on, who took that decision?' It is an in-house one and that is the biggest criticism of these two – they dominate the committees.[15]

TOGNONI: Havelange was a master of managing meetings. He was also a master of giving the people the feeling that they are important without giving power away. He was just a master of power.

FIFA is very democratic, but what is funny, until now or a few months ago, Havelange could appoint the members of the standing committee according to his personal desire, personal taste. First of all he was tough, physically tough, he was always the toughest guy and even when he was tired he didn't want to stop the meetings. To bring through something important you put it at point number 35 of the agenda, and people are tired, too tired to resist and so on, and what is also important is that he and Blatter, they were the only professionals in those meetings. I mean, Blatter as the general secretary and the president, as president, he was always fully informed about everything, whereas the members that came from, I don't know where, they were not professionals, they had to eat what was served, and it was the structure of FIFA. I do not say that it is wrong or right, I just stated he was like this. He had the power to do everything that he wanted.[16]

At one level, the wide spread of duties of FIFA committees and commissions has reflected the complex administrative demands of international football: the World Cup organizing committee; the referees' committee; the media committee; the committee for legal matters; the committee for security matters; the technical committee; the protocol committee: the medical commission; the committee for women's football and so on. At another level, by locating the expertise outwith the Executive Committee, it could be argued that the executive becomes increasingly toothless. In 1996 there were nineteen such groups, staffed by representatives from eighty-three different countries. No doubt all of these groups have had important functions to discharge. It is conceivable, though, that the proliferation of such sub-committees has been a mechanism which ensures that key members of the FIFA 'family' are kept within the fold, that is co-opted by the core of the organization which provides them with first-class international travel and five-star expense accounts. In many interviews with ageing 'former' football bureaucrats from the UK and elsewhere, it has been striking that even though they have 'retired' from their positions of primary responsibility, they have been found consultative roles on one or more of the committees of FIFA or the confederations, or sometimes, both; and so still retain busy international schedules at FIFA and/or confederational congresses, events and meetings.

Committees are formed and run by the FIFA president and general secretary in an essentially oligarchic style. Committee members are brought in from existing global networks. Dr Henry Fok of Hong Kong was one such figure, well established on FIFA's Executive Committee by the mid-1980s, and still there in the late 1990s. In the 1992 Annual Report of the Adidas company an important part of its future was summarized in the motto: 'To new frontiers in the East'. To this end, Adidas planned a trip to China to consolidate existing contracts, set up new production facilities and seek ways of opening up the whole Chinese market. The key entrepreneur in this strategy was Dr Fok, liaising with the Chinese Olympic Committee. Who was this Hong Kong Chinese figure whom Havelange had seen as so suited to the needs of Asian football's development? A profile provides a full answer:

> *Billionaire Henry Fok* is one of the most scintillating figures of the obscure financial world between Hong Kong and Beijing. He owns extensive real estate in the still Crown Colony, he operates hovercraft ferries running between Hong Kong and Macao. Earlier than others, Dr Fok sought contacts with the communist rulers in China and invested a great deal of money in joint ventures. He has a holding in the famous **White Swan Hotel** in Guangzhou and other luxury hotels in the country. In the meantime, Dr Fok also demonstrates his Chinese national awareness through the frequent use of his original first names **Ying Tong** and has integrated the middle initials Y.T. into his name. Should a cooperation of some kind develop between Adidas and Henry Fok, possibly plans would be realized which Henry Fok and, above all, his son **Timothy Fok**, had already discussed with the late Adidas chief **Horst Dassler**. It was long the wish of the Fok family to work with Adidas in the Far East and Fok junior would have liked nothing better than to become involved in activities of the Dassler-controlled **ISL Marketing AG**.[17]

Peopled by individuals at the centre of world business plans and expansionist markets, FIFA committees would obviously be acting for interests and motives way beyond those of simple football development. In 1994 a 'league table' of the membership of FIFA's executive and standing committees showed that 'Brazil comes out on top in the meeting-rooms just as it does on the field of play: with 11 individuals, including of course President **João Havelange**, holding down 13 seats, members from the world champion country are two seats clear at the top.'[18] The reshuffle of 1994, linked to France's successful bid to stage the World Cup Finals, placed the 1998 hosts in second place, with a different individual in each of the eleven places allotted to World Cup organizers. Germany had eight individuals in ten seats, Spain nine in nine, Italy seven in nine:

> The table is a sobering sight for **England**. The nation which still enjoys the title of Motherland of Football . . . can muster only two representatives: the venerable FA Chairman **Sir Bert Millichip** and, in the relatively uninfluential Media Committee, **David Miller**. Neighbours Scotland come off better with 7 seats, five of them occupied by **David Will**. Havelange has been nothing if not democratic with his distribution: the 239 seats have been allocated to a total of 174 individuals from no less than 84 of FIFA's 191 member countries. Democratic, but controversial, not always practical and certainly expensive, as so many members fly into Zurich for one single committee meeting.[19]

This allocation of committee places in the name of representative democracy within the FIFA bureaucracy, allied to the tameness of the sub-committees themselves, enabled the FIFA leadership to put in place a strategy of 'divide and rule' across the organization as a whole. The allocations were also based upon the usefulness of the member's potential contribution in wider networks of business. In 1986, for instance, long-standing Havelange ally, Guillermo Cañedo of Mexico, was on the Executive Committee as vice-president, was a member of the seven-man emergency committee, the five-man finance committee, chaired the media committee and was on the 1986 World Cup Organizing Committee for the World Cup in Mexico (he was to become chair of this latter committee when its German chair died just prior to the Finals). When he died in early 1997, Cañedo was FIFA's senior vice-president (in terms of the Statutes, Havelange's deputy), and in 1996 still held seats on the emergency and finance committees, and chaired the media committee and the two FIFA committees for World Cup France 1998. Cañedo had been prominent in FIFA work during his time as CONCACAF FIFA Executive Committee member from 1962–8, and assumed the chair of the media committee in 1972, two years before Havelange's succession to the presidency: 'a position in which his profound knowledge as a lawyer and television specialist stood FIFA in good stead'.[20] Cañedo's contribution and loyalty were movingly acknowledged by Havelange after his death, in a FIFA Internet announcement with a byline indicating how the 'FIFA President grieves for his old friend'. Havelange recalled how through all the 'joys' and the 'difficulty' of their work for world football, he could always:

> rely on his unflagging support. That is how one can recognise a truly admirable person of the highest calibre. The passing of my friend . . . fills me with profound sadness but I know that I shall always cherish his memory . . . [he was] a key figure in world football for several decades . . . above all a fond friend and close companion who was extremely dear to me.[21]

This personal and institutional tribute cemented a lifetime of collaborative work, sometimes involving mutual business interests as well as friendship and FIFA collaboration. When the crisis of Colombia's inability to stage the 1986 World Cup Finals was solved by Mexico stepping in as replacement host, and then this solution was threatened by an earthquake in late 1985, strong networks internal to FIFA and effective in the business and media worlds were vital to the plans to go ahead with the global media event.[22]

Although experienced European journalist and member of the FIFA media committee, Belgian Mick Michels, confirms the tokenistic nature of that committee – (in that Havelange and Blatter attend all meetings, advise on all agenda items, take all decisions and 'they always say "you are a member of FIFA, you are a member of the Committee, so you have to defend FIFA" ')[23] – clearly its long-time chair Cañedo was in a very powerful position as far as FIFA's media policy and decisions were concerned. Havelange, in an interview with Swiss magazine *Sport*, rejected the implication that he had the need to cultivate business interests around the 1986 World Cup:

> I am a businessman, and I have too much money to make even more from soccer. In my transport company, 3,000 buses carry 240 million people a year. I am a member of several supervisory boards, president of an insurance company, own a finance company, a factory for chemical products, I have shares in a stockbroking company, but neither in Brazil nor anywhere else in a TV network.[24]

Havelange's assumption that already rich people do not seek to get even richer is not borne out by the avaricious behaviour of those at the upper echelons of the business community in general. The FIFA president did not deny, though, the convenience of Cañedo's connections for conducting important committee business germane to FIFA's World Cup commitments. A combination of powerful and strongly networked individuals, and tame committees, was to prove effective for the implementation of FIFA strategies and plans.

■ Congress

In formal terms 'the Congress, the supreme body of FIFA' (Article 11) is the ultimate decision-making body of the organization, and the only source for organizational change: 'The Congress alone may alter the Statutes, the Regulations governing the Application of the Statutes and the Standing Orders of the Congress of FIFA' (Article 15, 1). The official minutes of the Congress are kept by the general secretary, and 'submitted for verification to five members specially appointed for this purpose by the Congress'. Congresses are scheduled to be held every two years, though at any time the Executive Committee could call an Extraordinary Congress; and one third of the affiliated national associations could request one in writing, to be held within three months of that request. Voting rights at Congresses are straightforward, each association having one vote and also the entitlement to be represented by three delegates. Confederations have no votes, but could be represented at Congress by three observers. Congress business, and congress elections, have been the focal point of FIFA politics. Voting for elections is by secret ballot, for any other item by show of hands. Amendments to the Statutes must receive three-fourths of the votes cast by delegates, from a delegation comprising an absolute majority of member associations: additions to an agenda, expulsion of members, change of the federation's headquarters, and dissolution of the federation, also require this. For the election of the president, two-thirds of the votes cast in the first ballot are needed for victory (any second ballot being decided on an absolute majority). On most other decisions, a simple majority is needed, though there are special cases. With most issues decided in public votes, and the three-quarter majority required for most business, FIFA is an inherently conservative organization. Consequently, to effect change in FIFA requires much lobbying, organizing and mobilizing of members and constituencies of interest. Getting the 'right' people in place has become increasingly important to power-wielding within FIFA and to the gaining and retaining of power.

The most famous example of the importance of this in FIFA's history is Havelange's challenge to the presidency of Sir Stanley Rous in 1974 (summarized in chapter 2 and covered in detail in chapter 6), the successful outcome of which, the journalist Brian Glanville has claimed, in his obituary of Rous in 1986, was premised upon Havelange's ability to 'appease the Afro-Asian bloc . . . Perhaps he [Rous] should have cast around, before 1974, for a younger European to replace him. As it was, he lost the Presidential election in Frankfurt in deeply disturbing circumstances. It was a *Sunday Times* observer who wrote of "small brown envelopes going into large black hands".'[25] This is not to say that Havelange bought his way to the presidency, but there remain unanswered questions about how the anti-Rous votes were marshalled. Any observer who has spent time around a FIFA or a confederation congress can confirm that, though the alleged practices of 1974 may not be at work – and certainly not in such crude fashion – the congress business is based upon intense trading and dealing of interests, and appropriate provision of incentives and benefits. An autocratic presidential style and what Belgian FIFA Executive Committee member Dr Michel D'Hooghe acknowledged as Havelange's omnipresence – 'he is everywhere . . . heaven and hell, like the Pope'[26] – operated as a form of patronage and surveillance throughout the committees and congresses of the organization.

■ Finances and Rights

The Executive Committee decides on the use of rights to live, deferred or excerpted broadcasts and transmissions of events, and can apply any 'special regulations', drawn up by itself, to the implementation of the appropriate Article 48. Regulations for World Cup competitions demand that a specified amount of gross receipts are 'reserved for development purposes'. Gross receipts of the World Cup Final Competition are made up as follows:

(a) the proceeds from ticket sales;
(b) the proceeds from the sale of the television rights by FIFA;
(c) the proceeds from the sale of the ground advertising rights by FIFA.
These three sources of revenue shall form the gross receipts and flow into the finance pool to be held in trust by FIFA.[27]

From these gross receipts, 19 per cent is taken for FIFA's general organization and administration over a four-year cycle. A 5 per cent contribution is directed towards a 'FIFA-administered fund for the development of football, 2% of which goes to the confederations'. An unspecified percentage goes to the general organizational expenses of the Local Organizing Committee. Of the proceeds of the sale of television rights, 2 per cent is reserved for contingencies. A 'special fund' also claims 1 per cent, 'the use of which shall be decided by the FIFA Executive Committee'.[28]

No separate article exists concerning marketing rights. The sale of FIFA's major product – the World Cup – seems, therefore, to have been traditionally in the gift of the Executive Committee and any special regulations that it might draft. Korean Dr Chung Mon Joon, new member of the Executive Committee and campaigner for the 2,002 World Cup, commented on this in late 1995, when he 'launched a scathing public attack on the way the Havelange administration conducted FIFA business. "Television and marketing contracts," he claimed, "are handled by very few people behind closed doors." '[29] The implications and consequences of such practices are presented in detail in chapter 4.

■ International Football Association Board

In its Statutes FIFA refers to this body as the International Board, or the Board. It is recognized in Article 2 that the 'Laws of the Game' are 'laid down by the International Football Association Board'. Linked to the Board's existence, within the Statutes, is the separate status as member associations and independent football 'nations', of the four British associations, England, Scotland, Wales and Northern Ireland. It is the historical legacy of the British Association's formation of the International Board which has guaranteed them a permanent vice-presidential position on FIFA's executive committee. The Board was established in 1886. Its 'purpose was to standardize the rules of the game and agree on definitions . . . also to regulate the intricacies of relations within a United Kingdom',[30] particularly on matters of the eligibility of players for international matches, and registration of non-national players for clubs in other national associations. In the struggle for supremacy in controlling the development of football, the Board initially rejected approaches from FIFA requesting representation on the Board, but in 1913, after lengthy discussions, a proposal by the FA to admit two representatives of the International Federation was accepted and 'Paris joined the likes of Portpatrick, Torquay and Llandudno as the Rest of the World's venue on the list of meeting places'.[31] Any changes in the laws could only be carried by an 80% vote, so (if working in harmony) the four British Associations retained the capacity to control business. The Board itself was a recurrent focus of dispute over several decades through which, 'led by England, the associations of the "United" Kingdom battled with the fledgling FIFA about who was to be the ultimate authority in world football'.[32] In a positive sense, the Board sustained working relationships between FIFA and the UK associations during the period of the latter's non-membership of the Federation from 1928–47.[33] The eventual compromise, resolved on the British Associations' re-entry into FIFA after World War II, preserved the UK countries' dominance on a Board with equal FIFA representation, and also guaranteed the four UK countries a permanent vice-president's position on the FIFA executive. A hundred and ten years on from its formation, the International Board still afforded the four UK footballing 'nations' the right to preside over the laws – and therefore the shape and the character – of the game, having four votes to FIFA's four votes. David Will of Scotland, for ten years a Scottish FA Board member before becoming (as vice-president and chair of the referees' committee) a FIFA representative in 1990, recognizes the anomaly of this:

> Yes, it is outwith FIFA, it is extraordinary, it is historical as you know, it is the four British Associations and FIFA, each of the Associations having one vote. They have three or four or sometimes five representatives at the meetings, who all put their oar in but at the end of the day they only have one vote. It is three quarters, six votes needed, to put anything through, so you can't put something through without FIFA and FIFA cannot put something through without at least two of the British Associations agreeing.[34]

The Board meets annually for a meeting that is usually of one hour's duration: as Will observes, 'the Board meeting is a rubber-stamp, now that is not to say that the Board meeting is not vitally important', representing as it does the formal outcome of extensive consultation and negotiation. Will recalls only two occasions over sixteen years in which the Board had gone to a vote. Much prior consultation has guaranteed that usually the annual meeting is 'the formal meeting to come to the conclusions that have been talked out by consensus for weeks before ... the end product of weeks of negotiation', as Will puts it. As full members of the Board, the UK associations can make any input at any time, but proposals from any other source must go to the Board via FIFA, which therefore sets the agenda. Will notes that despite the British predominance on the Board, the football world accepts it:

> The curious thing is that the Board is rarely under attack from outside. It is not something that is regularly attacked. Occasionally you will suddenly hear somebody say that this is ridiculous, the power that Britain has. It is hotly defended by Havelange and Blatter, one of the reasons being, I would have to say, that it is very handy, it is very useful for them to say 'Oh well, we can take that to the International Board', in the full knowledge that the Board will chuck it out, and then they can say 'I am sorry, we couldn't get that through the Board.' It is very useful for them to be able to kick it up the hill to the Board, but there is a surprising support for the British input to the Board in surprising places. You will find for example that many of the African countries, a great many of the Asian countries, are great supporters of the set-up of the Board because they recognize how conservative it is . . . I think it is a genuine recognition that the Board works.[35]

The International Board meeting for 1996 was scheduled to take place in Belfast, but as Havelange wanted to host and schedule a Board meeting in his home country, at short notice it was switched to Rio de Janeiro. The increased travel distance and time did not discourage delegates from attending the meeting. The Belfast meeting took place the following year, in March 1997, hosted by the Irish Football Association. The delegation stayed at the luxury Culloden Hotel for the weekend of the Saturday morning meeting. FIFA's president, general secretary and deputy general secretary attended unaccompanied. Vice-Presidents David Will and Abdullah Al-Dabal, and Havelange aide Peter Pullen, attended with their wives. FIFA had one further unaccompanied delegate. Football Association (of England) delegates Sir Bert Millichip, Keith Wiseman, Graham Kelly and Kenneth Ridden were accompanied by partners, and one delegate was unaccompanied. The Scottish Football Association was represented by six delegates, all accompanied by their wives. The Football Association of Wales sent four delegates, two accompanied by wives. The host association sent four delegates, all accompanied by their wives. The total delegation of forty-five guests relaxed after the morning meeting and press conference, able to enjoy the luxurious setting and anticipate the traditional banquet organized for the Saturday night. The Board's business was summarized by FIFA General Secretary Blatter, who also indicated some of the potential items for future consideration, such as the outlawing of the sliding tackle, a measure recommended by FIFA's medical and scientific committees. It was clear that though the Board had its independent status, it was very much dependent upon FIFA for its continuing high profile, its agenda-setting and its organizational functioning. As confirmed, too, by David Collins of the Football Association of Wales,[36] all four of FIFA's votes were, if needing to be cast, in the gift of just one FIFA individual – the President, Havelange himself.

■ Confederations

Whilst FIFA's 1994 definition of 'member' does not include the continental confederations, they nevertheless play a central role in world football. FIFA defines them as optional forms of organization for national associations: the latter, as long as they are 'affiliated to FIFA and geographically situated on the same continent may form confederations which will be recognized by FIFA'. Five such confederations are fully recognized, with Oceania being viewed as 'an independent geographical entity', to which the Executive Committee can grant some rights which are conferred upon the confederations.[37] The important division of labour between FIFA and the confederations is that the responsibility for competitions and tournaments at club and international level can be delegated to the confederations, whilst FIFA retains responsibility – via an appointed World Cup Organizing Committee – for the running of the World Cup Finals. That the 'Executive Committee of FIFA may, in specific cases, delegate some of its duties or powers to any confederation' is very convenient for FIFA. It can in effect delegate the arduous everyday tasks of developing and administering football throughout the world, whilst claiming the ultimate responsibility for the game, and controlling the structure of the game and the most shining jewel in the crown, the World Cup. This is a recipe for inter-organizational tensions, and has been generative of challenges and interventions, by the various confederations, to the ultimate authority on the game, as several chapters in part two dramatically demonstrate. In substance, the confederations are autonomous bodies, but their members must be affiliated to FIFA, and FIFA politics have become increasingly defined in terms of the interests of confederations, or of separate groupings within confederations, as well as the rivalries between and alliances among confederations. As FIFA became subjected to more scrutiny and pressure from the confederations during the later years of Havelange's presidency, meetings of the presidents and secretaries of the confederations with the president and secretary were established as an important forum, and were to become institutionalized into the organizational structure of the world body. It was such a series of five meetings in the autumn of 1995 that arrived at a compromise over UEFA's proposals in the *Visions* documents.[38] A seven point announcement from FIFA showed clearly the source of tensions and the points of negotiation central to the debates:

> Leaders of FIFA and the Continental Confederations have agreed on a series of points concerning the future of the FIFA World Cup and the organisation of world football administration, to be put to the FIFA Congress in Zurich on July 3 and 4 1996.
>
> The main points agreed at the meeting at FIFA House in Zurich are as follows:
>
> 1 In future, new National associations would apply first for membership of their respective Confederation and subsequently to FIFA (the reverse of the current system). Thus National Associations would in future be affiliated to FIFA via their respective Confederation.
> 2 The Confederations would be primarily responsible for dealing with political interference in football affairs, with FIFA becoming involved upon request or when no solution is forthcoming.
> 3 Similarly, the Confederations would be responsible for players' transfers within the same continent, with FIFA responsible for transfers of players between continents.
> 4 The Standing Committees of FIFA would in future be composed according to proposals submitted to FIFA by the National Associations through their Confederations.
> 5 Proposals for the rotation of the FIFA Presidency and of the FIFA World Cup were withdrawn at this stage, as were also proposals for the length of the FIFA President's mandate and the merger of certain Confederations.
> 6 The FIFA Executive Committee would contain a provisionally named 'Management Board' composed of the FIFA President and the six Confederation Presidents (including Oceania) as Vice-Presidents.
> 7 With regard to the commercialisation of the FIFA World Cup from 2,002, it was agreed that:
>> 1 revenue must be optimised, but not necessarily maximised.
>> 2 all National Associations should profit directly, with a system of distribution of funds to be worked out in detail.
>> 3 the Confederations should also share in such revenue, to a level exceeding any share received in the past.
>> 4 FIFA shall receive a share to cover its full financial requirements and costs incurred by FIFA development programmes. [39]

This was a radical list of innovations, illustrating the increased impact of the confederations upon FIFA, its organizational and leadership style, and its use of resources. The response at the FIFA Congress was to accept the broad principle of the proposals. Their implementation had the potential to produce truly significant changes in the workings of the FIFA organization and bureaucracy. To take them in turn: the anomaly of a national association being able to join FIFA, but not necessarily a confederation, would be eliminated. Sensitive international and political issues would be dealt with more immediately and in a more appropriate organizational context and geo-political setting. Player registration could be dealt with more closely in line with the conventions and precedents of particular legal systems. The composition of Standing Committees on the basis of proposals from confederations could bring to life what have been widely seen as dormant, time-serving and tokenistic levels of the FIFA organization. In exchange for these concessions, some status quo for the president was assured in not pushing for the rotational principle to be applied to the presidency and the World Cup Finals, and in leaving intact the existing confederational structure. But the confederations secured for themselves a pivotal role in world football administration by expanding the FIFA Executive Committee to ensure that it was more representative of the different constituencies of interest across the world. And the redistributive principle applied to World Cup income would benefit all levels of football organization, which, for smaller and/or poorer nations, could be revitalizing or transformative.

Although in a formal sense the Visions I and II documents were shelved, their substantial proposals offered a new framework for the future. The general secretary of UEFA, Gerhard Aigner, in his report to the European federation for 1994 and 1995, noted in his section on 'cooperation with FIFA' some 'regrettable indiscretions' in the 1995 discussions, when Havelange and Blatter publicized their views of the proposals prior to UEFA's schedule for the official announcement. Aigner described the proposals as:

> based on democratic principles in world football, placing responsibility for world football on the shoulders of both FIFA and each of the confederations, and freeing the attribution of World Cup final rounds from political tensions . . . I would also like to reiterate the official position that UEFA President Lennart Johansson has stated at every opportunity – Visions I and II are not criticisms of FIFA, and not personal attacks against FIFA's leaders. UEFA simply wants to show how it perceives the future of world football's governing body and of the World Cup. As the dominant force in world football, it is incumbent upon UEFA to have concrete views and ideas on the further development of our game. And at the end of the day, the essential decisions would be taken by FIFA's bodies.[40]

This is a skilful and diplomatic statement of the European federation's challenge to the autocratic and unaccountable style adopted and for so long established by Havelange and Blatter in running FIFA, and, in turn, of the Statutes that could allow an organization to function in such a fashion. But of course, why deny the charge in a forum such as this, in one's own back yard where one stands unaccused, unless one is seeking to put the public record straight? For, that FIFA should be in need of such reforms at all is itself a damning indictment of the way in which it was running world football; and it is a supremely confident form of reportage to concede that it is FIFA's bodies which must make the 'essential decision', knowing that, like never before, those bodies will be representative of the different geo-organizational constituencies of the world game, and that among that increasingly empowered company UEFA itself is 'the dominant force in world football'. For in his commentary upon 'UEFA and World Football' Aigner stated starkly that 'the confederations have grown in importance', in line with the 'basic precept of Vision . . . to integrate the confederations into FIFA as leading elements, and to involve them in an appropriate way in the key functions of world football's governing body'.[41] Underlying this, Aigner added, was the belief that the confederations and FIFA should work in harmony, complementing rather than competing with each other. UEFA's contacts with the other federations were described by Aigner. A long-standing 'friendly relationship with Oceania' was noted. Contacts with CONMEBOL (Central and North Americas) and CAF (Africa) were reported as 'becoming increasingly important'. And the South American and Asian confederations were not to be left out: 'a common field of activity has also emerged with CONCACAF and AFC'. The Vision proposals certainly emphasized democracy and organizational accountability. But the confederations generally had much to gain. Aigner could conclude, on this vital theme:

> All in all, an intensification of contacts between the confederations can be noted, which can only be beneficial to the positive development of world football.[42]

But the confederations knew what they were signing up for here in looking to revise FIFA's Statutes, and reshape the processes by which the organization worked. This was not some sudden political and global idealism. It was still about money and power. Redistribution of World Cup revenue would guarantee every national association member of FIFA an advance payment of one million Swiss francs, prior to the qualifying rounds of the 2002 World Cup Finals; and fuller participation within FIFA's Executive Committee would offer the opportunity to the confederations to engage more centrally, directly and frequently in the core business of the world body.

The 1995–6 debates and decisions were nevertheless remarkable in that they provided the possibility of breaking a style and a monopoly on the basis of which FIFA had been run by Havelange for more than twenty years. Guido Tognoni, head of public relations at FIFA from March 1984 to January 1995, sees 'the democratic intentions of UEFA' and its desire 'to give more power to the others' as being at the heart of the Vision proposals; but the proposals must also be understood as a 'political instrument against Havelange'.[43] For Tognoni, the challenges of the mid-1990s were no mere tinkering at the bureaucratic edges of the FIFA organization. Rather, 'this is a very interesting face of FIFA, it's the emancipation of the executive committee. They don't fear Havelange any more: he loses respect, he loses power.' Tognoni recalls, from a decade on the inside, that Blatter was a highly effective administrator for Havelange: 'He did a good job. It was never a real discussion in the meeting.' But by the early and mid-1990s Havelange, ill for a time and allegedly plotted against for the succession by Blatter himself, could no longer operate in the same style:

> Now the discussions start, led by the Europeans. Or Dr Chung from Korea, he has the courage to make a discussion, to challenge the president, to match the president sometimes, and this is new, this is a completely new development in FIFA. Johansson too. I call it the age of emancipation of FIFA, the emancipation of the Executive Committee in FIFA – they start to insist on something, they start to read the minutes, they start to correct the minutes. When Havelange says in Paris, during the meeting or the Executive Committee, we will inform you about the outcome of the negotiations with TV and marketing, they start to say, 'No, no Dr Havelange, we want to be not informed, we want to be consulted first.'[44]

At the end of 1993, Blatter had commented to a Swiss journalist, accurately and, given the way FIFA usually ran – just the way his president and he wanted it to – astutely, that the way the confederations went about their business was not FIFA's responsibility. The issue was that of the reorganization of the European club Champions' tournament, which offered Blatter the chance to clarify his understanding of the relationship between FIFA and the confederations:

QUESTION: Has FIFA no longer got UEFA under its control, in other words?
BLATTER: (He laughs) The question is phrased incorrectly. It is not FIFA's job to keep UEFA under control. Members of FIFA are the national associations, UEFA is not a member of FIFA. But UEFA is a conti-

nental organization which has had certain areas of competence transferred to it by FIFA. These also include the organization and implementation of club competitions.[45]

Two years on, though, with the consultation between the confederations and FIFA reaching their climax, this technically correct and rather dismissive interpretation looked out of place. Tognoni credits Havelange with more guile than this, for at precisely that time, with opposition to Havelange within the Executive Committee becoming more explicit, Havelange started to give the confederations more respect and recognition, and to work more closely with their presidents. Working with individuals at the top of those organizations was one way in which Havelange could buy time. It was to rebound on him, with the confederations collaborating over the Vision proposals, and most dramatically of all the decision that Japan and South Korea would co-host the 2002 World Cup Finals, but it was to allow him to choose the time and the terms of the announcement of his intent to stand down after twenty-four years in power. The Statutes of his organization had served him well, but clearly would not be able to be used in such dictatorial and autocratic fashion in FIFA's emerging future. Tognoni describes the context, nature and rationale of what was in essence one of Havelange's last stands:

FIFA always wanted to keep the confederations low key, for years and years, but when the emancipation in the Executive Committee started – and this was in [the] 90s, not before, and now it's more than ever – it was '93 when you really felt the opposition of some members towards Havelange. Then Havelange made a very smart move. He started to co-operate closer with the presidents of the confederations, with the individuals, because it was easier to manage four or five people than twenty people, and among these twenty were eight Europeans. So Havelange, he smelt that something could go wrong, that he should stay away from the Executive Committee. And without legal base, he started to consult more and more the presidents of the confederations. And how do you do that? You know the South American is anyway on your side. You have the Central American, he was easy to bring on your side. You had the African, as long as you give, you had him on your side. Then you have the Asian, who didn't care so much, it was anyway not a strong person. And then you had the European, and if the European would have opposed towards Havelange, he always would have been in [the] minority. So this was an extremely smart move, and I think was the last big move of Havelange, to give more power to the confederations. But now again, he wanted to give them one finger or two, now they took the whole hand, and now also the presidents of the confederations have smelt the power, and now they want more . . . So you have now a new group of people in the game. So far it was FIFA administration executive committee. FIFA administration were two people, Havelange and Blatter, of course Havelange being in most bodies. But now you have another political power in the confederation president. Havelange started with that business, to give more power, and to put aside the Executive Committee, but now among themselves these presidents, they start to make politics too. And at the end of the day, it will fall back on Havelange, in my opinion.[46]

And this is not only the opinion of an embittered former insider of FIFA. As confederations became more powerful in their own right and within the system of world football administration, and made such a contribution to the 'emancipation of the FIFA committees', so confederations' delegates to FIFA were likely to become more accountable and subordinate to the bodies from which they were elected. The immediate consequence of this was that individuals could be penalized as being too close to Havelange and the old FIFA style. This was the basis of the defeat of Poul Hyldgaard of Denmark, when standing for re-election to FIFA's Executive Committee, still the engine-room of the FIFA motor. Hyldgaard had been one of UEFA's elected members of the Executive Committee for more than a decade, and chair of the small and select Finance Committee (on which he was both the only European, and, effectively, the FIFA treasurer, at the time of his election defeat), for several years. At UEFA's Ordinary Congress in London in June 1996, both Hyldgaard and Belgium's Dr Michel D'Hooghe stood for re-election as the two European members of the Executive Committee of FIFA. Candidates from Turkey and Spain also stood. D'Hooghe was reselected comfortably with thirty-nine votes. Hyldgaard, though, polled only seventeen votes against the Turk Senes Erzik's twenty-six votes. FIFA's treasurer was thus removed from the FIFA committee structure by confederational priorities and politics. Dutch football journalist Ted van Leeuwen immediately commented that the Dane had been 'kicked out for being too close to Havelange'.[47] Hyldgaard himself, visibly shaken at his defeat, confirmed this,[48] but disputed the validity of the reason. Asked to explain his electoral defeat, he noted that 'there are plenty of reasons for me to be a bad boy', and stressed his consistent independence in all the work that he had undertaken for world, and not just for European, football. He elaborated on this with three of his 'plenty of reasons'. First, 'I'm European, not UEFA . . . I'm a European working for world football, not narrow organizational interests.' Second, 'I am a member of the FIFA Executive, I must defend FIFA, and I opposed co-hosting' of the 2002 World Cup. 'Japan and Korea did not want it, and [FIFA] should award it on merit.' Third, the FIFA representatives of UEFA should be from a

69

wider European base, for as things stand 'if you are not retired or a multi-millionaire you cannot be either for FIFA or UEFA'. Hyldgaard challenged the perception of his proximity to Havelange: 'They say I am close but, in thirteen years on FIFA Executive, [I have been] alone with Havelange for only thirty minutes'. This Hyldgaard response was to a UEFA challenge to FIFA from the European confederation, seen by Hyldgaard himself as being orchestrated by a scheming hardliner in UEFA's president, who insists upon 'following the party line' and is therefore not so open and democratic as is claimed. The surgent power of the confederation, Hyldgaard believed, had intensified long-standing FIFA–UEFA tensions: 'it is these tensions that have, in effect, robbed me of my independence'.

David Will describes how the increasing accountability demanded of its representatives by the European confederation worked against Hyldgaard's loyalties:

> A very honest individual and very honest to himself, a very brave man . . . courageous all the time, he spoke bravely and openly at meetings on his point of view but he made some very bad diplomatic mistakes . . . over the last two or three years there has been an increasing tension between UEFA and FIFA built up. Poul has stayed true to himself and his own views and remained a FIFA man, and would vote against the wishes of the UEFA Executive to support his views of what FIFA should be doing. And it would have to be said made some serious errors of judgement. It came to a head over these World Cup contracts and all the rest of it; that was really the last straw. He went all the time as the treasurer of FIFA, an office bearer of FIFA, he went always with the Havelange line over the last two or three years and opposed Vision 1 and Vision 2, categorically opposed in the UEFA Executive meeting where he was, like me, an observer, he had no vote but opposed it. He made a disastrous mistake in speaking at the Special Congress in Porto two years ago, speaking there publicly against Vision 1 and Vision 2, which meant he was attacking Lennart Johansson, a real attack, that he totally opposed, and that lead to his downfall . . . having reached a high position, FIFA treasurer, [he] was suddenly thrown out overnight.[49]

Michel D'Hooghe paid tribute too to Hyldgaard's important contribution to FIFA's work, but confirmed that if an elected representative of a body spoke out against that body, he could hardly expect not to lose support and votes.[50] General secretaries of two confederations also confirmed this shift in the power dynamic at the heart of world football. Chuck Blazer of CONCACAF,[51] and Peter Velappan of the AFC,[52] formulated a common view of the future of FIFA as one in which confederations like their own would come to assume more real power in football administration, alongside accompanying resources to channel back into football development in their geo-graphical regions. In Velappan's view, the confederations would then be the major developers and administrators of the world game: FIFA would be the guardian of the ideals of the peoples' game, its moral conscience. D'Hooghe's vision of FIFA's future was consonant with this: with more powerful and effective commissions (such as his own medical commisssion), alongside more accountable representation within FIFA by confederation delegates, FIFA's role for the future should prioritize its social – rather than economic – mission, devel-oping and celebrating social commonalities. In this sense the FIFA of the third millennium would champion the peoples' game, symboli-cally opposing extremities of religion, ethnicity or nationalism. But D'Hooghe also recognized the dangers of the increasing influence and potential power of FIFA's partners (marketing and sponsoring companies, and the mass communications industries). It is the gen-esis and impact of such partnerships which are reviewed and evalu-ated in the following chapter.

■ Behind the Democratic Façade

In formal terms FIFA is a democratic institution accountable to its members and to its congress. In reality, in the last quarter of the twen-tieth century it was operated more like a fiefdom or a mediaeval court, conveniently cumbersome to bring together as one, and based upon patronage dispensed from the centre and deference expressed in return.

It was from the outside that the institutional and organizational nature of FIFA began to be questioned, by the confederations, bod-ies that were an integral part of world football, but technically not members of FIFA, and therefore comparatively independent. FIFA's evolving relationship with the continental confederations produced a struggle for supremacy in the corridors of power of world football in the 1990s. Inter-confederational alliances (especially involving the three largest confederations, UEFA, CAF and AFC) led to challenges to the culture of the FIFA organization, and calls for internal reform. The essential features of FIFA were to remain intact. Those seeking to reform FIFA would have no interest in undermining its interna-tional non-governmental status, or the offshore-company benefits granted by its Swiss hosts. Football's rising global profile, and the escalating value of World Cups and associated rights, guaranteed that finding a way into FIFA was more than just a matter of working 'for the good of the game', as FIFA's logo put it. Throughout the century, and despite the football foci of its Statutes, FIFA became widely perceived as a source for the aggrandizement of nations and of individuals seeking recognition and Status on the global stage. It will be intriguing to observe how the democratic pledges and ideals of Havelange's successor will impact upon FIFA as it moves towards its centenary in the early years of the new millennium.

4

FIFA and its partners: media and markets

■ The Media and the Internationalization of Football

Within FIFA's most prominent confederational partner, UEFA, the role of the press, broadcasting and television became increasingly central in the modern media age, not least because of 'the great public interest in international competitions'—such as UEFA's Nations Championship, the Champion Clubs Cup and Cup Winners' Cup. In 1965 the UEFA Secretary, Hans Bangerter, asked how 'these powerful media could best be employed to serve the game?'.[1] He argued that the expert correspondent or commentator should act as guide or instructor, 'educating the public' on, for instance, interpretation of the Laws of the Game; that commentators should be sensitive to players, and censure gamesmanship. The reporter was portrayed as a moral agent, a communicator with the capacity to convert the unconverted to the values of the game:

> The football correspondents and radio and television commentators have the possibility to keep older and younger generations away from pubs, bars, dancings, teddy-boy mobs and other unhealthy entertainments of modern life, and to engage them in active sports, which is certainly a most important and gratifying mission.[2]

Over the following thirty years such sporting social reformism was to give way to a much more realistic appraisal of the impact of television upon the game. In March 1987 a full conference was held on football and television by UEFA's Committee for Problems concerning Radio and TV. Chair of the committee and UEFA Vice-President Freddy Rumo, of Switzerland, wrote that in a 'commercial war' of ratings, 'football has become an increasingly powerful instrument'. The committee showed an informed awareness of the new and aggressive forces within the media industries, and a realism concerning the protection of the value of television rights, particularly in a forthcoming era of scarcely regulated expansion of satellite broadcasting:

> The technology involved is becoming more and more refined; new satellites have been launched; commercial concerns have started to organize themselves; people from the media and owners of television stations have acquired stakes in big clubs in certain of the European member associations . . . Bearing in mind the lightning speed at which football has been developed, it must now make every attempt to batten down the hatches in the face of this commercial onslaught to protect itself from the deluge of pictures which could ultimately bring about its downfall.[3]

The football–television relationship was becoming much more the concern of the lawyers and the accountants, rather than the educationists, within UEFA. A decade on from this conference, UEFA in partnership with its marketing consultants (The Event Agency & Marketing, (TEAM), for the Champions League; International Sport & Leisure, (ISL), for the European Championship in England in 1996) was controlling the television product and exploiting it in highly effective fashion. For the twenty-fifth anniversary of its formation, UEFA's then press officer, U. Rudolph Rothenbühler writing on 'UEFA and the Mass Media', claimed that UEFA had a well-developed 'global perspective of an open-minded attitude towards the press', seeking to provide an 'active flow of information: in view of the investigatory research carried out by today's journalists, it would be illusory to try to conceal facts or decisions very long', and so the union 'tries to go about its daily business with the mass media as its partners'.[4] In line with this principle of accountability, the TEAM publication on the UEFA Champions League for 1995–6 provides illuminating data on the broadcasting of the event.[5]

■ The (European) Cup Floweth Over

The UEFA Champions League (UCL) is described as the 'world's most important football competition', with a cumulative television audience in the 1995–6 season of over 3.5 billion people in Europe alone. On each of the eleven match nights in 1996, an average 170 million viewers watched a live match. The final in Rome, in which

Juventus of Turin defeated Ajax of Amsterdam, was broadcast to 196 countries:

Table 4.1 Worldwide live TV coverage of the UEFA Champions League

Countries/Territories	Terrestrial	Satellite and Cable
Europe	46	3
Middle East	5	8
North America	2	1
Central America	4	27
South America	14	2
Asia/Oceania	8	27
Africa	35	14
Total	*114*	*82*

Source: TEAM/UEFA, *UEFA Champions League Season Review*, p. 37

ESPN delivered terrestrial coverage in Canada and the USA, and dominated world-wide 'additional live satellite' coverage, which it provided for the fourteen African countries/markets, the twenty-seven in each of Central America and Asia/Oceania, and the two in South America. The 'peak' audiences – that is, the highest recorded audience at any one time – guaranteed effective exposure for advertisers and sponsors: 20,666,000 in Italy; 10,085,000 in France; 9,462,000 in the UK; 7,265,000 in Spain; 6,630,000 in Germany; and 5,562,000 in the Netherlands. UEFA/TEAM commissioned Sports Marketing Surveys of Brussels to monitor television impact, and this confirmed that the 'audience levels ... positions the competition as the most popular annual sporting event in Europe'.[6] Over 1,414 hours of coverage was broadcast on the Continent, averaging forty-eight hours per country, and transmitted for the most part by 'the main national channel in their respective country, ensuring consistently high audiences and top market shares'.[7] Belgium (75 hours 40 minutes) and Switzerland (109 hours 33 minutes) figured among the top markets, as games were covered on several different language channels in those countries. The TEAM report notes this as further evidence of the 'universal appeal of this premier football competition', illustrating the '"must have" appeal of the competition to broadcasters'.[8] Israel's 105 hours, on its new commercial channel, comprised continuous repeat showings of matches. Apart from these three special cases, the top markets for cumulative broadcast hours were the UK (73 hours) and Italy (64 hours). The lowest were Hungary (29 hours) and Ireland (32 hours).

Covering the League throughout the season was an army of media professionals: 7,631 reporters, and 2,674 photographers. UEFA claims that the booming economy of this elite international competition has positive impacts:

> Football has benefited financially from the principle of solidarity and the concept of transparency with the revenues generated flowing back into football. A total of Swiss Francs 190 million was available for distribution to European football.[9]

Market penetration, as TEAM puts it, was truly global – 'complete pan-European television penetration coupled with significant coverage in every other continent on each of the 11 match nights'.[10] With build-ups to the live games, follow-ups and retrospectives, and highlights of other matches 'on a delayed basis', Wednesday evening television schedules throughout Europe were dominated on match nights by the event. The TEAM/UEFA achievement has been to standardize media cultures, to 'streamline' its 'on-screen graphic style', to 'mirror the on-air design across 35 stations in Europe alone'.[11] Squads of graphic specialists roamed Europe throughout the season, distributing packages of programme support material and background graphics. Juggernauts were dispatched throughout the Continent to deliver a standardized product. The competition logo and the opening sequence dominated the different host broadcasters' studio sets. Briefings were organized, and regular refresher briefings conducted throughout the campaign. There was little room for creative manoeuvre or innovation on the part of the broadcaster. In the August before the 1995–6 season began host broadcasters attended a workshop at the Hotel Noga Hilton in Geneva, around the time of the draw, a forum designed to build a 'bond between the family of broadcasters, enabling an exchange of ideas and viewpoints',[12] and stimulating discussion on new technologies and best practice. Directors and producers were able, in this forum, to 'determine for themselves' how to best develop the coverage. But they sound to have had little genuine scope for this:

> Broadcasters were also provided with a manual for the 1995–6 season which outlined the design concept, programme schedules, production issues, technical, commercial and on-screen guidelines plus information for venue procedures and contact details for all broadcasters, sponsors, clubs

and suppliers connected with the UEFA Champions League.

At every venue, representatives from UEFA, TEAM, the club and the Host Broadcaster would meet the day before the match to discuss all aspects of the TV production including camera positions, OB van areas, accreditation, and plans for any broadcast activity outside the match coverage itself. This ensured that all parties were fully informed of the timetable of events, essential for the effective organization of the live event.[13]

Planned with the precision of a military operation, this orchestration of the sporting spectacle aspires, as far as possible, to structure the environments of the football game, and control the cultural presentation of the event. It is a science of event management which manages not just an objective technical transmission of football, but which controls to the most minute detail the construction and presentation of the wholly commodified game in a colourful, ritzy yet standardized society of the mediated spectacle: 'The SPECTACLE is *capital* accumulated to the point where it becomes image.'[14] Control of the image and celebration of the commodity become one and the same. The UEFA Champions League and its brilliant partner TEAM has taken to its limits the 'unholy alliance' as Whannel has called it,[15] of sport, television and sponsors' interests. Such a development, it is widely believed, is as much the initiative of the marketing agency as of football's organizations: UEFA's concern that a pirate European Superleague might materialize played into the hands of TEAM's market opportunism.[16] This set of alliances around marketing and sponsorship is considered in a section below. It was the World Cup, as much as the Olympic Games, which showed what benefits there could be for sport in evolving lucrative partnerships with broadcasters.

■ World Cup Television Rights

World Cup Finals now provide some of the largest television audiences of all time. Television rights, as with those for the Olympics, have therefore become big business. The television rights world-wide, excepting the USA, for the 2002 and 2006 World Cups were awarded by FIFA in 1996, after consideration of the seven bids. These included Mark McCormack's IMG, and TEAM Marketing. Other offers were received from ABC Television (USA, owner of the cable network ESPN), Cable TV (Hong Kong), CWL (Switzerland). The European Broadcasting Union also coordinated an international consortium which placed a bid, of more than £1 billion: 'This consortium holds the current contract for World Cup TV rights for the 1998 World

Cup in France. The consortium's agreement with FIFA also covered the 1990 and 1994 World Cup Finals and includes a provision for priority negotiations, which have been continuing since last December', FIFA stated in its media release of 15 May 1996. The 1998 world-wide rights had been valued at 230 million Swiss francs in FIFA's agreements with the EBU, and with ABC-TV. These were expected to be far exceeded in the new agreement for 2002 and 2006, and the EBU's 'priority negotiations' were probably a hindrance rather than a help, involving the early revelation of its thinking. FIFA's Blatter added in a press release, on 31 May 1996, the day the bids closed: 'It is clear that the rights for 2,002, wherever the event is held, will show a substantial increase over the current contract. FIFA is very gratified by the interest shown in the World Cup by so many prominent companies.' Rupert Murdoch's News Corporation/Sky Television was not one of these, reputedly due to 'the widespread scepticism about the bidding process'.[17] IMG, with its English Premier League experience, was keen to establish itself in the wider European and world football markets, and submitted a $2.3 billion bid.[18] The successful bid came from an alliance of FIFA's long-term marketing partner, ISL in Switzerland, and the German Kirch's media conglomerate. Kirch could add World Cup football to his interests in film rights, pay-TV, his 35% stake in the Axel Springer publishing group including Germany's top tabloid *Bild*, his stakes in seven German radio stations, the Sat 1 private TV channel, and four other television channels. His interests in digital development showed in his partnership with TV tycoon and short-term president of his country, Silvio Berlusconi, in Italy.[19]

The ISL/Kirch bid was worth £1.45 billion, comprising £650 million for the 2002 finals, and £800 million for those of 2006. This enables ISL/Kirsch to auction World Cup coverage world-wide, but FIFA has retained a power of veto, which general secretary Sepp Blatter argued would be used to guarantee that the World Cup should 're-main accessible to viewers who do not possess expensive satellite or cable systems'.[20] This worthy sentiment was not likely to have been shared by the media moguls to whom a deregulated and fragmented sports media market meant more pricing options:

> Their interest comes not just from the bucketfuls of cash from advertisers and subscribers, but from the stratospheric income potential of the next generation of TV technology, with its digital services, computer links and, in the not too distant future, the advent of virtual stadia.[21]

The trend was established for the full exploitation of the media football market, and sports writer Keir Radnege could conclude that:

'The 1998 World Cup will be the last which European viewers can watch live, "clear" of some form of encryption.'[22] Within four years, Radnege predicted, football would be 'dictating a twin-track approach to football coverage', with the top games accessible only by cable, satellite or pay-per-view; and state broadcasters providing networked coverage on a late-night highlight model only. If Radnege were to be proved right, Britain would be once again leading developments in world football, with Sky's *The Match* and the BBC's *Match of the Day* providing the profitable precedent. As the 1996–7 European soccer season began, French football fans could pay 50 francs by credit card for their choice of any French First Division game, and call it up live onto their television screens via the Canal satellite service. Murdoch's Sky Television coup in gaining the rights for the English Premier League in 1992 helped the satellite company become 'the most profitable broadcaster in Western Europe, making pre-tax gains at the rate of £8 per second',[23] and showed how profitable football on television could become.

In 1996, for a renewal of rights in a four-year deal through to the year 2001, Sky paid the Premier League £670 million. The BBC paid £73 million to preserve its rights for its hugely successful Saturday night highlight show, *Match of the Day*. In 1983 the first ever contract for the transmission of live league football in England – a joint BBC/ITV deal – was based on an annual rights fee of £2.6 million. A competitive negotiation process in 1988 saw ITV win a four-year contract for exclusive rights, at the cost of £44 million. After a glamorous and high-profile World Cup in Italia '90,[24] and the move towards all-seater stadia in a post-Hillsborough England, Murdoch's move into the football media market changed the cultural base of the game for fans and spectators. It both extended and diversified the available modes of consumption of the football product. The senior press officer of the English Premier League summed this up accurately:

> It created a huge new source of income, it created more live coverage of football on television than ever before, it created a reinstated *Match of the Day* as a national institution and it created a new way of watching football in pubs and clubs.[25]

People could now follow the Premier matches live on screens in Johannesburg, Kuala Lumpur, Santa Cruz or Boston, Massachusetts, in preference to their own local league matches or more indigenous sports the inconvenience of a journey away. This was the reality of the globalized reach of the mediated football spectacle. The huge sums involved began to grip the game in an inflationary spiral, with obscene sums paid for individual players and salary contracts for top stars that would have been unimaginable just a few years previously. In the early summer of 1996, UEFA – on the eve of the Euro '96 tournament for Europe's national sides – announced that from the 1997–8 season onwards selected (strong, established) football countries could have two bites at the lucrative Champions League cherry. More games to sell, more revenue to raise for the television companies, more branding of the supranational elite model. In a dress-rehearsal for what many pundits saw as an embryonic European Super League, UEFA was cynically changing the very rationale for the Continent's major football competition. As the chief executive of the Football Association of Wales pithily put it: with two teams from a number of countries entering the tournament, 'well, it isn't the Champions League is it?'[26] Pride or misplaced provincial arrogance had kept Scotland away from the 1950 World Cup Finals, on the basis that as runner-up to England in the Home Championships of the UK associations, they were unworthy representatives of Europe in Brazil. In the inaugural season of a Champions League for non-champions, there would be no such principled withdrawals, in a political economy which bound together football, media and sports bodies in a golden triangle of mutual self-interest.

At the beginning of 1974, *FIFA News* reported that more than 2,100 press reporters, 750 photographers and 1,200 radio and television reporters had applied for accreditation to cover the Finals in West Germany.[27] The press and photographer applications came from sixty-six countries across five continents. Of those approved, Germany and Brazil had the highest contingents. On the eve of the World Cup, Rous wrote a piece on FIFA and made no mention of television, its potential and its problems.[28] Thirteen years later FIFA President Havelange dedicated his editorial in *FIFA News* (March 1987) to the issue of television, a statement of the recognition of its importance, and an announcement of FIFA's long-term partnership with the television industry.[29] The editorial opened with a nostalgic recollection of the first occasion on which World Cup football was seen on television, 'in the days when young Pelé was demonstrating his football skills', and contrasted those days of television as a luxury and an adventure with the technical advances which could relay 'the virtuosity of a Diego Maradona' to viewers all over the world. Havelange expressed his view of the reciprocal benefits in the relationship, for FIFA and its 'equally competent and loyal partners' in television:

Last June, people in 160 different countries watched the final between Argentina and the Federal Republic of Germany: surveys have shown that an estimated 580 million viewers were watching. The total number of people reported to have watched the World Cup Final Competition in Mexico is a gigantic 128 thousand million.

These figures reflect, on the one hand, the fascination of football and, on the other, the results of television's superlative contribution. The world's number 1 sport and the most prominent means of communication became partners during the so-called 'television age'. Each of these partners has contributed to the success of the other.[30]

FIFA's obligation in promoting world football, Havelange continued, is to provide the best possible television service, 'from the qualitative and quantitative point of view'. FIFA received 49 million Swiss francs for the television rights for the World Cup in Mexico in 1986, and though in 1986 it had very attractive bids for forthcoming rights from private television companies, it had decided to continue working with the European Broadcasting Union for the following three World Cups, the first time such rights had been sold on such a long-term basis:

> In view of its positive experience, FIFA has decided to conclude contracts not only for the next World Cup Final Competition but also for the 1994 and 1998 competitions at the same time. FIFA is convinced that the best possible broadcasting coverage for the next World Cup Competitions has thus been assured, FIFA will receive a total of Sfr. 340 million from the consortium for the broadcasting rights of all three World Cup Final competitions.[31]

This cumulative figure was broken down into 95 million for 1990; 115 million for 1994; and 130 million for 1998.[32] Critics of Havelange, including Ernie Walker of Scotland and UEFA,[33] have said that it was unwise and poor business to grant the rights for such a long period, and Tognoni comments that the 1987 deal was very good for the 1990 event, but would have been much higher for separately negotiated deals for 1994 and 1998. Whatever the business acumen or otherwise of the three-event deal, it undeniably secured the stability of FIFA finances, as Havelange himself claimed. In his editorial for the December 1987 *FIFA News*, Havelange confirmed this strategy, justifying it as 'a policy of continuity and stability with our former partners', and assuring 'FIFA's financial existence into the 21st century'. Coca-Cola sponsorship helped launch Havelange's 1974 development programme. Television money stabilized FIFA finances, around the ever more attractive and money-spinning event of the World Cup Finals. Tognoni, from right inside the FIFA organization

81

at this crucial point of consolidation of its global mission, evokes the critical importance of TV money to FIFA, and the simplicity of the money-making process once the television industry recognized the almost limitless potential of football's cross-cultural appeal and World Cup coverage:

> FIFA has never a problem finance wise, it's a monopoly enterprise, the money is always there. Maybe sometimes you put some money in a bad place but everything is under control, you had not to work for money you have to work for an idea. This is something beautiful . . . in FIFA you have not to sell product, product is a self-seller.
>
> FIFA is living from one event which is the World Cup and this event is living from marketing and television receipts, television money, and marketing money. Marketing money is only possible thanks to television, but it was not Havelange who invented television, it was not Blatter who invented television, it was not you and me who invented television, and made all this dream of money floating. It was the time, starting in the seventies where television got important then somebody invented publicity on television, the Dassler boards you know . . . Then in the eighties it started to explode, the money, and this is not the merit of Havelange and not the merit of Blatter, it is the merit of the circumstances of the time. In the monopoly sport like football and you have all the rights, then you can also praise yourself that you have done a lot of work for FIFA. I mean, Sir Stanley, he was president during a time when it was much more difficult to manage an international federation, and the people before they deserve a big respect. Havelange also deserves some respect, but he did not invent TV. He was just the right man at the right place in the right moment. And the moment was important, more than the players and the men, the moment was the moment when television grew and television made everything possible.[34]

Havelange was the ideal man for such a moment, though, for FIFA, football, friends and himself: his business links, personal networks and dictatorial leadership style meant that the moment was right for the man as well as vice versa. By the time of the 1994 World Cup in the USA FIFA could report, in its report on the 1994 World Cup, that 31 thousand million viewers had followed the event, across 188 different territories, as table 4.2 indicates:[35]

By the mid-1990s, FIFA also reported the football-television relationship as a more tempestuous partnership, due to the presence of 'new factors in an elusive equation'.[36] The major new factor was the 'boom in satellite television', transmitting the games of the great teams to all corners of the world, and making local or national coverage less attractive to broadcasters. Economically, too, the FIFA activity report notes, the television boom could have perverse effects: 'while TV rights change hands for ever more colossal sums at the top of the football pyramid in Europe, the smaller countries, far from being

Table 4.2 Worldwide Transmission of USA '94 World Cup

Continent/Region	Broadcaster	No of Territories
Europe	EBU	51
Middle East	EBU	5
Middle East	ASBU	11
Asia, Pacific	ABU TVB	23
Asia, Pacific	SBS	6
Africa	EBU	8
Africa	URTNA	36
North America	Various	2
South/Central America	OTI	19
Caribbean	OTI	18
Various	RFO	9

Source: FIFA, *Report – FIFA World Cup USA '94*, p. 197

able to capitalise on the knock-on effect of the sport's TV popularity, are often obliged to pay their national network to cover the local action to a neo-discerning public'.[37] Perverse or not, this did not stimulate FIFA to downplay the auction for the 2002 and 2006 rights just a few months later. It would not be too much of a simplification to note that at the heart of FIFA's problem – one might add inconsistency and hypocrisy – in this sphere is the tension between the resourced centre and the under-resourced periphery: the lived culture of the local gives way still more to the cultural prominence of the global. It is remarkable that in something so simple as the game of football, these disparate elements can be held together recognizably as part of the same overall cultural phenomenon. The broadcasting revolution has made the most developed examples of the peoples' game accessible on undreamt of scales: ironically it is the concomitant revolution, in sports marketing, that has done so much to redefine that access, and the culture and context of the game itself. FIFA's marketing partnerships are the focus of the following section.

■ FIFA Initiatives: Marketing the Peoples' Game

With the rising profile of the World Cups of 1950 (in Brazil), 1954 (Switzerland), 1958 (Sweden) and 1962 (Chile) it became increasingly clear that football, as a cultural product with world-wide appeal, could be exploited much more effectively for its business potential and financial profits. Sir Stanley Rous had shown awareness of this, but his own brand of internationalism was much more that of the missionary educator than the global businessman. FIFA was certainly in need of reform and modernization in the period immediately following on from World War II, and as a contribution to his belief in the role of football in international reconciliation, Rous – as secretary to the Football Association (England), and alongside his task of leading the British Associations back into FIFA membership – suggested a Great Britain versus Europe match to celebrate the re-entry. Approached by the president of the Swiss Football Association on the subject of 'FIFA's desperate financial problems', whilst holidaying in Switzerland, Rous proposed that the proceeds of such a celebration fixture should go 'to FIFA as our goodwill gesture on re-entry'.[38] A crowd of 135,000 filled Glasgow's Hampden Park stadium in 1947 as Great Britain cruised to a 6–1 win. FIFA received a £30,000 cheque which became 'the basis of FIFA's rapid financial recovery.'[39] During the 1950s, under whichever European president, FIFA did little to exploit such commercial potential. Rous himself knew the potential, but harboured deep reservations about the dangers to the game of an unbridled commercial logic and momentum. He could recall with pride the last World Cup Finals of his presidency, in Germany in 1974, as 'a spectacle which gave pleasure to millions worldwide . . . Such was the fascination of the competition that 74 countries between them sent 4,616 accredited Press, radio and TV representatives.'[40] But right to the end of his period of office, Rous was warning against 'the pressure of nationalism' and 'the menace' and 'pressure of commercialization'. In an address at an Olympic Congress in Varna in October 1973, he proposed that the International Olympic Committee should draw more upon the expertise of the international sporting fraternity and the federations in coping with these twin pressures. He proposed that the IOC, National Olympic Committees, and International Federations should join together as a 'trinity' working effectively and in co-ordination. Though for Rous the International Federations were 'the most important element in that trinity . . . the three parts of the trinity have a joint responsibility. They must present a united front to resist the encroachment of politics, nationalism and commercialization into sport.'[41] But at the very moment that Rous was seeking to cultivate or cement partnerships within extant sports organizations and administrative bodies, Havelange was campaigning across the planet. Here are some excerpts from Havelange's glossy campaign brochure in the build-up to the vote for the presidency:[42]

Characterized by firmness, culture and a quiet charm, Havelange will be the great leader, whom the football of a new world is expecting. Something of a Pierre de Coubertin, dignifying and completing the ideals of Jules Rimet . . . a name of high credentials, able to occupy a platform totally aimed at the development and magnitude of football on a world scale.

João Havelange as president of the FIFA? The European football, with the natural and foreseen exception of the British, says yes. It is a spontaneous yes, without restraints, based on the sympathy and esteem when it comes to a great Brazilian sports leader, that is, the man who took over the direction of the CBD and conducted the Brazilian football team to the triple conquest and definite possession of the world's most coveted trophy, the Jules Rimet Cup. Three championships won in a short period under the same direction, sometimes overcoming a lot of unfavourable incomprehensions in his own country, represent a performance which is not easy to match by any other sports leader in the world. Havelange managed to set up a perfect machine in the CBD and knows how to turn football into an unmatched attraction all over the globe.

This encomium was penned by an Italian journalist by the name of Renato C. Rotta, grandly labelled as 'President of the World Association of Football Enthusiasts'. Behind the hyperbole and the flowery and at times quirky translation lay some harsh realities for Rous and some serious messages for FIFA: a proven and thick-skinned ruthlessness of ambition and achievement; an explicit anti-Britishness; a hard-nosed approach to information-management (the claim to speak for almost all of Europe); and the commitment to expand the game, and its World Cup showcase, globally. FIFA's future growth and prosperity would come to depend upon the success of its marketing strategies for the world game, hand-in-hand with the marketing possibilities offered by FIFA and football to appropriate corporate sponsors: a symbiosis of impression management for both the football organization and the commercial company. If the marketing of himself in the campaign for the presidency was anything to go by, Havelange's election had placed the world body in good hands. Nevertheless, Havelange was faced with a huge problem on succession to the presidency. He had little chance of fulfilling his campaign commitments unless effective partnerships were established, and this was a dilemma indeed. The Olympic Games – despite the International Olympic Committee's (IOC) bank balance in the years of Lord Killanin's presidency having moved from the figure of $2,084,290 (1972) to $45,142,752 (1980)[43] – was still stuttering along towards the financial disasters of Montreal (1976) and the hidden subsidies of Moscow (1980). Los Angeles, in securing the Summer Olympic Games of 1984, had only one rival in the bidding process – Teheran: and it was not until the effective, successful and jingoistically American staging of those Games that the television bonanza took off to truly unrealistic levels, in the auctions for television rights. Sponsorship and rights marketing, Samaranch perceived, were the key to lucrative and stable forms of revenue, as opposed to dependency upon volatile television markets and unpredictable rights auctions. He learned much of this from the example of FIFA and Havelange. But in 1974, Havelange's commitments to the Third World allies who had helped him oust Rous had no economic base whatsoever. It was the German sports goods manufacturer Horst Dassler of Adidas, through the mediation of Patrick Nally, who secured Coca-Cola as a global partner for FIFA. This generated the expansion of the sports goods market, and accompanying forms of sports marketing, which became vital to FIFA's goals and achievements in the Havelange era.

Patrick Nally had been involved, with the sports commentator Peter West, in the early growth of sport sponsorship in Britain.[44] Through an advertising agency and then his own company WestNally, he had established sponsorship deals by brewery companies, Green Shield Stamps, and companies such as Benson and Hedges, Kraft, Ford and Esso, Cornhill Insurance: 'In those early days of sponsorship, when men like him were inventing the genre, he was the international cavalier for whom the British market was a base from which to conquer the world.'[45] Nally's marketing initiatives paved the way for remarkable marketing deals such as that achieved by ISL (International Sport and Leisure) for the IOC, in initiating the inaugural TOP (The Olympic Programme) scheme for the 1988 Seoul Summer Olympics. There were difficulties in this, but ISL succeeded in buying back from each National Olympic Committee the right to market the Olympics (and the IOC rule on this was accordingly amended); and sold exclusive Olympic marketing rights to 'nine companies: Coca-Cola, VISA, 3M, Brother, Philips, Federal express, Kodak, Time Inc. and Panasonic, for a grand total of . . . more than $100 million'.[46] The marketing bonanza was such that the South Korean Organizing Committee itself signed up ninety-seven Korean companies as smaller, national sponsors: 'the income from sponsorship, supply and licensed deals already then [a year before the Games] exceeded $150 million, $15 million more than the hugely profitable Los Angeles Games made from marketing'.[47] Wilson could conclude in the year of the Seoul Olympics that in the seven or eight years since Samaranch's succession to the Presidency, 'at least $2 billion has passed through' the IOC's 'Swiss bank account'.[48] ISL's negotiation of marketing rights, as much as the sale of television rights, was responsible for this. ISL was formed, Nally himself claims, as Dassler's own version of the WestNally Company and the Monaco-based SMPI (Société Monaquesque de Promotions Internationales) – this latter described by Wilson as 'Dassler's money and contracts allied to Nally's ideas and marketing experience'.[49] The model for ISL had therefore been the principle of exclusivity of marketing rights pioneered by Nally, on behalf of Dassler, for FIFA.

For Nally, the importance of getting a big name such as Coca-Cola into the soccer programme was twofold. First, it gave the right credibility and image for that sort of work. Second, 'if you're into Coke, you're into the biggest bluechip company on a global basis'. Bringing Coca-Cola into the sponsorship of world soccer 'became the blueprint for everyone who wanted to try and bring money into international federations through this source'. The multi-million investment package put together for FIFA concentrated initially upon the new world youth cup, which could guarantee Asian and African participation on the world stage. In order to be a political player, with voting rights within FIFA, a nation must participate in at least one FIFA competition, and so new competitions constituted an extension of FIFA's franchise.

Complementing the flow inwards of the development areas of coaching, administration and medical expertise, the competitive platform of the youth cup (first held in Tunisia in 1977) provided the opportunity to create a flow outwards, from Africa and Asia, of teams which could then compete at international level against European and South American nations. This was revolutionary, and though the champions of the first two youth (under twenties) tournaments produced established winners, in the Soviet Union and Argentina (the young Maradona scoring the decisive goal in the 1979 final in Tokyo, against the Soviet Union), by the third tournament the value of the new initiative was becoming clear for developing football nations: Qatar, though losing 4–0 to West Germany in the final in Sydney, had beaten Brazil (3–2) and England (2–1) on the way to the final. African nations were soon to emerge on this stage: Nigeria won the third-place match, in and against the Soviet Union, in 1985, and in Saudi Arabia in 1989 lost the final by just 2–0 to Portugal. Ghana lost only 2–1 to Brazil in the 1993 final in Australia, having won the 1991 Under-17 title in Florence, Italy, beating Spain 1–0 in the final. The Under-17 World Championship had been inaugurated in 1985, Nigeria beating West Germany 2–0 in the final in Beijing, having defeated Italy (1–0) and Hungary (3–1) en route to its triumph. However sceptical the established football nations might have been about such events (some seeing them as peripheral, in comparison to their own apprenticeship systems and fully developed professional leagues), the FIFA initiatives clearly offered valuable international experience and competition which were to stand Asian and African footballing nations in good stead on the larger world stages of the World Cup and the Olympic Games. These developmental initiatives would not have been possible without FIFA's Coca-Cola monies.

A world-wide skills programme was also created, to ensure widespread promotional activity for the sponsoring company. With the base established in the development programmes and the youth cup, a deal was then concluded whereby, at the cost of between eight and twelve million dollars, Coca-Cola was brought into the 1978 World Cup in Argentina, and 'financed and funded the whole of the marketing programme'. The external negotiations with Coca-Cola were conducted by Nally; the internal arrangements were accomplished by Dassler and Havelange: 'All the politics, he wanted handled through him and his team . . . the selection of putting Sepp Blatter in as gen. sec. of FIFA – the selection of Sepp out of [Swiss Timing] Longines, the training of Sepp at Landersheim . . . the convincing of Havelange to put Sepp in as the new development man as he then was – all that political selection of personnel was done by them.' Landersheim was the French residential base from which Dassler controlled his sports marketing and merchandising empire.

Nally and Dassler established the sponsoring of clients' exclusivity in all aspects of merchandising and franchising, not just in stadium advertising: 'Never again has FIFA released any rights to the World Cup from their central control', Nally observes.[50] By the first World Cup of Havelange's presidency, in Argentina in 1978, Nally had contracted six major sponsors to FIFA including Coca-Cola, Gillette and Seiko, though he was still juggling the advertising billboards of companies contracted with different national teams. This was soon to be streamlined, in FIFA's template for what became the TOP scheme in the case of the Olympics. From then on the only option open to sponsors was the complete marketing package: 'The sums were so vast that lots of companies couldn't touch it but it was a lot easier to work with the few who could', recalled Nally.[51] This new scale of football finance appears to have involved the acquisition and distribution of large sums of money.

Havelange had made major commitments to the development of African and Asian football. Dassler 'would commit himself to help Havelange to get the money' to, for example, 'take an event that's been running at 16 teams and go to 24 teams – to get the Spanish to agree to do it – politically it's important for the Africans and Asians'. It was then Nally's task to 'create a marketing programme to justify bringing big money into that sport to help Horst fulfil his obligations'. The cost of the marketing rights for international football were, therefore, unprecedentedly high because of the range and scale of deals needed to fuel this expansionist programme: as Nally alleges – 'because', for instance, 'Horst committed to give 36 million Swiss francs extra to Havelange to enable him to bribe the Spanish to take the World Cup up from 16 teams to 24 teams as part of his commitment to get more Asian and African teams in ... in Spain, in the Placo de Congresso, in the gentlemen's toilets, Horst said the going rate with the Spanish organizing committee wasn't going to be $4 million which I'd already negotiated and agreed, we had to pay an additional 36 million Swiss francs.' Nally sees the effects of such financial flexibility as 'good', evidenced by improving African and Asian performances in the World Cup following on from the developmental youth programmes, and such large amounts of money being poured in was made possible by the scale of the Coca-Cola investment: 'Coca-Cola if you like legitimized the industry, the amount of money that was going into soccer ... but I don't think ever quite realised the importance of their association and how it being abused enabled this club, this whole mafia going on within sport, to be really supported by them because they gave it all credibility.' Dassler got Havelange to impress the Coca-Cola people, at the company's world headquarters in Atlanta, by flying in on his private plane to meet with them. Nally argues that the Coca-Cola connection gives sports organizations an aura of respectability, generated by the Coca-Cola global image of corporate cleanliness: '[The federations] ... are in some ways, because of Coca-Cola, beyond reproach.'

One outcome of this new political economy of world sport, an important effect of the innovative form of partnership at the heart of this political economy, was the elevation in status of positions in sports organizations, as noted by Nally:

> It's suddenly becoming an extremely important and powerful position to be in, the President of an International Federation that is rich because there is money flowing in from the Olympic Games and other things. Now, it means trips, it means travel, it means awards, air tickets, it certainly beats sweeping out the back of the garden at the weekend if you're flying first class everywhere to major international events.

89

How did Horst Dassler hold together an operation on this scale? Clearly he provided lavish hospitality, the 'compulsory Adidas dinner' at every international sports federation meeting at a time when the federations were relatively impoverished and 'Adidas was the only company that ever supported them'; his own residential and catering complex at Landersheim, Alsace; and, allegedly mostly for Africans and Asians in Paris, his sports shop, and restaurant with other hospitality facilities in Montmartre. He retained useful individuals in bogus capacities – Harry Cavan, Northern Irish football administrator and FIFA vice-president, for instance, as 'shoe consultant'. And he made, and kept, commitments and promises that would catapult sport into a new phase of economically expanded and financially lucrative transnational practice. British former sports minister Lord Howell and his committee investigating sponsorship in sport were right to target Dassler as a pivotal figure in the evolving pattern of the global sports economy:

> I started by asking a question such as 'Can you give me any justification as to why a football boot manufacturer should wish to decide who should become the president of FIFA and control world football?' And his reply was that he had in his office a tremendous computer and records department which had every periodical and news letter issued by every sports body round the world and these were all tabulated. Therefore it was very natural that if anyone wanted to pursue a career like Havelange . . . they would come to him to get the names and addresses of all the contacts. That is what he supplied and the same facilities, he said, were available to Sir Stanley Rous, except Sir Stanley Rous didn't ask for them – and I don't suppose could have afforded to have made all these contacts around Africa and Asia, which enabled Havelange to get himself elected as president of FIFA.[52]

A major step in consolidating FIFA's commercial base was the setting up of ISL (International Sport and Leisure). Lord Howell learned of this as the Howell report was at the printers, and telexed some questions to the former British athlete John Boulter at Adidas (Boulter had accompanied Dassler during the meeting with Howell and John Wheatley, director of the Sports Council [London]). Howell recalls his committee's main areas of concern:

> The danger I saw was the danger that if you had a company which is going to be solely responsible for the advertising and commercial promotion of sport at FIFA level, would that then lead to commercial control of the government of the sport? I have to say that I don't think it has. Perhaps I overstated the dangers. But because Horst Dassler's company Adidas was very much at the heart of that exercise I felt it was something which had to be very closely watched.[53]

Lord Howell's concern was not shared by the Adidas representative. He 'received a reply from Boulter telling me that he was becoming increasingly concerned about the nature of my enquiries'.[54] 'When I raised' any questions or issues 'critical of Dassler, Boulter was threatening me with actions.'[55]

The formation of ISL was the masterstroke in Dassler's emerging monopoly of world sports marketing. Howell was unequivocally correct to express the concern that he did about such an initiative involving no process of open bidding or tendering; and Boulter was understandably nervous that such questions were being posed on the verge of what would be a major coup within the field of international sports marketing. By mid-1983, within a matter of months of its creation, ISL was handling merchandising rights and rights for stadium advertising for FIFA, UEFA and, embryonically at least, the IOC. By October 1983 the company had also signed to handle any of the Seoul Olympic Games Organizing Committee's merchandising, licensing, sponsorship and supplier contracts; and was publicizing, in a special supplement to *Time* magazine's European edition, its successes in attracting sponsors for its football marketing programme – not least, via advertising in the supplement reserved exclusively for the company's own regular clients such as Canon, Camel, JVC, Seiko, Fuji and Air France.[56] Andrew Craig, marketing manager of ISL Marketing, expounded the company philosophy on 'Globalisation, the Real Opportunity in Sports Marketing'. Craig argued that the multi-domestic system of management and control of international corporations, in which products are marketed locally by local management, is close to anachronistic in an age of accelerated communications, increased population mobility, and the growth of mass audience communication. However appropriate this system may have been in the past, 'the changing patterns of international business, the blending of market requirements and the resultant development of homogeneous world wide products suggest, that global marketing philosophy will ultimately prevail'. Craig then quoted his boss, Klaus Hempel, on how sport provides the ideal focus for companies seeking to impact in the global marketplace:

> the traditional media have been unable or unwilling to respond to the needs of global marketing companies. The result is that it is still extremely difficult for a major corporation to communicate a unified message on a world wide basis without first making a massive investment in both time and resources. It is up to sports marketing companies to fill this gap. ISL's Intersoccer 4 Programme for example makes use of soccer's world wide

91

appeal to create an immediate and highly flexible universal communications language for its sponsors.[57]

Globally minded corporations, as Hempel put it – such as Coca-Cola, Bata and Cinzano – could quickly see the benefits of the sponsor programmes, and ISL put these in place for its contracted clients for the 1984 European Football Championships in France. The main benefit was perimeter advertising in all of the stadia used during the tournament, guaranteeing world-wide television exposure. Exclusive franchising rights were also included in the package, and further exposure in event-based media. Sponsors also provided services to the media – a harried press person could loan photographic equipment from Canon, and photocopy on a Canon machine; take a refreshing drink of Coca-Cola; admire the ball-boy kit and opening ceremony equipment provided by Bata; check details on television monitors provided by JVC; and check copy deadlines and match timings via the official timekeeper Seiko. With its system in place – and despite the problems of Sport Billy Productions continuing to claim its contracted ownership of the FIFA emblem, trademark and mascots – ISL dominated world football marketing in this formative phase of the industry. At the World Cups from 1986 onwards the sponsors were as follows: [58]

- Mexico, 1986 – Anheuser-Busch, Bata, Canon, Coca-Cola, Cinzano, Fuji, Gillette, JVC, Opel, Philips, R. J. Reynolds (Camel), Seiko (twelve general sponsors with stadium advertising privileges). Two reserved sponsorship packages were granted to a selected group of Mexican firms to run local advertising; and to Arena Swimwear, as a result, it was claimed, of Anheuser Busch not taking up an option of supporting promotion measures. These extra deals certainly made sense to the main players: the man running the World Cup was Havelange's long-term ally, Mexican FIFA Vice-President Cañedo; Arena, of course, was an Adidas subsidiary.
- Italy, 1990 – Anheuser-Busch, Canon, Coca-Cola, Fuji, Gillette, JVC, Mars, Philips, Vini Italia (nine general sponsors with stadium advertising privileges). The sum raised from these sponsors was reported to be an estimated 100 million Swiss francs, to be shared between FIFA, the Italian Organizing Committee and the participating teams. Two further categories were sold. 'Official Suppliers' were Alitalia, Fiat, Olivetti, the Italian Post Office, Italian Railways, the RAI state TV Company and the INA insur-

ance company. And the title 'Official Product' was sold to a range of companies, including Adidas, Seiko, MasterCard, Barilla (pasta), Sagit (ice-cream), and Garan Padano (cheese).

- USA, 1994 – Canon, Coca-Cola, Energizer, Fuji, General Motors, Gillette, JVC, MasterCard, McDonald's, Philips, Snickers (eleven general sponsors).
- France, 1998 – Adidas, Budweiser, Canon, Coca-Cola, Fuji, General Motors, Gillette, JVC, Mars, MasterCard, McDonald's, Philips.

Fast foods and snacks, soft and alcoholic drinks, cars, batteries, photographic equipment and electronic media, credit sources – these are the items around which global sponsorship of football has been based, with their classic evocations of a predominantly masculinist realm of consumption: drinking, snacking, shaving, driving. The marketing of the commodities throughout the regions of the world game has clearly been effective. If it were not, companies of this stature would be unlikely to reinvest in ISL's recurrent Inter-Soccer programmes, or the equivalent schemes of its rivals.

After Dassler's death in 1987, it was confirmed that FIFA had signed all of the marketing and sponsorship rights for the 1994 and 1998 World Cup Finals to ISL, with an option included for the 2002 event, in a multi-million Swiss francs contract which also included the merchandising rights for FIFA's logos, which at the time were still held by Sport Billy Productions up to 1990. Continuity seemed to be the order of the day.[59] Dassler's long-time protégé, John Boulter, was installed as head of promotions at Adidas within a few months of Dassler's death. And the ISL operation worked prolifically and productively for FIFA, the IOC, the IAAF and other lucrative clients, wrapping up the global marketing of the world's highest profile sports. But power plays were under way in the boardrooms of Adidas and ISL. At the end of 1990 Horst Dassler's four sisters disposed of their 80% share of the Adidas company, and installed the husband of one of them as the president of the holding company which was the majority (51%) owner of ISL. Dassler's own two children became marginalized in this reshuffle. Within weeks, two key ISL personnel, Klaus Hempel and Jürgen Lenz had all but stopped work with ISL. Dassler's sisters placed Jean-Marie Weber in the chief executive's position, and by the autumn of 1991 Hempel and Lenz had formed their own rival operation. Their Hempel-Lenz & Partner AG cofounded The Event Agency and Marketing AG (TEAM), with backing from German industrialists. TEAM announced its aim 'to set new standards in the field of sports and cultural sponsoring on the basis of innovative concepts and thus make sponsorship an innovative marketing element'. Team Football Marketing AG was also established, and bids planned to UEFA and other sports bodies.

■ TEAM's Reframing of European Football

In the 1990s one of TEAM's major clients was UEFA, the European Football Union. ISL was still handling marketing for Euro '96, the European football championships staged in England in the Summer of 1996, and so had the English Football Association and UEFA as major clients. But the rights for the European Club Championship, widely known as the European Cup before being revised into a new format and relabelled the UEFA Champions League, were won by TEAM. UEFA's decision to introduce a league format prior to the quarter final stage of the tournament was seen by FIFA secretary general Blatter as 'exactly the opposite of our objective . . . with the new system the rich will become even richer and the poor poorer'. In an interview for Zurich's *Tages-Anzeiger*, Blatter went on to present FIFA as the guardian of the true spirit of the game, in contrast with the rapacious European Federation:

> It's always awkward expressing opinions about the position of FIFA and UEFA. Let me put it this way. UEFA is currently very concerned that lots of money is earned and the market exploited . . . It cannot be in the interests of soccer to earn as much money as possible. Commerce is important, but it cannot be allowed to dominate everything. FIFA and UEFA are not business-oriented organizations, they're not profit centers. Education and spectacle are their key tasks.[60]

This could have been Sir Stanley Rous speaking! The sub-text of Blatter's comments was the increasing challenge to FIFA from UEFA, and the strategy of looking to gain the high moral ground. Ironically, here, the forms of partnership established initially by FIFA – first with West Nally and then with ISL – were being driven to their logical financial potential by the powerful European union and its new marketing partner, the latter comprising erstwhile key ISL personnel. In this context, Blatter's moral defence of FIFA's global and redistributive objectives could be seen as cunningly disingenuous, if not an expression of sour grapes within the incestuous corridors of world football power.

Regardless of FIFA's reservations, the restructuring of the European club champions' competition went ahead, driven by a relentless commercial logic. It has become truistic to talk of sport as big business, but it is revealing to scrutinize the minutiae of this business in its marketing and merchandising manifestation. TEAM has provided illuminating documentation in its monitoring of its marketing of the event.[61] The UEFA Champions League brand was placed to dominate the studio sets of those broadcasters covering the matches, and all participating clubs must display the event's 'Starball' logo – a circle of seven interlinked silver five-pointed stars, connecting with a larger central star, resembling a spiky looking football or a crown of thorns – on their team shirts. The main broadcasters were well catered for – both literally, with 'the personal touch of snack boxes and hot drinks in their commentary positions or production vehicles a welcome luxury'; and in the spheres of self-presentation and profiling, with the provision of two advertising boards around the pitch, full page advertisements in the match programme, allocation of top match tickets, access to hospitality areas, mentions on banners in those areas, and 'branded recognition . . . on the reverse side of every match ticket and on the flash interview backdrops'. Part of TEAM's promised 'new standards' were no doubt most welcome to host broadcasters: their coverage could turn out to be as much of themselves as of the football event.

TEAM developed rigorous monitoring processes, commissioning telephone surveys of almost 3,000 15–44 year-olds 'with an above average income' in seven European markets. Awareness of the competitions was extremely high, and the Champions League was seen as offering the highest quality of football in Europe. This would all have been good news to the sponsors and licensees, for whom UEFA/ TEAM's report provided a full description of the underlying philosophy of sponsorship, marketing and licensing: 'The UEFA Champions League sponsorship concept allows communication in a clutter free environment and creates a pan-European package that delivers significant impact, acting as a prestigious platform delivering volume audiences in prime-time programming.' The exclusive group of eight sponsors for the 1995–6 tournament comprised:

1 Amstel (alcoholic and non-alcoholic beer)
2 Canon (office equipment and printers, cameras and accessories)
3 Continental (tyres)
4 Eurocard/MasterCard (electronic payment cards and systems, travellers cheques)
5 Ford (passenger cars, sports utility vehicles and commercial vehicles)

95

6 McDonald's (retail food service operation)
7 Philips (consumer electronics, audio and video software)
8 Reebok (sports and fitness footwear and apparel).

TEAM's philosophy emphasized the core principles of FIFA's early innovations: 'product category exclusivity and limited number of partners ensures optimum communication for each sponsor'. The package for sponsors was made up of 'a base package of Event Rights ... the entry level for all sponsors'. Options were then available in the categories of commercial airtime, broadcast sponsorship and an East European package. The Event Rights guaranteed extensive television exposure, and profiling in official printed material, throughout the tournament's sixty-one matches. Four advertising boards were available for each sponsor, each 'primary' board receiving twenty minutes of exposure per match. Flash interviews with star players and coaches had backdrops with sponsor identification. Official printed material featured the sponsors in match programmes, match tickets, accreditation cards, newsletters, press paper, statistic sheets, seat tickets and stadia signs. Sponsors could also erect product displays at all of the venues, and use the Champions League logo in all its packaging. At all of the sixteen venues a hospitality package was provided in 'a unique environment – The Champions Club'. This included tickets, soccer related sponsor competitions, speeches, prizegivings, entertainment and live music, forms of 'added value' climaxing 'at the final in Rome where 2500 guests were entertained in a first class Champions Village environment'. The Village itinerary included a fashion show and accompanying live jazz. Sponsors constructed displays, dispensed largesse from bars, arranged competitions and distributed banners and inflatables. For the most privileged of this elite of football spectatorship, it was not even necessary to leave the cocooned and pampered environment to see the final. Over 350 VIP guests had access to a Champions Lounge, where 'live match images' could be watched 'on a large vidiwall in the Lounge itself'. Official dinners and lunches preceded the match itself.

All major sponsors excepting Philips and Canon participated in the Broadcasting Sponsorship option. Their own creative treatments were integrated into the 'overall broadcast design concept'. Two sponsors per night could then benefit – dependent upon national regulations – from featuring in opening and closing voiceovers and billboards; 'breakbumpers', which are mentions or 'sponsor identification' at the start and the end of each commercial break; and, where permitted by local regulations, on screen credits throughout the live coverage. The Commercial Airtime option was purchased by all sponsors except McDonald's and Eurocard/MasterCard: for these, TEAM negotiated commercial airtime 'in and around the Champions League programme'. Amstel, Eurocard and Philips bought into the East European package, ensuring exposure in Russia, Poland, Hungary, Bulgaria, the Czech Republic, the Slovak Republic, Romania and Slovenia. UEFA also contracted exclusive licensing agreements for the product categories of sportswear and multi-media: more than 8,000 official licensed sportswear products were sold around the stadium in Rome on the night of the 1996 final. Sales continued after the final, across Europe and Asia, helped 'by the victorious Juventus players enthusiastically wearing these products in their celebrations just after the cup ceremony'. The report features in its main frontispiece photograph a shot of the Juventus star Ravanelli wearing one of these products, a black peaked Champions League cap.

The benefits for the commercial partners were clear enough, in both commercial and interpersonal terms. The benefits for the clubs were also clear enough – the champion, Juventus, received 18,150,000 Swiss francs from UEFA for its successful run. The least successful participating club, Grasshopper of Zurich, received 3,275,000 Swiss francs. UEFA planned, for the 1997–8 season, to include two teams from each top European country, increasing the scale of the League and, concomitantly, the level of revenue generated. FIFA began the process which has culminated in the European Champions League's lucrative inauguration. There are very positive sides to this. The 'presentation and organisation' of a sports event is 'likely to benefit from increased resources'[62] provided by the sponsor. Top European football is transmitted globally, and contributes to the continuing development of the game, and some of the income has been channelled back into national associations, with the smaller associations receiving larger sums than the European giants – a number of former Soviet republics' national associations each received 750,000 Swiss francs, and Switzerland 760,000, whilst Italy received only 400,000. But world football is also inflated by the new money, and the top clubs simply circulate it among themselves, in unprecedented salary structures for globally mobile superstars. Sponsorship of the game has helped restructure football environments, for instance by contributing to the funding of new stadia, shirt sponsorship, and match sponsorship. But the case of the World Cup, and of the quintessential UEFA Champions League, raises some serious questions concerning the extent to which football culture has become shaped by an inexorable commercial logic.

■ Conclusion

Football is a cultural product, and its meanings and significance are not wholly determined by its political economy. People in pubs or domestic lounges, as well as at live games at various levels of performance, can chant, sing, shout, speak and respond in their own appropriate ways as, with varying degrees of freedom and choice, they negotiate the expression of a particular cultural identity through the public culture of the game. But at the top level, football represents more and more graphically the triumph of the universal market,[63] and wherever it is watched – live or in its transmitted forms – it is an increasingly commodifed cultural product in a structured environment of an intensifyingly exclusive type. In its 1995/96 report, UEFA TEAM showed what camera positions were permitted at all of the sixteen stadia venues, and the final, specifying types and exact positions. Their marketing and licensing scope has begun to determine what can be bought in the environs of the stadium, and certainly inside it. To one expert observer, Dutch sports journalist Ted van Leeuwen, this is more than mere contextual detail:

> They say how the stadiums are, how you have to make your stadium, who sits where. They say where the cameras are, not the television. They sell the tickets, they make the programmes, now they say where you have to meet . . . they also decide who comes with a commercial on television in the country where the game is played . . .
> This special Champions League logo on the sleeves, you don't have to do it, but all clubs do it, and this guy [from TEAM] he says it's because they want to be part of the special world of Champions League. They just create a special world, and I asked where the success comes from. He says, 'it's a golden triangle, it's a field of power we call it – football, television and sponsors'. And TEAM and UEFA are the catalyst who make it happen.[64]

This golden triangle operates highly effectively at all levels of football consumption, transforming the basis of club affiliation and football fandom. If the three points of the triangle are represented as FIFA, television and sponsors, the ringmaster in the centre of the triangle is the marketing agency, an ISL or TEAM, mediating the partnerships and orchestrating the outcome. When, as in TEAM's case in the Champions League, and in ISL's case having secured television rights for the 2002 World Cup, such agencies feature as a crucial presence at all points of the triangle, their extensive power and influence can be gauged.

TEAM's concept of an expanding European Champions League has also served as a model for the raising of the profile of club football on other continents, such as Asia and Africa. Across Europe, hundreds of contractors and freelances co-ordinate the corporate image negotiated and constructed by TEAM, transporting advertising boards and displays to all the match venues, and checking on the layout of stadia and the attire of players. As young pan-European football fans buy the exclusively licensed products of UEFA or FIFA, relating to the Continent's and the world's top sides which they follow regularly on television, it is inevitable that their relationship to a local unfashionable and unsuccessful, or only modestly successful, club will be different to that of previous generations of fan, for whom the marketing of football meant a couple of billboards in the town centre and the gossip columns of the local sport pages. Commodification of the cultural product of football on the scale pioneered and developed by FIFA in the World Cup, and adopted and primed by UEFA in its Champions League, has contributed to the vicissitudes and the volatility that have constituted the lot of a newly cosmopolitan football fan, for whom fan support could be the mediated chant of the champions. The impact of this upon the perception of international football is complex, with Asian fans widely preferring to follow the fortunes of Manchester United rather than Malaysia, or Juventus rather than Japan. If the Champions League really is potentially bigger than the World Cup, the consequences for international football could be grave.

Watching FIFA and UEFA's hugely influential partners of the Havelange and Johansson eras – ISL, TEAM, or other equivalent agencies or personnel – police the commercial and company icons of the fully commodified modern football stadium, checking every detail of their constructed world like bodyguards protecting an American president, is to catch a glimpse of who controls international football's golden triangle in an expansionist phase of the peoples' game.

■ 5

FIFA's World Cup Finals: getting the event

■ Staging the Spectacle: Rising Stakes

Acquiring a World Cup Final has become an attractive – to some almost irresistible – proposition for many nations in an age of advanced media coverage and accompanyingly high forms of sponsorship. It delivers a rationale for revitalizing the communication and civic infrastructures of primary sites and locations; it provides a forum for the articulation and celebration of national pride; and for organizers of the later World Cups of the twentieth century it could deliver huge profits. With such projected and attainable benefits for powerful interested parties, the process of gaining the World Cup Finals has become unprecedentedly big business. The bidding process has been dramatically altered from a process in which, initially, the choice was largely pragmatic; succeeded by long-term plans laid on the basis of tentative submissions and fairly low-profile bids; and developing into an expensive, ruthless and many would say unethical contest between aggressive national delegations.

Things were not always thus. In the period after World War I, FIFA was to establish key presences, profiles and partnerships which would make it much more than a predominantly technical and regulatory body: and the watershed in this process was the institution of the World Cup, which relegated the Olympic Games's football tournament to a secondary status on the world stage. Uruguay's triumphs in the Olympic Games in Paris and Amsterdam in 1924 and 1928 respectively, and in the inaugural World Cup in Uruguay itself in 1930, have been summarized in chapter 2. Here, it is not so much the Uruguayan victory itself which is of interest; rather, the conditions of its staging illustrate the *modus operandi* of the world governing body in the period between the two World Wars. FIFA's main partnerships which made possible the first World Cups were, albeit indirectly and implicitly, political. There was no financial infrastructure available from media investment, corporate sponsorship and world marketing rights. The first two World Cups were staged by opportunistic hosts with political goals. In 1930 the Uruguayan government was keen to sustain its team's Olympic successes on home ground, in the centenary year of its constitution, and to display South American soccer strengths against Europe's top professional talent (which, for the most part, was not eligible for the all-amateur Olympic Games). The 1934 World Cup in Italy was one element in Mussolini's strategy to mobilize sport for the good of the nation: elite performers were developed, and key events targeted:

> Sport was a distraction and a means of indoctrination; a healthy pursuit and a preparation for the military; it was also an important organ of propaganda, inspiring nationalism at home by winning glory abroad. This meant the Olympic Games and after 1930 the World Cup in football. Private individuals and the State found plenty of money for football, its promotion and the building of impressive new stadia. At the same time the art of bribery and corruption as a means of dealing with the opposition, the *trasformismo* that had become almost a way of governing since the first days of unification in the 1860s, was developed to a higher degree, in soccer as in society. Italy was the host nation for the World Cup in 1934, and after some ugly exhibitions, strange refereeing decisions and egged on by fanatical crowds, they won the trophy.[1]

These early World Cups could hardly be international cultural festivals, bringing together cosmopolitan citizens of a co-operative cultural world order, underpinned as they were by a primitive transport and communications infrastructure. The Uruguayan government had committed itself to funding the expenses of travelling teams, and the four European entrants undertook a sea journey of two weeks to get to Montevideo. For fans within South America, overland travel was still more daunting. In 1919 the South American football championships had been held in Rio de Janeiro, Brazil, on the east coast of the continent: 'the few Chilean fans who attended travelled by boat, train and mule. It took them two months.'[2] The first World Cup in many respects climaxed as a regional metropolitan affair, around the major cities of Montevideo and Buenos Aires, separated by the River Plate. During Argentina's 6–1 victory over a USA team containing five Scots and one Englishman, 20,000 fans were estimated to have listened to the game 'over newspaper loudspeakers in the centre of

Buenos Aires'.[3] For the final, Argentinians in the capital city, Mason relates, huddled around radios in offices; or congregated outside newspaper offices to listen to broadcasts of the action and the atmosphere. Uruguay's 4–2 victory was followed by an all-night party throughout the capital, and the declaration, by the president, of a national holiday for the following day. In important ways, then, the first World Cups were as much national as international: they were supported by central authoritarian states; won by host countries; and reported most intensively at local and national level. FIFA had little control over them, or investment in them. The third World Cup of the 1930s was, despite a vigorous candidature from the Argentine Football Association, awarded to a second European host in succession, France – the home nation of the secretary and president of FIFA, whose organizational base was still Paris. This World Cup was hardly representative of developments and achievements in world football, with a mere three non-European countries in the line-up – two of which, the Dutch East Indies and Cuba, boasted no football pedigree at all. Brazil alone represented the South Americas. Dilemmas over professional and amateur codes and administration in Uruguayan and Argentinian football, and the recruitment of 'Italian' Argentine stars by Italian clubs (and, consequently, the national side on the basis of parental descent), had diluted the South American challenge, along with Argentina's sense of slight at not being awarded the 1938 tournament. If not explicitly political, the tournament was viewed as such by the Fascist states of central Europe. Germany fielded a side including players from Austria, the country that it had recently annexed, and whose entry, with perfect logic but sinister reality, was withdrawn. Italy defeated Hungary in the final. Its second World Cup triumph – following on from its 2–1 victory over Austria, with a winner in the second minute of extra time, in the Nazi Olympics in Berlin in 1936 – confirmed the primacy of state-initiated football development.

It has been argued that by the 1930s 'the time of the international football supporter had arrived', and though admittedly 'a pale shadow of what was to come, soccer had nevertheless arrived as a media event'.[4] But any fans taking advantage of hotel and railway packages to get to games in other countries would have been affluent and relatively privileged pioneers of sports tourism. It was the radio which offered more of a model for the participatory expansion of the high-profile international sports event. In France, Italy and Germany sports journals (in some cases, published daily) were established in the 1890s and the early 1900s; the 1934 World Cup drew

275 journalists representing the press of twenty-nine countries. Radio, though, was the medium through which the live drama of the football match was widely conveyed, and radio broadcasts of matches in homes and public venues became well established in the 1930s. Yet when Italy attempted to sell the broadcasting rights for the 1934 event, only the Dutch responded positively, though subsequent deals allowed people in fifteen countries to receive broadcasts of the event.[5] The World Cup was helped by such advances in communications technology, but it was not as yet dependent upon them. It was the political aspirations and posturings of ambitious and authoritarian states which created the basis of FIFA's inauguration and early institutionalization of its major product – confirming the central paradox of FIFA, that it has represented supranational and internationalist ideals by providing a platform for the display of nationalist identity and cultural superiority. As the profile of the World Cup expanded, the bidding process intensified into a race for ever higher political and economic stakes.

There is little evidence of any fierce fights over the hosting of the 1962 World Cup. At its Congress in Lisbon in June 1956, FIFA 'decided by 32 votes to 10 that the organization of the World Championship – Jules Rimet Cup – be delegated to the Chilean Football Association'.[6] The decision was still being made by a relatively broad body of the organization. Oliver marks the 1966 World Cup as the first one for which Western European nations seriously competed in the post-World War II period.[7] At FIFA's 1960 Congress in Rome England won a close vote over West Germany (FRG), Spain having withdrawn its bid just prior to the ballot. Sir Walter Winterbottom was England football manager at that time, and Sir Stanley Rous was the secretary of the English FA, and very active in FIFA and UEFA circles. Confirming the relatively low-key affair of the gaining of the 1966 Finals, Sir Walter commented:

SIR WALTER: Oh yes, but, well, it was our turn really, we hadn't had a World Cup you know, and the question is, we had the stadia, which had to be improved a bit . . .

QUESTION: Did we get awarded the World Cup when Sir Stanley was still in the FA, before he went to FIFA?

SIR WALTER: Yes, that's right, yes. But he was *in* FIFA, I mean let's be fair about it [several chuckles] . . . Stanley could use his influence. As I say, personality goes a long way. Yes, you looked at the friendships that grew up between himself and the powerful nations . . . the Treasurer of FIFA was Italy, somebody else was from Germany, and he had their friendship – not only their respect but their friendship, and he respected them. He was always talking to people

103

> and encouraging them, you know, he had this easy way of saying
> 'thank you very much, your idea' and so on, and the fellows but-
> tered up, to put it crudely, in a way that was quite amazing. They
> idolized him you know.[8]

It was, it seemed, 'Buggins' turn', for the British (in fact, the English)!
Long-term Rous PA and then latterly FA secretary Rose-Marie
Breitenstein recalls: 'It was awarded to him whilst he was secretary
of the Football Association, because he was well known all over the
world even then and that is how he got it really.'[9] It seems that re-
markably little had to be demonstrated of the planned capacity to
stage the tournament. Lord Howell recalls how he persuaded, with
a wild guestimate, the British prime minister Harold Wilson to commit half a million pounds towards the work that needed to be done,
during the first hours of the 1964 Labour Government.[10] In addition,
after England's home-based victory in 1966 (in 1997 England were
still the only World Cup winners to have won it only once – and
every game was played at the national stadium, Wembley), Howell
found that when he presented the details of the financial aid provided to the football clubs which had staged the matches outside
Wembley, there was not a murmur of objection in the House of Com-
mons or beyond.[11] Such ad hoc and emergency measures reveal the
superficiality of the bidding process at the time. But the nature of
that process was certainly changing, influenced by networks of interests in the emerging cultural and media industries.

The competition for the staging of the 1970 Finals was more intense. In 1964, as FIFA president, Rous was alarmed at the extent –
economic as well as interpersonal – to which Mexico and Argentina
were going in competing to stage the 1970 finals. Rose-Marie
Breitenstein, by then working closely with Rous within FIFA, recalls
how:

> they spent so much money. From then on he thought we should have a
> plan and money should not be wasted on campaigns – but unfortunately
> it has all gone haywire again – and then he did make a plan for the people
> who had applied, so that there was not too much competition.[12]

The planning model evolved by Rous – ('the long look ahead'[13]) –
was designed to give adequate notice to those committing themselves to major events. He had imported his strategic model of forward planning from his time at the English FA, 'to chart the likely
course of development'. At FIFA this translated into 'a twelve year
location plan for the World Cup so that countries concerned could

plan at leisure'.[14] This was accepted by FIFA at its 1964 Congress in Tokyo, with England reaffirmed for 1966 (becoming the blueprint for the more modern event in an era of advanced mass communications), and a future list confirmed: Mexico in 1970; West Germany in 1974; Argentina in 1978; and Spain in 1982. Columbia, for 1986, was added to this list in 1974. In Rous's planning, therefore, hosts would be able to plan twelve years or more ahead of the event, and this created the opportunity 'to study the "blueprints" and look in detail at the actual organization of the two previous finals'.[15] Unsuccessful but realistic bidders got their turn, to use Winterbottom's phrase, within Rous's planning framework: Germany for 1974, not 1966; Argentina for 1978, not 1970; Spain for 1982 after a long courtship.

Looking informedly back and astutely forward, Rous also anticipated problems concerning the escalating scale of the Finals event, with its demands upon pitches and stadia, press and TV facilities, accommodation and security. He considered that: 'FIFA should already be considering a long-term plan, and this should envisage zoning the Finals by splitting the games up between three or four countries.'[16] One example of such a co-hosting grouping had been suggested to Rous by a Yugoslav official, citing Austria, Hungary and Czechoslovakia as potential joint hosts. The Benelux countries and the Maghreb nations (Algeria, Tunisia and Morocco) were also suggested as a possible further grouping. Rous's reflections and projections proved perspicacious. The Low countries did indeed, in a UEFA initiative, win the 2000 European Football Championship. In chapter 7 it is recorded that the ASEAN nations have followed such logic. And the 2002 Finals were awarded to co-hosts, in June 1996, in a context considered later in this chapter. But the post-Rous FIFA proved less visionary, more commercially aware and businesslike, and perhaps more mercenary. Referring to the bidding processes from the aborted Colombian finals of 1986 through to the candidates for 2006, it is clear that by the later 1990s the disinterested 'long-term looks' of a Rous were long gone in FIFA House. As examples of the changing nature of bidding processes, practices and outcomes, the roads to Mexico (1986), France (1998) and Korea/Japan (2002) are reviewed, before a brief consideration of some preliminary skirmishes over the 2006 event (the 1994 World Cup is given extensive treatment in chapter 9).

■ Hustling for the Hosting Role: The Colombian Debacle and the Mexican Messiah

The Colombian bid for the 1986 World Cup Finals built up momentum in February 1973, when an official FIFA delegation visited the country.[17] The official delegation contained FIFA Vice-President Harry Cavan of Northern Ireland, and East German (GDR) and Costa Rican members. The Colombian committee also sent special invitations to the presidents of the African and South American confederations, and the head of finance of the North and Central American federation. There was no Asian delegate or guest. Civic and sports leaders of Colombia's five main cities met the delegation, as did mayors of all twelve cities proposed as venues for the sixteen team tournament (Havelange not yet having assumed power and moved towards implementation, in Spain in 1982, of a twenty-four team event). Dr Borrero, president of the Republic, also met the delegates and guests in a special reception in the presidential palace, expressing fervent government support for the initiative of the Colombian Football Federation. He declared:

> It is in everyone's mutual interest to demonstrate to the world that a country such as ours is perfectly competent to put this challenge to its sports administrators thus conveying to all other nations just how capable it is of organizing an event of this magnitude in 1986.[18]

In this simple declaration Borrero demonstrated the primary attraction, to underdeveloped countries, of hosting sports events: it was a commitment to the project of modernization and a chance to assert a progressive internationalism. For Colombia, staging the World Cup was seen to have other indirect benefits beyond just football: 'significance in all spheres, such as tourism, economics, material, etc.'[19] Colombia clearly had no adequate facility infrastructure, but mayors and governors were reported to have keenly declared: 'If it is necessary to construct new stadia, we shall do so with the people's backing in the knowledge of the Colombian's love of football.'[20] Fine words and ambitious intent. No budget but lots of bluff. Enough, though, for the FIFA Executive Committee to award the country the Finals. But the football administration could not deliver the dream of modernization and efficiency, for in Colombia 'drugs and bribery have been linked to football and the threats to referees, including at least one assassination, forced FIFA to intervene. The 1986 World Cup venue was withdrawn from Colombia when it became apparent that the mess in the domestic league was likely to be repeated as hosts to an international competition.'[21] A fuller account of the 'withdrawal' can be constructed from the reports in *Sport Intern*. In mid-1982 Colombia's newly elected president Belisario Betancur was still ready to give FIFA the guarantees it required, but FIFA leaders were increasingly unconvinced that Colombia could 'provide sufficient technical requirements', and it was becoming clear that a special FIFA commission soon to visit Colombia had 'no other intention but to prove that Colombia will not be able to organize the 1986 tournament'.

Supporters of a change of venue also argued that the event would not be in the poverty-stricken nation's best interests, as it would generate inflation. By the end of 1982 Colombia had returned its mandate, and the FIFA Executive Committee was faced with finding a replacement from among Brazil, Mexico, and the USA. The Committee postponed the decision for several months, *Sport Intern* claimed, due to Havelange's personal opposition to the re-election of the president of the Brazilian Football Federation. Havelange would only support a Brazilian bid if that president was not re-elected. If the president was re-elected, Mexico could therefore emerge as the favourite to replace Colombia, a Warner Communications-backed USA bid, and one from Canada, being seen as lacking any real support. Brazil did withdraw. Havelange's son-in-law, Teixeira, eventually was elected the president of the Brazilian Federation. On such personal and family loyalties and interpersonal rivalries are the major decisions of world football based.[22] In June 1983 Guillermo Cañedo was elected president of the organizing committee for the Finals, defeating the president of the country's football association 'after some violent tug-of-war behind the scenes'. Miller has referred to the process of Mexico's selection as 'the charade of the submissions',[23] in which no vote was taken. In fact, two and a half years previously, *Sport Intern* had mapped out the whole sham process with remarkable predictive precision:

> The 1986 Football World Championship will probably be given to Mexico if Colombia returns its mandate, a possibility which, in the meantime, is almost being counted on by the *International Football Federation* (FIFA). Even Brazil is considered in leading circles of the FIFA only as a 'second choice', even if FIFA President *Dr. João Havelange* uses all the prestige of his position to add weight to his homeland's candidacy. These circles view as 'completely absurd and almost ridiculous' the suggestion . . . to stage the championship in the USA. This even more so since the interest in soccer in the USA is noticeably declining. Some observers even see the existence of the *North American Soccer League* as being put into question.[24]

107

The stunning accuracy of this forecast, in the publication's first English-language edition, and following on from the Moscow Olympic Games and Samaranch's early days as IOC President, suggests the influence of the central figures in world sports politics such as financial figures like Dassler. There is no adequate explanation of the match between this prediction and the unfolding of the bidding narrative other than that networks of interests and powerful alliances could sway, influence and determine critical decisions. Sir Walter Winterbottom has referred to how Adidas had a lot to do with commercial developments in world sports, based on business contacts and the mutual interests of partners: 'It is done that way, it isn't a Mafia arrangement, it is a different way of looking at things. If you can get away with it, it is smart, you know, it is clever.'[25] Cañedo seems to have been very smart in capitalizing on Colombia's crisis, representing what English journalist Miller called a 'Mexican autocracy' in organizing the finals and generally 'running the committee as his personal private enterprise', as one Mexican observer told Miller.[26] Cañedo was also described as Emilio Azcarraga's 'man up front, Televisa's vice-president', a key link man between Azcarraga ('Mexico's communications Godfather') and the FIFA president.[27]

■ (International) Football's Coming Home

France was one of the prime movers in establishing FIFA, providing its main working language and its first president. Rimet initiated the first World Cup, and the European Champions Club Cup (the forerunner of the UEFA Champions League) was promoted by L'Équipe, the French sports daily paper. On its formation, UEFA was based in a room in the buildings of the French Football Federation. The bid from France for the 1998 Finals was, unsurprisingly, based upon this historical pedigree of footballing internationalism. To place a World Cup Finals tournament in France could therefore be validly claimed as a return to the birthplace of an influential internationalism in European and world football.

The FIFA president did not mark out France as a favourite in his early pronouncements on the race to host the 1998 Finals. In late 1986 – within five months of receiving a Nobel Peace Prize nomination from the president of the Swiss Football Association at FIFA's Zurich Congress – he praised Switzerland, stating at a press conference in Zurich:

Switzerland has all the necessary infrastructures (transport network, tel-ecommunications systems, hotels etc.), a stable currency, a strong economy, lots of know how and the enthusiastic soccer public, to be able to organize an outstanding World Cup as in 1954, but brought up to date. Only the stadiums require extensions and renovation, but given the financial strength of the country I can see no problem there.[28]

This was presidential style and favour indeed, comparable to the way in which bidding mania for the Olympic Games was stimulated by Samaranch's fulsome praise for just about any candidature. For within just weeks, in January of 1987, Havelange was welcoming the president of the French Football Federation to Zurich. The French were moving quickly to counter the Swiss momentum, and also feared problems in the relationship between their prime minister Jacques Chirac and Havelange. The FIFA President had backed Bar-celona over Paris in the race for the 1992 Olympics, and he was seen as part of a Latin monopoly of world sports leadership. In East Ber-lin in 1985 the then mayor of Paris, Chirac – seeking the support of the East European lobby – accused Havelange of bias, and 'was ru-moured to have threatened to use his influence in Africa to ensure that Havelange is not re-elected President of FIFA'.[29] Given the rec-ognized capacity of Havelange to 'create majorities within the IOC' from his power base in Central and South America, and his expressed favour for Falun in Sweden to win the 1992 Winter Olympics over Albertville in France, tensions had simmered between the two men since.

These relationships were interwoven with the dynamics of patron-age and persuasion at the heart of the bidding process for the Olym-pic Games. The Swedish city of Falun had sought to host the winter games on a number of occasions, and polled a promising thirty-one votes in the vote for the 1988 games, in a straight fight against Cana-da's Calgary, the favourite and winner with forty-eight votes. IOC members urged the Swedes to mount another bid: 'You will have my full support', Havelange wrote to them. In fact, victim of IOC president Samaranch's determination that Barcelona and not Paris should be awarded the 1992 summer games, the support for Falun drained away so that by the time of the vote Albertville won fifty-one votes against Falun's eleven. Jennings argues that awarding the games to Albertville in France was an IOC strategy which made it impossible for Paris to win the summer games (one country could not be awarded both games), and the sequence of the voting was reversed so that the decision about the winter games was taken first – so scuppering the Paris bid and putting Barcelona in prime position. If Havelange transferred support from Falun to Albertville, this was in essence therefore a move away from the greater French ambition to land the summer games. Even if his initial support for Falun was played down, Havelange could be seen to be blocking Chirac's ambitions.[30]

Clearly the bidding process involved sensitivities to overlapping networks of power and influence in world sport. In early 1988 Chirac used the 1998 Finals as a campaigning point, telling an election rally in Dijon that he had already discussed this matter with the FIFA president. Reminded by FIFA spokesman Guido Tognoni that it was FIFA and not a national prime minister who awarded the Finals, Chirac nevertheless restated that France had 'a good chance of being awarded the World Cup Finals. And I will do everything I can to ensure that we get them.'[31] There were still four years to go until FIFA was to make its decision. In France the media provided free advertising to the level of an estimated 25–30 million francs. After September 1991 the French Football Federation was ready, in the last stages of the bid, to disperse six to seven million francs in exclusively targeting the FIFA committees which were to award the Finals.[32] By November of 1991 Havelange was 'very, very unhappy' about the Swiss candidature, saying that FIFA could not accept the temporary tubular steel grandstands proposed for stadia. He was also stating that he believed that there was a logical case for the 2002 Finals being Asia's first, and noted that the Japanese had already submitted a 'magnificent plan'.[33] At the same time as he was dismissing the Swiss bid that he had so consistently encouraged in the previous five years, the French campaign was reaching a climax, as the same issue of *Sport Intern* reported:

> *Dr. João Havelange*, president of the **FIFA** world soccer federation, was inducted into France's Legion of Honour by the country's president **François Mitterand**. In a ceremony at the presidential palace Mitterand praised the 75-year-old Brazilian as 'one of the great figures of today's sporting world'. Disrespectful observers described the honoring of Havelange as just another attempt to win Havelange's support for the French bid to host soccer's **1998 World Cup Finals**.[34]

France's other main rival in the race, Morocco, was not giving up without a fight, and pressurized Havelange, Blatter and Cañedo to make a further trip to Morocco, to be received by King Hassan II. At its Congress in Zurich in July 1992, FIFA awarded the Finals to France. Morocco – seen as impatient by Havelange – had been disappointed before, in August 1988. For the 1994 Finals there were two runners

against the USA, Morocco and Brazil. Havelange and another Brazilian member of FIFA's executive committee abstained, and the USA
received ten votes, Morocco seven and Brazil just two. The committee justified its decision on the basis of the USA's facility infrastructure, transport and telecommunications, and praised the presentation
made by the United States Soccer Federation, under the presidency
of Werner Fricker, soon to be deposed by Alan Rothenberg, described
a decade on by a senior FIFA committee member as 'a quintessential
American entrepreneur, a hard-nosed LA lawyer . . . not a football
man.'[35] FIFA also reiterated its duty 'to inject life into football in the
USA',[36] where the sport was said to be growing more and more popular among several million young players.

The competition between France and Morocco had reached intense
levels, focused upon the individual members of the FIFA committee. Vice-president David Will, when asked whether there should be
more control over such practices, replied: 'Yes . . . I mean the last one
was bad enough, Morocco and France, that was bad enough, the pressures on that were terrible.'[37] Despite such pressures, the consecutive choices of the USA and then France over Morocco would clearly
please FIFA's corporate and media partners, guaranteeing that, after
the glitziest and most consumerist football spectacle in World Cup
history in the USA '94, following on from the conspicuous success of
Italia '90, world football would be once more coming home to the
established and most affluent markets of consumer capitalism.

■ Asian Delights: Japan, Korea and World Cup 2002

If FIFA vice-president David Will felt under pressure from the bidding nations in the race for the 1998 Finals, the race for the privilege
of hosting the first World Cup Finals of the new millennium, and the
first to be staged outside Europe and the Americas, was still more
intense and pressurizing. As Japan and (the Republic of) Korea moved
towards the decision due in the summer of 1996, the competitors
followed the French example of a last-ditch assault on key FIFA personnel. Will recalls:

> This was so dramatic, this one, this was just unbelievable . . . It was ri-
> diculous. I, about January of this year, I approached them. I said to Japan
> and Korea: 'Now, I am not coming to any more receptions, I am not ac-
> cepting any more gifts.' The stuff was arriving at the door here, and of
> course, what do you do? The postman delivers it. It's just ridiculous. The
> only thing that was missing was the cash in a plain brown envelope, you

111

> know it was unbelievable. And I am not accepting invitations to Japan or
> Korea, this is not out of discourtesy, I am stopping. And I know that most
> of the Europeans did the same. They just stopped.[38]

The UEFA president was one of those Europeans:

> Asked to confirm that FIFA's executive committee had endured bribery
> attempts by nations seeking to host the 2002 World Cup, Johansson said
> there appeared to be no limits.
> 'Yes, there were no limits. A bottle of whisky, a camera or a computer,
> everything was permissible', he said, adding he had been sent a computer
> that he returned.[39]

FIFA Executive Committee member Dr Michel D'Hooghe, of Belgium, described how hotel rooms were garlanded with flowers, and a lobbyist from one of the bidding countries even appeared in the seat next to him on a flight from Brussels to Prague, to take the opportunity to talk with him for the duration of the flight – 'could this be a coincidence?', he asked in a fashion that needed no answer.[40] An estimated 100 million US dollars was spent by Korea and Japan in their bidding campaigns.

Asia had long been seen as the venue for the 2002 World Cup, for to stage the first finals ever to be staged outside of Europe and the Americas was seen as an unprecedented boost to Asian football. No serious candidate was available from Africa, so in many ways the staging of the Finals by an Asian country would be a dramatic gesture by FIFA, fulfilling Havelange's pledge to raise the profile of the game in a continent in which playing standards were certainly improving, but whose teams were not yet as effectively competitive as were a number of national sides from the African continent. With no system in place or established precedent for a co-ordinated bid from single confederations, there was nothing to stop any number of national bids for the staging and hosting role. From the late 1980s onwards, the escalating scale of the bids from South Korea and Japan was to dominate FIFA and World Cup politics, culminating in the decision that the two bitter rivals should co-host the event. The way in which this decision was reached articulated the deep-rooted and simmering tensions between FIFA and UEFA, within the context of the positioning and implicit campaigning of potential successors to Havelange.

The Japanese believed that the World Cup Finals were within Havelange's individual gift. Havelange did not discourage this view and was very supportive of the Japanese bid. An Asian venue was very much in his thinking as early as 1986, when he gave an interview to the Swiss magazine *Sport*. Havelange reaffirmed the principle of the regular rotation of the Finals in Europe and America up until 1994, but 'expressed the wish' that the 'Finals in 2002 should be held in China'.[41] In the autumn of 1987 Havelange travelled to Peking, for further preliminary discussions with China's sports leaders. His encouragement of a Chinese bid was also linked to his belief – as experienced IOC member and catalyst for other South and Central American IOC committee members – that China would be awarded the Summer Olympic Games for the year 2000: 'Anyone who can organize Olympic Games is no doubt capable of hosting the Finals of Soccer's World Cup.'[42] Meanwhile, as the Chinese dwelt upon Havelange's overtures, Japan and South Korea expressed their interest in developing bids, at a meeting of the Asian Confederation. FIFA's general secretary Blatter had visited South Korea's soccer facilities earlier in the year, and the aggressive and uncompromising tone of the South Korean bid was set from the start of the campaign. A Summer Olympics the following year in Seoul was presented by the Koreans as a perfect illustration of the nation's abilities to stage such events, and the Korean press mobilized against the other potential bidders: China's low standard of living would bar it from meeting FIFA's financial criteria and Japan's main sport, baseball, would obstruct any Japanese plans to stage a World Cup Finals during the baseball season.[43] An effectively staged 1988 Olympic Games, and a concentration by the Chinese upon their bid for the 2000 Olympics, boosted Korean confidence in the race for the 2002 World Cup. By the summer of 1990 Havelange could tell the Xinhua press agency (speaking during Italia '90 in Rome) that as well as Korea, additional candidates for the finals were Japan, Saudi Arabia, China and Malaysia. Asian football standards were improving, he stated, and would be close to those of Europe and South America by 2000: an Asian venue was therefore ideal for 2002. But Havelange also erected a huge barrier against the Korean case, by saying that the reunification of the two Koreas should be a prerequisite for any successful Korean bid.[44] In a press conference in Rio de Janeiro, in November 1992, the FIFA president described Japan and South Africa as the 'most promising candidates' for the finals of 2002 and 2006 respectively.[45] During the World Under-17 Championships staged in Japan in 1993, Havelange gave the impression to the Japanese that they were the firm favourites: 'People he talked to in Japan gained the impression that it is also Havelange's aim to award the first World Cup of the third millennium to Japan.' Reservations remained,

113

nevertheless, over the lack of English-speaking expertise in Japan, and the rising costs of accommodation and transport.[46] At this stage, two and a half years before FIFA's decision was to be made, Japan appeared to be the leading contender for the 2002 Finals. Two critical, interrelated developments were to change this, to change world football and the World Cup from the fiefdom of Havelange, and move FIFA more towards new influences and alliances. One was the transformation of FIFA's own committee practices (see chapter 3 above); the other was the accession of the Korean, Dr Mon Joon Chung, to the Asian Confederation's vice-presidential place on FIFA's Executive Committee. Bound up with these developments was the determination of UEFA to see that Europe would not be outflanked again when the time came to contest the FIFA presidency.

In 1994, AFC Secretary Dato' Peter Velappan elicited a commitment from Havelange that FIFA would (after its Chicago Congress of the forthcoming summer) give serious consideration to the principle of awarding the Finals to two countries. A study commission was planned to investigate such a possibility, but no change was made to established rules. Velappan saw co-hosting as a solution to the fierceness of the Japan–Korea rivalry, for neither would lose, and a boost to Asian football as an extra host-nation would automatically qualify for the Finals.[47] At the same time, Tunisia, Egypt, Mali and Somalia were planning to present a motion to the Chicago Congress proposing a rotational principle for the World Cup Finals. FIFA general secretary Blatter told the CONCACAF Congress in New York that such a plan would fail, as very few countries in the world possessed an adequate infrastructure, technology, and economic basis to stage a thirty-two team tournament.[48] Regardless of the scepticism of the FIFA secretariat, such proposals coming from the confederations (including UEFA's discussion documents on the future of FIFA), was opening up debate in committees in ways that the dictatorial presidential style of Havelange could no longer stem. However confident the Japanese were in the bidding process, their reliance upon the patronage of Havelange, and upon their interpretation of and trust in the strength of his word, was to prove costly.

The second development was the Korean success in seeing Dr Chung elected onto the FIFA Executive Committee. A war of words had preceded the Asian Confederation's election for this position, with Dr Chung arguing that Japan's World War past rendered it unsuited to the role of World Cup Finals host.[49] Although four candidates lined up for the election, one Asian soccer official was reported to have described Chung and Tadao Murata of Japan's candidatures as a form of 'Tom and Jerry shadow boxing' in the build up to the bids to stage the 2002 Finals.[50] The two other candidates were Kuwait's Sheikh Ahmad Fahad, whose father was murdered by invading Iraqi troops and Mohamed Bin Hammam, of Qatar. The latter polled a promising vote, but Chung's eleven votes pipped Fahad's ten votes for the FIFA place. Murata received a humiliating vote of just two, and was in effect removed from office back in Japan's World Cup bidding organization.[51] After the 1994 World Cup, Chung announced that he would receive Havelange in Korea to show the facilities, and constantly took the opportunity to promote the Korean bid, and, somewhat disingenuously, to urge FIFA to act 'to prevent an escalation in the "unnecessary war of attrition" between Japan and Korea'.[52]

With FIFA committees open to new and uncompromising influences, the outcome of the bidding process for Asia's – and the new millennium's – first Word Cup Finals was becoming increasingly unpredictable – a gauge both of shifting power dynamics within and around FIFA, and of a relative decline in the power of the president. By the end of 1994 Havelange sought to stand back, cancelling trips to the Asian Games in Hiroshima, and the trip to Korea: 'Apparently, Havelange wanted to avoid straying between the fronts which separate Japan and Korea at this time, especially after he has generally been reported to favor the Japanese bid.'[53] With Chung, as Korean Football Association president, organizing the Korean Organizing Committee, and emerging as an effective voice within FIFA's major committee, the Korean bid was clearly gaining momentum.[54] The Japan bidding committee sustained its activities – such as sponsoring a course for youth-team coaches in Tunisia, at the time of the 1994 African Cup of Nations. This was a direct form of sponsorship of the African confederation, CAF, and was implemented by Sir Bobby Charlton's company, BCI (Bobby Charlton International). Although this was the first such event ever to be financed by a potential host committee, and could be seen as a form of incentive in the vote-gathering process, ethical concerns were soon dropped: 'As one insider official put it, if a candidate is going to woo votes, then financing youth courses is an infinitely more acceptable way of doing so than handing out lavish gifts or air tickets.'[55] Coaching courses were also held, during 1994 and 1995, in Botswana, Gabon, Uganda and Senegal: 'organized by Bobby Charlton International . . . to one of which elite coaches from every African country would be invited', all as part of the bidding committee's 'plans to intensify their promotional activities in Africa and at the same time . . . make a meaningful contribution to the development of African football'.[56] Every African country except Libyan Arab Jamahiriya accepted the invitations, and 120 coaches from fifty-two countries attended the four courses. Issa Hayatou, CAF president, attended the courses in Gabon and Senegal; and Slim Aloulou, chairman of CAF's technical committee, 'made a long journey to spend one day in Kampala' (Uganda), and also go to Senegal: 'In accordance with arrangements agreed with CAF, all participants were provided with Japan 2002 track suits, uniforms, training shoes and a Japan 2002 football, as well as a number of promotional materials highlighting Japan's bid to host the 2002 World Cup. Return airfares and the costs of accommodation and all meals of all participants were also met by the World Cup Japan 2002 Bidding Committee.'[57] At a meeting of the CAF (African Confederation) executive, during the African Cup of Nations in Johannesburg in 1996, some committee members clearly thought that they would be beneficiaries of another 'Japan-related event coming up in Yaoundé': a minute dashed such expectations, recording that 'Trips there would not be free, and it is clear that the occasion was not linked to Japan's bid for [the] 2002 World Cup.'

The competition for the 2002 finals turned into a merry-go-round of presentations, press conferences, receptions and hospitality events attached to the calendars of FIFA and the confederations; and mailings, deliveries and invitations to members of the FIFA Executive Committee. Confederation national championships and congresses were the platform for these, as football administrators and sports media personnel were invited to hear yet again the forceful rhetoric and hyperbole of the contestants. Japan's complimentary carrier bag was headed 'Japan Loves Goals', at the Japan Bidding Committee's reception for the 2002 World Cup in Sandton City, Johannesburg in January 1996, during the African Cup of Nations in South Africa. The bag contained a copy of the dazzling and futuristic video of Japan's vision of football for the new century; a folder of fact sheets and data on football in Japan, and a rationale for its World Cup bid; a glossy booklet on the joint initiative of the bidding company and Bobby Charlton International, in providing the coaching courses in Africa; a sticker of the bidding committee's logo, and a branded biro; a t-shirt with the bidding committee's logo; and a 2002 World Cup Japan/Bobby Charlton International football shirt.

The build up to the May, 1996 decision was an intensifying process of lobbying and promotion. General secretary and treasurer of CONCACAF, Chuck Blazer, commented: 'I have to say that the calls from the embassies and the consuls bordered on harassment, and surprised some members of the Executive Committee. The Japanese were a highly intelligent team, but I have to say that they as well were surprised at the intensity of the Korean approach.'[58] The stakes were so high, internally, in the bidding countries, that livelihoods if not lives were certainly at stake – FIFA vice-president David Will:

> You know, loss of face is everything in the East. I became seriously concerned for the effects. I was very much an advocate of co-hosting, very very much, very strong on it. Months before it came to be I was working on it. I was convinced that the effect on the countries would be devastating whichever country lost, particularly South Korea, a loss to them would have been a devastating thing, but also in Japan. It was going to be such a disaster for the one who lost, I actually was at the stage of becoming seriously concerned for the lives of people, if they lost, it was as bad as that.[59]

It would be a cultural misreading to underestimate Will's insight, for the stakes were higher than any intrinsic to the football world itself. The director of the Japanese Football Association, Murata, was demoted after failing to win the vote for the FIFA Executive Committee position. Chung and his compatriots, from Korea, as well as criticizing from the start the rival bids, discussed the Korean bid in terms of wider political projects and not just football. When in April 1996 North Korean troops entered the buffer zone separating the two Koreas, so violating the truce that ended the 1950–3 Korean War, General Song Young-Shik, the secretary-general of KOBID (the South Korean Bidding Committee) argued that such a situation reinforced Korea's case to be given the World Cup Finals: 'Hosting the World Cup can play a role in facilitating the reunification process', the General said, proposing football as a means to the resolution of one of the world's most long-standing conflicts.[60] Contribution to world peace was one of the Koreans' claims as to its suitability to host the Finals. The Korean bid – with the headline 'Dream for all – 2002 World Cup Korea' – offered five further reasons in answer to the question 'Why Korea?'. These were: because Korea was Asia's most successful football nation; the country has proven organizational ability; the infrastructure is there; the commercial support is established; and 'we have earned it'. In its 'advertising feature' in *Asian Football Confederation News*,[61] KOBID quoted the German head of the FIFA delegation that had visited the country in November 1996: 'I could not find any weak point in this bid.' A former British diplomat in Seoul might have described the Korean bid and claims as 'absolute nonsense – there's nothing there outside Seoul and Pusan',[62] but this did not hamper the visionary style of the General. Song was quoted in the feature extensively, emphasizing the affordability of accommodation and transport in Korea, the country's footballing heritage, and KOBID's pledge to 'donate some 230 million dollars to the global development of football' – over a million dollars per country for the member associations of FIFA. This was a commitment to return the organizing committee's 'entire share of FIFA World Cup profits back to the global development of football'. Japan's riposte in the following issue of the confederation's publication emphasized how the country could compete on accommodation, transport and subsistence, claiming: that – away from five-star hotels – accommodation was comparable in costs to US '94; that its range of indigenous and international fast-food eating outlets countered the myth of 'unaffordable food'; and that its discount rail tickets could compete with anywhere in Europe for value.[63] The prime minister was cited as pledging the strongest of support for the Japanese bid, and Ministry of Education, Science, Sports and Culture assistance was also cited. Further forms of support for African football – a medical seminar, for instance – were also reaffirmed. The Korean feature was skillfully written in a format disguised as feature journalism: General Song, and KOBID chairman Koo Pyong-Hwoi, were quoted as if speaking to an independent journalist. The Japanese feature was much more like an orthodox holiday brochure, though responsive and defensive, rather than assertive and authoritative, in tone: it did not cite its own personnel, and in its tentative tone left the reader with a quizzical thought as to why stronger voices did not pervade the feature.

In an 'Invitation to the World' the Koreans claimed to 'have earned the honour of hosting the tournament in our beautiful country . . . We also see a priceless opportunity to again make a major contribution to global peace and harmony, promoting unity among all people, including those of our divided nation.'[64] The Korean rationale for its bid expanded upon its and FIFA's dream, offering a World Cup to welcome the new millennium, to 'ignite the imagination of football fans around the globe', and 'to inspire every child who has ever kicked a ball', in an event 'which will unite the world through football'. The rhetoric rose to a crescendo in projecting the finals as 'a catalyst for peace', and linking 'the beautiful game and reconciliation'. A World Cup which contributed to the unification of the two Koreas 'would be in keeping with FIFA's commitment to promoting friendship and peace through football', and a way would be sought 'for all 70 million Koreans to enjoy the World Cup together':

If the first World Cup of the 21st Century could help erase the last vestige of the Cold War of the 20th Century, the tournament would be more than a milestone for football. It would be a milestone for mankind.[65]

The Japanese presented a more prosaic rationale, emphasizing infrastructure and facilities: 'Staging the World Cup is a complex assignment, and Japan demonstrates all the necessary infrastructure and financial strengths necessary to assure a successful FIFA World Cup 2002.'[66] FIFA's criteria were reported as being met, with government support at prime ministerial level. Facts, figures and testimonials on transport, security, accommodation, organization, finance, telecommunications and medical support services were presented, with an emphasis on extant facilities and organizational experience and expertise. A 'history of Japan's bidding activities' was outlined, implying that a strong relationship had evolved between FIFA and the country, and that its rival had really very little substance to its bid beyond its rhetoric and its promises. But the whole process became implicated in the power structure within FIFA, and especially the emerging challenge of Johansson to Havelange. Tadao Murata confirmed this, describing in embittered fashion the way in which the Japanese had become caught in the 'crossfire between the FIFA and the UEFA Presidents'.[67] The Japanese, believing that Havelange could still deliver his commitment, and 'refusing to distance themselves' (as Jim Trecker put it [68]) from a president whose dictatorial powers were being challenged as never before, were outflanked by a Korean operation which could not contemplate failure, and so expressed its willingness to accept co-hosting.

As the day of decision drew closer, it became clear that Korea, with the European members' support, could beat Japan in a head-to-head. The notion of co-hosting (proposed by AFC's Peter Velappan, but initially rejected outright by the FIFA secretariat) emerged as a theme around which Korean and European interests could unite, in liaison too with African and North American priorities. The Japanese – in their terms, playing strictly by the rules, that is, the FIFA Statutes, and interpreting them in terms of what they continued to see as a reciprocal understanding with the top man, Havelange – stuck to their principled but inflexible guns right through to the eve of the decisive FIFA meeting. In the two days before the FIFA meeting, it was reported, FIFA wrote to the Japanese asking them to consider the possibility of co-hosting; and former prime ministers of South Korea and Japan met as unofficial delegates of their respective governments, to seek a diplomatic solution.[69]

What determined the outcome of this drawn-out decade-long saga? Havelange, by all accounts close to what would have been a humiliating defeat for himself and for the Japanese bid, was at the last minute persuaded to support the co-hosting option. This had been strongly promoted by the Europeans on the committee, but Havelange remained, in Will's words, 'totally and utterly opposed' to the prospect: 'Forty eight hours before the vote he was saying "over my dead body"'.[70] Samaranch of the IOC was one source of advice prompting Havelange to give way,[71] and so avoiding a divisive vote. Chung's acceptance speech hailed 'democracy' as the real winner, and reiterated the peace-generating potential of football: 'I hope today can be a milestone for our two countries . . . and I hope the first World Cup of the 21st century can also be a catalyst for world peace.'[72] Other analysts see different motivations underlying the race. For instance, it is estimated that close to $1.5 billion was to be invested in South Korea, in stadia, transport and accommodation infrastructure; and the country's leading corporations – such as the so-called 'World Cup trio' of Hyundai, Sam Whan Camus and Hotel Shilla – were all due to benefit from this World Cup windfall.[73]

Chung's Japanese counterpart, Naganuma, spoke less effusively, stressing the problems, though 'respecting FIFA's direction'.[74] FIFA spokesman Keith Cooper confirmed this: 'This is not the end of the affair, merely the beginning of six years in which many problems must be overcome.'[75] Early tensions confirmed this, as the event became labelled 'World Cup 2002 Korea–Japan', Korea would stage the opening ceremony and match, and Japan the final. Faces and reputations were saved all round, though Korea, calling on French and Spanish spellings, manoeuvred itself the first billing in the name, as well as the opening credit of the tournament itself. Agence France Presse journalist Erskine McCullogh observed at close hand the ruthlessness of the Korean operation: 'the Japanese don't have any tradition for football. If Japan had lost the World Cup, socially it wouldn't have meant anything. If Korea had lost, the Japanese Embassy would have gone up in flames . . . to Korea the most important thing was to have their name before Japan, for historical reasons, mainly political reasons.'[76] Both Japan and Korea would have difficult decisions to make, in deselecting host towns now that only half the number of games would be played in each country. The Japanese did not share Chung's reading of the process and the outcome. For them, though political pressure from their government had led them to support the co-hosting compromise, it remained a highly unsatisfactory episode. FIFA statutes had been ignored, and their faith in the powers of Havelange had rebounded upon them, as the dynamics of Johansson's challenge to Havelange came to dictate the priorities of the FIFA Executive Committee.[77] UEFA had been clear in its position on the issue. The week before the decision was made at FIFA, press officers at the UEFA headquarters had been answering enquiries with the statement that 'UEFA confirms that they would support the idea of co-hosting . . . [they] favour that two countries – Korea and Japan – hold together the World Cup. It is a wish of the Executive Committee of UEFA that more than one hold the World Cup',[78] consistent with the principles underlying the joint staging of the 2000 European Football Championship by Belgium and the Netherlands.

■ World Cup 2006: European Spoils Again?

In early 1997 the English tabloid newspapers fell ravenously upon a story of England-German rivalry that fed into the xenophobic subconscious of its football-following populace. In ways that were to be echoed just a few months later in the Conservative Party's caricature of Labour Party leader Tony Blair as a small dummy on the lap of ventriloquist giant, Chancellor Kohl of Germany, confusion over bidding procedures pitched England against Germany in the corridors of power of UEFA and FIFA. The *Sunday Mirror* headlined the issue 'England in World Cup war' (2 February 1997, p. 1), and 'World at War! England fury as UEFA back German bid' (pp. 64 and 58).

The spark for this row was UEFA's championing of a German bid to FIFA for the 2006 World Cup, and the European body's claims 'to have taken a decision in favour of Germany', in 1993, of which there was no formal record or communication.[79] The UEFA secretary faxed the English FA, informing them of the UEFA support for a German bid. David Davies of the FA responded with a statement reporting support from the prime minister, and other political figures. The Conservative government's Minister of Sport, Ian Sproat, spouted that the 'undemocratic hole-in-the-corner way UEFA has acted' had caused him extreme concern.[80] Tony Blair referred to the issue as 'a cosy stitch-up', and England appealed to principles of openness and fair play. Davies wrote that the politicians and the sports administrators were:

> . . . deeply shocked by actions which run counter to all democratic instincts that we believe world football should stand for. Informal, unannounced pacts behind closed doors are no substitute for democracy and fairness.[81]

121

Sir Bert Millichip was clear that no (formal) deal or agreement had been made by him. Asked, two weeks before the UEFA fax was sent to London, whether he had formed an agreement with the Germans that England would not bid for 2006, he replied:

> I didn't have an agreement. It is false to say that I had an agreement with them. I am a very good friend, a very close friend of the president of Germany, I am also a friend of the French representative. Certainly it was I who persuaded England to go for the European Championship and not for the 1998 World Cup, because I thought that France had got the edge over us and the FA supported my consideration, and I think they are very pleased that we did do that. At that time, Germany said that we would like to announce now our interest to run at 2006. All I have to say is that I may well have indicated we will support you, at that time, but there was no agreement.[82]

No agreement, but clearly an understanding, and an arrangement. The 82 year-old Sir Bert was savaged in the English press. The *Guardian* recalled that his nicknames had been Bert the Inert and Sir Blert, and quoted UEFA media director Fritz Ahlstrom's confirmation that a UEFA executive meeting at which Sir Bert was in attendance had proposed supporting a German bid, had encountered no objections, but had not minuted the item.[83] Two further meetings were claimed as reaffirming the principle. Germany had placed a formal bid with FIFA, and as Ahlstrom said, 'it was "generally accepted" that Germany was the only European bidder, and Sir Bert knew that'.[84] In the seven months of the English FA's early campaigning in its £10 million bid, political support was granted in the form of forthcoming prime minister Blair's manifesto commitment that a new Labour government would support an English bid: 'We will provide full backing to the bid to host the 2006 football World Cup in England.'[85] With no record of discussions, though, UEFA looked foolish, and its decision-making and communication appeared unprofessional, resonant of 'smoky back rooms, dodgy handshakes and mutual back-scratching'.[86] FIFA, in its rivalry with its Swiss neighbour, commented that any backing of a single European bid by the European body would not affect the FIFA judgement on the candidates, and that from the FIFA perspective there was nothing to stop an English bid. FIFA's Blatter talked of a list of potential candidates comprising Australia, Germany, England, Brazil, Argentina, South Africa, Morocco, Egypt, Peru with Ecuador, and the USA;[87] within weeks, at a press conference following the Belfast meeting of the International Board, Havelange could add Russia to this list. The row over England's candidature was yet another example of the recurrent UEFA–FIFA tensions. It was technically correct for FIFA to remind the football world that the award of the Finals had nothing to do with a confederation, but realistically FIFA's key committees represented confederations' interests, and bids from several European countries would without doubt split any European vote when the decision was due in 2000. It would therefore have been foolish for UEFA not to act upon one of its principles in the *Visions* debate, that just one bid should emerge from a single confederation: to non-English Europeans, England's planning and outrage looked naive, and the British government-in-waiting's enthusiastic support was clearly under-researched and rather blandly and opportunistically formulated. The longest-serving non-Soviet European member of FIFA's executive committee, UEFA delegate Dr Michel D'Hooghe of Belgium, confirmed (in an interview at the Belgian Football Association's offices) that across Europe and UEFA the understanding that England would not rival a German bid was clear.[88] The English response to the eventual formalization of this understanding was widely regarded as ungentlemanly and arrogant, with Sir Bert Millichip the unfortunate butt of English anger. Away from the front and the back pages of the English tabloids and broadsheets, a sober editorial reminded readers that the whole row stemmed from the diminished power-base of British sport administrators:

> In rugby, cricket and of course football, the age of the gentleman amateur is supposed to be over. Welcome to the paid pro. But when it comes to governing these sports, especially inside those committees with international reach, we don't match up. That the Germans should be trying to stitch up the World Cup in 2006 says only that they are good at playing the game of committees and cronies. Instead of moaning, the English should get their act together, lobbying here, nobbling opponents there. That there is intense rivalry between FIFA and UEFA makes this game all the more open. Let's get on and play it, with greater skill.[89]

The mounting English campaign, with its self-righteous appeals, was clearly not in the spirit of the earlier European discussions. The FA's public defence of its late entry into the field centred on notions of fair play and open competition: 'In a world of tough competition we ask nothing more than an open and democratic appraisal of each country's bid according to its merits.'[90] Germany's national football coach, Berti Vogts, reiterated, in May 1997, the German view that England had not kept its word to stay out of the race, and Egidius Braun, head of the German Federation, warned that a double candidature from Europe could see a FIFA vote split, 'and a European country won't get it'.[91] Berti Vogts sat alongside other football figures, from Asia as well as Europe, and Johansson hosted Samaranch, at the final of the European Champions League in Munich – and Johansson perhaps recollected his seat next to United Kingdom premier Tony Blair at the FA Cup Final a couple of weeks previously. They were there not just for the football – they were contributing to the continuing saga of FIFA's complex relationship with increasingly prominent and assertive confederational organizations; and the undisputed importance of FIFA's World Cup in the contemporary politics of national pride and global status. Whether or not England's bid is successful, chief executive of the English FA, Graham Kelly, recognized the paramount importance of a strong English presence in UEFA's corridors of power.[92]

■ Hosts and Gifts

Early World Cup Finals tournaments were in the gift of individuals such as Rimet and tiny bureaucracies. Rous attempted to put in place a long-term plan, based on a combination of networking and the merit of bids. Havelange, from the decision regarding 1986 until his 1996 volte-face, which was greeted with such bitterness in Japan, seemed to many to act as if the venue for the World Cup Finals was his personal gift. With the Catalan Samaranch controlling Olympic affairs, Italian Nebiolo ruling world athletics, and Mexican media baron Rana in charge of the world's National Olympic Committees' umbrella organization, Havelange's apparent control of the biggest prize in world football consolidated what was widely seen as a Latin network of world sports autocrats. That getting the twenty-first century's first finals became more uncertain than the Japanese could ever have anticipated was an indication of changes in the dialectic of control in world football politics. New powerbrokers had emerged, from Asia, Africa and North America, to form alliances with European interests. This provided a basis from which to challenge Havelange's hegemony. For two decades Havelange had exercised considerable power and capacity to dispense patronage. The fact that Japan was not awarded the 2002 Finals was a personal blow to Havelange's status and position, and a triumph for European alliances with Asia and Africa. Within six months of that FIFA decision, having saved his position but lost face, Havelange had announced his decision not to stand for a further presidential term.

■ PART II

FIFA AND THE COLLAPSE OF EMPIRE

■ 6

FIFA and Africa

On 11 February 1990, Nelson Mandela, the leader of the ANC (African National Congress) was freed from Cape Town's Pollsmoor prison, heralding seismic changes in South Africa, culminating in the dismemberment of apartheid and the victory of the ANC, four years later, in the country's first democratic elections. Almost immediately upon his release, Mandela was presented to his supporters at Soccer City, a sprawling, modern football stadium on the outskirts of Soweto.[1] It was not simply the case that this was the biggest venue available in the vicinity. Football was and continues to be the black peoples' game, not just in South Africa, but throughout the continent. During times when significant gatherings of non-whites were either banned or heavily policed, South Africa's football grounds were one of the few places where, in significant numbers, blacks, coloureds and Indians could come together to celebrate common causes, either during the course of the game, or in more formally ordained political rallies. While the context may have been radically different, in earlier periods, from the Cape to Cairo and from the Ivory Coast to the Horn of Africa, football had played its part in the struggle against various forms of colonial oppression.[2]

Six years after his release, in January 1996, it must have been particularly satisfying for Mandela to return to Soccer City, in his capacity as president of South Africa, to officially open the finals of the African Cup of Nations, the continent's premier international football tournament.[3] As one leading South African sports journalist put it, 'After more than 40 years of isolation, this nations cup is the chance for the rest of Africa to get to know their lost sons, and for South Africans to learn something about the continent from which they have so long been alienated.'[4] Indeed, there was a lot to learn.

The 1996 tournament was the largest ever, with sixteen teams qualifying from a record of forty-five entrants. A depressingly large number of starters fell along the way. The first was Rwanda, which missed its rendezvous with the Central African Republic as civil war and carnage at home made football impossible. Burundi and Somalia likewise withdrew because of civil war and several countries, such as Zimbabwe, Malawi and Lesotho missed matches or sent depleted teams because of outbreaks of the dreaded ebola virus. Libya were forced out by an international embargo, whereas many others, such as Swaziland, Guinea Bissau, Gambia, Niger, Seychelles, Madagascar, Cape Verde, Equatorial Guinea and Benin failed to attend matches because of lack of funds.[5] As will be explored in some detail later in this chapter, Nigeria, the reigning African champions, failed to attend the finals because of political interference.

Seated alongside Mandela, surveying the opening ceremonies, and no doubt pondering the political and economic complexities of African football, were FIFA's President, João Havelange and Lennart Johannson, the head of UEFA. With a presidential election scheduled for the 1998 FIFA Congress, both the incumbent and his would-be challenger understood the significance of gaining the support of FIFA's fifty-one African member nations.[6] In order to mobilize this support, first they had to come to terms with the fundamental truth of African football: that it is framed totally by colonialism and the post-colonial experience.

■ African Football, Colonialism and the Post-colonial Experience

Football came to Africa on the wings of empires. European colonial administrators, military personnel, diplomats, traders and itinerant workers and fortune seekers introduced the game throughout the continent in the late nineteenth and early twentieth centuries.[7] In Ghana, for instance the game was introduced by British sailors and developed by the large numbers of British nationals who lived along the cape coast. There were not, however, sufficient numbers of expatriates to keep the game exclusive for a privileged, colonial white elite. Football became popular with the local population who formed their own teams in opposition to those established by their colonial masters. The semantics and semiotics of clubs with names such as Cape Coast Mysterious Dwarves and Cape Coast Venomous Vipers, formed long before the end of colonialism, indicates that football in

Ghana was more than simply a passive replica of the British game.[8] Likewise, in Southern Africa, football became a tool of political protest:

> In the soccer crowd there was a refuge for political and nationalist leaders constantly in fear of government spies or arrest. Soccer, popular among both the labouring classes and the African elite, became an ideal tool with which to win mass support from the majority of the population. African political leaders were not slow to exploit soccer in this way.[9]

In Egypt and Algeria football became embroiled in the struggles for independence from Britain and France respectively.[10] Dr Abdel Halim Mohamed of Sudan explained the way football was used in the struggle for independence in his country. The Sudan was used by the British as a training ground for colonial administrators and district commissioners. Almost all who came were public school educated and the vast majority were graduates of Oxford or Cambridge. The classification of their degrees was not as important as having earned a sporting blue.[11] Halim believed that the British used sport in the small number of secondary schools which they set up in the Sudan as a means of disciplining local young intellectuals and dissipating energies which may have been directed towards political protest. However, because football became so popular with the Sudanese masses, an educated Sudanese elite was able to harness it to a movement for political emancipation:

> We had our social clubs and we were talking about independence. The British accused us of being *afendeya* (elitist and bourgeoisie) – that we were not with the masses of the people, that we do not represent them. As a counter to this we started football clubs as social clubs where we would talk the principles of civics to the masses – that this is their country and that they have the right to independence. This helped to show that while it was we, the intelligentsia, who were the architects of the independence movement, we were backed by the people.[12]

In this regard, throughout Africa, football had a rooted political pedigree which was to become a critical feature of black-national identity in the post-colonial era and would raise the political profile of football in the world in general. In the words of Faouzi Mahjoub, football can 'provide a symbolic parallel for the difficult and tentative steps Africa has made forging ahead in the modern world'.[13]

The African Football Confederation (CAF) had been proposed in 1956 by Egypt, Ethiopia, Sudan and South Africa – the only independent nations on the continent at that time. The proposal to form an African Confederation met stern resistance from the South Americans who, misreading their own history, viewed the African nations as potential dupes of their former colonial masters. However, with strong support from Sir Stanley Rous and Valentin Granatkin of the Soviet Union, CAF was formally inaugurated at its first constitutional assembly in Khartoum in 1957.

In possibly the first use of sport as a political tool in the fight against apartheid, South Africa was suspended from CAF the following year when it insisted on sending either an all-white or an all-black team to the first African Cup of Nations in the Sudanese capital, Khartoum. As we shall see, the South African issue was to dominate CAF's political agenda for the next twenty-five years and have dramatic implications for the internal politics of FIFA.

With only three members throughout the following years, CAF was relatively insignificant as a political force within FIFA. However, by the early 1960s the situation changed radically as the European powers shed their colonial authority. In the absence of economic and military might, newly independent African nations discovered in football a medium through which to register their presence in the international arena both on and off the playing field. And as Ebo Quansah points out, 'application for membership of the United Nations, the Organisation of African Unity and CAF go hand in hand'.[14] In certain respects, African representatives at CAF and FIFA viewed their responsibilities in the same light as colleagues at the OAU and UN: that is, to establish and embellish the bargaining position of African nations in the market place of international relations.

We have also noted how, paradoxically, while the guardians of world football have a rhetorical commitment to promoting international harmony, in practice, international football often produces the opposite effect. One of Africa's oldest colonial legacies which finds clearest expression through football is the division between Arab Africa and sub-Saharan or black Africa – and, to a lesser extent, further divisions among nations colonized by the British, French and other European imperial powers.[15] The rift between Arab and black Africa is rooted in practices of intra-continental forms of imperialism, predating European intervention, via which more affluent Arab north Africans have preyed upon and exploited their less well off southern neighbours.

The extent of this antipathy was made brutally manifest during the 1986 African Nations Cup finals in Morocco. The semi-finals lined up Cameroon against the hosts and Nigeria faced neighbouring Algeria. Both games were extremely violent and in both cases the black

African players were subjected to extreme forms of racial abuse from predominantly Arab crowds. Witnessing these events caused senior sports writer, Rob Hughes, to question the facade of pan-African unity:

> This tournament threatens the dreams of men who live to promote African unity – men whose banner outside a Rabat hotel reads: Welcome to our African brethren. And the threat is exacerbated by Arab newspapers' suggesting that Morocco 'never again play black Africans'.[16]

A decade later in Bloomfontein, South Africa, one of the authors was on a coach with a group of Egyptian officials and supporters who had just attended their national team's defeat in the quarter finals by Zambia. As the coach left the stadium it was stoned by a mob of local black Africans. They spotted the Egyptian flags flying from the bus windows and, with apparent spontaneity, attacked the Egyptian party, which included several women and children, who were clearly terrified by the experience. Later, in the lobby of the hotel where the Egyptian team were staying, when it was suggested that FIFA might be considering South Africa as a venue for the World Cup 2006, in the presence of one of the authors, a disgruntled Egyptian official gave a sarcastic laugh and said, 'They (FIFA) would never trust niggers with the World Cup!'

Beyond pan-African divisions there are also serious problems within individual African nations, with implications for any understanding of football. Clearly, the history of post-colonial Africa has not been one of a smooth and progressive transition to self-determined democracy. On the contrary, it has been characterized by autocracy, despotism, political disorder and civil war. As South African writer, Rian Malan observes, modern Africa, 'is made up of artificial states ruled for the most part by the jumped-up and corrupt heirs of colonialists'.[17] These 'artificial states', over which a succession of dictators have ruled, are so riven by tribal factionalisms and ethnic rivalries that it has been all but impossible to construct meaningful and durable civil societies – that is institutional frameworks for the working up and maintenance of shared principles of equality and social justice, and counter-balances to the naked power of the state and its functionaries.

The general point being made here is that the potential liberalization of post-colonial Africa has never really materialized. Immature democratic experiments have, more often than not, perished, to be replaced by a range of authoritarian, military regimes and/or single party systems with little or no effective civil opposition. Jean-François

Bayart borrows a metaphor from Cameroon, 'the politics of the belly', to characterize the relationship between the state and immature civil societies in sub-Saharan Africa. He presents a model within which quasi-feudal traditions of power, patronage and exploitation operate in settings of bureaucratic rationality. Under such circumstances the abuse of political power and corruption have flourished and become institutionalized. Bayart works with two models of corruption: the *resources of extraversion* – command over or access to scarce physical and cultural capital; and *positions of predation* – the occupation of roles which provide opportunities for extortion. The administration of football in many African countries, is illustrative of how both of these models operate.[18]

Because football emerged from colonialism as one of the few institutions which captured the imagination of diverse populations, in the context outlined above, it became the target for political interference and economic exploitation by powerful political elites:

> In Africa, where the activities of military dictators and self-imposed iron-fist life presidents have stifled open political debate, the ordinary man's idea of self-expression emanates from the terraces . . . Such is the power of football that, the world over, aspiring and actual rulers whether constitutionally elected, military dictators or civilian autocrats, have tended to exploit the game's influence on the populace in order to buy time for their moribund administrations. Governments tend to look upon the game as the public relations wing of the ruling class. Administrators are often appointed without the interests of the game at heart, but according to how sycophantic they are and to the extent they can use the popularity of the game to further the interests of their rulers.[19]

Examples of heads of state taking an excessive and often manipulative interest in national football affairs would include Nkrumah and Rawlins in Ghana, Babingida and Abacha in Nigeria, Doe in Liberia, Numeri in Sudan and Mubarak in Egypt.[20] Dr Halim of Sudan recalls giving up his post as president of the Sudanese Football Association:

> In 1959 we had a junta government. They wanted to interfere in the work of the FA. They wanted to select the president and all of the committee members . . . I would not work in this situation. They put in a Minister for Sport who could have been my son! How could I be told what to do by a soldier?[21]

Detailed consideration of more contemporary forms of political interference and corruption will be looked at later in this chapter in the context of an unfolding story about the struggles within FIFA to contain and control the African theatre.

■ FIFA, UEFA and the Scramble for Africa: Part I

Despite the manifold intra-continental divisions and problems alluded to above, in its dealings with FIFA, as it grew, CAF managed to present a more or less unified front. There were two major issues which were to dominate CAF's dealings with FIFA: the World Cup and South Africa. There was a struggle to break the stranglehold which their former colonial masters had over the game's most prized competition. By the mid-1960s even though the membership of CAF had increased to more than thirty, African representation in the World Cup Finals could only be achieved via a play-off between the winners of the African Cup of Nations and the Asian equivalent. In protest against such obvious discrimination Dr Kwame Nkrumah, then president of Ghana, successfully persuaded CAF members to boycott the 1966 Finals in England. The final minute of CAF's submission to the FIFA Executive read as follows:

> We limit our demand, in the name of fair play and equity for one place of finalist to be granted to Africa, considering that this can and should be effected without hardships by reducing the allocation of Europe by one.
> and
> Otherwise, our FIFA Executive Committee members will take up this matter at its meeting in Tokyo, in the purpose of bringing it to appreciate that in the absence of this necessary adjustment African Associations cannot for the considerations stated above participate in the World Cup Jules Rimet Championship, 1966.[22]

This embargo 'shook the very foundations of FIFA which voted at its pre -tournament congress in London to allow African representation on their own merit'.[23] No doubt the fact that this boycott had been necessary in the first place was still fresh in the memories of many of the African delegates as they prepared for the 1974 Frankfurt congress. If it was not, Havelange lost no time in reminding them through the political machinery which he had put together to manage his African campaign. Shrewdly, Havelange was able to exploit the antipathy between the former British and French colonies. As the sixties wore on more and more African countries gained independence and as this happened, unnoticed by Sir Stanley Rous, the balance of power within CAF shifted from English speaking to French speaking Africa. One of Havelange's main collaborators in Africa was the Franco-African, Claude Ganga who was the first secretary of the Supreme Council for African Sport which was founded in 1966. There was little love lost between Rous and Ganga and the latter

133
■

appeared to be only too willing to use his influence to persuade fellow Africans to support Havelange.[24] Oroc Oyo, the first secretary of the Nigerian Football Association after independence explains:

> I remember the 1974 elections very vividly. There was this struggle [between Rous and Havelange] and I was in the centre of it. Dr Havelange mounted his campaign in 1971 and he produced a brochure on himself that was circulated around the world. I remember he attended the CAF congress in Egypt 1974. After the congress he invited African delegates to a cocktail party hosted by the ambassador of Brazil in Egypt. All of us were invited . . . The plank of Havelange's campaign was to ostracize South Africa, because this was the clarion call of African football. This was a carrot which Dr Havelange brandished before Africa. So Ganga mustered Africa.[25]

Of all Rous' miscalculations his misreading of the significance of the South African situation was the most serious. South Africa's suspension had been reiterated by FIFA in 1961, pending an investigation into the representative status of the mainly white Football Association of South Africa (FASA). Rous visited South Africa in January 1963 along with Jimmy McGuire, the secretary of the United States Soccer Federation and made a report in which he suggested that the FASA, 'was not – or by its rules should not have been – concerned with the government's policies and attitudes'.[26] His official report concluded, 'FIFA cannot be used as a weapon to force government to change its internal sports policy. To do so would wreck FIFA's true purpose.'[27] Rose-Marie Breitenstein, Sir Stanley's secretary, confirms that he believed that conditions for football in South Africa were such that facilities were widely available to all, whatever their background. He seems to have been resistant to facing up to the actualities of the apartheid system.[28]

Effectively, apartheid racially stratified football in South Africa and over the years a wide variety of governing bodies emerged to administer a segregated game.[29] In an attempt to appease the international community, in 1971 premier Vorster introduced a 'multinational' sports policy whereby officially sanctioned racial categories (whites, Indians, Africans and coloureds), under certain circumstances, could play against each other at an 'international level' and, exceptionally, play touring international teams. As Bose states:

> Only a white South African, steeped in the imbecile logic of apartheid could come up with such a tortuous policy. What the international community wanted was normal mixed sport where people of whatever race took part, as they did over the rest of the world. Vorster offered a unique

South African Solution: a wonderfully abnormal sporting solution for an abnormal society.[30]

A look at soccer in South Africa in the early 1970s reveals separate administrative bodies for Indian Soccer, coloured soccer, African soccer, non-racial soccer and white soccer, with the latter lobbying aggressively to be recognized as the commanding voice for South Africa in the international arena. The Bantuization of South African football can be viewed as the bizarre zenith of sporting apartheid. At one stage it led to an absurd proposal that South Africa would rotate the racial mix of the national team as it attempted to qualify for successive World Cup Finals. They would enter a black team for England in 1966, a white team for Mexico in 1970, presumably, a coloured team for Germany in 1974 and so on.[31]

Rous's dogged determination to stand by his views on sports politics flew in the face of pan-African sensibilities and eventually was to cost him the presidency. Mawad Wade, then secretary of the Senegal Football Association and a senior member of FIFA's technical committee, is clear about this:

> I was one of the men in the CAF who was in charge of making a campaign in our continent for Dr Havelange. Why? Because it was apartheid in South Africa. I was talking to Sir Stanley Rous in the Sheraton Hotel in Cairo. I told him, if you are elected, can you keep South Africa out of FIFA until apartheid goes down? He says to me, I can't promise you because I follow my country the United Kingdom. I say to him, in this case then we will never vote for you. Also when I meet Havelange in the same hotel he says to me, okay so long as I am in charge and apartheid still exists, South Africa will never come into FIFA.[32]

The South Africa issue was indeed a critical one, and Wade's impatience with the pseudo-neutral stance of Rous can be understood when the issue is scrutinized closely. From his earliest days in the presidency, Rous sided with the 'European'-based football establishment. In the early 1960s the Football Association of South Africa (FASA) faced a challenge from the South African Soccer Federation (SASF), and in the January 1963 visit to South Africa Rous's two-man commission held interviews with a wide range of sports organizations, and full submissions were received from the two football bodies. These submissions make remarkable and revealing reading. The FASA made plain its firm views early on in its submission:

> My Association is certain that FIFA, which is entirely non-Political, and will not allow the Federation to adopt the course which it has as its chief

aim for a number of reasons, but mainly because the political agitators who are now ruling the Federation behind the scenes, are merely using soccer as a catspaw for their own selfish ends, and they are not in any way interested in what is best for soccer football in Southern Africa, both for Europeans and non-Europeans ... The very large majority of the latter are uneducated, and not fit to assume positions of authority in any sphere of life. I do not desire to enter into any political discussions, as I am aware that your body does not allow politics to enter into any of its deliberations.[33]

Rous and McGuire 'unreservedly' recommended that the suspension of the FASA be lifted, and their report gave no credence to the claims of the SASF:

There is no other body which can take the place of the F.A.S.A. The members of the dissident Federation whom we interviewed, would, in our opinion, be quite unsuitable to represent Association Football in South Africa. Their attitude was one of destruction and not construction in any way. We found that they desired to hinder and to act contrary to Government Policy, which clearly indicates their inability to foster and propagate [sic] the game of soccer in that country.[34]

The Rous-McGuire recommendation was supported in the Executive Committee by thirteen votes to five, Rous referring, in correspondence with Aleck Jaffe of the FASA, to the nature of the vote: 'The votes against were all from the left wing and for the first time those members demonstrated their solidarity as a block. The President of Egypt made the most passionate speech of them all'.[35] At its Tokyo Congress in 1964, FIFA overturned the 1963 Executive Committee decision, and by forty-eight votes to fifteen suspended the FASA, for, in the formulation of the African Confederation, 'practice of racial discrimination'.

The South Africa issue was to haunt Rous throughout his presidency. At the VIIIth Ordinary General Assembly of the African Football Confederation in Addis Ababa, in January 1968, the president addressed the assembly, warning delegates against following the advice of sports politics activists from within South Africa:

I have noted that you attach undue importance to the SANROC [South African Non-Racial Olympic Committee]. In fact you should take no notice of their letter ... I know these peoples. I have been in South Africa to meet them ... In fact this group is more interested in communist politics than in football.[36]

In response, the Kenyan delegate spoke of 'the unwarranted attack of Sir Stanley Rous against the General Secretary and the AFC', on the South Africa question:

> In his declaration we saw the manifestation of old and dying colonialism. It is of no avail of him to say that the Football Association of South Africa has committed no crime because it is the government which is responsible of the apartheid policy. It is the government which controls the affairs of the F.A.S.A. We in Kenya wish to see that all means possible are used to bring about a change in South Africa so that our brothers there may enjoy the freedom of sports we have.[37]

As late as 1973 Rous was still seeking to bring South Africa back into the world footballing fold, through support – via a postal ballot supporting not the lifting of the suspension, but granting a 'special dispensation' – for a South African multi-racial sports festival. SANROC (South African Non-Racial Olympic Committee), from its exiled base in London, wrote to Rous condemning this as 'a dubious postal vote which is not in conformity with rules'.[38] Yet again, Rous mis-read the international response to such a gesture. Granatkin of the Soviet Union telegrammed Moscow's 'categorical' opposition to FIFA's support for the event. The African Federation roundly condemned the decision. When the dispensation was withdrawn – Rous and FIFA claiming to have been misled on the make-up of the teams – the damage was already done. Rous argued – in response to a query from Dakar – that 'this gesture was made as an experiment to overcome apartheid in sport'; however well-intentioned a gesture, it remained a naive one which was to undo Rous in the following months.

In this climate, Rous was ceding much moral ground to Havelange. In addition, Havelange promised the Africans that he would dramatically increase FIFA's efforts to develop football in their continent, particularly at youth level. Most importantly he promised to deliver more World Cup Finals places for Africa. Mawad Wade remembers Havelange's promises and how he intended to keep them:

> Havelange promised to make a plan to develop football in Africa by making coaching courses and to develop the youth football. This programme was good for Africa. Havelange delivered these promises. We are running coaching courses in all Africa. He got a sponsor, Coca-Cola. Coca-Cola they made a lot of money, some of which was used for the plan, for the programme, for Havelange.[39]

Right up to the vote in Frankfurt, just prior to the 1974 Finals in West Germany (FRG), the Europeans did not realize that they had been outmanoeuvred, and remained confident that Havelange's challenge would fail. A combination of UEFA's complacency and Rous's naïveté would cost European football dear. Ali summarizes this view well from the perspective of the African delegates at the meeting:

> Africa went to the congress with 37 votes. The 79 year old Sir Stanley Rous put his twelve year tenure of office and Europe's monopoly of the world body in the hands of 122 delegates. The balance of power was held by the AFC [CAF] bloc. In the vote it became clear that the battle was between the old guard and the third world with Africa playing a decisive role. The AFC's candidate, Dr. J. Havelange won the second vote with a clear majority.[40]

According to Brazilian, Peter Pullen, a senior official (Advisor for Special Duties) and a long time associate of Havelange (Rose-Marie Breitenstein recalled him as 'Havelange's agent in England'), there was a hidden irony in this result. Some time before he launched his own campaign for the FIFA Presidency, Havelange, in his capacity as president of the Brazilian Sport/Football Federation (CBF), had warned Rous of the increasing power of the Third World. Havelange counselled that Rous should consider changing FIFA's constitution in such a way that the votes of the more established nations of Europe and Latin America would weigh more than those of the newer members from Africa and Asia. Pullen believes that :

> Rous, thinking that he had the votes of the British Commonwealth nations in the palm of his hand turned down Havelange's proposal – a decision that was to haunt him after the Frankfurt congress.[41]

In fairness to Rous he had good reason to believe he had a sizeable proportion of the African vote in his pocket. In 1971 Oroc Oyo, then the secretary of the Nigerian Football Association, a man who had learned his trade under Rous during a sabbatical spent at the English FA in the late 1950s, promised Rous that Nigeria, perhaps the most influential country in West Africa and one of the Continent's strongest football nations, would support him. However, as Oyo himself explains:

> Sir Stanley saw it coming, but thought he could win because I had given him my word in Cairo. Even after Havelange's cocktail party I went to his room and pledged him Nigeria's support. I being British trained and since I had some tutelage under Sir Stanley Rous, I did not favour Dr Havelange's drive, I was for Sir Stanley Rous, but unfortunately, when they went for that election in 1974 I had a brush with the NFA and I was sidelined. I did not go to Frankfurt for the congress. The Nigerian delegation which went swallowed the bait of Dr Havelange and Ganga's Supreme Council and that was how he won the election.[42]

This result shattered Rous, whose response is recalled by his secretary, Rose-Marie Breitenstein, as 'certainly one of deep upset, and in some senses as a betrayal'.[43] The outcome also stunned his European colleagues. It signalled a sea-change in the affairs of FIFA as, largely through the intervention of the Africans, the balance of power in world football shifted from the northern to the southern hemisphere. Over a century earlier, the British prime minister, Disraeli had commented that Britain's African colonies had become as a 'millstone round our necks'. In the early 1970s, Disraeli's words resounded within FIFA's European inner-circle, a situation which the Latin Americans were more than happy to exploit to propel their man into the president's seat.

■ UEFA and the Scramble for Africa: Part II

Once more, because of the number of votes vested in that continent, in the 1990s, Africa became a critical theatre in the campaigning for the presidency in the build up to the 1998 congressional vote. Oroc Oyo compared this situation to the period leading up to the 1974 elections:

> We are faced with a similar situation now. . .Africa is now like the bride whose hand everyone is seeking. Johansson was here during the Congress [CAF, Johannesburg, 1996], so too was Havelange and each of them at every turn of the road was trying to make his case for the presidency. In every speech I was reading campaign strategies.[44]

Havelange, before he withdrew his candidature, tirelessly travelled the continent (in a repetition of his 1974 campaign), drumming up support for his re-election. His main strength was that he had delivered on his pre-1974 promises to develop the game in Africa and, as such, any promises he made this time carried considerable weight. Under his presidency African representation at the World Cup Finals grew from one in 1974 to five in the event in France in 1998. In this regard Havelange was considered to be a champion of the African cause. While, by 1996, many Africans believed that he had reached an age when he should retire gracefully, if he had stood, they may have voted for him out of a sense of duty:

> Africa may continue to support Havelange in 1998 – if only out of sentimentality and Africans are sentimental people. We are loyal to people who have helped us. Unfortunately, this is a trait that Havelange and many other individuals and groups are only too willing to exploit.[45]

139

Never a man to leave anything to chance, Havelange attempted to boost his popularity in Africa by suggesting that an African nation should host the World Cup Finals in 2006. Once more he played the South African card, but in an ideological setting which was the mirror image of the one in which he operated in 1974 when his platform had been the continued isolation of that country. Most observers agreed that when he spoke of 2006, Havelange had South Africa in mind and his statement eulogizing the 'Rainbow Nation' at the opening of the 1996 African Cup of nations in Johannesburg confirms this view:

> South Africa, with its superior infrastructure, modern transportation and telecommunications systems and beautiful facilities, has an important role to play in the future of African Football, in particular and sport in general. The end of South Africa's isolation can only serve as a further boost to making Africa an even more powerful sporting force on the World stage. I have no doubt in my mind that with her resources, facilities and expertise, South Africa could stage the 2006 World Cup Finals.[46]

UEFA officials had already declared an intention to support a European bid for the 2006 event and Havelange's intervention on behalf of Africa infuriated them. They viewed his comments in Johannesburg as shameless vote catching and as part of his attempt to split the growing alliance between UEFA and CAF.

While Havelange's backing for taking the World Cup to South Africa would have pleased Nelson Mandela, his declared affinity with Nigeria in the month leading up to the tournament was viewed less favourably by the South African president and many others throughout the continent and, indeed, throughout the world. The Nigerian case is worth dwelling upon because it offers a fascinating insight into how international football can be caught up in the internecine political problems of post-colonial Africa:

> The love of soccer is about the only thing on which there appears to be a national consensus in Nigeria's fractious polity. Successive administrations have shrewdly exploited this nation-wide passion for football.[47]

Nigeria had been scheduled to host the 1995 Under-20 World Cup Finals. In part this was a conciliatory gesture from FIFA to CAF, which was angered by the world body's decision to favour the USA over Morocco as the hosts for the 1994 World Cup Finals. It was also viewed as a gesture towards rehabilitation of the Nigerians, who had been banned by FIFA in December 1990 from all competitions for two years, after being found guilty of fielding ineligible players in international youth competitions. However, at short notice, FIFA rescinded Nigeria's status as hosts and switched the Under-20 tournament to Qatar. FIFA officials argued that there were too many health risks in this part of West Africa and that European teams in particular had been unable to obtain health insurance for travelling. Some observers believe that there was more to this decision than the risk of illness:

> The heavy hand of politics had a lot to do with that decision. It is an open secret that FIFA's action was a means of protesting against the continued detention of Mashood Abiola, the man who won Nigeria's Presidential Vote and who had been instrumental in getting facilities ready to honour the country's hosting pledge.[48]

Dr Halim of Sudan has a different interpretation, 'that is ridiculous! It was one of Havelange's nasty tricks. He had already promised it for Qatar. I don't know why'.[49] The inference being that Havelange had done a deal with the oil-rich Arabs at Africa's expense. Whatever the truth of the matter, because the main thrust to take the competition away from Nigeria had come from the Europeans, Havelange saw an opportunity to exploit the situation and improve his standing in Africa at the expense of Johansson. In November 1995 Havelange visited Lagos and met with the leader of the military dictatorship, General Abacha who fêted him like an important foreign head of state. Amidst a liturgy of glowing compliments about his hosts, Havelange apologized for the 1995 withdrawal and pledged to hold the 1997 Under-20 World Cup Finals in Nigeria.

There were three huge problems associated with this promise. In the first place the 1997 tournament was already scheduled to be held in Malaysia. To say the least Havelange's pledge infuriated the Malaysian Federation and seriously damaged the ageing president's reputation throughout the Asian confederation. Secondly, decisions of this nature can only be taken by the full executive and Havelange's ex-officio behaviour was a propaganda coup for Johansson and his supporters who were already campaigning on the grounds that Havelange was too dictatorial in the way he ruled. The affair reached crisis point in Paris on the eve of the 1998 World Cup Draw:

> What should have been a routine debate took on the dimensions of a crisis, as three and a half hours of acrimonious discussion failed to resolve the issue. For the first time Africa and Asia were forced to greet each other coldly. Europe and South America, those other long standing allies also found themselves on opposite sides of the table. The vote, when it was eventually taken, was split along straight regional lines: 11 in favour of

Malaysia (eight European plus three Asian) against nine in favour of Nigeria (three each from Africa and north/central and South America).[50]

The third and biggest problem for Havelange was the appalling timing of his Nigerian visit. Just as he was busy helping to legitimize the Abacha regime in Lagos, the writer and poet, Ken Saro-Wiwa, and eight other Ogoni dissidents were hanged at the General's behest. Saro-Wiwa and his clansmen were executed by the Abacha regime for leading a group of activists who were fighting for the rights of the Ogoni people in the face of the exploitation of their traditional tribal homelands by Shell Oil, who in turn, were one of the main contributors to the coffers of the Abacha military government.[51]

The international outrage at these executions was led by South African premier, Nelson Mandela. Previously Mandela had played a leading role in using diplomacy to bring Nigeria back into a democratic African fold. Now enraged, he made an emphatic call for oil sanctions against Nigeria and urged Shell to suspend its $4 billion liquified natural gas project in Nigeria as a mark of protest, warning, 'we are going to take action against them in this country because we can't allow people to think in terms of their gains when the very lives of human beings are involved'.[52]

One of the first things Mandela did was to persuade the South African Football Federation to withdraw an invitation to Nigeria to take part in a four nation tournament held in South Africa in December 1995 as a prelude to the African Cup of Nations. In related moves both the Netherlands and Israel refused to allow the Nigerian team to set up training camps and it was only through the personal intervention of Havelange (he threatened to call off the draw) that France were persuaded to allow Nigerian representatives to attend the World Cup draw in Paris on 12 December. An almost inevitable consequence of these embargoes was that Nigeria, the 1994 African champions, at the eleventh hour withdrew from the 1996 African Cup of Nations in South Africa. Oroc Oyo explains:

> Looking from the outside into the running of football in Nigeria the withdrawal from ACN had much to do with politics ... when this hanging happened it had a precipitous effect on Mandela and he reacted like one who was scorned. This led to a rift between Mandela and Abacha and so Nigeria felt they could use the withdrawal from the tournament as a means of hitting back at South Africa, particularly at Mr Nelson Mandela.[53]

As a consequence of Nigeria's withdrawal, CAF suspended them for the following two (1998 and 2000) African Cup of Nations and fined the federation £11,000.[54] Ironically, Shell Oil were one of the major sponsors of the African Nations Cup. During the final between South Africa and Tunisia a man in the crowd below the VIP box and Mandela held aloft a placard with a picture of Ken Saro-Wiwa on one side and Abacha on the other under the slogan, 'Abacha and Shell go to Hell!'. Meanwhile overhead, and also in full view of Mr Mandela, a light aircraft circled Soccer City in Soweto towing a banner proclaiming 'Go Well, *Bafana Bafana* Go Shell.'[55]

Whatever the impact of Saro-Wiwa's execution on Shell Oil, Havelange's proximity to it certainly seriously damaged his kudos throughout Africa, and dented his worldwide image. The Nigerian affair was considered by many as another example of his failing judgement. There is little doubt that the fall-out from this contributed to the decision he would take the following year not to stand for re-election. It is extraordinary to consider that the execution of a poet in Nigeria improved the chances of a Swedish football administrator getting a Brazilian's job in Zurich.

Ironically, in persuading Nigeria's Super Eagles, the pre-tournament favourites and the team which would go on to become Olympic champions in 1996, not to turn up, Abacha had really done Mandela a favour. With Cameroon in such disarray and with Ghana not playing up to their usual standard in Johannesburg's high altitude, South Africa were able to win the tournament with relative ease. What was made to appear as part of Mandela's and 'the new South Africa's' predestination by the international media, was, in fact, at least in part, determined by potent forces off the field of play.

At this stage, the main candidate to replace Havelange, UEFA's Swedish president, Lennart Johansson seemed to have a good chance of gaining Africa's support. There were two main planks to Johansson's strategy in Africa. To begin with there were the *Visions* proposals presented by UEFA which in summary suggested reducing the number of confederations from six to four and rotating both the presidency and the World Cup Finals around the four confederations every four years. The Africans were very displeased when Morocco's bid to host the 1994 World Cup was rejected in favour of the submission from the USA, a country with comparatively little tradition of professional football. The general thrust of Johansson's manifesto was in the spirit of the *Visions* proposals and suggested that he would be happy to see the Africans hosting the World Cup Finals in the foreseeable future. In fact the *Visions* proposals were nothing more than versions of ideas which have been talked about

143

in African circles for many years. Emanual Maradas, editor of African Soccer explains:

> Johansson's Visions proposals were originally a CAF initiative which, characteristically, were not taken seriously until the Europeans became interested.[56]

Also, strategically Johansson made overtures to the incumbent president of CAF, the Cameroonian, Issa Hayatou, a man with a growing reputation as a major player in FIFA. If Hayatou were to back the Swede's candidature for 1998 (and in doing so deliver Africa), then Johansson would step down in 2002, making way for Hayatou's bid for the presidency.[57]

However, Johansson's cause was seriously damaged when, in an 'off the record' interview with a Swedish journalist he made a series of remarks which, when reported in the Swedish newspaper, *Aftonbladet*, were widely construed as being racist. When asked what sets Africans apart as soccer players, Johansson responded: 'they have rhythm, emotions, dance. They move in that way we don't. I do not know what is built into the black race, but I have noticed that they don't seem to like swimming.' While his racial stereotyping was bad enough, it was his off-the-cuff remarks about meeting African officials which shocked most:

> When I got to South Africa the whole room was full of blackies and it's fucking dark when they sit down altogether. What's more it's no fucking fun when they're angry![58]

While not denying these statements, Johansson claimed that the problem lay in the translation and that he had not used the term 'blackie' in a racist way, a view supported by Sir Bert Millichip, who was present when the interview was given. The fact that Johansson was in Africa to accept an award from CAF for his work on development there added injury to insult. For a man trading on the Scandinavian reputation for openness and democracy, this interview seriously dented his reputation and nowhere more than in Africa.

■ Football in Africa and the Politics of the Belly

Johansson would have preferred to be remembered in Africa for his work to make soccer there more financially stable. A key proposal, which was introduced by Johansson and UEFA, was to give each

African team participating in World Cup qualification one million French francs ($80,000) to assist them with the competition and aid future development. This represented the second plank to Johansson's strategy. He pioneered a scheme through which any African country which participates in World Cup qualification would receive significant financial assistance from FIFA. Extreme poverty is the most serious obstacle to the development of football in Africa and regularly countries are forced to withdraw from international competitions because national federations do not have the money to send their teams abroad. As we have seen, in the qualification series of the 1996 African Cup of Nations, a combination of civil war and lack of funds led to sixteen countries dropping out. Mali let it be known that, owing to economic problems, they would not be able to take part in the World Cup qualifiers for France 1998. This situation, according to Maradas, is not helped by the approach of international aid agencies and the like:

> The main problem for football on this continent are the very weak African economies. With so much poverty, we simply cannot afford to fund football properly. The situation is made worse through the stance taken by the World Bank which has very strict criteria for money lending and equally strict monitoring procedures. It is not permitted to spend money on sport while money is borrowed from and owed to the World Bank.[59]

The financial misery of African football is accentuated through the corruption which so often goes hand in hand with the administration of football on the continent. Unlike so many other spheres of interest in Africa, football, because it is so popular, generates income through grants from sponsorship deals, television contracts, gate receipts and government subsidies. However, quite often the money which should be spent on football development ends up in the pockets of corrupt administrators and government officials. Maradas refers to this as 'the cancer of African football'. We could present material in support of this claim from almost every sub-Saharan African country, and for illustrative purposes we have chosen to dwell briefly on circumstances involving Zaire, Cameroon and South Africa.

Zaire with its mineral deposits was once one of the most prosperous countries in Africa. However, its post-colonial history tells of a progressive decline into despotic exploitation and economic chaos. Under the rule of the dictator Sesi Seko Mobuto Zaire's economy was ruined. In 1994 it was estimated that inflation was running at 6,000 per cent. For decades commentators have claimed that the country's natural wealth was being creamed off by the Mobutu family and there were no official denials that the President for Life had a numbered account in Switzerland containing more than $4 billion. When they were paid, the bloated army of civil servants which administered the country received as little as $3 per month. Under such circumstances it is hardly surprising that corruption was rife.[60]

During the African Cup of Nations in South Africa the Zaire national team checked into the hotel where the authors were staying. Almost immediately the rumour spread that $500,000 which was earmarked for the players' and manager's wages and bonuses had disappeared en route between Kinshasa and Durban where, it was further rumoured, the Zaire Minister of Sport had recently purchased a summer house. This was an outrageous tale that nobody we spoke to was prepared to disbelieve, especially when the Turkish-born coach, Muhamed Ertugal, resigned and several of the players refused to play in the next game until they were paid.

The image is conjured of one of the Zaire officials slipping away in the night carrying two battered suitcases full of used dollar bills. This becomes less of a fantasy when it turns out that most transactions in African football are conducted on a cash only basis. According to the captain of the Zambian national team, Kalusha Bwalya, many players do not have bank accounts and in Africa nobody trusts cheques anyway. When teams travel they literally do bring along with them sacks full of money. It is little wonder that, with so much poverty in Africa and so much hard cash lying around football circles, so much money goes missing.[61]

German Manfred Honer has worked in fourteen different African countries as a football coach and technical advisor, including managing the Nigerian national team. He was also staying in the same hotel and had no doubt that the Zaire story was true. He explained how it works:

> The thing is, back to corruption, I believe with all my experience that this is how it works: that the president of the federation or the government minister (sometimes they are one and the same) has all of the money in a safe in this hotel or another hotel and at the end, if everything works quite well, then he is paying some money to the players, but the biggest amount, more than 50%, is staying in his pocket. Not going back to the Federation, because officially he has paid the money to the players.[62]

Joseph Antoine Bell, one of Cameroon's goalkeepers in both the 1990 and 1994 World Cup Finals, also accepted the plausibility of the Zaire story. Like Honer and Maradas, he believed corruption to be endemic within African football. He should know. Famously, Cameroon had qualified for the World Cup Finals in Italy in 1990. Prior to the competition the Cameroon squad had gathered at a training camp in the former Yugoslavia. According to Bell, they only had eight footballs to practise with, 'and only one ball was any good'. The team doctor and trainer had no medical gear and the players had to have a collection to buy bandages and other essentials. Yet Bell knew that the federation had already received a sizeable subvention from FIFA to help the team's preparations. Bell, who was then a senior professional in southern France (and so was well placed to understand corruption in football), decided to act to protect the players' interests. He got the team to agree that on the eve of the first game in Italy, the opening match against the host nation, they would refuse to play unless the federation paid them their wages in advance. Bell was experienced enough to know that if they were not paid in advance the money would disappear into the pockets of federation officials and politicians back in Yaoundé, the capital of Cameroon.

In the meantime he persuaded the players to train and prepare like European professionals, instigating a system of fines to ensure that players turned up on time to practices, meals and so forth. Bell's strategy worked to the extent that at the eleventh hour the federation came up with a proportion of the team's wages and they went on to make Italia '90 a truly memorable competition. However, player power was not enough to prevent the president of Cameroon imposing his personal friend, Roger Milla, on the squad (perhaps just as well as he turned out to be the team's most influential player), nor could it spare Bell from being dropped as first-choice keeper because of his shop steward's role. That year Cameroon got far enough in the competition for the players to earn sizeable bonuses which they never received because, after the event, the threat to withdraw labour became meaningless.

Bell explained that the USA '94 endeavour was just as chaotic and corrupt. In the build up to the tournament the papers were full of stories of a repetition of the 1990 stand off over players' wages, and in America itself the situation deteriorated. 'For two days, Henri Michel, our coach, couldn't sleep because he was constantly taking calls from here in America and from Cameroon . . . It is people trying to interfere. Trying to be big men with the team.' Demoralized and in total disarray, Cameroon lost the final match of their involvement in USA '94 6–1 to Russia, another under-achieving team which likewise was on its way home. After the competition, the vast majority of an estimated $4 million which should have accrued to the players and been used for football development in Cameroon disappeared.[63]

The Cameroon government responded by disbanding the federation and imposing a politically accountable regime, which, according to Bell, was as likely to be as corrupt as the outgoing body. FIFA's response to this political *coup d'état* was to suspend Cameroon until a democratically elected federation resumes control. It was only through the intervention of CAF that Cameroon were allowed under a special dispensation to participate in the 1996 African Cup of Nations.[64]

For the 1996 African Cup of Nations, the Cameroon team got their flight tickets to Johannesburg late and lost a night's sleep over a flight delay. Thus, they had to play South Africa at altitude in the opening match less than twenty-four hours after arriving in the country. Not surprisingly they were hammered 3–0. This added a further twist to Cameroon's story when, much to the dismay of team manager, Jules Nyongha, two days after this defeat the former Brazilian captain, Carlos Alberto Torres, arrived at the team's hotel to be introduced as the new 'technical advisor' to Cameroon. He had been flown from Brazil by MBM Multimedia, Inc., the company which brokered Nike's $7 million sponsorship of Cameroon football. Torres, who had previously worked as technical advisor for Nigeria for eight months without getting paid, said that he was not committing himself to anything until a contract was produced which guaranteed substantial remuneration.

Nyongha got a stay of execution when his team managed to scrape a 2–1 victory over Egypt, but Yves Yopa, the MBM representative and Torres' chaperon, was confident that after the tournament, Carlos Alberto would be installed as Cameroon's new manager. Nike's directors were eager to see a return on their $7 million investment and believed that a world-respected figure such as Carlos Alberto would be good, both for Cameroon football and for headlining their products. This could have been the first case of an international team manager being appointed by the sponsors. As it turned out, unable to get the assurances he wanted, Carlos Alberto rejected the Nike/Cameroon proposal.

It is not unusual to view big corporations such as Nike as villains in the political economy of world football. However, Yopa explains that in order to receive instalments of the $7 million sponsorship, the Cameroon Federation must adhere to a carefully structured budget which ensures that most of the money is spent on football and related projects. In a context where 'the politics of the belly' pertains, intervention and financial control by the multinationals may be one of the few things which could help to stabilize African football.[65]

However, this apparent instance of corporate morality has to be balanced with a more cautionary tale of what happened in South Africa after their 1996 triumph. As Mark Gleeson put it, 'after just four years back on the world stage, revelations of corruption and farcical on-field incidents have threatened to retard this remarkable progress after almost 30 years of apartheid-enforced isolation'.[66]

At the centre of these scandals was Solomon 'Stix' Morewa, the president of SAFA and the man who, next to Mandela, had bathed most in the after-glow of the national team's ACN triumph. It also seems that he gained most financially. After serious allegations of corruption and mismanagement, Sports Minister, Steve Tshwete, appointed a supreme court judge, Benjamin Pickard, to investigate the affairs of SAFA and related football bodies. According to John Perlman:

> Judge Pickard found that the SAFA President . . . had sold out to an Irish-based marketing company 'virtually every asset it had to earn money'. In return for a modest fixed fee, the company which was called Awesome Sports International – you'd think the name might have given some advanced warning – cashed in on all ticket sales, advertising sponsorships and TV rights. One report said that ASI had transferred some R28 million into its European accounts – SAFA's total annual budget rarely tops R10 million.[67]

In return for his 'co-operation', Morewa received a R500,000 'loan' from ASI, as well as accepting from a sponsor a new Mercedes Benz worth R40,000. In addition, Morewa was found to have paid himself a performance bonus of R45,000. This was unlikely to have been checked by the SAFA executive who, after the ACN, voted themselves R15,000 bonuses. Moreover, despite being warned of the dangers of selling out to the multi-nationals by Judge Pickard, SAFA voted to retain ties with ASI and went on to strike a deal with a US-based marketing company to promote South Africa's bid for the 2006 World Cup.[68]

In the light of the rumours of bribery surrounding the South Korean and Japanese bids for World Cup 2002, it is worrying that somebody with Morewa's track record was a member of FIFA's bids inspection team. However, Morewa's graft and pickings looked paltry compared with those of former South African league president, Abdul Bhamjee, who was sent to prison in 1992 for embezzling R7.4 million.

If the above scenarios are typical of the administration of African football it must be questioned whether or not Johansson's initiative will succeed in having an impact at the grass roots of the game there. It seems equally likely that a sizeable chunk of the one million francs per nation will be rerouted. As Maradas concludes:

> Hopefully, the new money for development promised by FIFA will make the national FAs stronger and more autonomous, but there is an equal chance that this initiative will only lead to more corruption.[69]

Either way, it is possible that Johansson's initiative could pay dividends for him on polling day, as those who stood most to gain from FIFA's largesse were precisely those who would vote on behalf of their national federations.

■ Conclusion

African football has come a long way since Egypt, Ethiopia, Sudan and South Africa came together to found CAF in 1957. At that time, the rest of the continent remained chained within colonialism and in a global context, African football was viewed as irrelevant. By 1992, with the readmission of South Africa, CAF had fifty-one members and had become a major force in world football, both on the field and in FIFA's corridors of power. In this chapter we have traced the dynamics of this growth. While, inevitably, growth would have happened in one way or another, there can be little doubt that Havelange's critical interventions accelerated the rate of development of African football. It is equally clear that the reluctance of the Europeans to facilitate the emergence of their former colonies onto the stage of world football was seized upon by Havelange as an opportunity to launch his bid for the presidency and consolidate his position thereafter.

Likewise, Havelange's would-be successor, Johansson (unlike Sir Stanley Rous) recognized the need to harness Africa, through whatever means available. In both cases, football in Africa stood to gain from a transfer of resources from Europe and beyond. However, because of 'the politics of the belly' it is by no means certain that football has been the main beneficiary.

We are not suggesting that corruption in sport is a uniquely African problem. On the contrary, like sport itself, corruption is a global phenomenon. What is special about the African case is both the extent of corruption and how taken-for-granted it is in many parts of the continent. As Bell observed:

> In France you might expect that for every $100 coming into football, $10 might disappear, in Africa for every $100 coming into football, $90 disappears![70]

Africa may, from time to time, yield teams of world-beating potential, such as Cameroon in Italia '90 or Nigeria, Olympic champions in 1996. And, yes, Africa may indeed one day win the World Cup. But, so long as 'the politics of the belly' continues to characterize the administration of football in Africa – with critical resources controlled with no accountability, by ruthlessly self-seeking individuals – the tremendous potential for sustained development across the continent will never be realised.

■ 7
FIFA and Asia

■ Asian Football: From Amateur Leisure to Professional Development

The roots of football in Asia are comparable to those in South America and Africa. The game was, as observed by Mason, taken to newly expanding and colonized countries and markets by 'some Englishmen and Scotsmen abroad'.[1] Thus, in the South Asian sub-continent, the oldest established football association was the Calcutta-based Indian FA (1893) (though the All India Football Federation was not established until 1937). In South-East Asia football made some early institutionalized impact, Singapore's football association dating from 1892. Little detail is known of this body's history, but the Football Association of Singapore is certain that 'the game was dominated by the British companies and the British forces that were stationed in Singapore during the colonial days', and that 'Inter-Business Houses football matches started in the early part of the twentieth century', involved in which 'there were many expatriate players, mostly from England'.[2] Occupying forces and international business were the seminal influences on what was then known as the SAFA (Singapore Amateur Football Association). Indeed, this legacy lives on, at least in the sphere of tradition and cultural heritage, in the context of Singapore's modern professional league, the S-League, modelled explicitly upon Japan's J-League, but with deeper historical roots. The top and bottom clubs in the Pioneer Series B programme of fourteen matches during Singapore's inaugural professional season in 1996 were, respectively, Singapore Armed Forces Football Club, and Police FC.[3] Much had happened in Asian football in the intervening century to indicate that, though tradition might live on in matters of nomenclature and labels, the meanings, motivations and aspirations underlying the game at the end of the twentieth century were a world apart from those which stimulated the pioneers of the game in the continent. This chapter examines this transformation, and identifies the major influences upon the growth, spread, and impact of the game in the world's largest continent. The scale of this transformation and growth was captured by the tigerish comments on Asian football by the general secretary of the Asian Football Confederation (AFC), in December 1996:[4]

> Football is a serious business. We need to reorientate our thinking to treat Asian soccer as a product which needs to be researched, produced and marketed on a planned and sustained basis through every available means throughout the continent.

Football in Asia has acquired – in this seriously developed, produced and marketed form – a wider global profile, in line with some very ambitious objectives. For the general secretary, Peter Velappan, increasing success in FIFA tournaments at world-class level – particularly in younger age-group categories – has demonstrated genuine development and authentic potential. This has been so much the case that Velappan believes that 'by 2,005, Asia will be the equal to Brazil in terms of standards'.[5] Much of this notable pace of development has required the promotion and management of change – organizational and cultural, as well as sporting – in and among the forty-four (as in 1996) member associations of the confederation. The AFC's own modernization – driving 'towards a more professional approach to football management and an improved and efficient communications system'[6] – has generated a set of objectives for itself and its member associations:

> The following measures are now being initiated within the AFC to further **enhance** its image:
> - The push towards well-structured national associations
> - Professional management of the Associations
> - An effective communications system between the Confederation and National Associations
> - Well-structured professional leagues
> - Coach Education Programme
> - Youth Development Programme
> - Referees Development Programme
> - Promotion of the game through the Media, TV and newsletters
> - Sports medicine and its contribution towards high-level performance

- Stadia Security
- Fair Play drive

With the above in view, FIFA and AFC have been working very closely in assisting the National Associations through the introduction of various programmes, seminars, study tours, and inspection visits. This is to ensure that the National Associations are professionally managed, the leagues well structured and the various programmes implemented.[7]

The claim being made here is a far from modest one. It is proposed that, in a new era of professionalized and more systematically developed football culture, FIFA and the confederation can work together to lead the transformation of a cross-continental sporting infrastructure – that between them the two federations can operate as a successful facilitator of supra-national initiatives. They are global initiatives – despite the relatively low profile of Asian football in the football world's biggest showcase, the World Cup – because of the sheer scale of the confederation's brief, geographically, demographically, politically and culturally. In this context, the question of 'Asia' as an entity raises many substantial issues.

■ Asia on the World Football Stage

The Asian presence in world football at its highest levels was most dramatically announced by North Korea's successes in the World Cup in England in 1966, most notably its defeat of Italy.[8] But that was prompted above all by the sporting imperatives of a Communist regime (other social formations were developing their football cultures and systems much more unevenly), and by that country's opportunistic response in going to England when the mass of Asian and African nations withdrew from the qualifying rounds. The succeeding thirty years saw some outstanding successes in football development. In November 1996, according to the FIFA/Coca-Cola Asian rankings, the more prominent Asian national sides were as follows (for this purpose, only those Asian nations featuring in FIFA's top 100 World Ranking are listed opposite). [9]

It is striking, in table 7.1, that (apart from Thailand and Iran) the top ten is dominated by either Arab Gulf states in the Middle East (Saudi Arabia, Qatar, United Arab Emirates, Kuwait and Oman), or established or aspirant superpower societies of the Far East (China, Japan and Korea). Thailand's ranking was based in part upon its prominence within the South-east Asia region – the ASEAN (Association of South-East Asian Nations) grouping – having triumphed

Table 7.1 FIFA/Coca-Cola Asian rankings, November 1996

Asian Ranking		World Ranking	Change – Oct–Nov '96
1	Japan	22	− 2
2	Saudi Arabia	40	0
3	South Korea	46	− 1
4	Thailand	57	− 3
5	Qatar	64	− 2
6	UAE	69	+ 4
7	Iran	77	− 6
8	China	78	− 12
9	Kuwait	79	+ 7
10	Oman	88	0
11	Malaysia	92	0
12	Singapore	94	− 1
13	Lebanon	99	− 2
14	Myanmar	100	− 2

Source: *Asian Football Confederation News*, vol. 3 no. 1/97, January 1997, p. 6

in the inaugural Tiger Cup. Its bubble, though, was soon to be burst at the 1996 Asian Cup in the UAE, where it suffered confidence-shattering defeats at the hands of Saudi Arabia (0–6), Iran (1–3), and Iraq (1–4). Iran re-emerged as a regional power, in the wake of persisting problems even six years after the end of the Iran–Iraq war. But the dominant regions, performing frequently and consistently enough to make a mark in world rankings, were the oil-rich societies of the Gulf, and the thrusting capitalist and emerging tiger economies of the Far East. Performance on the World Cup stage has also reflected such patterns.

Asian national sides did not immediately follow up the 1966 success of the Korean Democratic People's Republic. As the AFC general secretary reflected: 'Asia did not take the cue that Asian teams had the potential and the capability to take on the best in the world. Asia continued to slumber.'[10] To put this point less poetically, but in a more explanatory way – no other Asian side was as yet supported by a centrist infrastructure, in the North Korean case along para-Soviet lines; nor were any yet undergirded by a supportive infrastructure from within a capitalist economy, or a corporatist alliance of social, political and economic interests. It is the societal type, and the deployment of resources within the society, which has promoted football enough to heighten levels of aspiration and raise levels of performance – along with an increased presence within FIFA and confederational organization, administration and politics.[11] Along with CAF, AFC has doggedly pursued increased representation on the Executive Committee of FIFA. Many Asian countries were to experience, in periods of post-colonial independence and adaptation, the same type of developmental problems as were newly independent African nations. The collapse of empire also meant the withdrawal of forms of organization and resources. Football could hardly be immune from this. Unless newly formed nations could provide substantial resources, and scrupulous and efficient administration, there was little chance of them reaching world-class performance levels. The record of Asian teams in World Cups testifies to this basic but critical point:

Table 7.2 Finishing position of Asian sides in World Cup Finals

World Cup	Year	Asian Side	Finishing Position
Switzerland	1954	Korea Republic	16/16
England	1966	Democratic Republic of Korea	8/16
Argentina	1978	Iran	14/16
Spain	1982	Kuwait	21/24
Mexico	1986	Korea Republic	20/24
Mexico	1986	Iraq	23/24
Italy	1990	Korea Republic	23/24
Italy	1990	UAE	24/24
USA	1994	Saudi Arabia	12/24
USA	1994	Korea Republic	20/24

Source: compiled from *Asian Football Confederation 1954–1994*, p. 48

Clearly, on the levels of performance among the established, developed elite of world footballing nations, Asian sides have been the minnows in the global sea. Two performances in particular have been hailed as breakthroughs: the Saudi performance throughout USA '94, in which it beat Belgium and Morocco, and shook a complacent Germany with a late rally in a quarter-final knock-out game; and a non-World Cup performance, Japan's defeat of Brazil (1–0) at the Atlanta Olympics in July 1996 (Brazil nevertheless advanced in the tournament, losing the final to Nigeria). Opinion is divided as to the realism of these claims. Otto Pfister, experienced German coach to African and Asian national sides including the famous 'Black Stars' Ghana team of the early 1990s, remains unconvinced: 'Asia is far behind . . . Look, I take ten football games, nine times I lost, and won in one game. This game is in a big competition? It is not typical, it is not typical.'[12] The resounding fact for Asian football remains – whatever the level achieved, anticipated or predicted – that its leading countries have *systematically* produced the continent's elite squads, in some cases in astoundingly short-term phases of development. China's vast resources, for instance, could be harnessed behind sport, so enabling its footballers to set up a training camp in the Brazilian jungle, in the belief that there was something to be learned from proximity to and immersion in the football culture that had produced the most successful international side in the history of the World Cup.[13]

In this sense Asia is as divided as ever. Velappan has not ignored the question of the diversity of this vast 'entity'. Indeed, it would be absurd so to do in a continent and confederation including both China and Guam:

> Asia is a fascinating continent. There is tremendous **diversity** of culture, tradition, religion as well as political and social systems. This diversity in a continent that also holds 50% of the world's population gives it an unique strength. In recent years Asia has forged ahead economically. Asia accounts for 25% of global exports, 22% of global imports and has 33% of global international reserves. By the turn of the century there is expected to emerge a new Asia – and for football **unlimited possibilities**.[14]

For understandable reasons of professionalism, tact, diplomacy and harmony, the AFC general secretary stressed here the positive side of such diversity. But he was also realistic, recognizing that 'it is going to take a **new breed** of Asian Football administrators to make that push for excellence in the new millennium', and that this push could not be made evenly across the continent. In his own tripartite division of the continent in development terms, the huge variations in resources available for football were clear to see: the petrol-rich oil states, the less well-resourced and at times inefficiently and corruptly administered South-East Asian states; and the powerful states of East Asia, where Korea 'has the leadership, the resources, the support and the base for even better football'; and all of this compounded by the entry into the confederation of five former Soviet republics.[15] Velappan was realistic enough to recognize that neither his confederation nor FIFA could change the material circumstances of nation states, and his message was primarily one of encouragement to modernize, to professionalize expertise and administration. His emphasis on diversity as strength, though, was less realistic, and the nature of difference – of background, culture, motivation and objective – underplayed in his harmonizing and unifying mission. For the huge continent of Asia has been fraught with social, cultural, political and economic tensions that inevitably operate at supra-national levels, and rebound on the development of football across the region. The following section considers some examples of such intra-confederational strife.

■ Asia: An Elusive Unity

Two controversies over the most high-profile Asian football events – the World Cup Finals themselves, and the confederation's championship for national sides, the Asian Cup – illustrate the deep divisions of interest within the confederation. Behind the facade of continental harmony and a rhetoric appealing to the unity of the 'Asian football family', the decision, in December 1996, of the AFC's Executive Committee to award the XIIth Asian Cup Finals, for the year 2000, to the Lebanon, and the decision, in May 1996, of FIFA's Executive Committee to award the 2002 World Cup Finals to both Japan and South Korea, threatened to split the AFC asunder. The higher profile issue was obviously the notorious co-hosting decision by FIFA (for a fuller account and exploration of this, see chapter 5). But the lower-profile case is equally revealing of the deep divides within the confederation, and of the frailty behind the public discourses of unity. Difference is celebrated as colourfulness, so that Havelange, in his message to the UAE and its guests, could write: 'The variety of countries in this vast continent has always promised to produce a sporting spectacular of special richness, so diverse are the ethnic backgrounds of the teams and the characteristics of their players. No other continental championship can compare with the Asian Cup in this respect, and it provides this event with a flavour which certain other continental tournaments may sometimes lack.' The exotic is stressed here, and long-standing international hostilities such as in the Arabian Gulf and South-East Asia are recast through football as competitive but co-operative rivalries. At the draw for the tournament, Iraq and Kuwait were kept apart. In administering this, AFC general secretary Dato' Peter Velappan combined the diplomacy of the negotiator and sensitive visitor with a pan-Asian rhetoric of harmony and the realism of an impresario of the spectacle: 'Certainly the Asian football family is looking forward to being in the United Arab Emirates for the XIth Asian Cup to experience the rich hospitality of this beautiful country . . . Football is peace and football is entertainment.'[16]

For the football politicians of Asia, the culmination of the Asian Cup 1996 was not so much the final between Saudi Arabia and the United Arab Emirates (UAE), but rather the executive meeting on the morning of the match (effectively, the last day of the event). The lobby of the Sheraton Hotel in Abu Dhabi was alive with gossip. Rumours that had been circulating throughout the tournament built to a climax as the AFC Executive Committee met to award the 2000 finals. The bidding national associations were, in the fullest, earlier line-up, China, Hong Kong, Korea Republic, Lebanon and Malaysia. An acknowledged, though not formally constituted, principle within the confederation was that the Asian Cup should rotate from East to West, or at least across the different sub-regions of Asia. The UAE had itself argued its case around this principle when bidding successfully to stage the 1996 finals.[17] The decision on the hosting of the Cup was taken in 1993. The UAE's strategy is recalled by Salem:

> In the interest of friendly relations that exist among member countries of the AFC, the UAE delegation tried to convince the South Koreans to withdraw their candidacy to host the tournament and avoid a contest.
>
> It argued that the 10th championship had been held in the east and, hence, it was logical that the next should be held in the western part of the continent. The UAE, therefore, ought to stage the 20th century's last Asian Cup finals.
>
> The arguments proved futile. The Korean delegation insisted on solving the issue by vote. The Executive Committee of the AFC granted Korea's demand.[18]

A recurrent characteristic of the football politics of South Korea was exhibited here: an inflexibility of negotiation combined with a confrontational style. The AFC awarded the finals to the UAE by twelve votes to four. Three and a half years later, Arab solidarity was to dash Chinese and Malaysian hopes as the UAE's arguments of 1993 were jettisoned. Prior to any presentations by contenders, the seven

Arab members of the AFC executive were reported to have met and decided that they would back the Lebanon bid: India and Sri Lanka were said to have taken the same position. In negotiations during the last week of the tournament, South Korea (which was already confirmed as co-host of the 2002 World Cup) and Hong Kong withdrew their candidatures. Malaysia made a presentation but asked not to be considered. The contest therefore came down to Lebanon versus China. It was clear that the unwritten principle of rotational hosting, scorned by South Korea in 1993, would be equally irrelevant as alliances emerged to award the 2000 tournament to the Lebanon, its officials having convinced 'AFC's executives that the war-ravaged country is on the path to recovery'.[19] The confederation secretariat would not be drawn upon what was really accruing in the process of deal-making. It could always, in public pronouncements, take refuge in its role of civil service, operating neutrally behind the scenes of negotiation and conflict fronted by the national associations. The outcome of the Abu Dhabi vote was an overwhelming majority of 14–2 for the Lebanon against China, even in the light of the AFC's marketing wing's views, for which the choice of China would have made much more economic sense. The Chinese football establishment appeared stunned, and was clearly enraged at the lack of support forthcoming from within its own continent. This was less traumatic than the defeat inflicted upon Beijing by Sydney in the IOC vote for the 2000 summer Olympics. But it was similarly indicative of the problems facing the Chinese in world sports politics, over human rights issues, and as a consequence of its own lack of experience of deal-making and its lightweight presence in the corridors of power of world sport. In June, 1996, at the AFC's General Assembly in Kuala Lumpur, the vote for a new Asian seat on FIFA's executive committee showed the power of the Arab presence. Mohamed bin Hammam Al-Abdulla of Qatar had been nominated by nineteen countries, his rival Timothy Fok by just Hong Kong and China. The Qatari secured the vote comfortably by twenty-seven votes to ten. China was clearly marginalized in the football politics of the confederation.

Malaysia had recognized the way that the Asian Cup 2000 issue was going, and withdrew after its pride-salvaging presentation. In the words of Dato' Paul Mony Samuel of the Malaysian federation: 'We pulled out of it to avoid any unnecessary complication for the Asian Football Confederation.'[20] This is a view from the inside, confirming the necessity to concede ground to preserve harmony. For the Malaysian bid was a serious one from a nation with an expanding sporting infrastructure, the responsibility to stage the forthcoming 1997 World Youth Football Championships and the 1998 Commonwealth Games, and whose president – His Royal Highness Sultan Ahmad Shah – was also president of the AFC. The Football Association of Malaysia's general secretary's defence of the decision to withdraw portrays the pragmatism and realism driving the politics of football development in Asia:

> In the absence of some sort of ruling, right, you have to depend on, let me say, moral positions. That's always bad, because when you have to make a decision on some other criterion rather than rule and regulation, yes, an unwritten principle . . . In the absence of a ruling, in the absence of a statutory statement to say one should be in the East and the other in the West, it is always difficult to expect everybody to follow an unwritten principle. Yes, we went in and thought we stood a very good chance, and then we knew that emotions were running so high that a decision is not going to be made on merit, or on an unwritten principle. So once you know that things are done by emotions then you know that *you* might deserve it, but you're not going to get it.[21]

In the name of co-operation, mutual understanding, 'whatever you call it' Samuel stated, the Malaysian bid was withdrawn, even though this was not necessarily 'for the good of the game'. 'Passions, emotions, lack of common sense' – these are the forces identified as swaying the situation and determining the decision. Clearly, a dominant faction of Middle Eastern states made it clear, this time round, that the unwritten principle of rotation meant little or nothing. The composition of the AFC's Executive Committee was such that a united Middle East grouping could dominate decision-making.[22] South and South-East Asia could muster seven members of the committee (though one of these would be the non-voting president); the Far East three; and the Middle East seven. With the history of hostility between Japan and Korea precluding the possibility of any common approach from the Far East members, and India and Sri Lanka showing no support towards their South-East Asian or Chinese neighbours, a show of solidarity and lobbying from the Middle Eastern delegates retained the event in their part of the continent. In retrospect the outcome looked inevitable, but made a mockery of the bidding process. Off the record, some senior football politicians were fuming at the process and the outcome. The Malaysian bid was well-documented, well-prepared and presented and yet it was withdrawn; the Chinese bid was very serious, but hardly taken seriously; the Lebanon bid was more tentative, little documented, but based on an emotional appeal to the rehabilitation, through football, of a war-ravaged society. A South-East Asia official commented that 'there are no principles . . . we knew a three-way fight would win it for the Arab countries', and confirmed that the Chinese bid 'was not taken seriously'.[23]

The decision over the Asian Cup 2000 was seen as a successful political coup by and for the Arab countries. Velappan presented a brave civil-service face on this, seeing the Asian Cup in the UAE as 'a great success with tremendous organization . . . conducted with a magnificent spirit of fair play and friendship', and called upon a well-rehearsed philosophy of international bridge-building and peace promotion in looking forward to the 2000 event:

> Asian football is reputed for building bridges of peace for those countries at political odds. This Asian Cup was no exception. The games involving Saudi Arabia, Iraq, Iran and Kuwait not only provided outstanding matches and spectacular goals but they were played in harmony and friendship and they were examples to a troubled world.
> Lebanon will, I'm sure, prove to be a worthy host of our premier tournament in the year 2,000. We all know that the country has had to endure political upheaval but we are hopeful that football can play a major part in helping the country return to its former glory.[24]

This is an illuminating passage, balancing as it does the explicit recognition of the political tensions of Asia and its regions, and the driving mission of the confederation to resolve differences, to stress the common need to pull together for the good of the continent. At the same time, there is an air of grudging compliment to the Lebanon and its Arab allies and mentors. *Will* it prove to be a 'worthy host'? What doubts lurked or surfaced in the mind of the AFC secretariat to even raise the issue of whether the Lebanon vote was 'the right choice'? The passions and emotions mentioned by the Malaysian Association's general secretary were powerful ones, without doubt. But what had actually convinced South-East Asian and Far Eastern delegates to go so far as to support the Lebanon? Lebanon's success was announced at a press conference just prior to the Asian Cup final.[25] Velappan stated that: 'They presented the design for four stadia which will be built by the end of 1998 in order to be ready for the year 2000', a 'futuristic vision', as an AFC publication generously expressed it, given that, as Velappan noted, the country was 'in the middle of total reconstruction of the nation' after seven wars and just seven years of peace. China had been seen as the favourite, and confirmed that they would be able to 'organise the Asian Cup tomorrow if necessary because they have all of the stadia and all of the facilities'. Velappan himself would soon – but more privately – acknowledge the complexity of the situation, referring to the outcome as 'regrettable' and 'undesirable'.[26] This is not to say, though, that the discourse of commonality, co-operation and reconciliation so frequently employed by the AFC general secretary was mere rhetoric.

Within the context of the AFC itself, conflicting factions have indeed shared common goals, and common resentments concerning the supercilious ethnocentrism of the European football authorities and, to a lesser extent, those of South America. Sometimes this is best expressed in the apparently innocent and neutral technical sphere. General Bouzo, treasurer to the AFC and doubling up as commissioner for referees, spoke vehemently of Eurocentric assumptions concerning the higher quality of European referees. He asserted forcefully that the European Championships of 1996, in England, had refereeing performances which were of lower quality and consistency than those of Asian referees. It was not possible to disagree with him, given the victory of which the Spanish side was robbed in its game against England, when a perfect goal was disallowed for offside; and a fair and legitimate goal scored by Germany within extra time against England was ruled out for no good reason at all. Bouzo went on to say:

> We don't need you – Europe – any more. For 100 years you have thought that we needed your level, but now we are as good as you. Our decisions are as good. Yet you Europeans refuse still to accept an Asian referee for a big European match. The Europeans just laughed at that.[27]

The unity of the Asian football family may be shown all to easily to be a fragile one, but it is authentic when understood in the light of wider global cultures, politics and prejudices, particularly *vis-à-vis* a Eurocentric West. This elusive unity would be further tested into the new century, in the build up to the first-ever co-hosted World Cup, 'World Cup 2002 Korea and Japan'. The process whereby this decision was arrived at by FIFA, and detailed accounts and responses of FIFA, Korean and Japanese personnel are considered in chapter 5. Here, it is intended merely to document the deep divisiveness within the confederation over the decision. Two members of the FIFA Executive Committee, who joined it after the May 1996 decision, expressed their scepticism. Mohamed Bin Hammam, former president of the Qatar Football Association, was reflectively trenchant on the matter:

> The decision of co-hosting the World Cup 2002 is I feel an unfair decision for both Korea and Japan. I am quite confident that each of the two coun-

tries deserve to organize the World Cup and if they had been given the opportunity to singly host the World Cup then that particular event would have created a landmark event in [the] history of football. Actually, the co-hosting decision was an insulting one to Asia and it was as good as somebody telling that no country in Asia has the qualification and capability to host the World Cup independently, which is in my view totally incorrect.[28]

Chuck Blazer, the general secretary of CONCACAF, expressed the view that a certain level of compromise needed to be reached, given the intensity of the campaigning.[29] Smaller, less fully-resourced or wealthy nations were more open-minded about the principle of co-hosting. Dato' Paul Mony Samuel recalled that the Malaysian association had made such a proposal, informally, to FIFA:

> We made that suggestion. We made that suggestion because if the World Cup is only going to be played in one country, then out of 195 countries who are members of FIFA, more than 80% or 90% are ruled out because they don't have twelve cities, they don't have the population, or they don't have the infrastructure that could manage a World Cup. Why should the World Cup only go to countries that have the infrastructure that could manage a World Cup? And just because you're small, and just because you're economically lower than the others, and just because you can't achieve that twelve-city status, you don't get the chance. So we wanted to work for 2002 on that principle. ASEAN [the Association of South-East Asian Nations] could do it. Now we have got Bangkok, we have got Singapore, Malaysia, and there are enough stadiums to host a World Cup.[30]

FIFA deflected this ASEAN initiative, by offering Malaysia the 1997 World Youth Championships. But the case is convincingly put, particularly given the Malaysian general secretary's further emphasis that – to avoid the unnecessary 'hassle' of seeking to solve problems and find solutions retrospectively – 'the countries that want to host it must join together and bid it from the beginning', in order to avoid 'bad blood'.[31] These perspectives on Asian football's contribution to world football and the World Cup reflect both the positive unity and pride of the confederation, and the conflictual dynamic that characterizes such an heterogeneous organization. First, there are common interests of aim and aspiration – Dato' Paul is 'proud to be part of Asia' in opening the doors for the first time to the co-hosting model among the members of the confederation.[32] Second, opinion will continue to be led by regional interests, and the schemings and manipulations within and across intra-confederational power blocs. This was further spiced by the confederation's acquisition of five new members from Central Asia after the disintegration of the former Soviet

Union – Kyrgyzstan, Tadjikistan, Turkmenistan, Uzbekistan and Kazakhstan – disgruntled as some of them were that they were not to be affiliated to the much wealthier European confederation, UEFA. Underlying all the machinations and power-building of Asian football politics was the stark fact of the differences of political and economic power among Asia's sub-regions. The case-studies in the following section are testimony to these socio-economic, cultural and political realities of Asian football. The UAE and Japan are selected as 'polar types within a broader category',[33] the understanding of which will illuminate the larger whole comprising those categories and types.

■ A Gulf Apart: The Case of the UAE

The UAE – as World Cup qualifier in Italy in 1990 (finishing with the poorest record of all the participants in the finals), and hosts of and finalists in the XIth Asian Cup in December 1996 – provides one of the less well known stories of successful football development. It is considered here as a revealing case of the conditions and nature of football development in the Arab Gulf states.[34]

The UAE was founded as a nation only in 1971, and the UAE Football Association affiliated to FIFA the following year. Within nineteen years the national side was playing in the World Cup Finals, and was regularly a serious contender for honours in continental Asia and sub-regional Asian tournaments such as the Gulf Cup. For a nation with such a small population – in 1995 a mere 2,377,453, 66.5 per cent of which were male – and with a heritage of sports much more resonant of the nativist sports of the Arab ruling class, and the imported sports of the former ruling classes of the British Empire, this was a remarkable achievement. How, and why, was this achieved? Football was developed consciously in the UAE for political purposes, in order to express parallel status with other Gulf states and, if success were achieved, to raise the profile of the UAE across the world.[35] The way in which this was done was to deploy the power and resources of an (enlightened) despotic corporatist state in the realm of public culture. Football was developed, not just as a potential career for young athletes, but as a form of service to the nation, and a contribution to its further development.

Football was introduced into the Emirates – seven separate Emirates were united into a federation in December 1971 – by British merchant sailors, playing the game in their free time in port, and soldiers based in the various statelets. Emirate nationals also encountered the game, filtered through British colonials, in India. The first school-based football side is said to date from the late 1920s, and neighbourhood-based youth sides developed in the 1940s. This provided a basis for some growth and expansion of the game, but the critical date for the development of UAE soccer was two weeks to the day after the formation of the UAE, when the UAE Football Association was established within the new Youth and Sports Ministry. The UAE president, HH Sheikh Zayed bin Sultan Al Nahyan, saw youth as having a major role in the development of the new nation, and from the very beginnings of the new country, 'sport became an official movement countrywide', and the major task of the football association was to build a national side capable of competing effectively in international tournaments. Vast resources have been poured, from the coffers of the oil-rich ruling family, into this project.

In the context of such a one-ruler dynastic state, sport came to play a major part, with ruling family appointees placed in key positions in the body responsible for sport policy, the Ministry of Youth and Sports. General fitness and exercise was promoted, reputedly for the population as a whole. But international events (snooker, tennis, power-boat racing, golf) were attracted, and particular sports targeted for development, to bring the new nation, its modernization and its riches, to the attention of a wider world. The UAE Football Association was chaired in 1996 by HH Sheikh Abdulla bin Zayed Al Nahyan, under secretary of the Ministry of Information and Culture. This was a high profile indeed for football administration during the finals of the Asian Cup. But to the visitor arriving in Abu Dhabi during the tournament, it soon became clear that the event was merely part of a national celebration of a more important moment, the 25th anniversary of Sheikh Zayed's accession, and the extraordinary illuminated trimmings on Abu Dhabi's office blocks and high-rises, and the bright lightbulbs along all the length of the airport road into Abu Dhabi city, were not in the name of Asian football.[36] They celebrated the supremacy of the president. Very little publicity on the Asian Cup adorned the streets and thoroughfares of the city. Some young children in the city centre might be playing football in an alleyway, enquiring of foreign journalists 'Will we win, will we win?', but as the UAE progressed to the final football remained very low-profile within the public culture of the city. It could only be concluded that to a large extent the football culture was a manufactured one, lacking – despite full stadia for UAE games, the crowds made up in part of bussed-in schoolchildren and security and military forces – a deep-rooted historical and cultural vintage and passion. Football's development was fuelled by patriotism, diplomacy, veneration of national institutions, and moral approval for the blend of sports and youth.

Technically, the UAE League players in 1996 were neither full-time nor professional. But in actuality, the league was a version of classic Soviet models of central promotion and sponsorship of sports and athletes in the service of the state.[37] The Minister of Youth and Sports was in charge of all the sports associations in the country, and stadia and clubs of the top division were sustained by government funds, each club receiving a regular revenue allocation. The UAE permitted no foreign players to play in its league, nor any UAE player to leave the country. Officials claimed that players from Gulf countries like the UAE did not want to play abroad, well remunerated and provided as they have been in their own countries. Whatever, a player simply would not be permitted to play elsewhere. Playing for one of the UAE's top clubs guaranteed a job for life, with related work available after playing, and generous testimonials also providing for the future. All presidents of clubs were sheikhs, and provision for players was comprehensive. The government provided a free home for all locals and nationals[38] – 'very nice houses, free electricity and free water . . . quality and security in the UAE is very very good, top of the world', as Hassan stated. Nominally, UAE players are part-time, holding down jobs, and play as amateurs. In fact, they are generously sponsored, and close to full-time athletes. In 1996 there was some debate about the prospect of developing a squad of more explicitly full-time professionals in the UAE, along the lines of neighbours Saudi Arabia. It was recognized that coaches can find it difficult coaching amateurs many of whom would be working at something other than football in the morning. There was no doubt that such issues would be raised and decided upon at the highest level of government policy, the football association president being at the heart of the state apparatus.

Football has benefited in the UAE from the patronage of the corporatist state.[39] In corporatism, the functions of the state, the economy and the civil society are coterminous. The direction and nature of policy are dictated by a sense of clear objectives, the achievement of which is seen to justify any choice of means. With the support of the highest echelon of the state itself, Sheikh Zayed, and in line with his support for the improving welfare of the people and the world-wide image of the nation, football was developed in the UAE as a means of profiling the qualities of the new nation, and presenting an image of progress and excellence to the wider world. That the football association of the country can be given to a 21-year-old as a birthday present was further testimony to the integrated nature of the political-cultural project. FIFA affiliation, and FIFA and AFC approval of the state-of-the-art facilities in which events could be held, became hallmarks of modernity for a state and a society in which the legacy of Arab culture remained central – camel racing, eagle breeding and flying, were prominent in the sport sections of UAE official literature for 1996. Sports which were legacies of the colonial imperialist days – rugby, golf and tennis – continued to sustain a higher regular public profile than did football, even though the latter could claim to be the country's most popular spectator sport. It is the internationalism of football that has placed it at the centre of UAE policy.

The UAE has offered the world sports calendar some of its richest events – the Dubai golf classic, tennis open and snooker tournaments, for instance. And the UAE's public relations policy has been imaginative. On his return from successful medical treatment in the USA, Sheikh Zayed was presented with the biggest birthday cake in the world, and such gimmicks could lay claim to mention in the *Guinness Book of Records*. The Asian Cup itself was in many respects no more than just another side-show to the worship of the Sheikh. Football, though, could deliver the international audience. In the continental and world terms of AFC and FIFA respectively, football could provide the opportunity to profile both the nation and its own sporting culture. Any means to such an end could be justified, on the basis solely of the corporatist project. The price might be high for perceived failure. Nowhere in the UAE's own histories are the results of Italia '90 mentioned – eleven goals against, two goals for, and three defeats in three matches. And veteran Sudanese world sports leader Dr Halim, citing the UAE as an instance, has commented that the price of some forms of extremism and cultural and political fundamentalism, that can lead to public humiliation, shame and disgrace for players and officials returning to their home country, is unacceptable.[40] Certainly those Iraqi players who, after a World Cup qualifying defeat by Kazakhstan in a home fixture in Baghdad in June 1997, were reported to have been tortured by Saddam Hussein's son Uday, head of Iraq's football association and Olympic Committee, would agree with Dr Halim. After the defeat, the players were taken to a prison in the desert, where 'they were whipped across their backs and on the soles of their feet. The punishment was carried out by one of Saddam's cousins, Ahmed Sulaiman al-Majid.'[41]

But these are the prices demanded in the corporatist societies for which football has been developed as a serious political commitment and cultural project. Away from the field of play, the not-so-enlightened despot or the far-from-benevolent dictator, could cull the football establishment at will – in the name of national pride, honour, and all 'for the good of the game'.

■ Making Culture – Japan's J-League Experiment

'Olé, olé, olé, olé', sung repetitively, droningly and loudly behind a football goal, by young fans of mixed gender bedecked in the expensive replica shirts of the successful football team. This was an unimaginable scene in Japan before the 1990s, and the formation of the professional J-League. The growth of football in Japan and the professional experiment can be seen as interesting examples of the globalization of sport.[42] Top world stars from Eastern Europe and Brazil were imported to set the level; commercial sponsors and government backed the League, which was seen as crucial to the improvement and maintenance of the level of the national side; and the formation of the League was seen as an integral part of the bid, by Japan's national football association, to host the 2002 FIFA World Cup Finals. All the paraphernalia of fan culture was promoted in an attempt to reproduce a professional football culture in a setting where its historical base was negligible.

This was an attempt to take football out of its amateurist, educational framework and professionalize it in modern form.[43] Football had featured in the school curriculum of the Shizuoka Prefecture from the beginning of the twentieth century, and has been taught there ever since. Football was introduced into the country as a consequence of the opening up of trade with the British in the late nineteenth century.[44] An Englishman, Lieutenant Commander Douglas of the Royal Navy, is said to have introduced the game, and football came to feature in some schools, particularly in British-oriented educational institutions. Generally, though, baseball was the compulsory sport in Japanese schools. It was the international impact of the Olympic Games that gave football a higher profile in Japan, and the Japan Football Association was founded in 1921 with a view to Olympic participation, a cup competition starting in the same year. The first winner was the Tokyo Club, and most winners throughout that inaugural and the following decades were university teams and clubs, from Tokyo or other major cities. Admission to FIFA came in 1929.

But it was the international stage of the Olympics, and especially the country's staging of the 1964 Summer Games, that provided the platform for a fuller development of the game at a higher level of international performance. In 1960 widely experienced FIFA coach, German Dettmar Cramer, was hired to prepare the national team for the Olympics. A solid showing – victory over Argentina on the way towards the quarter finals, where Czechoslovakia won 4–0 – created a wave of enthusiasm for the game, and the following year the Japanese Football League was established. At the 1968 Olympics, in Mexico, the national team went undefeated until its 5–0 semi-final defeat by Hungary, but recovered well to take the bronze medal by defeating the Mexican hosts 2–0. This was the basis of football's development in Japan – an improving record of performance and achievement at high, but still amateur, level.[45] The heavy Olympic defeats in 1964 and 1968 were, of course, at the hands of Eastern European, state-sponsored athletes – full-time professionals in all but formal status. The Football Association of Japan was convinced that the next stage of development required a more sustained exposure to top international levels of performance. By the turn of the 1970s and the 1980s, the association was bringing the world's top national and club sides to Japan, in the Kirin Cup (for invited national sides) and the Toyota Cup (for the club champions of Europe and South America). Recognizing the widening interest in the game, the JFA saw the next logical stage as the creation of a professional league, linked to the plan to bid for the first World Cup ever to be staged in Asia.

JFA officials, sensitive to this evolutionary and incremental development of the game, recognized that it needs to be established in clubs and communities, not just imposed from above at elite level. This was stated clearly in the declaration of 'goals in establishing the J. League':

1. **To Promote Football as Culture**
To spread the love of Japanese football more widely, thereby promoting the healthy and physical growth of the Japanese people and generating a rich sporting culture. To promote friendship and exchange with international society.
2. **To Strengthen and Foster Japanese Football**
To invigorate Japanese football, improving the level to the point where Japan can qualify regularly for the Olympic Games and the World Cup, and to raise the status of football in Japan.
3. **To Raise the Status of Players and Coaches**
To provide top-level players and coaches with worthwhile opportunities in the sport and to promote their standing in society.

4. **To Foster Stadium-development and other 'Home-town' Ties and Facilities**
To establish close ties between clubs and their communities through the provision of stadium and other facilities that enable local residents to experience first-class football at first hand.[46]

This amounts to an ambitious project, at the levels of both community and nation. It is also a sophisticated conception, recognizing that the task is one of cultural innovation not just policy implementation, one in which inroads had to be made into established values. There are elements of social engineering within the vision too – the cultivation of the healthy body, healthy mind, for instance – along with the sense that this can create conditions conducive to the production of national and international excellence. As J. League chairman and chief executive Saburo Kawabuchi put it, 'we are also determined to build a new sports culture for Japan'.[47] Such a culture would reposition Japan within the international sporting community, so contributing – as stated by Ryo Nishimura, of World Cup 2002's Communications Department – to the post-World War II project of rehabilitation.[48]

Local government, industry and companies proved to be responsive partners in the J. League initiative. The league itself set up a number of independent affiliated companies to handle visual rights (video and stills), and commercial rights, logo sales and the like. Specialist outside companies, in 1996, dealt with data analysis of match records, result services and schedule/match communications. All clubs in the 1996 line-up were sponsored (see table 7.3).

The business and company names were consciously dropped from the team titles, to emphasize community and locality roots and identities.[49] Such a line-up of influential and prominent industrial and commercial sponsors, and substantial support from local and regional government, enabled the J. League to develop from its solid start in 1993. It had been planned in the context of a booming 'bubble economy' in the second half of the 1980s, benefiting from a climate of buoyant support from corporations. *Mécénat*, the sponsorship of sport and culture by corporations, provided the basis of its economic development.[50]

At the end of its third season, Kawabuchi commented that 'we anticipated continued growth and excitement in 1995 and all of us are thrilled that we achieved our goals'.[51] This 'thrill' sounded like a sigh of relief that the league was still prospering after a Japan-less World Cup in the USA the previous year. The Japan national side, having defeated its greatest rival South Korea, conceded a last-gasp equalizing goal to Iraq in Qatar, so allowing Korea to

Table 7.3 J. League Club Sponsors, 1996 Season

Club	Sponsors/Founding Funder
Kashima Antlers	Local government and companies
	Sumitomo Metal Industries Ltd
Jeff United Ichihara	Furukawa Electric Company Ltd
	East Japan Railway Company
Kashiwa Reysol	Hitachi Ltd
Urawa Red Diamonds	Mitsubishi Motors Corporation
Verdy Kawasaki	Yomiuri Shimbun
	Nippon Television Network Corp
	Yomiuri Land Company Ltd
Yokohama Marinos	Nissan Motor Co. Ltd
Yokohama Flügels	All Nippon Airways Co., Ltd
	Sato Kogyo Co. Ltd
Bellmare Hiratsuka	Fujita Corp.
Shimizu S-Pulse	Local companies
Júbilo Iwata	Yamaha Corp.
	The Shizuoka Broadcasting System etc.
Nagoya Grampus Eight	Consortium of 20 major local companies
Kyoto Purple Saga	Consortium of local companies (core Kyocera)
	Local government
Gamba Osaka	Matsushita Electric Industrial Co. Ltd
Cerezo Osaka	Consortium of 17 Osaka companies, including Nippon Meat Packers Inc., Capcom Co. Ltd, Yanmar Diesel Engine Co. Ltd
Sanfreece Hiroshima	Consortium of 47 companies, including Hiroshima Prefecture, Hiroshima City, Mazda Motor Corporation, Chugoku Electric Power and Hiroshima Bank
Avispa Fukuoka	Consortium of 44 local bodies and companies, including Fukuoka City, Kitakyushu Coca-Cola Bottlers and Sanyo Shimpan

Source: J. League Profile (1996), pp. 8–15

qualify for the USA Finals: this traumatic moment became known in Japan as the Tragedy of Doha. Despite the 1995 growth, though, the 1996 season saw a decline in attendances, and a lessening of television interest – interestingly, in the context of the league's first experience of a European-style single stage schedule for the championship, and FIFA's decision mid-way through the season that the 2002 World Cup be co-hosted with Korea. The league reverted to the two-stage system with play-offs for the 1997 season, and sponsors remained committed. But a poor performance by the national side at the XIth Asian Cup (going out in a 0–2 defeat by Kuwait) had frayed the nerves of the Japanese football establishment.[52] Nevertheless, the first four years of the J. League could be adjudged an overall success, particularly in the light of the longer term project for cultural change. Such success demonstrated the value of integrated planning and development based upon commercial, political and organizational alliances and partnerships.[53] This was acknowledged by the AFC when its general secretary Velappan described Japan's 'dedicated officials and players' as 'definitely on the march with a promising new era ahead', and praised the JFA as 'well structured and professionally managed, with good coach education, youth development, orderly crowds and, certainly Asia's, first professional women's football league'.[54] It is FIFA, and the Havelange programme, which could encourage football developments in Asia, and the AFC which could assume a closer facilitating and monitoring role. But it was private capital and state commitment, often working in tandem, which was required to put in place the J. League blueprint.

■ Rous, Havelange and the Development of Asian Football

The Third World was promised much by Havelange in his drive for the FIFA presidency. This is not to say that Asia had not benefited from FIFA during Sir Stanley Rous's leadership of FIFA. Velappan describes Rous's contribution: 'mainly on the technical development programmes. With his assistance we organized the Asian academies for coaches, referees and always he had a very ready and open heart to receive whatever Asia's needs were.'[55] Rous's relationship with FIFA's Asian constituency was not exclusively technical and administrative. His stated aim was 'to maintain the sporting unity of football', even wherever 'politics were apt to intrude as in the Djakarta games of 1962.'[56] In this case, Israel and Taiwan were refused visas to enter Indonesia, and all Rous's diplomacy could not get the bans lifted. Rous's solution to the Israel problem was to work towards the relocation of its national association into Europe. In a letter, marked confidential, to the AFC secretary Koe Ewe Teik in Penang, Malaysia, in September 1970, Rous voiced privately his view of how the problem might be solved, and new allies within FIFA carefully courted:

> In view of the possible 'bloks' in FIFA becoming more solid I wish to talk to you, when we next meet, about strengthening the position of Asia. Is there any possibility of you eventually succeeding one of the present members? You have done so much to develop football throughout Asia that you ought to become one of the leaders within FIFA. Do you agree that in the Olympic Games and the World Cup, in future, we should put Israel in a European group? If we do, I am told by the leaders of Kuwait and Bahrain, more Arab countries would participate and we might be able to find influential leaders in those states.[57]

So in appropriate circumstances, Sir Stanley was not averse to playing Jew off against Arab. Such negotiations developed over the next two years, and the Kuwait Football Association proposed to the AFC that 'Israel be excluded from future AFC tournaments'. Z. Bar-Sever, chair of the Israel Football Association, registered his astonishment at this proposal, in a letter to Rous dated July 1972, recounting his association's long service to the cause of Asian football, and its representation of the continent at the Olympic Games of 1968, and the World Cup Finals of 1970 (both in Mexico):

> You will agree that this ridiculous proposal is against the principles, objects and ideal of the A.F.C., as stated in the A.F.C. statutes. It seems that those who are demanding equality in sports are, themselves, ruthly [sic] ruining the term and aim of sportsmanship and fairness, and are trying again and again to involve politics with sports.[58]

The Israeli condemned the Kuwaiti proposal as a mockery of the first principle of 'world sporting organizations . . . that there will be no racial or any other discrimination in sport'. Clearly, behind his own resolute defence of FIFA statutes, Rous was not above some political pragmatism of his own. Israel was actually ejected from the AFC in 1976, two years after the end of his presidency, and 'flitted from Europe to Oceania in search of a home',[59] before stabilizing its affiliation in UEFA in 1992. Rous himself had been willing to recognize the pressing claims of the emergent Arab nations. and sacrifice

Israel on an altar of FIFA *realpolitik*. He could concoct no such potential solution to the Chinese issue, and this would prove costly to him.

China had left FIFA in 1958 because it continued to recognize the association from Chiang Kai-Shek's Taiwan. The communist Chinese were particularly offended by the fact that FIFA allowed Taiwan to operate under the name it used within the United Nations: National China. As the influence of communist China spread, particularly throughout Asia and Africa, in the early 1970s there was a growing lobby outside of Europe and South America, which held the view that not only should China be readmitted, but that Taiwan should be expelled. Rous argued that while it was perfectly acceptable to readmit China, this could not be done at the expense of Taiwan as this would be contrary to FIFA's constitutional position which stated that: 'So long as a country was internationally recognized to exist [*i.e. was a member of the United Nations*] and had a reputable national Association . . . FIFA's rules required us to give recognition'.[60]

Rous realized that by taking such a stand he may have alienated potential voters from the Third World and the communist bloc, but still he chose to hide behind his cherished, philosophical and publicly stated belief in the separation of sport and politics. 'It was made clear to me that some delegates would vote against me unless Taiwan was expelled, but I was not amenable to that sort of pressure.'[61]

Despite Rous's close ties with South-East Asia, Velappan was one of the delegates (as secretary of the Malaysian Association) at the 1974 FIFA Congress to have taken Sir Stanley by surprise and voted for Havelange. Rous's footballing persona was beyond doubt, Velappan recalled, but 'I think Sir Stanley did not take the election too seriously. He didn't believe in campaigning. But Dr Havelange and his people did a lot of groundwork, and specially promising Asia and Africa many benefits, such as more places in the World Cup, more places in the Olympics and also the introduction of youth tournaments, technical aid programmes and so on, and obviously he carried the day. He has achieved all that, he expanded the World Cup, he introduced the youth tournaments for the Under-17 and the Under-20 years, the women's tournament, and now the FUTSAL development programmes. And so he has given enormous contribution to football and I am sure in 1998 when he officially retires everyone will be very, very thankful for his contribution.'[62] One of Velappan's successors, Paul Mony Samuel of the Malaysian Association, also commented on this scale of Havelange's contribution to Asian football, adding too that it is important that FIFA has broadened the game world-wide at less elevated levels than just the World

Cup Finals: 'I think he's done a fantastic job. It will not be easy for a successor to do it. But a precedent has been set.'[63] FIFA Executive Committee members echoed these sentiments. Dr Chung of Korea observed that Havelange has 'achieved a great deal', so that now 'FIFA is one of the most prestigious international sports organizations'.[64] Mr Mohammed Bin Hammam of Qatar (former president of the Qatar Football Association) says that football in Asia 'has gained a lot by the presence of Dr Havelange as top man of FIFA. I always regard him as a big brother to me and I believe his feelings towards me is nothing less than a father's feelings towards a son. It is his attitude towards all the presidents of National Associations. Without doubt I respect his personality and character. He is one of very few people in the world who is a born leader and when he talks people listen to him.'[65] Hammam also pointed to the 'undoubted fact' that sport and football in the Gulf states have 'grown tremendously and strengthened . . . by the great efforts and support from the government of these Gulf states. Huge amount of monies have been invested to develop the youth sport activities in this region and one of the major activities is football.'[66]

There is clearly a deep-rooted and widely held respect for the achievements of FIFA and Havelange in the development of Asian football. A rounded and realistic appraisal of the conditions favouring strong growth identifies FIFA more as facilitator than funder, and private capital and national government (in varying intensities of close relationship) as the key determinants of football's successful development. With more and more monies coming into Asian football through FIFA's World Cup and the AFC's marketing initiatives, by the turn of the century a number of nations will have received more direct economic support from the continental and international football federations. As the cases considered in this chapter have indicated, though, this is likely to have little effect upon the balance of power and achievement in Asian football, for the potent combination of economic muscle and political power within a nation gives a resource base to football development that FIFA and the AFC cannot begin to match.[67] The most powerful and successful footballing nations need FIFA least, except in the role of legitimizing authority and event manager (the most lucrative event being, of course, the World Cup). Havelange and the FIFA that he has moulded facilitated the expansion of Asian football. But its firmest foundations were laid by political motives and a political will that are internal to those nations, as well as private capital keen to be associated with the promise of globally profiled success or to seize the opportunity to profile products in new markets. It could be said that FIFA itself, or a confederation, is used as a means of internationalizing a nation and a figure – such as Sheikh Zayed of the UAE, appending the Asian Cup to his solipsistic celebration of the nation's birthday; or Dr Chung of South Korea, representing the intricate intertwining of political, economic and sports interests.

■ Future Developments

In 1984 Velappan wrote that progress over the previous thirty years had only been modest, and pointed to four main problems: the different levels of the game country by country; the distances separating nations; the lack of professionally trained manpower; and the status of players.[68] Ten years later, the general secretary referred to the same four problems as 'gradually being minimised', but could still summarize progress 'over the last 40 years' as 'modest'.[69] What would really transform the basis of development, he observed, was the realization of the marketing potential of the game across the continent.

In its fortieth anniversary publication, the AFC printed a message from the FIFA president, 'Dato' Dr João Havelange':

> The AFC is to be commended especially on its dynamic leadership and its success in uniting, through the mediary of our sport, the most diverse countries and cultures. This is an exemplary achievement which merits our highest recognition.
>
> As FIFA and AFC travel alongside towards the end of the century, it is our most sincere wish that the close relations which bind our organisations may grow even more stronger, for the promotion of peace among our peoples, and for the glory of our sport of football.[70]

In this diplomatic encomium the essence of FIFA is distilled: its capacity to dispense patronage (in the collective personal pronoun of the royal 'we') and approval; its claims to contribute to global cultural initiatives for peace; and its ideological universalism in speaking for the peoples of the world. But just as FIFA needed its own partners to realize Havelange's 1974 programme, so Asian football would need to forge its own effective commercial partnerships for the needy nations to experience real progress and development, whilst the rich, and sometimes politically authoritarian, nations, continued to use the FIFA framework as a means of realizing their own social and cultural projects and experiments. Many of the less well-resourced members of Asia's football family in a world of disintegrated empires and revived and multiplied nationalisms would observe this with a combination of envy and resentment.

From the perspective of the extended football family across the world, whilst the astuteness, ambitions and aspirations of Asian football administrators might command increasing respect, the opposite could be said of its players. As the co-hosts of World Cup 2002 tumbled out of the Asian Cup in 1996, and Gulf sides occupied all semi-final places, commentators wondered whether Asian football standards were deteriorating rather than improving.[71] It was not just Asian outsiders who reflected on this issue. Behind the scenes Asian insiders were raising such questions. A top figure in the Korean Football Association agreed that the team's performance had been poor, in attack as well as defence, and noted that there was no instant explanation for this, either from his own perspective or that of the Korean media;[72] a coach to a national side in the Antipodes noted a severe dip in the developmental profile of the game in Asia;[73] and a top football official from South-East Asia agreed that standards were falling: 'I agree, yes, I agree. I see it with my own eyes ... I was a player. You tell me, who are the young stars here?'[74] Well, this was a good question. But for the impressive Iranian forward Ali Daei (who at twenty-seven was far from young), who bagged four against Korea, few names stuck; and memories of leaky defences persisted.

So, at the end of Havelange's presidency, where stood the peoples' game among more than half of the world's population? In many ways it depends where you looked. The big guns of the Far East, the toothless tigers of December 1996, were certainly on a different plane to the societies of South-East Asia; and what, really, united them with the nations and countries of the Middle East? As a widely experienced European coach noted, the Middle East and the Far East have limitless resources but restricted potential; some societies of South-East Asia have massive potential, but problematic infrastructures and limited resources.[75] More effective coordination of sponsorship and marketing of the football product was generating more reliable forms and higher levels of income which could help further develop the game in poorer countries. AFC Marketing Limited, the marketing company of the confederation, paid US$10 million for the marketing rights to all of the AFC's events over a four-year period from 1993: 'We said to the AFC, we will guarantee you a lump sum which will ensure you financial security for the first time', as Charlie Charters, senior manager in AFC Marketing, and top executive in related communications and television companies, put it. This contract was won in competition with the Japanese company Dentsu, and a Saudi Arabian sports marketing company. In December 1997 AFC Marketing won the rights for the following four-year cycle, when the AFC accepted a bid of more than US$20 million.[76] However dramatic this level of increase in the confederation's revenues, it would be unlikely to alter the balance of power of the continent's football.

Contrary to the AFC's claims that the East deserved the 2002 World Cup (and, with co-hosting, could have five of the thirty-two places for the Finals) because domestic football there was catching up with Europe and South America, if UEA '96 was anything to go by, the lack of a deep-rooted tradition in the game and its consequent levels in world terms suggested that the Orient was destined to remain in the third division of international football. Relatedly, in the power politics within FIFA, it could be argued that Asia had become disproportionately influential. No doubt the UEFA president, Lennart Johansson, reflected on these matters in December 1996 as he sat in Zayed Sport City alongside Dr Mong Joon Chung from Korea and Mr Abdullah Al-Dabal from Saudi Arabia, watching relative mediocrity (echoes, here, perhaps, of Soccer City, Soweto, in the first month of the year during the African Cup of Nations?). Was he thinking that, if in the near future the control of world football did not return to Europe through the election of a European (him) to the FIFA presidency in 1998, perhaps it would be the time for the Europeans to pick up the ball – which through history and money they believed to be theirs anyway – and take it home, leaving the rest of the world to play with themselves? A successful, but persistently uneven, development of the game world-wide in such circumstances would reiterate the dominance of the traditionally powerful centres of world football, reminding us of the local and regional hierarchies that have continued to characterize the game's global culture.

■ 8

FIFA and the former Soviet Union

■ Introduction

A map of Eastern Europe in the mid-1990s bore more resemblance to the one which existed before Peter the Great's reign in the eighteenth century than to the one that existed before the collapse of the Soviet Union. Clearly, the most potent forces in the break-up of the Soviet state were perestroika and glasnost. However, in this chapter we argue that football had a deeply subversive potential which these broader political and economic reforms helped to release and this has had serious ramifications for FIFA and UEFA.

In November 1989 the Berlin Wall was pulled down, preempting the official reunification of Germany the following year. This event was a powerful symbol of the break-up of the communist system in Europe and, with it, the ending of the Cold War. At that time, many of us who had lived with super-power confrontation and the threat of global nuclear war, believed that a new era of universal peace was dawning, a view reinforced by moves towards reconciliation in the Middle East and South Africa. However, what we had perhaps failed to realize was that for nearly half a century the Cold War had frozen a multiplicity of more ancient rivalries and suppressed a large number of nationalistic aspirations which otherwise could have led to widespread conflict in the post-war period. Albeit perversely, and largely through the perceived threat of mutual mass destruction, the Cold War had preserved a balance of power among the world's leading economic and military powers. Moreover, because of the mutually respected pro-rata influence which the super powers had over neighbouring or historically connected regions in the post-war period, the indices of confrontation and conflict between and within less powerful nations had not been as high as they might.

This is particularly true of the political orbit of the former Soviet Union, which, within its post-war boundaries and through its potent influence over nations around its borders, held together a commonwealth which contained most of the subjugated lands of the old Russian Empire and most of the remnants of the Austro-Hungarian dominion.[1] The collapse of the Soviet Union was, at least in part, precipitated by the reassertion of nationalism in some of these republics and neighbouring countries and the creation of new forms of nationalism in others.[2] Within a context of considerable conflict, beyond Moscow's enforced leviathan, nationalist sentiment in and around the former Soviet Union has been given free rein, with both geographical and ethnically based claims to sovereignty leading to a proliferation of 'new' nations and yet another redrawing of the map in Eastern Europe.

■ Football and the Idea of Nationalism

Until the events of the late 1980s it was quite widely believed that nationalism – the mobilization of popular sentiment around the theme of shared national identity – was becoming less potent as a defining characteristic of modernity.[3] In Western Europe, for instance, the member states of the European Union, at least through their political representatives, were evolving policies through which national boundaries were to become less and less significant. At the same time, as was noted separately by both authors, sport in general and football in particular, were standing against this grain by continuing to provide transnational competitive structures through which existing nationalisms could be reaffirmed and nascent notions of national identity communicated and displayed,[4] sustaining the important contributions of bodies such as FIFA and UEFA to the process of 'national self-imagining'.[5]

The point made here is that in addition to the political and institutional frameworks within which nations are enshrined, popular culture plays an important role *vis-à-vis* the articulation of nationalism. In nation states which are internally stable, and during tranquil periods of international relations, the relationship between popular culture and national identity tends to be a passive one. This dynamic becomes more pronounced when there is either a perceived threat to an established nation state, for instance during times of mobilization for war, or during periods of internal instability when sizeable sections of a given state (a) question the basis of national sovereignty; and (b) share an idea of national identity which is different from and in opposition to that embodied in the existing regime.

Central to this thesis is the *'idea* [our italics] of nationalism', which Greenfeld argues is, 'the only condition. . .without which no nationalism is possible'.[6] Greenfeld's main point is that national identity must reside in the psyche of the people before it can be mobilized in the making of nations. This is similar to Anderson's notion of the imagined community and its relation to national identity. One of the levels proposed by Anderson of the nation's imagining is as follows:

> [The nation] is imagined as a community because, regardless of the actual inequality and exploitation that may prevail in each, the nation is always conceived as a deep, horizontal comradeship.[7]

The question is, how is this 'deep, horizontal comradeship' generated and collectively conceived of as nationalism? For Greenfeld nationalism is a dialectical process,[8] emerging through a collective dialogue whereby the idea of a sovereign community develops both in concert with, and in opposition to, surrounding political and economic structures and competing cultural traditions. When discussing the dynamics of nation making, Greenfeld draws heavily on the concept of *ressentiment*: the individually felt and communally shared sense of status frustration cultivated when a group of people perceives that what could or should be 'theirs' is being thwarted by the activities of other social categories:

> The creative power of *ressentiment* – and its sociological importance – consists in that it may eventually lead to the 'transvaluation of values', that is, to the transformation of the value scale in a way which denigrates the originally supreme values.[9]

In this sense, in contexts where structural conditions lead to widely held perceptions of inequity, *ressentiment* becomes the catalyst for social movements and through them the progenitor of social change. Greenfeld uses historically located case studies of England, Germany, France, the USA and Russia to show how such change can be directed towards reform and revolution within an existing state or to the reshaping of the existing nation, leading to the emergence of new nationalisms and, ultimately, new nations. In the latter case, according to Greenfeld, such change is often directed in opposition to overarching social formations

> where the emergence of national identity is accompanied by *ressentiment*, the latter leads to the emphasis on the elements of indigenous traditions – or the construction of a new system of values – hostile to the principles of the original nationalism.[10]

This does not fully answer the question about precisely how such counter-hegemonic principles are worked up and communicated. A critical intervention into the debate about the preconditions of the making of modern nations has been made by Richard Sennett, who argues persuasively that significant social change is predicated upon popular participation and shared communication.[11] In other words, for it to act as a catalyst for change, *ressentiment* must have a publicly accessible vehicle, or as John Tomlinson puts it, 'a mass vernacular'.[12] Tomlinson and Anderson have argued that in the characteristically populous and complex societies of late modernity, print and televisual media, more than anything else, have been the mass vernacular of nationalism.[13]

While up to a point we can accept this, we must also argue that there are other significant cultural gathering points and sources of mediated action and interaction which can operate as crucibles of *ressentiment*, and where ideas about different versions of nationalism can be generated and passed around (particularly when some of these can themselves become transmitted through the mass media).[14] Certainly, in authoritarian societies, where the mass media are under the strict control of a single dominant group, it is unlikely that dissenting sections of the population will easily be able to share their disaffection through the popular press, mass literature or through film and television.

Instead, they must seek other avenues for its expression. Typically, this can involve two styles of subversive communication: clandestine, or duplicitous. The first takes place outside of the gaze of the authorities, normally involving the face to face interaction of small numbers of people only, and often leading to the production of covert methods of communication in the form of secret meetings, underground presses, pamphlets, news sheets and the like. Taken in isolation, in terms of its spread clandestine subversive communication, which by definition could not take place in public, can only have limited impact. Duplicitous subversive communication occurs when officially sanctioned arenas of popular interaction become the sites for the working out and articulation of dissent. (This is a process which itself may be informed by ideas generated by those engaged in more clandestine forms of subversive communication.) This is another way of arguing that in totalitarian societies, in which the state has a surveillance and control over non-political spheres of public life (civil society) such as the mass media, popular dissent and resistance (counter hegemonic struggle) can still take place, but often in ways which exploit conditions created for entirely different purposes.

Sport can be perfectly situated to accommodate the forms of duplicitous subversive communication alluded to above. It has proven to be a very flexible medium for the working up and transmission of a variety of ideological positions – sets of values working in the interests of particular social groups. In the context of international relations it has been well established that sport can often be used by different countries to represent dramatically different world views.[15] It has also been argued that within nations sport can be used differently by separate social groups to define their distinctiveness and contest established models of national identity. Importantly, it has been discovered that sometimes this can happen in the face of the 'official' functions assigned to sport by ruling groups.[16]

Within the boundaries of the corporatist, multi-national and multi-ethnic nation state which was the Soviet Union, how did passive 'ideas' of distinctive national identities become collectivized and mobilized as nationalism and how did these 'ideas' resonate with particular forms of subversive communication? Contrary to the official role assigned to it as a force for pan-Soviet integration, football developed as a theatre for duplicitous subversive communication, making a contribution to the working up and circulation of the multiple ideas of nationalism which hastened the break up of the Soviet state.

■ Soviet Football and the Promotion of the Union

Reflective of the way through which the game became established globally, football was introduced to Russia mainly by British, German and French industrialists, artisans and diplomats at the end of the nineteenth century.[17] However, given the relatively low level of industrial development in Russia at that time, football, a game which had its roots in the urban landscapes of the new industrial age, took hold initially in and around St Petersburg and Moscow and in a small number of other industrial cities and sea ports such as Kiev, Odessa and Kharkov.[18] This represented a tiny corner of the Romanov empire, which when Russia affiliated to FIFA in 1912, stretched from Vladivostok, on the Sea of Japan in the Far East, to St Petersburg harbouring the Baltic Sea in the West, a distance of almost 7,000 miles across eleven time zones. It was populated by approximately 140 million people who formed a patchwork of distinctive ethnic groups, religious communities, colours and cultures. Many of these geographic/ethnic entities, such as Armenia, Moldova (part of Bessarabia) and Georgia, had, in their previous histories, existed, albeit fleetingly, as independently sovereign countries and in terms of national identity, were at best ambivalent towards their Russian status, particularly since that status was quite often brutally enforced.[19] As Riordan has argued, without the disaffection of these national minorities, the Bolshevik Revolution would not have succeeded in bringing down the old regime.[20]

Thus, when they came to power in 1917 the Bolsheviks were well aware of the problem of national integration which the fledgling communist state had inherited from mother Russia.[21] In 1926, when the first Soviet census was taken, there were 178 officially recognised nationalities.[22] Moreover, the formal annexation of the Baltic states of Estonia, Latvia and Lithuania in 1940, added further ingredients to the Soviet Union's reluctant melting pot. According to Marxist orthodoxy, in theory, forms of stratified social conflict based on ethnicity, race, religion and narrowly defined nationalisms were to be resolved once the more pressing question of class inequality had been answered through a proletarian revolution.[23] In reality it was unlikely in a country with a huge illiterate and semi-literate populace that these time honoured sub-national differences would be 'forgotten' without the intervention of the state.

During the immediate post-revolutionary period there was an official toleration of national diversity which bordered on encouragement. As Gitelman observes:

> In the 1920s the Soviet leadership declared that Russian chauvinism was the main problem in nationality relations and that the non-Russians, having been discriminated against for so long, should be assisted in developing their cultures.[24]

In theory, Lenin believed that the cultural articulation of local nationalisms was a necessary part of the dialectical process through which the idea of nation could be superseded by that of international communism. Furthermore, there was also an orthodoxy which held that so long as the major economic and political institutions of the state were under the centralized control of the Soviet Communist Party, cultural nationalism, which, after all, was merely a 'superstructural' phenomenon (and as such of relatively minor significance when compared with the more determining institutional spheres of political economy), could not threaten the construction of a pan-Soviet state. Indeed it was Lenin who oversaw the establishment of a Commissariat of Nationalities, the brief of which was to devise ways of stimulating the appearance of ethnic and national self determination within the embrace of the Soviet Union.[25] Ironically, the man placed in charge of this operation was an up and coming party bureaucrat from Georgia, Joseph Stalin, who, once he succeeded Lenin as Communist Party Chairman, did more than any other single figure to repress national and ethnic minorities.[26]

Riordan has established the ideological underpinnings and aims of sport in Soviet society which he summarizes as being for promoting 'health and hygiene, defence, labour productivity, integration, emancipation of women, international recognition and prestige'.[27] Until Olympism became elevated as the most significant vehicle for the Soviet sports creed, football was to be the main sporting agent of social change. This was logical, since in 1917 football was the only sport with any real mass appeal and the only non-elitist activity which had a recognisable infrastructure.[28] As such, in the mid-1920s the Russian Football Association along with the private clubs within its orbit were, for all intents and purposes, 'nationalized' and incorporated within the Soviet state. At this stage, however, Lenin and the Bolsheviks had more pressing matters to contend with and the restructuring of the game would have to keep. As such the prerevolutionary and localized structure of football remained largely unchanged until the mid-1930s.[29]

It is argued that for a relatively short period in the 1920s the Soviet Union verged on the edge of a historic break from autocracy.[30] After the civil war there was a window of opportunity for the dictatorship of the proletariat to give way to genuine forms of participatory democracy. However, the combination of economic collapse, political isolation and the oligarchical tendencies of the communist party ensured that rather than wither away, the state became stronger, less accountable and more authoritarian.[31] By the 1930s the facade of democracy in the Soviet Union had been removed to be replaced by the dictatorship of a party elite which itself was dominated by Stalin.

Stalin's answer to the problem of Soviet political sovereignty was the construction of a repressive and authoritarian state apparatus within which open dissent was brutally repressed. Social engineering during Stalin's reign (of terror) was given added impetus through the operational mechanisms of the party. An economically driven version of socialism, stripped of any idealism, was now introduced as a pan-Soviet collective goal. Under Stalin, debate and dissent were no longer tolerated, 'the national effort was so comprehensive and inclusive that there could be no questioning of its aims or method.'[32] Mechanisms such as the Five Year (industrial) Plan, launched in 1928, and the collectivization of agriculture, begun in 1929, were geared towards the systematic acceleration of the Soviet Union's economic output. Activities defined as counter revolutionary – that is, anything which appeared to stand in the way of Stalin's political and economic programme – were met with imprisonment, exile and execution. In the great purges of the 1930s, millions of Soviet people perished in the gulags or died at the hands of Stalin and his functionaries as 'the goal of promoting national cultures yielded to the overarching aim of rapid industrial development at any cost'.[33]

Allied to these developments were initiatives designed to generate a supportive political and cultural product. Even during Stalin's reign of terror attempts were made to promote popular consent around the central concerns of the Soviet state, one of which was the promulgation of Soviet nationalism.[34] In the context of football this meant that the otherwise unpredictable and largely localized structure of soccer was dismantled to be replaced by the first All-Union league within which all leading Soviet cities would have representative teams – as was the case with all other Western European nations – and from which the national team would be selected.

The social pressures brought about by 'war communism'[35] led to massive problems of population mobility, increased tensions between urban and rural workers (who were a residual peasantry) and still deeper fissures in community relations.[36] Just as decades earlier reformers in Britain and the United States had proselytized the virtues of organized sports in combating some of the social and health related problems endemic to the industrialization,[37] so too did the Soviet authorities see in sport potential opportunities to off-set some of the worst effects of economic dislocation and aid in the construction of the new Soviet citizen. At a time of rapid population growth, industrialization and urban expansion soccer continued to be viewed by the Soviet authorities as an important stabilizing and transforming influence in a society in a state of flux.

Equal importance was attached to the sport's perceived capacity to 'reinforce the sense of cohesion in the far flung multinational state that the USSR had become'.[38] In the 1920s there were some early attempts made to use football as a form of cultural cement to help bind the city with the country and the far-flung periphery with the

Moscow-centric core of Soviet society.[39] From the centre football was viewed as an anodyne replacement for traditional games and folk festivals which were heavily redolent of the cultural distinctiveness of the old country. However, in ways which were to portend difficulties ahead, the introduction of football into parts of Central Asia backfired as local religious leaders denounced this essentially alien game as a harbinger of secular corruption and exploited its imposition for the purposes of anti-Russian propaganda.[40] Initially, this hostility was exceptional and limited to republics in the outer periphery, particularly in the south. However, soccer had revealed a subversive potential which in later years would become much more widely manifest.

■ The Internationalization of Soviet football

There can be little doubt that when the new, pan-national league kicked off in 1936 the majority of Soviet citizens welcomed the opportunity to see the best players from cities such as Moscow, Leningrad, Kiev, Odessa, and Tbilisi competing against each other on a regular basis. Furthermore, the reorganization of domestic football and the rise in standards rendered a return to international club competition viable. In the late 1930s visiting teams from Turkey and the Basque region of the Iberian peninsula attracted vast crowds. For their part teams such as Dinamo Moscow were well received when they toured neighbouring states such as Czechoslovakia shortly before the outbreak of World War II.

After the War, when on tours of Scandinavia and the United Kingdom a strengthened Dinamo Moscow team took on and beat teams then widely believed to be among the world's best, the Soviet authorities felt confident enough to re-enter international football.[41] The Soviet Union joined FIFA in 1946 and won its first international match 2–1 against Bulgaria. When the final whistle went in their last international match, a 3–0 victory over Cyprus in Larnica in 1991, the Soviet Union had played 391 matches, winning 217, drawing 96 and losing just 78. On paper this appears to be a proud record, but it disguises the fact that (other than in erstwhile 'amateur' Olympic tournaments) the Soviet Union conspicuously failed to equal the achievements of the world's leading professional football nations such as Brazil, Italy and West Germany.[42]

The record of the Soviet Union in the World Cup underlines this lack of achievement at the highest level. In Chile, in 1962 they were beaten 2–1 by the hosts in the quarter finals. In 1966 they lost by the same score to West Germany in the semi-finals in England. In Mexico in 1970 they lost 1–0 to Uruguay in the quarter finals. They failed to qualify for the finals again until 1982 in West Germany when they were edged out of a semi-final place by Poland on goal difference. Back in Mexico in 1986 they were put out by Belgium, losing 4–3 after extra time and in 1990 in Italy, in their last World Cup as the Soviet Union they failed to qualify for the second phase after consecutive 2–0 defeats by Argentina and Romania. More often than not it seemed that the Soviets would run a good race only to fall at the last one or two hurdles. The resounding message here being that when the Soviets competed at the highest level in the professional sport which the West took more seriously than anything else, even more seriously than the Olympics, they failed. The Soviet state's own obssesion with Olympism seriously undermined their capacity to achieve in international football. As Edelman observes, 'the official insistence on the across-the-board excellence needed to dominate the medal counts restricted soccer's capacity to attract the nation's best athletes'.[43]

The Soviets themselves favoured a more conspiratorial excuse for soccer's under achievement. The Soviet Union failed to qualify for the 1974 World Cup after they were thrown out of the qualifying tournament by FIFA for refusing to play their away fixture against Chile in 'the stadium of death' in Santiago, where the dictator Pinochet had tortured and executed communists after his military take over in 1973.[44] The attitude of FIFA over this and, at that time, its continued resistance to the membership of the People's Republic of China helped to fuel suspicions that there was an anti-communist conspiracy at work in the corridors of world football's governing body. The Soviet Union's regular narrow defeats in the big games of important tournaments (by last minute goals, disputed penalties and, on one occasion, the toss of a coin) has also been used as 'evidence' by conspiracy theorist in support of their claim that during the Cold War, a pro-Western FIFA plotted against the Soviet Union and allied countries. Alfonso Marraquin, former coach of the Colombian national under-twenty side has stated that 'in the international competitions the democratic countries always wanted the communist countries to lose. This is a fact. The agreed first target was always the Soviet Union. They couldn't be allowed to win the World Cup. It wouldn't look good for free enterprise. So the referee chosen for their matches was always "the best man for the job".'[45]

■ Chile vs Soviet Union, 1973

Conspiracy or not, after studying the documentation and correspondence which the Chile/Soviet Union incident generated, it is hard not to conclude that the Soviet Union were shabbily treated by FIFA over this affair. In October 1973 FIFA sent a delegation to Santiago led by Vice-President, Mr A. D'Almeida and General Secretary, Dr H. Käser. The FIFA officials were put up in one of the capital's finest hotels and provided with a chauffeur-driven limousine for the duration of their two and a half day visit. Studying the 1973 report which was submitted to the FIFA executive upon their return it is obvious that the delegates were totally insensitive to the broader political context of the situation.[46] As the following extracts reveal, D'Almeida and Käser made no serious attempts to probe beneath the surface of the guided tour provided for them by Chilean officials:

GENERAL IMPRESSIONS:

From short conversations with inhabitants we gained the impression that they were happy and that they felt that life was worth living again and everybody is back at work. The only apparent restriction seems to be the curfew in Santiago at 22.00 . . . Dr Käser took advantage of the car at his disposal to visit other parts of the city where the situation seemed to be exactly the same as in the centre . . . The queuing up was very orderly and everyone quietly waited his turn.

VISIT TO THE MINISTER OF NATIONAL DEFENCE, VICE-ADMIRAL PATRICIO CARVAJAL PRADO:

In reply to our precise question concerning the stadium, he said that in a couple of days the stadium will be at the disposal of the sports organisations as it is expected that the interrogation of the remaining detainees will be terminated and most of them will have gone home.

VISIT TO THE NATIONAL STADIUM:

As mentioned before, the stadium is at present being used as a 'clearing station' and the people in there are not prisoners but only detainees whose identity has to be established (a large number of foreigners without valid documents) . . . The stadium is under military guard and entry is only with a special pass. Inside the outer fencing everything seemed to be normal and gardeners are working on the gardens. Inside the stadium itself the seats and pitch were empty and the remaining detainees were in the dressing and other rooms. The grass on the pitch is in perfect condition as were the seating arrangements ... Outside the stadium approximately 50–100 people were waiting for news of relatives who were still detained.

CONCLUSION:

Mr. D'Almeida and the undersigned came to the conclusion that, based on what they saw and heard in Santiago, life is back to normal and the guarantees given by the government are such that the World Cup Preliminary match Chile vs. USSR can be carried out on 21 November 1973.

Without hesitation the FIFA executive accepted these recommendations and immediately upon his return to Zurich Dr Käser sent a telegram communicating the same to Mr Granatkin of the Soviet Football Federation. The following day, 27 October, at his London home, the FIFA president, Stanley Rous, received a telegram from Granatkin, the verbatim extracts from which clearly communicate Soviet anger and suggest a markedly different interpretation of the situation in Chile:

WELL KNOWN THAT AS RESULT FASCIST UPHEAVAL OVERTHROWN LEGAL GOVERNMENT NATIONAL UNITY NOW IN CHILI [SIC] REVEALS ATMOSPHERE BLOODY TERRORISM AND REPRESSIONS COMMA ... NATIONAL STADIUM SUPPOSED BE VENUE HOLD FOOTBALL MATCH TURNED BY MILITARY JUNTA INTO CONCENTRATION CAMP PLACE OF TORTURES AND EXECUTIONS OF CHILEAN PATRIOTS STOP ... USSR FOOTBALL FEDERATION ADDRESSED FIFA WITH PROPOSITION HOLD MATCH IN THIRD COUNTRY AS SOVIET SPORTSMEN CANNOT AT PRESENT PLAY AT STADIUM STAINED WITH BLOOD OF CHILEAN PATRIOTS STOP NEVERTHELESS FIFA NEGLECTED KNOWN WHOLE WORLD ABOMINABLE CRIMES OF MILITARY JUNTA AND TAKING AS BIAS ASSURANCES OF SELFSTYLED CHILI DEFENCE MINISTER ... STOP USSR FOOTBALL FEDERATION ON BEHALF SOVIET SPORTSMEN EXPRESS DECISIVE PROTEST AND ... REFUSE PARTICIPATE QUALIFICATION MATCH AT CHILI TERRITORY AND MAKES FIFA LEADERS RESPONSIBLE FOR IT STOP[47]

In suggesting that the game be played in a third country the Soviet Federation pointed to the precedent of the game between Northern Ireland and Bulgaria in 1973 which was relocated from Belfast to Sheffield, England, because of the unstable political situation in Ulster, but FIFA continued to be unimpressed.[48] FIFA received many communications objecting to its ruling, none more graphic than a personal letter to Stanley Rous from a youth football organization in the German Democratic Republic, which compared the situation in Chile's National Stadium to that of the Nazi death camps, and asked the FIFA President, 'would you carry out sport qualifications in sports-wear at the concentration camp Dachau or Sachsenhausen?'[49] For his part, the president of the East German (GDR) Football Federation made a heartfelt personal plea to Sir Stanley, using the theme of sport and world peace to argue that it was unreasonable to expect any nation, let alone the Soviet Union, to send its athletes to perform, 'under the present conditions in the sports arenas of Santiago de Chile and the whole country which are saturated with the blood of noble and honest men'.[50]

Similar missives were received from parts of Africa and Latin America imploring Rous to convene an extraordinary meeting of the FIFA Executive to reconsider its 6 October decision in the light of further evidence.[51] Such overtures had little or no impact on Sir Stanley or FIFA who took refuge in FIFA's Statutes (Articles 4 and 22 of the 1973 Statutes) before reiterating the original ruling. Article 22 stated 'If a team does not report for a match – except in the case of *force majeure*, accepted by the organising committee – . . . the team shall be considered as having lost.' The Soviets must have wondered what exactly constituted a *force majeure* if playing in a country during the after shock of a military coup, and in a stadium which only days before had been used as a prison camp and interrogation centre, did not count.

Whether this outcome was the result of genuine naïveté on behalf of FIFA or, as the Soviets believed, part of a broader pro-Western conspiracy is open to question. Whatever the answer, a scenario such as this could be used by the Soviet authorities to galvanize support for the national team who, in the Cold War era, were portrayed at home as victims of a pro-capitalist bias within world football. Certainly, when the national team took the field in their red shirts, under the red flag with its hammer and sickle emblem, there is every reason to believe that until the last years of the Soviet Union a large number of Soviet citizens recognized them as 'their' team. At a time of relative economic prosperity, when the Soviet Union appeared to be winning the space race, and was perceived as a military match for Western powers, it was fashionable to support the national team. Many Soviet fans rejoiced and mourned their team's victories and defeats in much the same way that fans of England, Spain and Argentina empathized with the exploits of their own national teams.

This, according to Edelman, was only possible because of the multiethnic nature of Soviet representative teams.[52] In as far as this was true it can be said, in terms of the intended outcomes of the Soviet authorities' social engineering, at least to some extent, that the integrative function of Soviet football met with a measure of success. Recent history has taught us, however, that such displays of Soviet national unity were at best ephemeral.

The further away from the Russian centre the less likely it was

that Soviet sport drew local support. In the Baltic republics of Estonia, Latvia and Lithuania, which were annexed by the Soviet Union
in 1940, there was little if any good feeling towards Soviet football.
In Estonia, for instance, according to Tarmo Ruulti, a former player
and assistant manager of the post-1991 Estonian national team, in
his lifetime, he remembers nothing but ill-feeling towards the Rus-
sian-dominated Communist Party, which had done much to undermine the place of football in Estonian society since the Soviet takeover.
Estonia had been a member of FIFA since 1923 and was established
in international football. Clearly, Moscow viewed the lingering
memory of 'national' football as a threat to Estonian assimilation into
Soviet society and proceded to dismantle the local football infrastructure. For this reason, Ruulti and others like him, 'prayed that the
Soviet Union would lose every time they played . . . also in [ice] hockey
I remember we supported Canada and not [the] Soviet Union'.[53]

Glen Hoddle, the former England international player and national
team manager, recalls playing for England in 1986, in a World Cup
qualifying match against the Soviet Union in Tbilisi, Georgia, when
the 'home' fans rejected the national team:

> At that time they were under the USSR and really wanted to be a Repub-
> lic. England played well on the day and the crowd turned against their
> team and cheered us, which was an unusual situation.[54]

At that time, David Petriashveli played for Dynamo Tbilisi. Now he
is the international secretary of the Georgian Football Federation and
he recalls being in the crowd that day and cheering for England. 'The
stadium was incredible, because all of the people supported England! Georgians are quite different from Russians, our culture is ancient, older than Russia and, next to Christianity, our football
expresses this.'[55]

From a purely technical point of view it has been suggested that
combining so many 'nationalities' in one team led to tactical problems on the field of play. During the 1950s and early 1960s Sir Walter
Winterbottom coached several English teams in matches against the
Soviet Union. While he believed them to be supremely fit and technically superb, an overriding lack of commitment to the idea of the
Soviet nation led, in his words, to a 'disparateness and lack of cohesion in the team itself and this caused them to underachieve'.[56] At
one stage it seems that the Soviets themselves reached a similar conclusion. In the mid-1970s the national team was built around one
team, Dinamo Kiev, the Ukrainian club side which had won the

European Cup and the world Super Cup in 1975. However, a gruelling schedule which saw the same squad of players playing in national league and cup competitions, European club championships, the European Nations Cup, the Olympic Games and the World Cup was itself doomed to failure.[57]

If it proved to be difficult to put together a multi-national, multi-ethnic football team, it was a problem on a different scale altogether to hold together and progress a multi-national and multi-ethnic political society. It is to the role played by club football in the unravelling of the Soviet Union that we now turn.

■ Club Football, Political Dissent and National Fragmentation.

In totalitarian societies the distinction between political institutions (in this case the Communist Party and its various organs) and civil society is minimized to the extent that the former, wherever possible, seek to infiltrate and influence the contents and conduct of the latter. However, when the legitimacy of the state is widely questioned, the terrain of civil society becomes fiercely contested between political authorities and those groups who harbour different views on the issue of sovereignty. As has been demonstrated elsewhere,[58] in the modern world sport is an important theatre in this struggle over meaning and culture, in what is a contest for hegemony. It is in this light that we can view the growth and development of Soviet domestic football under Stalin and in the decades after World War II.

Almost all of the big clubs were affiliated to and controlled by one or other state institution (political, military and industrial). For instance: Dinamo = ministry of the interior, incorporating the KGB; TSKA = Central Branch of the Red Army; Krylya Sovyetov= aviation industry; Lokomotiv = railway workers; Torpedo = ZIS motor works. Each team had their party sponsors who would often go to great lengths to ensure that their favoured teams were successful, augmenting a tendency for corruption,[59] and alienating sections of supporters who, in the wake of the Stalinist years, became increasingly disaffected with anything associated with the Communist Party and its bosses.[60]

Even during the darkest days of Stalin's tyranny, football was one of the few public gathering points where privately held resentments could be shared and expressed simultaneously as public aspirations. What we are suggesting here is that even under conditions of extreme surveillance football stadia could serve as theatres for the communication of ideas which could contribute to the subversion of the state. Of course, the state did not passively accept challenges to its domination of this increasingly important sphere of civil society and as Riordan discovered, 'sport was not exempt from the arrests and persecution that permeated all walks of life from the mid-1930s'.[61] He goes on to detail the infamous interventions of Lavrenty Beria, Stalin's chief of secret police and honorary president of the Dinamo Society, in the running of Soviet football and his particular victimization of Spartak, the one high profile sports organization which had no direct affiliation to a state institution.

The Spartak sporting club had been formed by the Starostin brothers who had a strong belief that sport should be free from any direct government interference.[62] It was precisely because of the lack of a paramilitary profile that Spartak attracted numbers of athletes and supporters who were disillusioned with the quality of life in the police state that the Soviet Union had become. If football was the people's game then, in Moscow at least, Spartak was the people's club. As Kuper observes, supporting Spartak 'was a small way of saying "No"'. Kuper develops this theme in a conversation in Moscow with anthropologist Levon Abramian who reflected upon the role of football in the former Soviet Union:

> 'In a communist country,' he said, 'the football club you supported was a community to which you yourself had chosen to belong. The regime did not send you to support a club, and, perhaps, excepting western sides, you could chose your team. It might be your only chance to choose a community, and also, in that community you could express yourself as you wished. To be a fan', concluded Levon, 'is to be with others and to be free'.[63]

In a society where opportunities for public gatherings and open debate were severely restricted, football provided rare, out-of-structure experiences, arousing popular passions 'in ways that could be uncontrollable and therefore undesirable',[64] with potential for the articulation of collective *ressentiment* – the sharing of an idea that things should and could be different. Of course, under circumstances when often a cordon of soldiers and police stood between the fans and the pitch, the level of public dissent at football matches was bound to be strictly limited. Nevertheless, as Edelman argues, sometimes, simply choosing to 'be there' can be read as a gesture of resistance:

> Those who sought 'fun' in spectator sports were not simply engaged in a search for the apolitical in an overpoliticized society. In looking for entertainment, Soviet citizens were doing more than simply avoiding the mes-

195

sages of the state. They were also making choices about which entertainments they accepted and which they rejected. By doing this, they could, in limited but important ways, impose their own meanings and derive their own lessons from sports and from other forms of popular culture as well.[65]

Major structural strains began to show in the Soviet Union in the 1980s when, through the twin thrusts of perestroika and glasnost, Mikhail Gorbachev introduced wholesale economic, political and cultural reforms, leading to a relaxation of the iron grip which the state had on the everyday lives of ordinary Soviet citizens. After decades of oppression, and mindful of the military debacle in Afghanistan, the Soviet people took full advantage of new found freedoms to display their opposition to the old order. In the early days of what was to turn out to be another major revolution in Soviet society, in the absence of other venues for public engagement, the All-Soviet Football League was perfectly situated to act as a medium for popular dissent and political protest.

When the All-Soviet League was set up in the 1930s every major city in every republic had a team in one of the four national divisions. Given the multi-national and multi-ethnic nature of the Soviet Union this meant that teams were often representative of distinctive social groups, many of which had suffered the worst excesses of Russian-centred totalitarianism and harboured the desire to break free from the Soviet Union. This was particularly the case with some of the smaller republics, wherein 'one team, usually from that republic's capital, represented the hopes and dreams of the nation'.[66] In effect these teams were in all but name the national teams of the disaffected republics and their team colours often closely resembled those which were to represent the nation in years to come. Ararat became Armenia; Minsk, Belarus; Tallinn, Estonia; Tbilisi, Georgia; Riga, Latvia; Vilnius, Lithuania; and, so forth. Dinamo Kiev, the most successful non-Russian team, contested for the mantle of the Ukraine with other senior teams in the region such as Dnepr of Dnepropetrovsk and Karpaty from the extremely nationalist centre of Lvov. Moreover, as the All-Soviet League matured, the non-Russian teams got stronger and the pre-eminence of the big Moscow clubs could no longer be guaranteed.[67]

A regular season of home and away league and cup fixtures provided the perfect opportunity for the implanting and transmission of the idea of nationalism. During the glasnost years, both planned and spontaneous displays of nationalist fervour increased at football matches. Flags and banners proclaiming non-Soviet national identity were waved and traditional folk songs and protest ballads were sung. In matches between teams from republics which were both seeking independence, supporters would sometimes engage in singing and chanting which expressed mutual solidarity. These became double-edged demonstrations when Russian teams, particularly from Moscow, visited the provinces. Anti-Russian *ressentiment* fed the flames of national self-determination, sometimes generating fan violence inside and outside the stadiums. Kuper offers the example of supporters of the Armenian team, Yerevan Ararat:

> Then, under Gorbachov, the republics began to scent independence. At matches against Zhalgiris, or against an Estonian team, the Yerevan fans would chant 'Lithuania!' or 'Estonia!' to show solidarity with their opponents. When a Russian side visited a southern Republic, a local policeman would often suggest to the Russians that if they won there would be a regrettable riot.[68]

Pavel Katchatrian, the general secretary of the Armenian Football Federation (1997), recalls that when Ararat won the Soviet league and cup double in 1973 they did so with a team which was ethnically 100 per cent Armenian. The nationalist celebrations in the streets of Yerevan were even more passionate than when Armenia finally gained political independence from the Soviet Union almost twenty years later. 'To gain independence was truly a great achievement, but to beat the Russians at their own game seemed even better!'[69]

Significantly, in the 1970s, hooliganism emerged as a problem in the Soviet Union. The Soviet authorities dismissed the hooligans as a minority of 'pathologically aggressive teenagers',[70] who mimicked the excesses of their corrupt Western neighbours. Edelman argues to the contrary that, 'nonconformity in the Soviet Union was a more serious choice, precisely because of the use the state sought to make of sports. In that sense, gang violence and other forms of fan misbehavior do have a political dimension.'[71] Moreover, the fact that the 'worst offenders' were fans of the non-aligned Spartak Moscow may suggest that these crowd disturbances were in some way linked to wider forms of political dissent.

During the 1980s, as hooliganism became an increasing problem in Soviet football, it developed a pattern which indicated that, at least in part, fan violence was being fuelled by nationalism.[72] In 1987, for instance, serious disturbances took place on the streets of Kiev when visiting fans of Spartak Moscow were attacked by supporters of Dinamo Kiev and in the same year there were riots in Vilnius, the capital of Lithuania after a match between local club, Zhalgiris and TSKA, the central branch of the Red Army club.[73]

Clearly, in the build up to independence football did not passively reflect events in the wider social and political environment, rather it made a decisive contribution. In certain cases football federations declared their 'national' independence before political sovereignty had been established:

> On the eve of the 1990 season, the Lithuanians and Georgians, pushed by their struggles for national independence and enflamed by violence in their streets, announced that their teams were quitting all Soviet competitions in all sports and that their players would no longer represent the USSR. They announced plans for separate Georgian and Lithuanian soccer leagues.[74]

■ FIFA, UEFA and the Eastern European Assistance Bureau

Once the final break up came, in the wake of the 1991 Moscow *coup d'état*, the example of Lithuania and Georgia was followed by eight other former republics (Armenia, Azerbaijan, Belarus, Estonia, Latvia, Moldova, Ukraine and, of course, Russia itself) who proclaimed independence, withdrew from all-Soviet competitions and formed their own soccer leagues. Almost immediately they were recognized by the European and World governing bodies of football, UEFA and FIFA, as independent national associations, which, with the exception of recognition by the United Nations, is the clearest possible statement of arrival at the high table of international relations.

There is a persisting tendency in the former republics to blame the Russian Federation for the ills vested upon them during the Soviet era. Whenever possible efforts are made to settle old scores. Football is no exception and events during the 1996 FIFA Congress were indicative of this. The former Soviet Union used to be guaranteed one vice-presidential seat in the inner circle of the FIFA Executive. Dr. Viacheslav Koloskov, the president of the Soviet Football Federation held this post, but when the Soviet Union dissolved he lost his automatic seat and had to stand for re-election in his new status as the president of the Russian Football Federation. Ironically, he was only re-elected on the strength of the votes cast by Western European nations. The former republics of the Soviet Union all voted against him because of lingering resentments towards things Russian.

The precarious condition of football in Eastern Europe has presented both FIFA and UEFA with big challenges. Once the former Republics became independent, so long as they had viable football federations, they had to be admitted to UEFA and FIFA, becoming eligible to take part in international football competitions. UEFA were reasonably content to help with the global development of the game so long as it was kept at arms length in Africa and Asia. Waking up one morning to find football's 'Third World' camped in their own backyard – while the back door was wide open into the Champions League, the European Football Championship and European World Cup qualification tournaments – was another matter altogether.

Once they got over the shock, UEFA provided a more measured response. In the light of the new motto, 'we care about football', UEFA has embarked upon a mission to assist in the global development of soccer, providing technical support and financial assistance to developing football countries in Africa and Asia, in addition to that already supplied by FIFA. However, it is upon the 'new' countries of Eastern Europe, particularly those which emerged from the wreckage of the former Soviet Union, that most efforts have been centred. The vehicle created to administer this initiative is the Eastern European Assistance Bureau (EEAB). Under the headline, 'helping the newcomers to our family', the *raison d'être* of the EEAB is clearly stated by the UEFA president:

> The aim of this programme is to assist and support these new associations in the areas of administration and management, infrastructure, commercial matters and the popularisation of football, with the objective of integrating them into the UEFA family as quickly as possible, and of promoting and developing football by reinvesting footballing revenue into the game.[75]

To this end the EEAB has five main objectives:

- Provision of urgently needed material, such as football equipment, stadia equipment, office equipment.
- Organisation of training courses and seminars for administrators, coaches, referees, doctors, etc.
- Promotion of youth football in any possible form (including street soccer, Futsal, beach football etc.).
- Assistance in contract negotiations on TV and advertising rights, kit contracts, international player transfers.
- Assistance in the search for sponsors, and in the establishment of partnerships between EEAB member associations and renowned international companies.

For the purposes of this book it is necessary to make three broad points. Firstly, the EEAB package has a strong economic thrust which attempts to bind the East European members to commercial mechanisms already under the control of UEFA. While initially this will undoubtedly benefit UEFA's fledgling members, in the long run, as each nation becomes more self-sustaining as a football entity, UEFA's general economic position (and that of its business partners) will be strengthened as will its control over its new membership.

Secondly, and related to the latter point, the greater the influence which UEFA has over these new constituents the stronger will its position be *vis-à-vis* its relations with the other confederations and, critically, with FIFA itself. For instance, each 'new' member represents one vote in the FIFA congress. This is especially important with regard to the selection and election of the FIFA president. Given FIFA's adherence to the democratic principles of one country one vote and equal weighting among voting members, the votes of members such as Belarus, Moldova, Armenia are as valuable as those cast by Germany, Brazil and the USA. As such, it is important for UEFA to be able to count on the ballots of Eastern Europe as it seeks to wrest control of FIFA from the Latin Americans and their allies. In this regard UEFA has clearly decided that, in the long run, the fragmentation of Eastern Europe can be used to its advantage in any significant power play *vis-à-vis* FIFA.

Thirdly, by shoring up an area of popular culture which can be so readily used as a vehicle of nation building, UEFA's mission in Eastern Europe, will undoubtedly contribute to the future stability of these new nations. Furthermore, there are those who belive that UEFA's mission in Eastern Europe has other, more far-reaching, political objectives. Edigus Braun, the president of the German Football Association, certainly believes this when he says:

> Had we excluded these countries, associations and people from the European competitions we would have caused immense political damage. And if we fail to create more humane living conditions in the former Eastern Bloc countries, there will be serious consequences, maybe not for you or me, but certainly for our children and grandchildren.[76]

Ernie Walker, former secretary of the Scottish Football Association and now a consultant with UEFA, was instrumental in the setting up of the EEAB. He remembers visiting Georgia in the early 1990s and being whisked from the airport to meet the new president, former Soviet Foreign Minister, Eduard Shevardnadze, who was struggling to keep control of the then war-torn country. 'I told him to put less money into arms and more into football. Developing the national team would put Georgia on the map. Only then, when you play the likes of Germany or England, will the rest of the world realize that

Georgia was an independent country and not a state in the USA!'.[77] Despite their 2–0 defeat, Georgia's appearance at Wembley in 1997 more than fulfilled Walker's predictions.

More than a hundred years after the establishment of football in Europe it appears that the game's administrators have not strayed too far from the proselytizing of their Victorian forefathers. To some, such as the UEFA president, football continues to be more than a game: it makes nations, brings peace and, as the following words suggest, shows politicians the way forward in international relations:

> As far as the integration of the new associations from Eastern Europe is concerned, football has once again proved that it is more capable of achieving such integration. Football has succeeded – long before the politicians, scientists and technocrats – in creating a United Europe. And we should all be proud of this.[78]

■ Conclusion

In retrospect it can be seen that one of the consequences of the imposition of a pan-Soviet league was to provide a structure through which the ideas of old and new nationalisms could be nurtured and expressed, accelerating the downfall of the Soviet Union and all that it stood for:

> The experiment to promote a 'Soviet', supra-national 'nationalism' . . . patently failed. The failure has been made all the more lamentable by the alacrity with which the 'fraternal peoples' of the Soviet Union have distanced themselves from the past three score years and ten and reverted to nationalism based on a single ethnic group – and often a petty state – reinforced in its new freedom by racial contempt and even hatred for its one-time Soviet fellows and even team-mates.[79]

The failure of the CIS (Commonwealth of Independent States) to mature much beyond a weak trading alliance, bears out Riordan's underlying point that by the time the Soviet Union split asunder there was so much *ressentiment* towards the old Russian centre, and so much suspicion and mutual hostility between neighbouring republics, that there was no chance that a united states of the Soviet Union could ever succeed, either in politics or in sport.

Since the dissolution of the Soviet Union, football (and sport in general) in that region has been in pronounced decline. There are some obvious reasons for this not the least of which are: economic collapse and poverty; the decline in competitive standards since the demise of the All-Soviet League; the emigration of top players; and the dismantling of a sports-benevolent central bureaucracy.[80] The latter brings to our attention the paradoxical notion that even though football was used as a vehicle for duplicitous subversive activity before the collapse of the Soviet Union, it was nevertheless a state-sponsored activity, and, as such, was something to be scorned once independence had been secured.[81] Once independence had been achieved it was no longer necessary to exploit football as a theatre of resistance. When party and national affiliations could be expressed openly through more direct political and civic institutions (such as political parties, trades unions, newspapers, partisan movements and so forth) in the short term at least, there ceased to be a need for duplicitous forms of communication around football. If the only reason for being there was to watch football, the people stayed away.

■ 9
FIFA's final frontier: USA '94

■ FIFA, CONCACAF and Soccer in North America

Sepp Blatter, FIFA general secretary, delivered a very positive verdict on the 1994 World Cup Finals, staged in the USA: 'The 1994 World Cup produced a turnover of $4 billion with 32 billion television viewers. I mean no disrespect to other sports by saying that even the Olympic Games cannot compare. The World Cup was a fabulous success.'[1] It is apposite for the modern FIFA that its chief executive's primary criterion for the adjudging of the event's success was economic, and based upon the statistics so vital to its commercial and media partners.

For FIFA, penetrating the soccer-starved US sports market has been its biggest and its final challenge. Rous, as FIFA president from 1961–74, was fully aware of the solid basis for the development of the game that existed in the country, and was keen to promote a stronger US soccer presence within the North and Central Americas confederation, CONCACAF, which he saw as 'effective', rather than strong, and as under the primary influence of Mexico. The confederation was based in Guatemala City, from its formation in 1961 up until 1992 when it was relocated in Manhattan, New York. Prior to 1961, 'there had been a confusion of bodies claiming responsibility over the game in the region, or various parts of it'.[2] These had included congresses and associations representing central American and Caribbean countries, and a 'North American' confederation (1939) comprising the USA, Cuba and Mexico. Some of these included South American nations as members. With the South American confederation unwilling to sacrifice its long-standing status and independence, with guaranteed World Cup Final places, the rationalization of the central and north American interests was clearly necessary. Bringing a stronger US presence into CONCACAF business and politics would clearly have the potential to counterbalance what might become over-dominant Mexican interests. For CONCACAF could be a vital source of entry into world football politics. It was CONCACAF that provided the power base from 1962 onwards for Guillermo Cañedo of Mexico, and at an Ordinary Congress of the Confederation in Trinidad in November 1971 'la votación favoreció al Senor Guillermo Cañedo para Vice Presidente de FIFA por parte de CONCACAF'.[3] He was to become senior vice-president, chair of FIFA's media committee, and Cañedo's last major task for FIFA before he died was to chair the organizing committee of the USA World Cup Finals. Not all members of CONCACAF's football family were happy about the outcome of this meeting, at which Mordy Maduro of Curaçao was, in his absence, ousted from FIFA. He learned of the decisions from his football association's delegate:

> It seems that quite a few irregularities have occurred, so much so that some football associations are even considering calling an extraordinary congress in order to put forward a motion of no confidence against some members of the Executive Committee of CONCACAF . . .
> I was quite astonished to learn that Jimmy McGuire, who I always considered as a friend, actually voted against me. His attitude really has me baffled and I do not know what to think of it . . . To add insult to injury also Eric James of Trinidad voted against me. It is really bewildering to receive a stab in the back by allegedly friendly people.[4]

FIFA could do little about such complaints. Even when it was suspected that results of matches in World Cup qualifying tournaments were manipulated, the CONCACAF administration appears simply to have ignored the letters referring to a particular country's protest. FIFA General secretary, Dr Käser, writing to Rous, commented that: 'Quite a number of "incomprehensible decisions" were taken in connection with this CONCACAF tournament but all of them were finally endorsed by their Congress with the exception of the above mentioned Surinam vs. Haiti case which happened after the Congress was over.'[5] It was clear that by the early 1970s key positions in confederations and FIFA itself were being pursued by powerful individuals representing interlocking sets of interest within and across confederations – the dialectic of control characterizing FIFA was on the verge of transformation. Rous himself, backing strong and efficient confederations, unwittingly contributed to this transformation.

He had addressed the CONCACAF congress in June 1971, in Caracas.[6] Intriguingly, the confederation president and the secretary general were both absent, though all member associations were represented. Rous urged the confederation's administration to 'see that all financial resources were used to best effect', and referred to the wastefulness of 'bad administration, which was out of touch and spent money in the wrong ways ... It was of course important to FIFA to see that all financial and other help made available was properly used, and it was of great importance to see that money was well spent.' Rous reminded delegates to take their responsibilities seriously and become involved in the business and decision-making of the confederation: 'When nominating people, especially referees, only the best names should be forwarded.' He stressed the need for strong organizational backing that 'truly reflected the membership of the Confederation. It was important to make sure that the Executive was balanced and reflected the different areas, especially that the English speaking and Spanish speaking areas were properly represented. It was also important for the expeditious discharge of business, to use 'bureaux' or sub-committees to carry out certain of the jobs of the Referees' or the Executive Committee. Anything which would increase the efficient charge of business was important.' Financial irregularities and inefficiency; dubious refereeing appointments and dodgy delegates; organizational unaccountability – there was not much else that Rous could list in what amounted to a sub-textual manifesto for reform. Over the next two years such reforms were put in place, with incumbent confederation office-holders protesting at the proposal that delegates be officers of national associations. This protest was based upon the record of input of such members, claimed as 'deplorable', and the argument that such positions were so unstable within member associations that the nature of a confederation made up of such delegates would be of 'implicit anarchy, the end of CONCACAF's stability which is the support of its institutional nature as an entity which rules football activities throughout the circuit'.[7] Despite such passionate protests, the momentum of reform which modernized, bureaucratized and, on the surface, democratized the CONCACAF structure and practices was sustained. However, by early 1973 Joaquin Sorvia Terrazas, the president of CONCACAF unable to be at the Congress addressed by Rous, was writing to the FIFA president explaining the basis of reports that 'Sr. Joa [sic.] Havelange' had been invited to attend the confederation's forthcoming Ordinary and Extraordinary Congresses. Terrazas denied that CONCACAF had invited Havelange to take part in or attend the congress, and claimed that the Brazilian had not been present at any of the confederation's meetings: 'Unfortunately, his spontaneous visit to the Mexican Football Federation coincided on the same dates as our Congress.'.[8] Little more than a year later, Havelange had replaced Rous as FIFA president.

■ Gloryland: Soccer, USA Sports Space and Globalization

It was the work and commitment of Havelange and CONCACAF's Cañedo which were to secure the World Cup for the USA, if not as replacement for Colombia for the 1986 Finals, then for the 1994 Finals. The USA had performed well and reached the semi-finals at the first World Cup in 1930 (six former British professionals, five Scots and an Englishman were in their team, and 'gave an impression of crude vigour . . . formidably strong athletes with thighs like tree-trunks'.[9] And when Rous himself, as secretary of the Football Association, ushered English football out of its insularity, it was the USA team at the 1950 World Cup Finals which 'inflicted that humiliating defeat on us in our first World Cup attempt'.[10] Sir Walter Winterbottom was coach/manager to the national side at that historic game in Belo Horizonte, Brazil:

> You cannot make excuses, we got beaten, but really it is ridiculous. Now that was a referee who was badly influenced by the crowd. The crowd were all for America simply because they were the underdogs . . . it wasn't a big ground, it didn't hold that many spectators at all. Why we had to play there God only knows, but the pitch was in dreadful shape. The grass was high and thick, it was Bermuda grass growing in small clusters and it spreads and it sits the ball up. We hadn't had any practice on it of course, what is happening is the ball is teed up and you are hitting shots over the bar, they were going over the bar . . . Maurice Smith, who was writing for *The People* in those days, he was doing statistics on the match and he said we hit the woodwork eleven times. Eleven times, that's absurd. We were shooting in, virtually, and they were doing all kinds of things. They were handling Stanley Mortensen outside the penalty area, you know, tackling, rugby tackling him when he was running through. But we scored a genuine goal Mortensen claims, and all our players do. What happened was that the goal was going into the net but Mortensen decided he'd head it, and he deflected the ball and the goalkeeper fell back into the goal, he was a basketball player, he caught the ball in one hand and threw it out from the back of the goal, and the referee didn't give the goal, oh dear . . .[11]

Whatever, the result entered the record books and the country that gave the people's game to the world was humbled by a makeshift team of immigrants from a country where the game 'seemed doomed to remain a marginal activity . . . far . . . from the mainstream of American sport'.[12] Nevertheless, the result had been achieved, as had those of 1930, and Rous was insightful and correct in noting that the USA was more than 'an emergent nation' in football. He was over-optimistic, though, at the initial success of the North American Soccer League (NASL) in its boom years in the late 1970s, the presence of Pelé at the New York Cosmos constituting 'the breakthrough I had hoped for when I told American promoters earlier that they would have to show their public the real skills of the game before they would be hooked on it'.[13] But the soccer boom of the late 1970s and the early 1980s was short-lived, and financial backers as well as fans withdrew as the New York Cosmos all-star, international but ageing side was not replaced by players of comparable world stature, or high-level homegrown 'home-town heroes', as NASL press man of the time Jim Trecker recalled:

> We did not develop enough American players and despite the free movement of players around the world you need a home base in any country, you can't just stack your team with all foreigners. There weren't any home-town heroes, and so when Pelé retired, Beckenbauer got a little older, Carlos Alberto retired – this great gallery of stars that the fans loved – there was no-one to take their place. The league lacked any of its sparkle, lacked any of its glory.
>
> The second reason is financial instability. Expenses and revenues became so out of whack that ultimately, like any business, it began to collapse, and the League just sort of imploded on itself in financial instability.[14]

Carlos Alberto (Torres) himself, Brazil's captain in its World Cup winning team of 1970, links the financial issue to FIFA and World Cup politics, and the question of who should replace Colombia as host for the 1986 World Cup:

> Very few people know why soccer in the United States finished. The problem was in 1982, four years before the 1986 World Cup. The US was the candidate. Soccer in the US was high and [backed by] Warner Communication. The people from Warner Communication didn't believe it [the FIFA decision that Mexico replace Colombia], because Mexico was the host before in 1970. The World Cup the Americans would like to host wasn't in 1994, it was in 1986. If FIFA makes the 1986 World Cup in the USA, this was the best market. When FIFA decided on Mexico, Warner Communications say 'I finished. I don't put money in.'.[15]

There was indeed deep disappointment among the US delegation when its serious bid lost out to a barely documented Mexican bid.

Whilst Dr Henry Kissinger was making an hour-long sophisticated presentation incorporating detailed commercial analyses, the Mexican delegation was in the lobby of the Stockholm hotel, already following up its eight-minute presentation with preparations for a celebration and victory reception. It turned out that 'Havelange had gained the executive's approval of the special commission's recommendation – Mexico – at breakfast time.'[16] Outraged at the way in which the USA's bid had been rejected in favour of Mexico, Kissinger is said to have considered suing FIFA. The FIFA decision, and the manner in which it was reached, were both disappointing and humiliating to the US soccer establishment, including Warner, the financial backers of the NASL. With escalating costs and falling revenues at home, and this snub from FIFA and the deal-making networks of world football, it was hardly surprising that Warner withdrew its support.

The false dawn of the NASL meant that soccer at its highest level would have a low profile in the USA until it was selected by FIFA to stage the 1994 finals, and its national side did well enough, in the build-up to 1994, and in the absence of Mexico from the qualifying process, to qualify for the World Cup Finals in Italy in 1990.[17] An evaluation of the context of production, and the impact, of USA '94 provides a revealing focus for assessing FIFA's continuing influence upon the culture and political economy of world football.

In June and July 1994, then, the major event in television sports across the world was the football World Cup, the world championships of soccer, as the host nation of that year preferred to call it. Yet in the USA itself there was still much scepticism about this event, for the USA has never embraced soccer as a major competitive, spectator-based and high-performance sport. Alongside baseball, American football and basketball (the big three) – and the claimant to entry into a Big Four, ice hockey – soccer has looked unquestionably minor league. And yet at the World Cup Finals of 1994 ticket sales exceeded those of any previous World Cup; the games were widely recognized as splendidly entertaining, and television recording and reproduction techniques guaranteed high-quality coverage of and feedback on almost any aspect of the game, its players and the tournament. How was this possible? And what was the impact of the successful staging of the tournament upon sports culture in the USA? And upon soccer itself? The answers to these questions have far-reaching implications for an understanding and theorization of the impact of FIFA, and for an understanding of football's place in a globalizing world.

In his seminal work on globalization Robertson argues that the concept 'should be applied to a particular series of developments concerning *the concrete structuration of the world as a whole*', and should address 'the question of *the actual* form of recent and contemporary moves in the direction of global interdependence and global consciousness'. International competitions – 'e.g. Olympics, Nobel Prizes', to which can be added, of course, FIFA's World Cup – contributed to an earlier phase of development of global density and complexity. The final phase of the globalization process, for Robertson, is one of 'uncertainty', with intensifying forms of global consciousness achieved in a 'consolidation of global media system[s]', alongside an increase for many societies in 'problems of multiculturality and polyethnicity'.[18] FIFA's growth has been based on such parallel developments, yet some trends within globalization continue to embody the aspirations and ambitions of particular individuals, and forms of *concrete structuration* can be identified as the projects of networks and alliances of powerful individuals. FIFA's global networks would only grant the World Cup to the USA when such a decision fitted the interests of these networks and alliances.

Hobsbawm has noted the importance and distinctiveness of sport, in its complex relationship to political domination and cultural standardization. In his survey of 'The Arts 1914–1945' he asserts that in 'the field of popular culture the world was American or it was provincial', but with one exception: 'The unique exception was sport.' He recognizes soccer as a 'genuinely international' sport: 'The sport the world made its own was association football, the child of Britain's global economic presence ... This simple and elegant game, unhampered by complex rules and equipment, and which could be practised on any more or less flat open space of the required size, made its way through the world entirely on its merits.'[19] But not in the USA.

In the USA, Markovits has argued, the lack of American response to soccer World Cups (particularly when the Finals took place in a contiguous neighbouring country) has been intriguing. He noted that when the 1986 World Cup Finals were hosted by Mexico in 1986, 'this event failed to capture the imagination of the American public', and described the American interest in 'the world's most important media event' as 'strikingly minute in comparison to that exhibited in virtually every country in the world'.[20] His explanation for the failure of soccer to gain a hold in US sports culture revolves around a notion of *sports space*, and the argument that in the formative period of US nation-building three vigorously characteristic American sports took shape – baseball, American football and basketball. This had the consequence that 'America's bourgeois hegemony and legacy of the 'first new nation' . . . contributed substantially to the continued absence of the world's most popular team sport as a major presence in American popular culture'.[21] The *sports space*, Markovits eloquently and convincingly argues, was occupied early in the USA, so that a fully matured form of association football or soccer (as developed formatively in Britain and its imperial and trading networks) had little chance of gaining any serious foothold in the USA's sports territory. Soccer was crowded out, from below by baseball, with its myth-like resonance of rural community; and from above by American football, with its initially college-based rationalistic personification of the new industrial order. Indoors, basketball also took a hold on the sports consciousness of the expanding nation – very much, though Markovits does not touch upon this, in waiting for its development in its professional form by black Americans.[22]

Where soccer took some hold, prior to World War I, it 'remained closely associated with immigrants, a stigma which proved fatal to soccer's potential of becoming a popular team sport in the "new world"'.[23] And even on its reintroduction as a university/college sport in the latter half of this century, 'soccer has remained largely the domain of foreigners and recent immigrants, both as players and spectators'.[24] Fuller explorations of soccer's relationship to nativist US sports, and popular retrospectives on USA '94 by the journeyman professional and the literary fan,[25] bear out the continuing relevance of Markovits's thesis. A review of the impact of FIFA's World Cup, which gave elite soccer its highest ever profile within the USA, will illuminate the extent and nature of sport's contribution to the globalization process, and the relationship of sport and sports space to trends within globalization.

■ USA '94: The Build-up – Some Themes and Discourses

FIFA awarded the 1994 World Cup Finals to the USA in 1988. The United States Soccer Federation's (USSF) bid 'received more votes than Brazil and Morocco put together',[26] supported as it was by an infrastructure of stadiums, hotels, transport networks and projected sponsors. African sports leader Dr Halim, of the Sudan, recalls that the USA's bid was always going to succeed, for Havelange had assured US former secretary of state Dr Henry Kissinger that the USA would be considered favourably,[27] – no doubt making up for the slight suffered by Kissinger several years earlier when Mexico was awarded the 1986 event in such non-competitive circumstances. The business interests of both the FIFA president, and especially the senior vice-president Cañedo, also now stood to gain from locating the Finals in the biggest media and consumer market in the world.

The choice of the USA as host for the World Cup Finals was greeted with a combination of disbelief, hoots of derision, and scepticism among journalists, commentators and professionals, both within and beyond the USA. The draw for the tournament was held in December 1993, and even at that stage, just months before the event itself, print media columnists could seek to mobilize nationalist sentiment against the most popular sport in the world, on the basis that it was very strange indeed to give so much credence to a sport which was based upon the skillful manipulation of a round ball by the foot. Tom Weir commented that spectators in the USA are thrilled most of all by action from the waist up:

> all arms and hands, things that happen from the waist up . . . The World Cup draw is Sunday and admit it, you don't care. And no matter how much this event gets crammed down your throat . . . you still won't care. But don't feel guilty about it. There's a good reason why you don't care about soccer, even if it is the national passion in Cameroon, Uruguay and Madagascar. It's because you are an American, and hating soccer is more American than mom's apple pie, driving a pickup or spending Saturday afternoon channel-surfing with the remote control.[28]

Such rhetoric is of course fuelled by the columnist's eye for controversy, and there are many other places beyond the USA where pick-up driving and channel-surfing are well established and extremely popular. But the implication is that (however globalized they have become) these are quintessentially *American* activities, and that soccer is not. The sub-text to Weir's tirade is a separatist and nativist one.

If US journalists were dismissive of soccer on the basis of an ethnocentric celebration of their own culture, other writers were uncritically celebratory of soccer and dismissive of US culture and mores. One British journalist, for instance, stressed the more absurd side of the draw in a puritanical piece on Las Vegas/US culture:

> filthy lucre it is that bought one of sport's great events for a nation of philistines who continue to treat it with yawning indifference . . . the American organizing committee called a media conference for 12 noon, and arrived 65 minutes late. What followed was truly Pythonesque, with Roy Post, of the US Mint, treating the world's football writers to a lengthy dissertation on his commemorative coin programme.[29]

Monty Python's Flying Circus (the classic surrealist British comedy series), Mickey Mouse and Disney – these were the cultural references and metaphors with which Lovejoy made sense of the draw. Though the metaphor of the 'circus' is multi-faceted, evoking notions of festival, fun, entertainment, daring, as well as clowns and ridiculousness, British journalistic responses to the draw touched more upon the clownishness and the absurdity – as well as a perceived tackiness – of the event. Other British sports journalists were sceptical about or dismissive of the stages of the build-up,[30] and the media events such as the draw (though nothing could be less slick, sophisticated or engaging than the televised draw for the English FA Cup, even in its revised prime-time format as launched in autumn 1995).

The draw itself was broadcast in the UK on the obscure Eurosport cable channel, in a mid-evening slot up against the competitive schedules of the terrestrial network channels. It opened with a series of welcomes from apparently high-profile television, film and sports celebrities, including the movie stars Jessica Lange and Jeff Bridges, and several sports stars. 'Hello world, welcome to the USA' was the repeated line as these celebrities performed, for the most part, limited tricks with a soccer ball. The US president, Bill Clinton, then appeared to state that the country was 'proud and excited' to host the World Cup, and that 'World Cup fever' had gripped the whole nation right through to the White House. He then relayed some participation statistics which showed that soccer was the fastest growing youth sport in the USA. Three thousand guests at the Las Vegas draw were then offered snippets on the world profile of the game, with movie celebrity Faye Dunaway co-hosting the programme. Dr João Havelange, president of FIFA, was welcomed for what the host acknowledged as 'one of the most complicated draws' ever to have been conducted, linked as it was to a seeding system and the demographics of ethnic and immigrant communities across the venue cities and regions. The holders of the World Cup trophy passed the cup to Havelange, and he passed this on to Alan Rothenberg, lynchpin of the organization World Cup USA '94. Rothenberg stated that it was with 'pride and humility' that he accepted the trophy for the period of the Finals, which would he was convinced 'establish a legacy for USA soccer to flourish at every level of play', including at the level of a new professional league – the proposed Major League Soccer – which would soon rank with any other in the world, and for which Rothenberg himself was responsible. Soon after awarding the Finals to the USA in 1988, Palmer reports,[31] FIFA had been active in campaigning against the USSF's incumbent elected president, Werner Fricker, and was directly implicated in the election of Rothenberg as his successor. Palmer reports Rothenberg on this: 'The World Cup was dead in the water when I came in . . . There was even talk about taking it away from America'.[32] The draw, and the line-up at the draw, were testimony to Rothenberg's revivalist impact.

Roberto Baggio of Italy was presented with not just the Player of the Year award, but also with the Adidas Energizer trophy, and then a few welcomes were shown from some of the host cities. Mickey Mouse introduced the viewer to the attractions of Orlando, Florida; night life, cars and people were highlighted as the special qualities of Detroit, for instance. Nike, Delta and Opel graphics then led into a sustained Nike advertisement – 'You can't live without . . . Just do It' – which conflated soccer, sex and youth style, before the event returned to welcome the top FIFA careerist Sepp Blatter. The razzmatazz of the build-up anti-climaxed in singer Diana Ross's penalty kick at the Opening Ceremony in Chicago on 17 July. She struck the ball with a jerky mechanical swing of the leg. The ball rolled painfully and apologetically wide, and simultaneously the goal itself collapsed. Ironically, the Italian star Baggio was to shoot the deciding penalty of the final over the bar in Pasadena just a few weeks later.

Nevertheless, early concerns at the staging of the event in the USA were assuaged by the time of the later stages of the build-up. It had been feared that, in order to create more high-scoring games, the goals would be enlarged; that, to accommodate US television advertising, single matches would be divided into four time periods; and that matches would be played upon artificial surfaces rather than turf. But the goals stayed the same size; and the matches were played in two forty-five minute halves, on grass. Indeed, scepticism among some was tempered by an eager anticipation of the effect of some brave innovations by FIFA: a subtle amendment to the offside law which would favour attacking play; the stricter interpretation of foul and violent play, which would inhibit the more physically intimidating side of the game, especially among defenders, and so promote creativity; a strict line on how to deal with injured players; and the award of three points to teams for first-round wins. These innovations matched the image of soccer in the USA which sponsors were keen to promote – a free-flowing, creative game with few of the trappings of overt aggression and violence characteristic of other top-level professional team sports.

■ USA'94: The Event and its Legacy

The World Cup had a bigger media impact in the USA than many pessimists had anticipated, hailed as 'the surprise sports story of the year', with television ratings '20%-30% higher than many expected'.[33] Live games on the ESPN cable channel attracted viewing figures equal to the rating for prime-time Wednesday Major League Baseball games: 'The July 17 championship final, Brazil vs. Italy, drew an unprecedented 9.5/24 (8.95 mil.) on ABC plus another 1.62 mil. on Univision, the Spanish network available on cable and off-air TV.'[34] Press coverage also exceeded expectation.

In the light of this profile of the event, substantial impact was widely assumed. Claims have been made that the 1994 World Cup has generated a high level of interest and recruitment to the grass roots of the game. The United States Youth Soccer Association reported that in the follow-up to the World Cup its membership increased by 9 per cent to 2.1 million; the American Youth Soccer Association's membership was claimed to have increased by 14 per cent to half a million.[35] And certainly young people comprised the primary marketing target – 'The US Soccer Federation claims 16m registered players – more than any other FIFA member – of whom most are children.'[36] But the professional game continued to face difficulties in 'attracting investors, finding adequate stadiums and local franchise control'.[37]

The professional game was fragmented, with the five-year-old American Professional Soccer League (APSL) continuing to plan its own expansion from seven to twelve teams, at the same time as the proposed full-time Major League Soccer (MLS) initiative was stalling. Yet the highest average gate in the APSL, in the 10,000 capacity California State Fullerton stadium, was 5,300, following the Los Angeles Salsa; followed by averages of 4,200 and 4,873 for teams in a different country, the Montreal Impact and the Vancouver 86ers respectively.[38] The situation a year on from USA '94 did not augur well for the future of professional soccer in the USA, as Paul Gardner's overview has also indicated.[39] The new professional league (Major League Soccer) which had been pledged to FIFA when the Finals were given to the USA had still not started up, and its starting date had been put back from the postponed date of April 1995 to a further postponed date of April 1996. Ten teams were planned, but only eight sites had been found by April 1995. Gardner describes a divided, factionalized part-time soccer culture in the USA, with four existing leagues (two of these indoor) currently in existence, and none of them willing to give up any share of the soccer market. The US public is also used to paying to see the best, and to hailing its indigenous sports as 'world-class'. An English professional soccer star with many years of experience of the game in the USA, Rodney Marsh, pinpointed this, three years before the event, as a problem for the future of the game after the World Cup: '1995 will be the kill or cure year . . . Assuming the World Cup is a success in soccer terms . . . assuming the football captures the American imagination, the pro clubs here will have to show a big improvement or go under. Once people have seen the best there is no way they'll go back to watch second-rate stuff.'[40] The ever acerbic football journalist Brian Glanville reiterated this point after the Finals: 'Having watched the World Cup, Americans were never going to settle for junk soccer.'[41]

Where soccer did thrive in the immediate wake of the USA '94 adventure was where it had thrived before – in the schools, among particular ethnic communities and among some women.[42] This is where the sponsorship had already been targeted. The banana retailer Chiquita Brands International sponsored the Chiquita Cup, Fair Play, Clinics and Soccer Challenges, essentially grass roots programmes for youth soccer. Chiquita was also an Olympic soccer and US soccer sponsor. But its World Cup marketing drive confirmed soccer's specific market: 'According to Chiquita the company will be focusing on its soccer sponsorship through World Cup '94 . . . Chiquita Brands target 3 demographic groups: children ages 15–16; women ages 25–34; and adults 55+ . . . [it] looks for quality events with a 'healthy image' and family image.'[43]

But thriving Mexican Leagues playing their matches in Southern California; Hispanic crowds flocking into Los Angeles stadia for an El Salvador versus Denmark match;[44] healthy and athletic women (even if world champions, and potential gold medallists at the inaugural Olympic women's soccer tournament in Atlanta in 1996); and senior citizens and children – whatever commitment to soccer they might represent – all of these groups would be unlikely to guarantee any inroads by soccer into the core sports space of the USA. In this respect the business community was focused and realistic concerning where soccer's potential in the US market really lay – belying the rhetoric of Rothenberg and the like.

Staging the event well was a matter of civic pride for many and massive personal profit for a few. There are direct comparisons with the Olympic Games here. In Los Angeles in 1984 armies of volunteers were recruited to help stage the Summer Olympics at the peak

215

of global Cold War politics. Controversies raged over whether these volunteers could be provided with working lunches; the Los Angeles Organizing Committee reported a surplus of $225 million. At the World Cup Finals ten years on this same productive – and certainly from some perspectives exploitative – dynamic provided the base for the spectacular staging of a global event of staggering profitability. Tony Mason has summarized the impact of that World Cup.[45] Crowds averaged 68,604, and the aggregate spectator figure was 3,567,415. The 94,194 spectators at the final in the Rosebowl, Pasadena paid $43.5 million for their tickets, an average price of nearly $462 per ticket. Three million dollars' worth of World Cup merchandise was sold at airport and hotel gift stores operated in the USA by the British W H Smith company. And Univision, the Spanish-language television network, generated twice as much advertising revenue as during the previous World Cup, Italia '90.

This outcome was not merely accidental or a stroke of serendipity for the organizers. Scott Parks Le Tellier was featured in the British press in 1993 as not just 'the managing director and chief operating officer' of USA '94, but also as a missionary (well-based with a Mormon background), visionary and evangelist – for football.[46] He became keen on soccer whilst watching the World Cup in Germany in 1974, Lawson reports. Along with a 'surviving hunger of commerce for new outlets', it was the Le Tellier-style 'new breed of evangelists' who helped secure the soccer World Cup for the USA. Lawson presents Le Tellier as a force outside of that 'hunger for commerce'. In fact, on closer scrutiny, Le Tellier and other key players in USA '94 were catalysts for that hungry commerce, not merely complements to it.

Le Tellier, speaking to journalist Ken Reich in the post-Olympics euphoria in early 1985, spoke less idealistically about his involvement in and motivation for the soccer cause in North America. He had spent his honeymoon in Spain in 1982 'at the World Cup championships learning how to run a major soccer tournament so we could do it two years later'. He had actually moved to Los Angeles to try to get involved in the 1984 Olympic Games, having been in Montreal in 1976, and as an ambitious young attorney had met sports entrepreneurs on the appropriate sports and professional circuits. In discussion with Reich he noted the pressures of multi-commitments in the case of Alan Rothenberg, co-commissioner for soccer in the 1984 Olympic Games: 'Alan was the original commissioner, but he was so tied up doing other things ... they figured that the job wasn't going to get done.' Le Tellier relates how he had joined the Olympic

Organizing Committee in July 1981, after having become the tennis partner of Mike O'Hara, head of the sports department in the organizing committee. By the end of the following year he was concentrating on three sports (soccer, baseball and equestrian events) and later worked in the finance department. After the successful Games bonuses were paid to employees, in three categories of $2,500, $1,500 and $700, Reich asked Le Tellier 'Do you think the bonuses paid the employees were adequate?' Le Tellier replied 'No, and I'm sure I'm not alone in feeling that way . . . It is unfathomable to me that with that kind of surplus that you wouldn't want to leave a little bit better taste in some of the people that had been around for that period of time, and what led them to think, I wasn't in the discussion, obviously, at that stage, I don't know who was.'[47] No doubt Peter Ueberroth, the man behind the organization of the Games, was.

A decade on, and working with Alan Rothenberg in a team that seemed to have survived the bitterness and tensions of the Olympic exertions, Le Tellier reaped a richer harvest. Three months on from the final game of USA '94 the *Los Angeles Times* reported that 'Alan Rothenberg will receive $7 million in compensation for serving as the World Cup Organizing Committee's chairman and chief executive officer',[48] out of the event's preliminary projection of a $60 million surplus. The seven million comprised a three million bonus and a four million 'deferred-compensation package for "back-pay due", calculated at $800,000 a year, running from August of 1990 through next year'.[49] Prominent in defence of this decision was board member Peter V. Ueberroth. Cart also cites one board member who was not so supportive, and stated to her that 'I'm against paying a guy for a volunteer job.' Le Tellier, chief operating officer of the World Cup organizing committee, was voted a $500,000 bonus.

For the fifty hours a week reported for 1991 (for roles of secretary, managing director and chief operating officer), Le Tellier's documented annual 'compensation' was $174,000, with a further $148,697 reported for 'other allowances'.[50] Le Tellier's address in this return is a Virginia one. For his 0.5 hours per week as honorary chairman and director Henry Kissinger claimed nothing. For his 20 hours per week as chairman, chief executive officer and president Alan I. Rothenberg is documented as receiving no compensation, and just $2,500 in 'other allowances'. In the following year Scott Le Tellier, still working fifty hours a week, received $186,000 'compensation', and $414,291 for 'other allowances' – 'Mr Le Tellier's other allowances include the accelerated payment to him of certain vested post-1994 World Cup salary continuation benefits and of expenses and allowances associated with his relocation from Virginia to California.'[51] In this same return Alan I. Rothenberg was documented as receiving no 'compensation', as in the previous year, and $30,000 in 'other allowances'. But the Treasury was also informed that: 'The Board of Directors has authorized the payment of salaried compensation to Mr. Rothenberg. Mr. Rothenberg has elected to defer the compensation pending a determination that a sufficient surplus exists from World Cup USA 1994, Inc. operations to satisfy all other obligations'.[52] Perhaps the World Cup organizing committee's board members did not all recognize the full implications of this authorization, made as it was at a time when Rothenberg, as Cart reports, declined a salary offer of $350,000 per annum.[53]

Rothenberg had taken over responsibility for the World Cup organizing committee soon after election as USSF president, and assumed a central position in the tangled networks of the USA's soccer developments. Palmer comments: 'What bothers some people is that MLS, which is headed by Rothenberg, received £500,000 from World Cup USA, whose chairman is Rothenberg, to pay for its business plan which it submitted to the USSF, of which Rothenberg is president . . . No-one was very surprised when MLS beat two other bids to set up the national league and then was given $3.5 million by World Cup USA for start-up costs.'[54] No-one seemed very surprised either when Rothenberg's claims about the legacy of the World Cup event looked to have little foundation.

This detail of the financial transactions at the heart of the USA World Cup administration is not an indulgent excursus, a mere empirical aside. It is fundamental to understanding the basis on which the USA World Cup was staged. Like the 1984 Olympics before it, the event was staged to celebrate the ways in which the United States of America could meet a challenge and put on an efficient and spectacular global show. But it was also a gold rush for a thrusting and entrepreneurial professional elite, whose commitment to soccer development has been questioned. A former English professional soccer player, Graham Ramsay, has said of Rothenberg that: 'All the reasons for him being involved are financial. He's not there for the sport. The World Cup is like a big circus going through town.'[55] British football journalist Brian Glanville questions Rothenberg's, as well as Havelange's credentials: 'Havelange . . . has this much in common with the Czar of American Soccer, Alan ($7 million or more) Rothenberg: neither has any real feeling for the game'.[56] Enterprise and business acumen have clearly been the primary strengths of such football entrepreneurs. Off the field, there could be no doubt whatsoever about their commitment to the administration of soccer.

As has been noted, 'the World Cup provided a terrific sampling opportunity among American viewers'.[57] And some cash will certainly have flowed to the grass roots of the game: 'The estimated economic impact of the circus on the USA was a cool $4 billion, with a direct profit of over $20 million to the US organizers.'[58] But the real legacy of the USA World Cup, once the circus has left town, has been the model of mean, lean and immensely profitable event management that the organizers of the 1996 Atlanta Olympic Games sought to replicate. You don't have to like sport to do that. It helps if you do, but the driving force behind USA '94 was a combination of local pride, global posturing and personal ambition.

This evaluation of the nature and impact of USA '94 shows that the Markovits thesis on the fullness of the sport space in the USA is not undermined by the success of the event. For the event was in many ways, whatever its profile in the Summer of 1994, marginal to that space. Even when the established sports space of the USA was disrupted and so rendered theoretically vulnerable by strikes in major sports, in the immediate wake of the World Cup in the autumn/ winter of 1994/95, this could not be seized as an opportunity to establish professional soccer, for the public and the sponsors remained sceptical about the place of soccer within the canon of US sports culture.

■
The Final Frontier Reached?

USA '94 confirmed that a country which hosts successfully a global sports event need not be one of the top competitors in that sport. This certainly encouraged future bids from emergent soccer nations such as Japan and South Korea (fiercely competing into 1996 for the 2002 World Cup Finals), which claim to have the economic, transport and communication infrastructure in place for the hosting of an event of this scale. The USA World Cup reaffirmed the profile of spectacle in the global sporting calendar, and the persistent problems for professional soccer in gaining any significant foothold in the territory of dominant US sports.

World soccer culture penetrated only partially and unevenly the sports cultures and space of the USA, but analysis of the impact of World Cup '94 is also a reminder that central to some major trends in the globalization of world sport is a political economy that merges the interests of trans-national bodies such as FIFA, multi-national corporations, and national and regional elites. These interests merge to produce economically profitable outcomes that are both entirely intended and, as our analysis demonstrates, identifiable. In this light the analysis is offered as an example of the study of an *actual form* of a globalizing tendency, to paraphrase Robertson, and of, again in Robertson's words, the *concrete structuration* of one of the world's premier sports events. The analysis is also testimony to the relevance of the economic and the culture-ideology dimensions of trans-national practices,[59] for an understanding of globalizing sports. The false promises of some of the prophets and makers of USA '94 can only really be explained as examples of the ideological – the masking of real interests and values geared towards a set of particular interests – exploitation of the situation.

The embryonic soccer culture of the USA was never likely to make significant inroads into the established sports space of that culture. In the MLS's (Major League Soccer) first full season, three million fans watched the matches, including a record-setting 92,216 at the Rose Bowl in June 1996. This success met with a realistic response. As MLS commissioner Doug Logan put it: 'I think it is to us an impressive start, but we see it as just the beginning, we don't see it as an end. And I at least have the perspective of permanence and of leaving a legacy that will outlive what I call the fragile attraction that our sports audience has to specific sports.'[60] Tognoni, FIFA's former PR man recalled: 'It was never a condition of FIFA that they had to set up a league. It was a mutual understanding that it would be desirable and it is more important that you have a stable project than a quick project.'[61]

For FIFA, USA '94 was, in Havelange's words, a source of 'great pride' in its own 'reputation as a dynamic and progressive body alert to modern currents of thought and deed'. Havelange expressed all-round satisfaction at the event, with the 'historical mandate' of the organization to develop the sport world-wide as the long-term goal:

> FIFA can reflect upon . . . universal acknowledgement of its exceptional success . . . it vindicated totally FIFA's decision to award the Finals to a country whose tireless efforts to promote our sport have long earned our respect . . . The short-term objective – to stage a spectacular World Cup with thrilling football, full stadia, fair play and a peaceful atmosphere – is beyond question.[62]

Cañedo, chair of the organizing committee, wrote that the event 'was organized to a degree of perfection befitting the prestige of the tournament itself',[63] so that some concerned voices about the capacity of

America to cope with cultural and logistical problems were silenced. Football administrators in the USA were still triumphalist about the scale of the success years after the event. Hank Steinbrecher, of the United States Soccer Federation, comments on the sceptical climate with which he and others had to contend:

> It was considered a joke, and I heard all the criticisms for so long – the United States could never pull off a successful World Cup, they would never get fans into the stadiums, they never sold sponsorships, they would cut the game into quarters, they have no passion, they have no idea of what it is like to play. Oh, and by the way, their team sucks – well, guess what? All the European press had to eat crow.[64]

Cañedo also added that new technological standards were established in organizational structure, and for reporters and the media as well no doubt. Nowhere in his forward did he refer to the welcome viewing figures for his own television company, and the Report made no comment on Rothenberg's bonus, described by Hank Hersch of *Sports Illustrated* as an 'unconscionable' level of personal remuneration for an individual purporting to work in a voluntary capacity for a supposedly non-profit organization.[65] Three years on from the World Cup, Rothenberg's management of World Cup USA '94 Inc. was in the spotlight of the Californian courts, in a case in which he was being sued by a former World Cup employee for breach of an employment contract. Rothenberg's own firm, Latham & Watkins, had handled the World Cup's legal matters, and in December 1996 a column in *Sports Illustrated* described him as 'a shameless self-promoter and a smug . . . profiteer', and called his hiring of his own law firm a 'blatant misuse of power'. Rothenberg was called upon to explain his 'multi-million dollar compensation, the use of Latham & Watkins as World Cup's legal counsel, the hiring of his son and a licensing contract between the organization and his wife'.[66] But on the field of play, USA '94 was indeed a glorious spectacle, and did defy the cynical and world-weary doomsday predictions of soccercentric non-Americans and soccerphobic Americans. And for some professionals it was the crowning glory of their careers. Tognoni recalls a disappointing scoreline in the goalless final:

> But it was a wonderful event and a full stadium, and I think you know it will never be . . . I was in the plane and I said to myself 'first of all I will never, I can never do more for an event as I did for USA '94.' And maybe it may not be as beautiful again because we will never have, until we go to the US, we will never have the big stadium again.[67]

Tognoni was not alone in this sentiment. Hank Steinbrecher, of the US soccer federation, hailing Havelange as 'the father of the rebirth of soccer in the United States', insisted that 'this giant is starting to stir', and that 'by the year 2010 the United States will host and win the World Cup'. The USSF/Organizing Committee made sixty million dollars: 'that is our cut. We made a lot of money for FIFA, hundreds of millions', he further stated, giving profit pride of place in any hierarchy of qualities for future host nations.[68] World Cup '94 undoubtedly awakened sports entrepreneurs to the cultural variety and vitality, global profile and commercial potential of soccer. Doug Logan, former promoter of Pink Floyd, Rolling Stones and Madonna concerts, has developed a logo for the MLS which celebrates not just the kick (at the expense of the manual dexterity so critical to mainstream US sports), but a 'Pan Americanism not Americanism', with the dominant green and blue of the logo symbolizing the sky and the pitch of a global game 'played in 192 countries throughout the world'.[69] As 'Glory Land' played over the PA in the Pasadena Rosebowl, where the proceedings of the Final had included football ambassador Pelé skipping onto the pitch hand-in-hand with singer Whitney Houston, not only football fans were basking in the sunshine. Despite CONCACAF general secretary Chuck Blazer's conviction that the Finals could not feasibly take place again in the USA in the forseeable future,[70] given the credibility of the claims of other FIFA members, the Mr Fixits of FIFA, and self-confessed 'brash American' soccer entrepreneurs and popular cultural promoters, were in all likelihood already counting the benefits of returning to CONCACAF's biggest member for another World Cup bonanza.

■ 10

Conclusion: who rules the peoples' game?

■ Football and FIFA: Beyond Imperialism and Towards a Global Marketplace

An adequate theorization of FIFA's impact must consider the extent to which football can be viewed as a symbol of economic and cultural imperialism; and the role FIFA has played in the brokerage of forms of neo-imperialism. The answers to these questions inform the context of Rous's downfall and Havelange's ascendancy; and, through the contextual analysis, give some indication as to FIFA's developmental direction, as a globally powerful INGO (International Non-Government Organization) and OFC (Off-Shore Financial Centre), as it approaches its second century.

It is estimated that globally the football industry is 'worth two hundred and twenty five billion dollars annually'.[1] The FIFA general secretary expands on this:

> The success of the game virtually throughout the world . . . its social ramifications and its economic impact make of it a phenomenal force. The figures alone speak for themselves: 200 million persons actively involved and an estimated 1.2 billion directly or indirectly, an annual turnover of some 200 billion Dollars, far larger than corporate leaders such as Mitsubishi or General Motors . . . And the end is not yet in sight.[2]

The emergence of such a political economy of world football has been traced in this study in the story of FIFA's developing partnerships with corporate sponsors, marketing agencies and the media industry, culminating in its apotheosis at the 1994 USA World Cup. In a development of some earlier, collaborative work,[3] Darby has presented a convincing synthesis which shows how dependency theory and world systems theory can be utilized to make some sense of FIFA's global presence in the industry of football. He focuses on Africa to show how, in a variety of ways, football and FIFA feature in the post-colonial exploitation of emergent nations by an elite 'core' of European and South American countries.[4] Much of the evidence presented in the preceding pages would suggest that such arguments with regard to economic and cultural imperialism are valid, but we believe that the full story needs to incorporate the idea of FIFA as a body which *also* articulates the interests of the Third World. That is, the extent to which FIFA serves as a forum for resistance, by the Third World, to First World domination or hegemony, needs to be assessed.

To further explore this it is useful to compare the situation of FIFA with that of comparable institutions. The Food and Agriculture Organization (FAO), founded in 1945 as the UN's (United Nations) largest agency, and based in Rome, was formed to combat world hunger by compiling and disseminating research and data, and providing advice to governments on food production. In the mid-1990s its annual budget was $700 million. Beckett sees the half-century history of this body as typical of a swing in power away from Anglo-Saxon dominance towards the Third World:

> Its first Director-General was Sir John Boyd-Orr, a Scottish nutritionist who smoked a pipe and took tea with his staff every afternoon. Then came decolonisation and the emergence of a Third World, with its own opinions and demands for representation. A gradual redistribution of power took place: at the FAO a new American head was succeeded by an Indian and, ultimately, a Lebanese Director-General who courted Africa and ignored the West. The same pattern transformed world sport: FIFA's Sir Stanley Rous, a reserved former referee, gave way to a Brazilian mining magnate called João Havelange.[5]

Another of the United Nations' important sub groupings, UNESCO (United Nations Educational, Scientific and Cultural Organization), was founded in 1946. There are also striking similarities between the development of UNESCO and that of FIFA. UNESCO was formed with the broad aim of forging global educational and cultural links: 'for the purposes of advancing . . . the objectives of international peace and the common welfare of mankind'. Initially there were twenty affiliated countries and membership and executive power was dominated by the Europeans and the USA. By the 1970s membership had grown to around 150, largely as a result of the end of colonialism. As

John Tomlinson correctly points out, 'political independence did not, of course, mean economic independence or anything like global political power'.[6] In the absence of such, he argues that, 'to have a voice in the world as represented at UNESCO means to be a nation'.[7] In this way, the UN, and particularly UNESCO, became a political assembly point for the development of and promotion of Third World interests.

At the same time that the Brazilian, João Havelange, was organizing the Third World in a bid to unseat Sir Stanley Rous as FIFA president, at the UN similar alliances between South America, Africa and parts of Asia were mobilized to give the Third World a greater say in world affairs. This was to lead in 1974 to a call for a 'New International Economic Order' within the UN itself, and a parallel call for a 'New World Information and Communications Order' within UNESCO. The former verged on a formal declaration by the UN that the Third World was being exploited by the First, and called for the introduction of mechanisms which would redress that imbalance; the latter challenged the domination of the world's media services by a handful of US and European conglomerates. These initiatives and Havelange's power play within FIFA were intimately connected in as much as they were all part of a wider political struggle through which the non-aligned or 'Third World' sought to have an impact on international affairs with the ultimate objective being to 'eliminate the widening gap between developed and developing countries'.[8]

Of course, both the UN and UNESCO are heavily dependent for material support upon the core nations of the developed world and this seriously undermines their power to challenge the status quo. As Tomlinson argues, economically dominant nations exercise limits to their tolerance of radical debate concerning the world order, and this is particularly the case for right-wing administrations.[9] As UNESCO became more and more critical of neo-colonialism in the early 1980s, the response of two of the premier targets for that criticism, Britain and the USA, was to withdraw their subscriptions to that organization. As for the UN, the world's leading economic and military powers can veto any decision taken by the general assembly. For instance, in 1996, feeling that under his stewardship, the UN was not acting in America's best interests, the United States vetoed a further term of office for the incumbent general secretary of the UN, the Egyptian, Boutros Boutros Gali. The Americans also withheld their considerable contribution to the organization's budget.[10] In this respect, as Tomlinson points out, the voice of the Third World

225

in these IGOs has been, at best, a 'provisional' one, which has not seriously threatened the global balance of power.[11]

There are both differences and similarities with the case of FIFA. Firstly, as evidenced by four times world champions Brazil, it must be pointed out that 'power' in football is not entirely determined by combinations of economic, political and military might. Eyeballing the FIFA rankings suggests that there is some correlation between performance in international football and levels of economic development. Certainly, in the Asian Confederation, the prominence in the FIFA rankings of Japan, South Korea, Saudi Arabia, Kuwait, the United Arab Emirates and (to a lesser extent) Thailand, indicates the importance of economic resources for football development at the highest competitive level. However, as confirmed by the research of Stamm and Lamprecht, while GNP (Gross National Product) is a factor to be considered in the interpretation of FIFA's international rankings, it is by no means the only determinant of achievement. 'Money cannot buy success in world football.'[12] Proven playing ability and 'tradition' are also important parts of a complex equation which permits certain less well-off nations to command high status in world football, and thereby have a say in the global running of the game.

Secondly, there is nothing equivalent to the UN's veto in FIFA's statutes. An established elite of football nations cannot block decisions taken at the FIFA congress. On the basis of the one vote per nation rule, this has meant that as Third World membership of FIFA has expanded, their political influence has grown concomitantly. This has been reflected in many ways, including in the make-up of the organization's most influential committees, the allocation of places for World Cup Finals, and, indeed, in the occupancy of the presidency by a South American for almost a quarter of a century.

However, there are certain 'disguised' similarities with the situation *vis-à-vis* the UN and its bodies such as the FAO and UNESCO. It is the Europeans who feel that their interests have been most damaged by the progress of the emergent nations in FIFA. UEFA claims that football in Europe generates almost 80 per cent of the game's global turnover and makes by far the greatest contribution to FIFA's coffers. Given its current scale of operation, FIFA would struggle to survive without European support. Indeed, there have been serious informal talks in the corridors of European football about a UEFA withdrawal from FIFA,[13] and from future World Cup competitions.

It is in this context that the campaign for FIFA's presidential election in 1998 was fought. One year before the Paris Congress at which that election would take place, it looked most likely that Havelange, who in December 1996 announced that he would not stand for re-election, would be succeeded by a European. At least three of the confederations indicated (in interviews with authors) that the ideal outcome for FIFA and 'the good of the game' (FIFA's verbal logo) would be a candidature of one; and the six confederation presidents were due to meet in the Summer of 1997 to discuss and negotiate such principles and strategies. A European succession to Havelange was the means of removing the threat of a UEFA secession from FIFA. On the other hand, an election for the presidency contested in a climate of intrigue and deal-making was bound to fragment confederational alliances. If the post-Havelange presidency passed into the hands of another South American or a figure from one of the non-European confederations (such as Hayatou from Cameroon or the South Korean, Chung), the prospect of World Cup 2002 in Japan and Korea being played without the Europeans could have become more than mere conjecture. As Tomlinson points out, with reference to UNESCO, the Third World's impact is limited by the nature of the distribution of global economic power, and in the global order of capitalism access to the debate itself is limited in terms of resources.[14] So long as the financial centre of world football continued to be in Europe, the prospect of FIFA continuing to promote the development of football in the Third World at UEFA's expense would seem to have been limited.

■ FIFA's Legacy: Globalization, Cultural Reproduction and Resistance

Robertson has argued that an historical, comparative and interdisciplinary social science framework can be developed if social theory is 'refocused and expanded so as to make concern with "the world" a central hermeneutic, and in such a way as to constrain empirical and comparative-historical research in the same direction'; for Robertson, the concept 'should be applied to a particular series of developments concerning *the concrete structuration of the world as a whole* ', and with 'the question of *the actual* form of recent and contemporary moves in the direction of global interdependence and global consciousness'.[15] With these concerns and questions in mind, Robertson offers 'in unavoidably skeletal terms' a fivefold classification of 'the temporal-historical path to the present circumstance of a very high degree of *global density and complexity*.' Early 'germinal' and 'incipient' phases are

227

followed by a third phase which Robertson labels the 'take-off phase', covering the last quarter of the nineteenth and the first quarter of the twentieth centuries. In this phase, instances of international communication and international relations escalate, and global competitions are developed – 'e.g. Olympics, Nobel Prizes' – to which can be added, of course, FIFA's World Cup. Robertson's fourth phase is a 'struggle for hegemony', running through from the 1920s to the mid-1960s. The final phase in his model is one of 'uncertainty', with intensifying forms of global consciousness achieved in a 'consolidation of global media system[s]', alongside an increase for many societies in 'problems of multiculturality and polyethnicity'.[16] FIFA's growth has been symptomatic of this intensifying uncertainty and complexity.

While there can be little or no doubt that the FIFA story coincides with the rise, fall and reincarnation of forms of imperialism, and that this must be accounted for, it is also the case that football has provided an important public gathering point at which local, national and regional versions of popular culture can be celebrated in the face of globalizing tendencies. As Golding and Harris point out, 'the global culture we may presume to observe is itself the transnationalization of a very national voice, the universal triumph of a supremely local and parochial set of images'.[17]

In this way FIFA can be viewed *both* as a transnational body which promotes globalization (and transnational capitalism), and as a locus for resistance to entrenched forms of imperialist domination, and emergent forms of international and capitalist power.[18] However, we must be careful not to overstate the case for football and counter-hegemony. We are reminded that 'the rediscovery of the resistant and creative, even subversive, power of audiences can too easily slip, even within self-consciously radical discourses, into a romantic celebration of the cultural insubordination of consumers'.[19] In any corrective to forms of Marxist economic reductionism, Golding and Harris add that ephemera should not be exclusively focused upon at the expense of persisting forces of political economy.

With this warning in mind, we need to record three *major* qualifications to the consideration of FIFA as a vehicle for forces of resistance to imperialism, as a champion of the Third World. Firstly, for the post-colonial Third World, affiliation to FIFA and participation in international football represented a tacit acceptance of the deep structure left behind by the colonists. Football was a European game and, while some of the names might have changed, the shape and ethnic contents of the new nation states which affiliated to FIFA were the same as those imposed by the old colonial powers a century earlier. By playing international football, countries like Sudan, Nigeria, Malaysia, Singapore and South Africa are confirming a social and political map imposed by the first world. As Billig reminds us, this is critical to any understanding of how forms of cultural imperialism persist in the post-colonial age.[20]

Secondly, FIFA's expansion could not have been achieved without the considerable support of major commercial sponsors. It has been an economic as much as a political and cultural phenomenon. FIFA's development and growth is an instance of a trans-national practice impacting strongly on the level of the cultural-ideological: 'the major locus of trans-national cultural-ideological practices is to be found in the culture-ideology of consumerism'.[21] The development of a global media, the international economics of the television industry, and media-related forms of sponsorship, have been fundamental to FIFA's expansion. The Third World in general and Africa in particular, where manifold social, political and ecological problems undermined the strength and stability of national governments, offered great opportunities for unfettered market development by multi-national companies and their trans-national, financial partners.[22] Havelange recognized this and it was his partnership with companies such as Adidas, Nike and Coca-Cola which helped to finance FIFA's initiatives in the Third World.[23] Thus, while on the one hand FIFA has served as a forum for Third World resistance, on the other hand, it has undoubtedly aided and abetted neo-colonialist forms of economic and cultural exploitation.

Finally, the conditions which generate the need for resistance and inspire the institutionalized expressions of this resistance can be exploited for reasons which have nothing to do with 'fighting the cause'. The World Cup and the world-wide development of soccer by FIFA and those social actors/human agents within and associated with FIFA can be seen as a revealing source for the study of globally resonating cultural politics. The structure of world relations as they have unfolded during the last century, and the generic conditions of exploitation and dependency, created opportunities for individuals to use FIFA and the confederational sub-structure as sites for the construction of personal fiefdoms, while at the same time appearing to carry forward FIFA's global mission. Some trends within globalization embody the aspirations and ambitions of particular individuals and some forms of *concrete structuration* can be identified as the projects of networks and alliances of powerful individuals. This conclusion does not represent a naive lapse into an agency-structure dichotomy. On the contrary, through our study of FIFA, we have

229

shown how interpersonal politics and transcending social forces work together to construct and change institutional practices which themselves are generative of wider social and political change.

History will no doubt record that under Havelange's guiding hand football became global in ways never envisaged during the era of Drewry and Rous, and that the greatest beneficiaries of this development were the emergent nations. It is likely that less attention will be paid to the fact that this expansion enabled Havelange to wield unprecedented power within FIFA and experience a lifestyle akin to that enjoyed by eminent world politicians and royalty. In our study of the man himself, we, like many others who have scrutinized Havelange's reign as FIFA President, are convinced that it is this, rather than being a champion of the oppressed, that has provided him with his driving ambition.[24]

Who, then, rules the peoples' game? Locally, the alliances of interests between a particular government and the cultural industries, and the capacity for cultural autonomy of a populace, obviously vary. Thus, the answer in the USA will be different from the answer in the United Arab Emirates, different in South Korea to in Scotland. Transcendent, but also manipulative of, such regional variations, for almost the whole of the twentieth century FIFA has successfuly survived, and prospered, as the primary agent of football's global development. A widening world-wide recognition of this fact has led to an increasing number of powerful players looking to FIFA as the forum through which to engage in the contest for world football.

It would be easy to romanticize an earlier phase in the world game as being one in the hands of the people, but this would be a mystification, obscuring the truth about the dialectics of control. In terms of ownership, in its modern form, football has never been the peoples' game. Since its formation in 1904 FIFA has been the power base for a small, mainly white and exclusively male elite. For most of the twentieth century it was those who held high office within FIFA who benefited most from the prestige and patronage which went along with running the world's most popular sport. However, as it sought to fulfil its global mission, and serve the personal ambitions of its leaders, FIFA became more and more dependent upon partners outside of football. In turn, powerful corporate entities came to see that there were increasingly lucrative gains to be made through the use of FIFA. Prominent partners in the commercial, cultural and media industries assumed more power than political partners as the century progressed. By the turn of the twentieth and twenty-first centuries there was only one sure answer to the question 'Who rules the peoples' game?' – and that was 'certainly not the people'. They just play it, or stand on the periphery of the increasingly mediated and commodified football spectacle, watching twenty-two players struggle for control of the ball. Elsewhere, behind the closed doors of their international non-governmental organizations and off-shore companies, football politicians and marketing men plot their partnerships and coups in the continuing contest for the control of world football.

Afterword: FIFA and the Future of World Football

International politics are framed by dynamic contours and fluid channels of economic and political relations. Likewise, the global politics of FIFA are seldom static. In the preceding pages we have presented an account and interpretation of the current status of world football through the lens of its global governing body. Necessarily, this interpretation is provisional, inasmuch as the FIFA story is itself ongoing and the political cultures which provide the settings for world football are always evolutionary and, sometimes, revolutionary. In order to demonstrate both the dynamic nature of FIFA's political persona, as well as confirm (perhaps, modify or reject) the more durable themes identified in this book, in this afterword we have sought to corroborate our findings by speaking directly with the leading protagonists in the unfolding FIFA story.[1] We interviewed them around FIFA's Executive Committee meeting in Cairo on the eve of the World Under-17 Championship Finals in early September 1997.

This afterword features interviews with Dr João Havelange, the president of FIFA; Lennart Johansson, the president of UEFA; and Issa Hayatou, the president of CAF. These main commentaries are supported by information and views provided by Charles Dempsey, president of OFC and Chuck Blazer, general secretary of CONCACAF. Mostly, we have let them speak for themselves.

■ Long Live the King? João Havelange

Havelange only faces inquisitors on his own terms, and, when matters have a potential for controversy, on his own turf. On separate occasions, Mark McCormack and Rupert Murdoch, two of the world's most powerful media and marketing businessmen, have experienced Havelange's imperious approach to appointments. As the president told us:

> I heard that Mark McCormack wanted to meet the president of FIFA, either in Rio or Zurich. Mr McCormack was going round the world and part of this itinerary was to take a boat from Buenos Aires and would pass by Rio. I said, 'No, I'm sorry that doesn't suit me, why don't you come to Zurich because I'm not just going to fit myself into your schedule – you want to see me so it is for you. I don't just simply want to be a convenient stop on your journey, if you want to talk business, we talk business but not just because you happen to be there on a boat.' On another occasion, a couple of years ago at the final between Brazil and Mexico of the CONCACAF Gold Cup in Los Angeles I was in the VIP box and saw a gentleman whom I did not know come into the VIP box. He was presented to me and I was told that Mr Murdoch would like to speak to the president, but then added that he could only spare fifteen minutes! Well, I told him that I was here to watch this football match and if he would like to have a meeting, then I would be happy to receive him any time in my office in Zurich – no problem. So Murdoch left for the airport and flew back to New York and that is the last I heard of that. I consider myself important, and I am important, but FIFA is important also and people should respect FIFA. I, as president, made Mr Murdoch respect FIFA in a certain way.

Keith Cooper, FIFA's director of communications, confirmed the president's preoccupation with protocol in matters such as these:

> Havelange hates people to be late. I remember once in Madrid, at a time when both France and Morocco were bidding to host the 1998 World Cup Finals, King Hassan II of Morocco kept the president waiting for two hours because he was held up in a meeting with King Juan Carlos of Spain. Havelange was furious, and did Morocco get the World Cup?

Cooper's story is obviously a dramatic enhancement, and there were many other factors which worked against Morocco's bid. Nevertheless, the impact of King Hassan's breach of protocol, in Havelange's eyes, should not be under estimated.

We had waited for more than two years to be granted an audience with the FIFA president. In early 1997 we had received a message from FIFA headquarters, inviting us to interview the president while he was attending the international board's annual meeting in Belfast, Northern Ireland, in March. Twenty-four hours before the interview, the president called it off. In summer 1997, prior to conducting fieldwork in South America, we made a final request to

233

see Havelange, and, since we were in the neighbourhood, suggested his Rio de Janeiro office. He declined this request (learning of his snub to Mark McCormack made us feel better about this), but on our return we received a further communiqué from Zurich inviting us to interview the president on 4 September in Cairo.

Unlike the King of Morocco, we arrived respectfully early for our appointment with the president. Thus it was, after walking nervously past several heavily armed guards (standard issue ear-pieces and compact sub-machine guns), we found ourselves entering Havelange's opulent suite of rooms and offices in the Cairo Sheraton. While no one should doubt the aura of supreme authority which surrounds the man, particularly when at the centre of the FIFA empire, he was, at the same time, disarmingly courteous, charming and accessible (he moved our seats around and instructed his secretary to block his phone calls). However, he created the atmosphere of an audience rather than an interview, and one which reminded us of one of the opening scenes in Francis Ford Coppola's film *The Godfather*- apposite given the number of times 'the family' had been evoked as a metaphor for FIFA and its networks.

Our conversation was structured around four related themes – the Havelange biography; FIFA's commercial basis and business partners; his role as politician and world statesman; and his view of FIFA in the post-Havelange era.

Understanding Havelange's own background is of critical importance in comprehending the way he modelled FIFA during the twenty-four years of his reign. We had read much of his biography in official publications, but it was only while listening to his own version of it that it dawned on us that the developmental model which he adopted for FIFA was deeply rooted in his own past: his knowledge of global commerce, gleaned as a child from his father; his experience in building companies; his work in the Brazilian Sports Federation, and his notion of what it is to be Brazilian:

> My father and mother were both Belgian. My father was a mining engineer at the mining university in Liège which is very famous. My mother was from a family which was involved in copper mining in the Liège region. My father then left Belgium in 1902 to become professor of a mining university in Peru. He was there for ten years and then returned to Belgium to get married. They moved to Brazil as representatives of the United States Steel. He was a representative of several American and Belgian companies in Brazil. Also as a representative of the cotton industry from Britain. He was also representing an Australian company also in the textile industry. Also representing armaments companies, particularly French. My father was not a wealthy man, but nevertheless I had a comfortable childhood.

Already as a young teenager I was going to my father's office and helping decoding the then current telegram system – no faxes of course, but a
system of decoding international messages so I was already helping in
my father's office as a young teenager. My father died when I was eighteen. I went to work, went to study and paid for this study, although I
wasn't earning very much, but I was learning something for life. I went to
speak with a company which had a Belgian link – iron and steel construction company. I served a kind of self-imposed apprenticeship in this company doing all the administrative work but also dealing with the workers,
receiving clients, everything to do with the organization of this company
for about ten dollars per week. After six years I went to the boss of the
company and said, 'I'm resigning. I never want to work for another boss
again in my life.' I have never had another boss in my life, except maybe
my wife! I then served as a lawyer for a couple of years before becoming
managing director of my own transport company. Twenty million people
a year are transported by my company which I have now been with for
fifty-seven years (fifty-three years as chairman), also being the director of
the biggest insurance company in Brazil – when I became president of
FIFA I had to take a step down in that company.

I had the good fortune to be born a Brazilian, which is a multi-racial
society, Indian, blacks, Arabs, Jews, European, Japanese, Korean, Latinos,
everything. All the various races of the world joined together to make a
multi-racial world. In São Paulo and Rio there are streets with Arabs living on one side and Jews on the other side and they live in the same street
in perfect harmony. One of my closest business associates and friends
since boyhood is a son of a Jewish father and they have been the closest
possible friends since childhood and one of the lawyers in his automobile
company is Arab. Brazil is the eighth industrial power in the world and
São Paulo is a city just like industrial Germany, it is absolutely an industr-
ialized world. There are various European ethnics in the south of Brazil,
who are developing that area very rapidly. Northern Brazil is a little like
Africa. It has a more wild terrain and is less developed, but is evolving/
developing quickly. It was an advantage for me when I became president
of FIFA that since a small child I have lived together with all the different
races and understood their mentalities. It is nothing new for me to be in
FIFA's multi-racial environment.

Brazil lives for football. What Brazil wanted more than anything else
when I became president of the Brazilian federation was to win the World
Cup, but they weren't organized. I brought with me the entrepreneurial
skills/the business skills from my own company to the federation. For
instance, when I arrived at the motor bus company we had 200 buses now
there are 3,000. When I started they were just urban routes but now inter-
city routes, for example between Rio and São Paulo my company runs
sixty trips a day between the two cities – 460 kilometres in six hours. I
developed an administrative side to the bus company – and applied the
same principle on coming to the Brazilian Federation. To begin with there
were just coaches, but I brought in specialist doctors, administrators for
the federation to give it a wider basis. This is what made the difference
and why they won the World Cup in 1958, 1962 and 1970. So, when I
came to FIFA, I had the experience first hand of organizing a team on the

235

field, but equally importantly the administrative side of how to build up a whole administration of the federation.

Havelange emphasizes his steeped commercial acumen and how critical this has been to his approach to the administration and development of world football. This he believes to have been absolutely necessary in an era during which football has grown to be one of the biggest commercial markets on the planet and, significantly, in his eyes, an important area of employment:

There is nowadays in football a very important economic financial aspect to the game. Economically speaking we mustn't forget the huge problem which exists in the world today which is unemployment. Football directly involves/employs some 200 million people around the world which is a major factor in the world-wide fight against unemployment. You could say it is the biggest multinational organization in the world. Unemployment is a huge problem and football goes a long way to resolving that problem. Machines are taking over the world if you like. But there is no place for machines in football, they can't play, they can't referee, they can't coach, they can't be doctors and they can't spectate. Football is the reserve of human beings. You could say that football generates a turnover of 250 billion dollars. General Motors is 170 billion dollars. It puts in perspective the inevitable importance of football economically speaking. You can watch football on television anywhere, anytime now along with its publicity content. You have to multiply by five the number of people directly involved in football to see the full extent of its economic reach, (and this factor of five has been studied and confirmed) then you get to 1.5 billion people world-wide involved directly/indirectly in the game.

Havelange prioritizes the significant expansion in world football during his period of office as the most important part of his legacy, while at the same time recognizing the commercial dynamics behind this:

Without doubt the most important thing has been the development of the game itself and the game itself particularly through the growth of the competitions. Not only the World Cup itself, which indeed has become amplified up to thirty-two teams now, but also the introduction of the two youth championships. We have the whole development of women's football, indoor football of course, the Olympic football tournaments, which have taken on a new dimension, a new importance – both of them – men's and women's. And a new departure now which is interesting to follow a new phenomenon which is beach soccer . . . There are all these sponsors because it is attractive – football in every form is attractive. So this is an illustration of how football is always moving from one thing to another. But we should also mention the courses, the football development courses as another aspect of my accomplishments. The growth of the interest in the game with accumulated TV audience in 1994 of some 32/34 billion and projected for France of about 41 billion this is absolutely unique. You can send a man to the moon or have a visit from the Pope, but it doesn't compare with this. I will not stand again as president of FIFA next year, that's my decision – I will be eighty-two years old. But by the time that I leave office on the basis of the contracts that have either already been signed, or will be signed by the middle of next year, I am proud to be able to leave a heritage for FIFA, for world football, of four billion dollars (five billion Swiss Francs).

Havelange recognizes that the expansion of football by FIFA under his leadership could not have been achieved without forging links with powerful commercial partners such as Coca-Cola. He also recognizes the significance played in such partnerships by the late boss of Adidas, Horst Dassler:

When I became president there was hardly twenty dollars in the cash box and now it gives me great personal satisfaction to know that things have moved on from there. I will leave with the cash box substantially filled with four billion . . . Mr Dassler gave his total support to me. There was already a relationship of a kind between Adidas and FIFA, which was then accelerated or increased so that the development programme that I had in my 1974 manifesto could be realized. Mr Dassler opened the door for me to Coca-Cola through Mr Killeen, who was the President of Coca-Cola. The contract was signed with Coca-Cola in London in 1975 and since then, for almost a quarter of a century, FIFA has worked with Coca-Cola through a coaching development programme which has served more than 40,000 participants. This illustrates the strength and influence of football in the commercial sphere. At that time, twenty or so years ago, Coca-Cola didn't exist in China or the Soviet Union or in the Arab countries. It was largely thanks to the FIFA Coca-Cola Cup and the obligation of host countries to accept Coca-Cola into their territories that Coca-Cola got their foot in the door, so to speak, of these countries. It was through the FIFA competitions in China in 1985, the first under-16 World Championships, and the FIFA Coca-Cola Cup in the Soviet Union, also in 1985, and in Saudi Arabia in 1989, that Coca-Cola was able to access these important markets. It shows the value and the strength of FIFA as a promotional partner for the commercial partner. This relationship has never been a problem because both sides know that FIFA is responsible for football and Coca-Cola is responsible for Coca-Cola and the two respect each other and know their parameters and their limits. The day when the partnership is only in favour of only one partner there is no more partnership.

We moved on from biography and commerce to discuss the political and diplomatic dimensions of the president's period of office. Havelange's attitude towards the mixing of sport and politics is interesting. Rhetorically, he adopts the old Sir Stanley Rous line that football and politics should not overlap. He consigns to the realm of diplomacy the fact that much of his time as FIFA president has been spent dealing with political issues, believing that, 'if you can use football to solve a political problem then it is entirely justifiable'. To illustrate how he operated as a diplomat, Havelange highlighted three problematic areas which he had confronted as president: China, South Africa and the Middle East.

Twenty-five years before I became president, China had pulled out of FIFA. In 1975 there was an Executive Committee meeting in Senegal. I asked if, as a new president with this diplomatic status so to speak, I could go to China to try to bring them back in again. I arrived in Beijing on the 4th May 1975 and met with the Chinese leaders – meeting for more than seven hours and every time the conversation came back to a political aspect. Mao Zedong was still in power and negotiations were very, very difficult. I put forward six ideas during this meeting and they rejected all of them. Halfway through this meeting when they were rejecting everything I said, 'Excuse me, I would like to go and make a telephone call' and they said, 'To whom?'. I said, 'I want to call my Brazilian ambassador here', and they said, 'What for?' I said, 'well as you don't seem to want to talk about football you only want to talk about politics, it is better that the ambassador is here and not me – I've got nothing to do with this conversation', so they immediately changed their attitude and said 'Now wait a minute I'm sure we can find a solution'. So I then – having exhausted the first six proposals the meeting took this turn – I then took out the seventh proposal which I had been holding back, which was a sporting/diplomatic solution not a political one. It took four personal visits to China each year for five years specifically to resolve this problem.

The problem with the Chinese revolved around the nature of the people of Taiwan – it is not that they wanted to take over Taiwan, but that they wanted for the world to consider it as all one country. I understood the sensitivities between mainland China and Taiwan and that had to be respected in order for China to come back into FIFA. It was important to call it China Football Association for mainland China and Taiwan was not allowed to fly its own flag nor play its own anthem – in competitions. The Chinese agreed to that principle in Beijing. I flew to Hong Kong and Taipei and met with the military commander, General Chung, who was also the president of the federation. He refused to sign because he wanted to be called China also. I went to my briefcase and took out something which had been made in Taiwan with the label on it 'made in Taiwan' and said, 'If you are really China why do you say made in Taiwan?' He signed straight away. In the Zurich congress of 1980 the congress accepted both China and Taiwan by a unanimous decision. That was another political problem put away.

In the preceding pages we have stressed how significant the South African issue was in the downfall of Sir Stanley Rous. The following represents Havelange's recollection of events and subsequent developments in African football:

In 1960, when I was president of the Brazilian Sports Federation, the Brazilian football team went to play a match in Cape Town. There were some coloured players in that team and when they arrived in Cape Town the authorities would not let them land. As a result of that experience upon returning to Brazil I said, 'OK we have no more sporting relationships with South Africa.' Many times since I had to pass through Johannesburg to go to other countries in southern Africa, and contacts slowly built up without a great deal of publicity and then obviously accelerated somewhat when Nelson Mandela came to power. I went to see Nelson Mandela to congratulate him and thank him for all that he had done to liberate his own country, to promise support – they have the African Cup of Nations and it is my personal opinion that Africa and more specifically South Africa should have the World Cup in 2006. All the political problems of South Africa are truly in the past and I would like to think that I have also played this little part in the rehabilitation of that country. There aren't many people, if any, who have visited all the fifty-one countries of the African continent as I have done, and most of them at least three times, to show a personal attachment. Really this is unprecedented and I feel that this is an important part of my mission. African football has increased enormously in quality and respect, hundreds of African players have played in Europe, played very well – the fruits of twenty years of work with FIFA.

One of the first 'diplomatic' issues which Havelange confronted as president was the dispute over territory and sovereignty between Israel and Palestine. This has been an ongoing concern for FIFA and he sees this area as his last great political challenge:

You will remember the PLO's attack on the Israeli athletes at the Munich Olympics in 1972? When I became president of FIFA I was determined that such a thing would never happen in football. In '75 I was at the final of the Asian Cup Final in Tehran between Iran and Israel. Eighty thousand spectators in the stadium in Tehran, Iran beat Israel 1–0 and you could say 'thank God' that they did because it is difficult to imagine what may have happened otherwise. Next day I had to leave for Montreal in preparation for the Olympic Games, to go and look at the football stadium, and then back to Brazil. Then I had to leave to go to Israel and meet with the prime minister and the president of the republic and the president of the football association. I proposed that because of what I had just seen (in Tehran), and this constant tension with Israel and the Arab countries, the best thing to do would be for Israel to be taken out of the Asian Confederation and put together with Oceania, geographically distant of course, but politically more acceptable. The Israelis accepted and I flew back to Brazil, changed the passports again – two passports because of the stamps – and arrived in the eight Gulf countries, to tell them of this idea. At first they were not very convinced, but finally they came to that way of thinking and agreed, voted in favour of that, even though it was strictly speaking against the statutes. That really solved the problem because they never came into direct contact with each other again. Later, once the precedent had been set, we were able to move Israel into UEFA.

239

Already when I first took office in 1974 the Saudi Arabian Football Association wrote to me asking that FIFA recognize Palestine. My reply was that according to the statutes FIFA could not do that because Palestine was not a political entity, a political territory which the statutes demand. A year or so later, when I was building-up this relationship with the Arab countries, they wrote again – the same thing. I said, 'OK, we can do this if you take part of your Saudi Arabian territory and designate that as Palestine which otherwise doesn't exist and then you can make that the federation.' I never got a response to that letter!

One day during the World Cup (USA '94) I had a telephone call from Al Gore [vice-president of the United States]. At that time Gore was involved in negotiating for a peaceful settlement in the Middle East. Mr Gore said he really had no experience of football before, but he was amazed that the World Cup could be so perfectly organized and that so many people could become so passionately involved. He was greatly inspired by this and asked would it not be possible to have a match between Palestine and Israel, organized by FIFA? I replied, 'No – we are sport we are not politics in that sense', which didn't please Mr Gore, who became very upset. Because of his reaction I said, 'Okay, we can look into that and see if it is possible.' So then I wrote to Saudi Arabia and asked for an audience with the King. Through the intermediary of Prince Faisal, King Fahed [of Saudi Arabia] said he was delighted to hear this initiative and offered to give the Palestine Football Federation 100 million dollars to get them going. Now things have moved on and Palestine is a more clearly defined political entity and is in the process of obtaining full FIFA membership. Next week I will be in Jordan to meet the Palestine Football Federation officials. (I can't go to Palestine itself because it is still complicated to travel in some of those areas.) The project now is indeed to have such a match, Palestine versus Israel, ideally in New York – New York being the seat of the United Nations – just to show the politicians that football can do things which they cannot!

As we have seen, Havelange believes that he will leave FIFA in a much healthier state than he found it. He has some interesting thoughts on FIFA's future, the qualities which should be looked for in his successor, and insights into the work regime required of one of the world's most powerful sports administrators:

Football will continue to progress, it will never go back. My successor should have no problem to administer FIFA because of the depth of the financial resources and the strength of the game that I have left behind. There is no doubt about it, the World Cup must remain the pre-eminent event, it must continue to enthrall people world-wide because it is central and fundamental to FIFA's own continuing financial well-being – that is the main source of FIFA's income. Whoever follows me must not think only about money, he must see it on a wider level. Football must continue to develop in these various ways that we have discussed in order to reach out and touch and to help as many people as possible and not just those who are already well off.

As to my successor, first, he must have an administrative skill – most essential. He must understand figures and money in the way that I have understood that you must turn red figures into black. Those financial and administrative aspects are only really important as long as football continues to develop. Second, he must continue to spread the game, and courses and competitions are fundamental. Ten years ago or so when these youth competitions were starting it was difficult sometimes to find countries that were ready to organize it, but now we've got New Zealand and then Trinidad and they seem lined up until 2003 which shows the success of these initiatives. It is the same thing with the under twenties for 2006 and 2010. Third, my successor has got to consider FIFA as a family – one which works to keep a balance and equilibrium across all the regions of the world. Fourth he must be dedicated and tireless. My home is in Rio, but 300 days a year I am not there. Fifteen times a year just to Zurich, 340 hours in an aeroplane just to Rio and Zurich, you can add onto that another 460 hours for the rest of the world. Sitting in an aeroplane for 800 hours a year, an average of ten full working days a month dedicated to FIFA, apart from those days. No matter where I am, there is a call that goes to FIFA every day and these calls are backed up by fax communications so that there is a file and everything is documented. There are replies, of course, a record of everything is retained. So the mentality has to be 'to serve' and not to think of any personal glorification or personal benefit. If you are not ready to serve in this sense and depth you cannot be president.

Apart from a brief mention in his biography, during our interview Havelange was conspicuously quiet about the development of the game in his own continent, South America. Indeed during our fieldwork in Latin America it became clear that Havelange was by no means universally popular. In Argentina and Uruguay he was perceived as being both a self-serving agent of international interests and too pro-Brazilian. Ironically, within Brazil itself, the president is not unanimously respected for his achievements in football administration. While we were in Brazil the breaking story was of Havelange's latest confrontation with Pelé, now Brazil's sports minister, over the financial and administrative reform of Brazilian football and FIFA's stance against it, threatening to the expulsion of Brazil from FIFA and the World Cup.[2]

■ The Man Who Would be King? Lennart Johansson

We had to negotiate hard to get an interview with the UEFA president, Lennart Johansson. However, during the course of these negotiations, with him and his team, something must have encouraged him to believe that his campaigning for the presidency could not be damaged by speaking with us and thus making a contribution to this book. We are quite sure of this because upon entering his suite of rooms in the equally opulent Cairo Marriot, the first thing he did was to offer us an exclusive copy of his election manifesto which would not be released to the press for several months. We were given this document on a handshake agreement that we would use it only in this book. We have kept our word and the full document is appended to this afterword. Many of the answers which we sought originally are contained in this document. What follows are mainly Johansson's views of things which are not spelled out in his manifesto.

The biography of the man who would most dearly like to succeed Havelange is, in some ways, similar to that of the Brazilian, and in other ways very different:

> I was brought up with six children, my father was a carpenter, I had to learn what I have learned in the nights and work in the daytime, that gives me a view of reality and made me believe in democratic ideas and this is part of my vision. For forty years I was involved in a business, a national concern (trucking) and a member of the international management so I also have sound business views. I think this is important. But, I also know the smells in the dressing room and this is more important. It's not that I was a first division player [but] I played football (and ice hockey and handball). I was born to the sport, I was dedicated to the sport, I experienced small clubs, I became president of a big club, president of a national association, then of the European confederation – that generates 80%–90% of world football's income, we had seven teams in the quarter finals of the last World Cup, so I think we know a lot also about this type of business (FIFA).

During our interview he continually stressed his democratic credentials, part of his Swedish heritage, and this informed his veiled criticisms of Havelange's regime and his suggestions for the reform of FIFA:

> I try as much as possible to avoid criticism of a man who has earned so much respect . . . I think that he must be given quite a lot of credit for the development of football within these years since 1974. He has first of all seen to it to keep the family together, the whole football family together, he has seen to it that those involved in our game pay respect to football and its rules and regulations, he has upgraded the image of football . . . You will always have to start with giving him credit for what he has done. But that was his time, and that's another story, there's time for certain changes now for the next decade.

Johansson was particularly critical of the system of autocracy and patronage through which, he believed, Havelange had manipulated

FIFA's extensive committee structure. He cites the example of Havelange's close friend and business associate and media giant, the late FIFA senior vice-president, Guillermo Cañedo's stewardship of FIFA's media committee as an example of potential conflict of interest:

> Mr Cañedo for sure was in the media business and he was high up in the FIFA hierarchy. He made a certain kind of business through his position. If someone in the future is in that position, it would be most important that he was not involved in the decision-making process [about the awarding of media contracts]. This would not be correct.

He was also critical of the way, under Havelange, the FIFA general secretary, had become powerful in ways which were less than accountable, attributing this more to the way Havelange ran FIFA, than to Sepp Blatter's personality:

> He [the general secretary] is supposed to do what the Executive Committee tells him to do and to handle the administration of organization. He is not the 'godfather' of football. With all respect to Mr. Blatter, who does he think he is? In fact it's not his fault, it's our [FIFA's] fault to let him make these statements.

But his harshest criticisms are directed towards Havelange's use of the Executive Committee to rubber stamp decisions which the president has taken alone or with close confidants, such as Blatter:

> The procedure through which decisions are made must be different than it is today. It's not acceptable that you get a bunch of papers the same morning as you have a meeting that you are supposed to take a decision on, matters that have a long term effect. These are things that can be changed.

He realises the significance of the African vote in terms of the politics which swirl around the forthcoming election, but is reluctant to admit that any closeness between UEFA and CAF has any bearing on his candidature. He views UEFA's 'special relationship' with CAF as one which is based upon mutuality:

> By culture and by tradition we are closer to Africa than any other continent. We have an agreement about co-operation which comes from us and it's not to gain votes, it's because you see the need for the development of the African sector. It's fair of us, we think, to give a contribution to Africa within fields which perhaps are a little bit less advanced than our own. This doesn't exclude co-operation with other confederations, it's only that the Africans, on the whole, while there are exceptions, are

243

still in a very poor situation. They are in the same need as the former Soviet Union countries and the Baltic states. It's good for football that we help Africa. Football is not a self-playing piano and we have to protect football for the future. We have to go for development from the grass roots, from the amateurs, that's very important. We have a tendency to concentrate the focus on top class football. Without the base you have no summit and vice-versa. We have learned this.

Johansson was one of the main protagonists for the co-hosting arrangement between Japan and South Korea for the World Cup Finals in 2002. We asked him how and why this decision had been reached and his answer contains elements of pragmatism and diplomatic mission:

> Now we are no longer, as in Stockholm in 1958, eight teams in the World Cup, no longer sixteen teams, no longer twenty-four, we are thirty-two teams, there are a limited number of countries that can arrange such an event. Now we have the experience of women's football – Sweden and Norway took the Women's World Cup and we are looking forward to the co-hosting of the European Championships in Belgium and Holland, 2000. I can see that this is a solution that can be used. We have to gain experience and this is an excellent opportunity to do so. Why did I and UEFA and all the others support co-hosting, and finally why was it proposed by the president, who originally gave favour to Japan? In the first place, it was because these two spent billions and billions in their attempts to win the right to host the world cup. Our committee who went there came back and said, 'these two are equal, cast a coin!' We said this is crazy, why not here try something that we have already prepared and partially had tried in our area. So that was the decision. This was not the only reason. With relations politically strained – you know we don't interfere with politics, we look at realities – we could see that Japan and Korea has tried since the Second World War and earlier to come together again, but there was no chance. By picking one or the other we would have created a bigger mess with one big loser and one big winner. South Korea was prepared to join us and Japan came to me late at night. Then I knew the situation and I said, 'I'll give you strong advice to support the idea' and they did. Both parties, not only in football but in the political area, through the ambassadors, had thanked us for this decision. I am naive enough to believe that this will be a success, that this will be something that will be followed.

Whether it is something which will be followed by Germany and England in 2006 remains to be seen. On this matter, Johansson was unequivocal in his criticism of the English FA's approach:

> Why did we give preference to Germany and not to England? Because we had a gentleman's agreement on this. All the big nations were present, you can go to Spain you can go to any of them and they know that we said, 'Let's go for England Euro '96 and for Germany World Cup 2006, to

avoid that we have more than one candidate.' A new management set up in the English FA did not appreciate this 'gentleman's' agreement.

In the months building up to the Paris 1998 FIFA Congress, it was by no means certain that Johansson would be elected unopposed to FIFA's top post. To do so he would have to convince people like Chuck Blazer, the general secretary of CONCACAF (thirty votes) that his election would be more than a confirmation of Eurocentric interests. Likewise, Charles Dempsey, the president of Oceania (ten votes), a newly confirmed full confederation which has greatly benefited from Havelange's alliances with less developed regions, fears that Johansson's candidature could herald a return to Europe's imperious control over the destiny of world football. Johansson's response to such concerns is characteristically candid and realistic:

> They criticize me and say that I focus on European football. That is true to a certain extent because this is what the statutes tell me, to represent European football in the Executive Committee of FIFA. When I become FIFA president I can only promise them that the minute I become president of FIFA it's the global focus that I will adopt immediately. The risk is, that in order to demonstrate my objectivity I will go too far, and perhaps this will be a disadvantage for the European football.

It is clear that Johansson's campaign for the FIFA presidency is built on a platform which prioritizes openness and honesty. He sees it as an open race but wonders where his competitors will come from:

> I welcome anyone who will stand up against me, but it is late. Most of those who take part in the election they are interested in the game, they are fascinated by the game, they are dedicated to the game and they like to know who the candidate is, what does he stand for, is he prepared to give a full statement to which he is bound for the future? I am prepared to do so (I have given you a copy!). I read about a number of names who may stand against me, but none of them themselves stood up, they were mentioned by others. The media produce some candidates in order to get something to write about. The fact is, I told them about a year ago, when I was asked to stand, so there is no doubt about giving the chance to anyone to come forward and oppose me . . . If anyone is better he might step up. I don't say that I am that good, but I've been asked to go for the presidency and I think I can do a good job. I'm prepared to make my public declarations about my visions for the future, and then, may the best man win!

■ King Maker? Issa Hayatou

In 1988 Cameroonian, Issa Hayatou, was elected to the presidency of CAF after the death of the legendary Ydnekatchev Tessema the previous year. Tessema was a powerful role model. It was he, more than anybody else, who was responsible for modernizing CAF and making sure that Africa took its place as a partner rather than a supplicant within FIFA. Above all, Tessema was a tireless campaigner for African rights in the international arena and against political interference and corruption within African football itself. It is significant that CAF's Cairo offices, at El Borg, on an island in the centre of the Nile, have diplomatic status and all of the rights, immunities and privileges that go with it. This protects CAF from the political intrusions which are frequently experienced by football federations throughout the continent. It was at CAF's headquarters that we met Hayatou, who had managed to squeeze us in between a meeting with Havelange and FIFA's top brass and a surprise visit by the Nigerian foreign minister.

Hayatou is continuing Tessema's fight against political interference and corruption, seeing these close relatives as African football's biggest problems:

> This is the main problem facing African football – the instability of the federations caused by the interference of governments. This is a problem for the majority of federations in Africa. We are trying with FIFA to control this. It is only with stability that the African federations will develop and only then will an African nation reach the final of the World Cup. Another major problem concerns material resources and other infrastructural concerns. This too is partially a problem of instability.

Despite such problems, Hayatou still believes that Africa should have its turn to host the World Cup Finals:

> Apart from Europe and South America, the World Cup has already been organised by CONCACAF [USA '94] and by Asia [Korea/Japan 2002]. It is only fair that Africa has a chance also. Dr Havelange stressed the principle of rotation and that it should come to Africa. He proposes South Africa because it is the most experienced country for organizing this kind of thing. Also, where we are here, Egypt, is capable of hosting the World Cup with its first class hotels, transport, telecommunications and everything.

He believes that the Western media distort and exaggerate the nature of Africa's problems, and that when it comes to things like host-

246

ing the World Cup and other FIFA competitions, First World countries conspire against Africa to suit their own interests. The transfer-
ring of the Youth World Championships from Nigeria to Qatar in
1995 is an outstanding example of something which was perceived
by all Africa as an imperialistic affront. Hayatou spells out his concerns with regard to a potential South African bid to host the World
Cup in 2006:

> The media has a point of view about South Africa saying that it has no
> security, but security is no better in many other big cities – take New York,
> for instance, robberies, murder, Mafia and such like, but it hosted games
> during the 1994 World Cup. When it comes to Africa the media exagger-
> ates the problem. We had the African Cup of Nations in South Africa and
> nobody was killed! Also, the Rugby World Cup was held there and no-
> body was killed! When it's Africa, the media presents it as a special prob-
> lem, why should this be so? Whose interests does this serve?

Hayatou acknowledges the considerable progress which has been
made in African football during the period of Havelange's reign,
particularly through FIFA (and Coca-Cola)-sponsored development
programmes in 'administration, para-medics and coaching'. He recognizes that with the expansion of African places in the World Cup
Finals – increasing from three to five and FIFA Executive members
rising from three to four – that in the Havelange years Africa's status
in world football has been significantly enhanced. Nevertheless,
Hayatou recognizes that Havelange has not always acted in Africa's
best interests. For instance, in July 1992, FIFA rejected for the second
time Morocco's bid to host the World Cup Finals. Hayatou was in-
censed:

> Where is democracy? I am ready to fight for the prevailing of justice within
> FIFA. I regret that Mr Havelange has not behaved as a judge as he should
> have. But why doesn't he also say that he is wearing a shirt and playing
> instead of the Africans?[3]

Significantly, many of the gains made by CAF, particularly in the
last decade, Hayatou attributes to a growing alliance with UEFA:

> These proposals [to increase World Cup places and Executive members]
> came from CAF, not FIFA. FIFA proposed four World Cup places for Af-
> rica, but we proposed five and we got five because of the support of UEFA.
> Also, it was only through the support of the Europeans that we got an
> extra Executive Committee member. Now CAF has a very good relation-
> ship with UEFA. Only this year [January] 1997 we signed a protocol of co-
> operation with UEFA [the Europeans pledging wide-ranging support for

247

the development of African football, independent of FIFA's own work].
Yesterday there was a meeting between UEFA and CAF which went very
well.

There was an apparently strong base for this new level of co-operation. Hayatou declared in Lisbon, after the first 'conjoint meeting' of
the two confederations: ' "From now on both Federations are running on the freeway of the international football development. They
are the pillars of FIFA, the focal point of the football planet". '[4] Such
levels of co-operation between CAF and UEFA can only work to the
advantage of Johansson in his attempt to be elected to the FIFA presidency in 1998. Hayatou was reluctant to be drawn on this issue, saying that who Africa intended to back for the presidency was a matter
for the CAF congress in February 1998. (Chuck Blazer and Charles
Dempsey were similarly guarded in their assessments of how their
own confederation's block votes would be delivered.) Significantly,
however, he more or less ruled himself out as a candidate, saying
that, while he would not dismiss the idea of his own candidature in
the future, 'this moment was not right' for an African candidate.
Hayatou's circumspection did little to discourage the view that a deal
had been done whereby if he delivered Africa for Johannson in 1998,
the Swede, when he stepped down, could deliver Europe for Hayatou.
As Charles Dempsey told us, if Hayatou can deliver the African vote
and Johansson can count on the backing of his fellow Europeans, no
matter how ill at ease Havelange may feel about being succeeded by
the Swede, come the FIFA Congress in Paris in June 1998, mathemat-
ics decrees that there will be nothing that the Brazilian can do to
prevent it.

■ Conclusion

Has anything in this afterword led us to alter our overall conclusions to this book? We think not. Our fieldwork in Cairo reinforces
our view that Havelange must take great credit for the reform of
FIFA, an organization which had become moribund towards the end
of Stanley Rous's career. Perhaps someone other than Havelange
would have been able to pioneer the global development of the game
and its massively increased commercial foundation. Likewise, maybe
somebody else would have championed the cause of football's poor
relations in Africa, Asia, Oceania and North and Central America.
However, in our interview with him we became convinced that his

background and his personality (a charismatic Brazilian business-man with a global gaze, an autocratic manner and a considerable ego) made him ideally suited to spearhead and force through a nec-essary revolution in world football. In development terms there can be no doubting the depth of this legacy. Perhaps the outstanding question remains: what will be the cost for the future of the game, of the wider and wider opening of FIFA's door to the media and mar-keting people?

Having given such recognition to Havelange's achievements, we are equally convinced that the time for change has come. If the no-tion of football as the world's most popular sport – the peoples' game – is to be more than a rhetorical gesture toward democracy, FIFA needs to be reformed in such a way that its global presence is re-flected in the manner through which decisions are made and imple-mented. It is only through openness and accountability that an organization, which, by its own admission, has grown into one of the world's biggest income generators, can truly be seen to be work-ing in the best interests of football and football people. There is a delicate balance to be achieved between football development, com-mercial success, diplomacy and democracy. Havelange will be a very hard act to follow. We must hope that whoever succeeds him will have the vision and capacities to achieve such a balance, 'for the good of the game'.

■
Appendix

August 1997

VISION for the Future Governance of Football
by Lennart Johansson

Preface
"Football can only maintain its leading role if our world-wide movement retains its spirit of solidarity'"

It is my firm belief that, in the future, football will be challenged in several different ways. Many steps have to be taken to guide the world-wide football movement towards modern structures. Football has a glorious past and a wonderful present, but the success stories of the past are of little relevance to the problems of tomorrow. The challenges that lie ahead cannot be tackled by one person alone, in his capacity as FIFA president. What is needed is an international, democratic network based on trust, transparency, loyalty and solidarity. These fundamental elements will lead our sport successfully into the next century.

The world football movement is a community. For this reason, FIFA has to further strengthen its democratic governance, as the United Nations of world football. In order to strengthen the democratic spirit and establish a fair system of balance between FIFA, the confederations and the associations, a revised structure must be openly discussed and then implemented.

Besides democratic governance, the professional management of the world-wide football movement is also of paramount importance.

It is for this reason that I am presenting this VISION paper, with the following five fields of action and the key objectives:

1. *Football at Grassroots Level*
   Strengthen the entire world-wide football movement
2. *Football at Professional Level*
   Define clear objectives and monitor the development of top-class football
3. *Football at Management Level*
   Involve the representatives of the national associations and the confederations in all FIFA activities
4. *FIFA and the Confederations*
   Redefine the role and functions of the confederations in the FIFA statutes
5. *FIFA and the National Associations*
   Strengthen the national associations politically, financially and structurally

In this VISION paper, FIFA's tasks are defined as those of a global nature, whereas the Confederations would assume all functions which can be better dealt with at a continental level, taking into account the growing importance of the Confederations since their foundation, and the associations would assume all functions which can be better dealt with at national or even regional level.

This VISION paper describes the most important criteria to which I intend to lead the world football's governing body FIFA into the next century. I will be able to fulfil this task with the help of all those who support the ideals of solidarity and democracy within the family of football.

Lennart Johansson

VISION for the Future Governance of Football

1. Football at Grassroots Level
Strengthen the entire world-wide football movement

- Increase participation in every country and in all sectors and levels
- Facilitate access to football for everyone, regardless of sex, ability and age

- Launch world-wide grassroots programmes in co-operation with the associations, clubs, schools, communities, sponsors and media
- Improve educational standards of coaches, referees and officials at all levels
- Increase awareness of the social importance and responsibility of football in every single country

2. Football at Professional Level
Define clear objectives and monitor the development of top-class football

- Establish, promote and enforce detailed code of conduct for all participants in the game
- Define the legal structure of professional clubs and leagues and their relationship with the national associations, confederations and FIFA
- Ensure a fair share of the confederations in organising final rounds of FIFA competitions
- Implement a fixed match calendar for qualifying competitions in co-operation with the confederations. The present World Cup format remains unchanged, i.e. 32 teams
- Ensure co-operation with the Olympic Movement
- Create an Under-20 competition for women at world level
- Create the logistical and financial base to permit inter-continental competitions for national and club teams

3. Football at Management Level
Involve the representatives of the national associations and the confederations in all FIFA activities

- Ensure a fair share of leadership within FIFA. The number of presidential terms to be limited by a statutory amendment. The maximum duration of the presidency to be set by the FIFA congress.
- Meetings between the FIFA president and the presidents of the confederations will take place at least four times per year
- The presidents of the confederations will automatically become members of the FIFA Executive Committee and vice-presidents of FIFA
- FIFA Executive Committee members will chair a FIFA committee in accordance with their specific capacities

- Members of FIFA committees will be proposed by the national associations to their confederation, which will then propose them to FIFA
- All committee member appointments will be approved by the FIFA Executive Committee
- The chairmen of committees within the confederations should automatically be members of the respective FIFA committees
- Development of a long-term financial and marketing plan for FIFA by the Executive Committee
- The general secretaries of the confederations will attend FIFA Executive Committee meetings in a consultative capacity

4. FIFA and the Confederations
Redefine the role and functions of the confederations in the FIFA statutes

- FIFA president to have regular meetings with the Confederations
- Allocate an appropriate contribution from the World Cup to the confederations, to strengthen each of them in their aim to promote football by investing in sporting, technical and administrative matters
- Support the confederations to complete and train their full-time staff in the following sectors:

  * management
  * technical development/coaching
  * development programmes
  * marketing/PR
  * medical services
  * competitions
  * refereeing
  * legal matters
  * media services

- FIFA to delegate all areas where the confederations can act independently, namely in all continental related business matters
- FIFA to support the confederations to set up their own development programmes
- FIFA to entrust the confederations with the task of ensuring that the higher income from the World Cup will be used by the national associations for increased investment in grassroots and other development programmes

5. FIFA and the National Associations
Strengthen the national associations politically, financially and structurally

- FIFA to maintain the "one country-one vote" system
- Defend the integrity, authority and independence of national associations from external interference
- Strengthen the position of the national teams of the member associations
- Defend the principles of ethics and fair-play in the game, and strengthen the social importance of football within society.
- Reserve a substantial part of World Cup income for distribution in equal parts to all member associations. This allocation will not be less than one million US dollars per association and is to be used for concrete projects, grassroots programmes, participation in competitions, education and technical equipment. The projects will be defined in co-operation with the confederations according to the needs of each association.

Notes

CHAPTER 1 INTRODUCTION

1 Walvin, *The People's Game* p. 186. Walvin's 'people's' refers to the popular working classes in Britain. Hereafter, our use of the term recognizes the global importance of the game for the 'peoples' of the world – hence the use of the plural possessive.

2 MacAloon, 'The Ethnographic Imperative', p. 117.

3 Sugden, 'Fieldworkers Rush In'.

4 See Douglas, *Investigative Social Research*.

5 On the theoretical rationale for this, see Thompson, *Ideology and Modern Culture*.

6 Murray, *Football*; Mason, *Passion of the People?*

7 Waters, *Globalisation*, p. 113.

8 Ibid., p. 112.

9 Hampton, 'Where Currents Meet', p. 78 and 'Treasure Island or Fool's Gold?', p. 237.

10 Sklair, *Sociology of the Global System*, p. 6.

11 This list is compiled from the *FIFA Directory*, 1996.

12 Turner, *Orientalism*, pp. 29 and 34.

13 Herren (ed.), *90 Years of FIFA*, p. 75.

14 Turner, *Orientalism*, pp. 105–14.

15 Interview with authors, Glasgow, Scotland, 27 March 1997.

16 Tomlinson, J., *Cultural Imperialism*, p. 87.

17 Though it can stimulate conflict. In 1969 hostilities between El Salvador and Honduras were ignited in the course of World Cup qualifying matches. Though the war lasted only 100 hours, 6,000 people lost their lives, 50,000 their homes and fields. See Kapuscinski, 'The Soccer War', p. 23.

18 Tomlinson, J., *Cultural Imperialism*, p. 85.

19 Edelman, *Serious Fun*.

20 See Meisl, 'The F.I.F.A.', p. 301; and Tomlinson, A., 'Going Global'.

21 International Board, Minute 7, 1886 Minutes.

22 Cited in Meisl, 'The F.I.F.A.', p. 301.

23 The International Board still exists, meeting once a year and continuing to

have the last word in the rules of world football. At least six of the eight voting members must vote in favour of any proposed change, theoretically giving the home nations' four members a collective veto over football's regulations. However, because of the absence of consensus among the home nations, in practice this body is easily controlled by FIFA.

24 The preceding discussion draws upon Mangan, *The Games Ethic*, Holt, *Sport and the British*, Mason, 'Some Englishmen and Scotsman Abroad', and Perkin, 'Teaching the Nations How to Play', on sport in the British Empire; Sugden, 'USA and the World Cup', on US sports scene; Sugden and Tomlinson, *Hosts and Champions*, Lee, 'World Cup Co-hosting', and Mason, *Passion of the People?*, on the impact of football in countries not colonized by the British. See, too, Duke and Crolley, *Football, Nationality and the State*, pp. 94–5, on Eastern Europe; Sugden and Tomlinson, 'The Price of Fame', and 'FIFA, UEFA and the Scramble for Africa'; Lee, 'World-Cup Co-hosting', and Lim, 'Sport and Modernization', on Korea.

25 On the main theoretical issues involved in theorizing these dimensions of FIFA, see also Sugden and Tomlinson, 'Theorizing FIFA's Transnational Impact'.

26 Burke, *Popular Culture in Early Modern Europe*, p. 84.

CHAPTER 2 FIFA, EUROPE AND SOUTH AMERICA

1 FIFA, *History of FIFA*, p. 26.
2 In Herren (ed.), *90 Years of FIFA*, p. 3.
3 Ibid., pp. 4 and 6.
4 Interview with authors, Zurich, Switzerland, 21 May 1996.
5 See Tomlinson, A., 'Going Global', and 'FIFA and the World Cup'; Duke and Crolley, *Football, Nationality and the State*, pp. 12–14; Meisl, 'The F.I.F.A.'; Moorhouse, 'One State, Several Countries'; and Byrne, *Football Association of Ireland*.
6 The Bohemian case is provided by Bonini Gherardo, in a personal communication, 3 February 1997.
7 Holt, *Sport and the British* and *Sport and Society in Modern France*.
8 Rous, *Football Worlds*, p. 95.
9 Ibid., p. 134.
10 Ibid., p. 131.
11 Guldemont and Deps, *100 Ans de Football*, p. 19.
12 Marx, 'The Eighteenth Brumaire', p. 103.
13 Murray, *Football*, p. 115.
14 Mason, *Passion of the People?*, p. 27.
15 Ibid., p. 29.
16 Oliver, *The Guinness Book* (2nd Edition), p. 578.
17 Mason, *Passion of the People?*, p. 30.
18 Ibid., p. 36.
19 Ibid., p. 39.
20 In the inter-war period, largely on the back of a booming beef export industry, Uruguay was one of South America's wealthiest countries – often described as the Switzerland of Latin America.
21 See Oliver, *The Guinness Book* (2nd edn), pp. 6–7; Mason, *Passion of the People?*, pp. 38–42; and Murray, *Football*, pp. 128–31.

22 Rous, *Football Worlds*, p. 133.
23 Rous papers, SCAIR.
24 Käser letter to Rous, 18 November 1969, SCAIR.
25 CONMEBOL Official Bulletins, Year 6, nos 23 and 24. The tribute is on p. 53 of no. 24.
26 Oliver, *The Guinness Book* (2nd edn), p. 43.
27 Avignolo, 'Argentina Bribed Peru'.
28 Ibid., p. 3.
29 Ibid., p. 1.
30 Interview with authors, Cranleigh, Surrey, UK, 24 November 1996.
31 In CONMEBOL News no. 44, March/April 1996, p. 3.
32 Ibid., p. 66.
33 Ibid., p. 68.
34 J. Crahay, quoted in Rothenbühler, *25 Years of UEFA*, p. 76.
35 A. Franchi, writing in the *Official Bulletin of UEFA*, no. 87, June 1979, p. 21.
36 S. Rous, writing in *UEFA Bulletin*, no. 16, April 1961, p. 50.
37 Rous papers, SCAIR.
38 Rous papers, SCAIR.
39 FIFA Congress Minutes, 1970, in Rous papers, SCAIR.
40 UEFA minutes, IVth Extraordinary Congress, Monte Carlo, June 1971.
41 Ibid.
42 Ibid.
43 Ibid.
44 The radio interview was on BBC Radio 4, 22 April 1985; the latter point was made in interview with authors, Cranleigh, Surrey, UK, 24 November 1996.
45 Rous, *Football Worlds*, p. 24.
46 Rous, 'Post-war development', a 'memorandum prepared by the War Emergency Committee for the consideration of the Council', May 1943; and 'Post-war development – an Interim Report', October 1944. Both of these papers are in the minute books of the Football Association's Council.
47 BBC Radio 4, 22 April 1985.
48 Glanville, 'World Cup At Risk', p. 18.
49 BBC Radio 4, 22 April 1985.
50 Ibid.
51 Rous, *Football Worlds*, p. 203.
52 There is a village in Belgium called Havelange, and the Brazilian has numerous cousins in the country. The Belgian football establishment has been proud to report this connection.
53 From Havelange's campaign programme, Rous papers, SCAIR.
54 Ibid.
55 Havelange reported this in an interview in *Playboy* (Brazilian edn) in 1985.
56 Simson and Jennings, *The Lords of the Rings*, pp. 39-40.
57 Ibid., p. 53.
58 Glanville, 'FIFA knows', p. 14.
59 Ibid.
60 Glanville, 'World Cup at Risk', p. 18.
61 FIFA, *History of FIFA*, p. 82.
62 Ibid.
63 Ibid.
64 Simson and Jennings, *The Lords of the Rings*, p. 47.

65 Arbena, 'International Aspects of Sport', p. 153.
66 Guttmann, 'The Diffusion of Sports', p. 134.
67 Malam, 'Mother is alone'.
68 Lovejoy, 'World Cup 1994'.
69 Interview with authors, Zurich, Switzerland, 21 May 1996.
70 Tomlinson, A., 'Going Global', p. 97.
71 Interview with Havelange aide Peter Pullen, Cheam, Surrey, UK, 11 November 1996.
72 Interview with authors, Zurich, Switzerland, 21 May 1996.
73 Giddens, *The Constitution of Society*, p. 9.
74 Ibid., p. 12.
75 Ibid., p. 15.
76 Ibid., p. 16.
77 Anderson, *Imagined Communities*.
78 Rous, *Football Worlds*, p. 204.
79 *FIFA News*, July 1988, p. 3.
80 This *Sunday Times* report was cited in *Sport Intern* vol. 9 no. 19, 12 September 1988, p. 4.
81 Burns and Harverson, 'Rivals Jostle', p. 16.
82 Interview with authors, London, 12 June 1997. This relationship was cemented in January 1997 in Lisbon, when the presidents of the European and African Confederations signed an 'agreement of cooperation in all spheres of football'. See 'Lisbonne – Le Sommet UEFA/CAF', in *CAF News - Official Publication of Confédération Africaine de Football*, no. 61, May 1997, pp. 19–21.

CHAPTER 3 FIFA: AN ORGANIZATIONAL AND INSTITUTIONAL ANALYSIS

1 The version cited throughout this chapter is the one signed off by the president and the general secretary, on behalf of the FIFA Executive Committee, dated June 1994 in Chicago.
2 For the notions of front-stage and back-stage so central to an ethnographically sensitive dramaturgical sociology, see Goffman, *Asylums*, and *The Presentation of Self in Everyday Life*. We are indebted to Berger and Luckmann, *The Social Construction of Reality* for the notion of mutually reinforcing individual and social influences which generate social phenomena.
3 Personal faxed communication, 1 July 1997.
4 The Bosman case concerned the Belgian player Jean-Marc Bosman's fight against restraint of trade, from 1990 to 1995, in the context of RFC Liège's control of his contract. On December 15 1995 the European Court of Justice's judgement concluded that: 'The rules on transfers of players and the limits on the numbers of Community players in inter-club matches are contrary to the Treaty of Rome.' See Radnege, 'Foreigners Rule Could Go Now'.
5 FIFA Communications Department, Zurich, 24 November 1995.
6 FIFA Communications Department, Zurich, 15 December 1995.
7 Interview with authors, Zurich, Switzerland, 21 May 1996.
8 The version signed off by the president and the general secretary, on behalf of the executive committee, dated Berne, August 1993.
9 Interview with authors, Zurich, Switzerland, 21 May 1996.
10 Duke and Crolley, *Football, Nationality and the State*, pp. 19–23.

11 Ibid., p. 21.
12 FIFA Communications Department, Zurich, 15 August 1995.
13 Interview with authors, Cardiff, Wales, 18 April 1997.
14 Interview with authors, Brechin, Scotland, 9 October 1996.
15 Ibid.
16 Interview with authors, Zurich, Switzerland, 21 May 1996.
17 From *Sport Intern*, vol. 25 no. 6, 1 March 1993, p. 6. Havelange himself has referred to Mr Fok's global business activities as stretching way beyond Asia: 'Henry Fok has the sea commute concession to Macau. He is enterprising. Even though he holds the exclusive concession for the maritime line to relieve traffic in the region, he built underwater tunnels. It is a First World job that merits a visit. The fact that he is a member of FIFA and my friend favours the invitation to invest in Brazil,' p. 114 of Farah, *Young Havelange*.
18 Compiled by *Sport Intern*, vol. 26, no. 23, 30 November 1994, pp. 3–4.
19 Ibid., p. 4.
20 FIFA On-Line, Zurich, 21 January 1997.
21 Ibid.
22 These networks are elaborated upon in *Sport Intern*, vol. 6, no. 22, 20 November 1985, p. 1.
23 Interview with authors, Johannesburg, South Africa, 1 February 1996.
24 Cited in *Sport Intern*, vol. 7 no. 12/13, 7 July 1986, p. 4.
25 Glanville, writing in the *Sunday Times*, was cited in *Sport Intern*, vol. 7 no. 14a, 1 August 1986, p. 4.
26 Interview with authors, Brussels, Belgium, 3 June 1997.
27 FIFA, *Regulations FIFA World Cup France '98*, signed 'for the FIFA Executive Committee', by the president and general secretary, dated 31 May 1995, Zurich, p. 21.
28 Ibid.
29 Watts, 'Seoul Survivors?', p. 24.
30 Moorhouse, 'One State, Several Countries', p. 59.
31 Ibid., p. 67.
32 Ibid., p. 70.
33 Meisl, 'The F.I.F.A.'; Joy, 'The Broken Time Problem', p. 454.
34 Interview with authors, Brechin, Scotland, 9 October 1996.
35 Ibid.
36 Interview with authors, Cardiff, Wales, 18 April 1997.
37 At its Congress in 1996, FIFA conferred full confederational status upon Oceania, and this will be incorporated into revised Statutes.
38 The proposals called for a review of the structure of FIFA's organization, in terms of principles of democracy and accountability, and increased responsibility for the confederations; and open tenders for major World Cup contracts, linked to profit-sharing among all the confederations and their member associations.
39 FIFA Communications Department, Zurich, 20 November 1995.
40 Aigner, *Report of the General Secretary*, pp. 33 and 34.
41 Ibid., p. 43.
42 Ibid.
43 Interview with authors, Zurich, Switzerland, 21 May 1996.
44 Ibid.
45 Cited in *Sport Intern's inside soccer*, Issue Zero, 15 December 1993, p. 6.

46 Interview with authors, Zurich, Switzerland, 21 May 1996.
47 Interview with authors, Queen Elizabeth Hall, London, 29 June 1996.
48 Interview with authors, Park Terrace, Royal Garden Hotel, London, 29 June 1996.
49 Interview with authors, Brechin, Scotland, 9 October 1996.
50 Interview with authors, Brussels, Belgium, 3 June 1997.
51 Interview with authors, Manhattan, New York City, 20 February 1997.
52 Interview with authors, Kuala Lumpur, Malaysia, 12 March 1997.

CHAPTER 4 FIFA AND ITS PARTNERS

1 *UEFA Bulletin*, no. 32, October 1965, pp. 329–30.
2 Ibid.
3 *UEFA Bulletin*, no. 129, December 1989, pp. 20 and 21.
4 Rothenbühler, *25 Years of UEFA*, pp. 252 and 254.
5 TEAM/UEFA, *UEFA Champions League Season Review*.
6 Ibid., p. 42.
7 Ibid., p. 42.
8 Ibid., p. 43.
9 Ibid., p. 6.
10 Ibid., p. 25.
11 Ibid., p. 28.
12 Ibid., p. 30.
13 Ibid., p. 30.
14 Debord, *The Society of the Spectacle*, p. 24. For an application of some of Debord's ideas to trends in the contemporary political economy of sport, see Gruneau, 'Canadian Sport in the Society of the Spectacle.'
15 Whannel, 'The Unholy Alliance', passim.
16 Authors' interview with Dutch sports journalist, Ted van Leeuven, Johannesburg, South Africa, 25 January 1996.
17 Burns, 'Murdoch Quits Race for World Cup TV'.
18 Jonathan Hill, of IMG's football division, provided this background. See Moore, K., *Global Sports Marketing*, pp. 62–9. Hill further commented: 'ISL gained their contract for a figure less than that, so I think it's fair to say that there's something of a very special relationship between ISL and FIFA', p. 66. Hill was interviewed by Karina Moore on 25 April 1997.
19 Guest and Law, 'The Revolution Will Be Televised', p. 15.
20 Radnege, 'Cashing In', p. 25.
21 Guest and Law, 'The Revolution Will Be Televised', p. 15.
22 Radnege, 'Cashing In', p. 24.
23 Henderson, 'Clouds Begin to Gather on Sky's Golden Horizon', p. 11. On the unruly scrap for the breakthrough deal in which Sky secured English Premier League rights, see Tomlinson, A., 'Whose Game Is It Anyway?'; for some of the implications of the deal, see Williams, 'The Local and the Global in English Soccer'.
24 See King, *The Premier League and the New Consumption of Football*.
25 Cited in Henderson, 'Clouds Begin to Gather on Sky's Golden Horizon'.
26 Interview with authors, Cardiff, Wales, 18 April 1997.
27 Reported in *FIFA News*, no. 129, February 1974, pp. 82–3.
28 Rous was writing in *FIFA News*, no. 131, April 1974.

29 Havelange was writing in *FIFA News*, March, 1987, p. 1.
30 Ibid.
31 Ibid.
32 Breakdown provided by Guido Tognoni, in interview with authors, Zurich, Switzerland, 21 May 1996.
33 Interview with authors, Glasgow, Scotland, 20 December 1996.
34 Interview with authors, Zurich, Switzerland, 21 May 1996.
35 FIFA, *Report – FIFA World Cup USA '94*, p. 197.
36 FIFA, *Activities Report April 1994–March 1996*, pp. 50–1.
37 Ibid.
38 Rous, *Football Worlds*, p. 96.
39 Ibid., p. 96.
40 Ibid., p. 205.
41 *FIFA News*, no. 130, March 1974, p.109.
42 From Havelange campaign programme, 1974, Rous papers, SCAIR.
43 These figures are reported in Jennings, *The New Lords of the Rings*, p. 54; and in early issues of *Sports Intern*.
44 Unattributed quotes in the rest of this section are from Nally transcript, Simson and Jennings papers, SCAIR. Nally was interviewed by Simson and Jennings in 1991.
45 Wilson, N., *The Sports Business*, p. 176.
46 Ibid., p. 27.
47 Ibid., p. 28.
48 Ibid., p. 29.
49 Ibid., p. 179.
50 Ibid., p. 181.
51 Ibid., p. 182.
52 Interview with authors, Birmingham, England, 8 October 1996.
53 Ibid.
54 Howell, *Made in Birmingham*, p. 353.
55 Interview with authors, Birmingham, England, 8 October 1996.
56 *Sport Intern*, vol. 4 no. 20/21, 31 October 1983, pp. 1–2.
57 Ibid., p. 6.
58 The details in the following list are compiled from *Sport Intern*, vol. 7 no. 9, 15 May 1986, p. 1; *Sport Intern*, vol. 10 no. 18/19, 15 October 1989, p. 5; FIFA, *Report – FIFA World Cup USA '94*, p. 202; and faxed information from FIFA's communications department, 22 October 1997.
59 The following summary of post-Dassler developments is culled from the following issues of *Sport Intern*: vol. 8 no. 19, 11 September 1987, p. 1; vol. 23 no. 1, 15 January 1991, p. 1; vol. 23 no. 2, 6 February 1991, p. 3; vol. 23 no. 16/17, 15 October 1991, p. 6; and vol. 23 no. 20/22, 30 November 1991, p. 3. Though the authors sought an interview with ISL chief Jean-Marie Weber for over a year, his stated willingness to agree to this never materialized into an appointment.
60 The interview was reported in *Sport Intern's inside soccer*, Issue Zero, 15 December 1993, pp. 1 and 6–7.
61 TEAM/UEFA, *UEFA Champions League Season Review*. The data and quotations reported and cited here are mainly from the sponsorship and related sections of the review, pp. 48–65.
62 Barnett, *Games and Sets*, p. 182.

63 On the concept of the universal market, see Braverman, *Labour and Monopoly Capital*; for discussion of the spread of the universal market into more and more spheres of everyday life and popular culture, see Philips and Tomlinson, 'Homeward Bound,' pp. 12–15.
64 Interview with authors, Johannesburg, South Africa, 25 January 1996.

CHAPTER 5 FIFA'S WORLD CUP FINALS

1 Murray, *Football*, pp. 97 and 98.
2 Mason, *Passion of the People?*, p. 27.
3 Ibid., p. 40.
4 Murray, *Football*, p. 90.
5 Ibid., pp. 87–9.
6 Interim report on FIFA Congress, to the FA Council, July 1956 – Football Association Minutes.
7 Oliver, *The Guinness Book* (2nd Edn), p. 28.
8 Interview with authors, Cranleigh, Surrey, UK, 24 November 1996.
9 Interview with authors, London, 27 November 1996.
10 Howell, *Made in Birmingham*, pp. 142–43.
11 Ibid., p. 175.
12 Interview with authors, London, 27 November 1996.
13 Rous, *Football Worlds*, p. 213.
14 Ibid., p. 212.
15 Ibid., p. 213.
16 Ibid.
17 See *FIFA News*, no. 101, April 1974, pp. 160–4.
18 Ibid., p. 162.
19 Ibid., p. 163.
20 Ibid.
21 Murray, *Football*, pp. 123–4.
22 In early May 1997, the BBC World Service broadcast an item on corruption in the administration of domestic football in Brazil. A senior official with responsibility for refereeing appointments had been recorded on the telephone, involved in the bribery of referees and so the fixing of matches. The president of the federation, Havelange's son-in-law Teixeira, made a statement to the effect that he felt betrayed. Pelé, with a governmental portfolio for sport, was reported as feeling 'disappointed but not surprised'.
23 Miller, 'The Head Boy From Brazil', p. 8a.
24 *Sport Intern*, vol. 1 no. 25, 31 October 1980, p. 4.
25 Interview with authors, Cranleigh, Surrey, UK, 24 November 1996.
26 In *The Times*, cited in *Sport Intern*, vol. 6 no. 6 1985, p. 2.
27 Chapman, 'Don Emilio has some goals of his own', p. 29.
28 Cited in *Sport Intern*, vol. 7 no. 21/22, 8 November 1986, p. 5.
29 *Sport Intern*, vol. 6 no. 11, 1985, p. 2
30 On the Falun issue, see Jennings, *The New Lords of the Rings*, chapter 11, esp. pp. 117, 123 and 127 ff.
31 Cited in *Sport Intern*, vol. 9 no. 5, 28 March 1988, p. 2.
32 *Sport Intern*, vol. 23 no. 7/8, 15 May 1991, p. 2.
33 *Sport Intern*, vol. 23 no. 18/19, 5 November 1991, p. 3.
34 Ibid., p. 4.

35 Interview with authors.
36 *FIFA News,* 7 August 1988, p. 6.
37 Interview with authors, Brechin, Scotland, 9 October 1996.
38 Ibid.
39 Haydon, Reuters Sports Report.
40 Interview with authors, Brussels, Belgium, 3 June 1997.
41 Cited in *Sport Intern,* vol. 7 no. 12/13, 7 July 1986, p. 1.
42 Cited in *Sport Intern,* vol. 8 no. 13/14, 25 June 1987, p. 1.
43 Cited in *Sport Intern,* vol. 8 no. 17, 15 August 1987, p. 2.
44 Cited in *Sport Intern,* vol.11 no. 14/15, 30 June 1990, p. 2.
45 *Sport Intern,* vol. 24 no. 22/23, November 1992, p. 7.
46 *Sport Intern,* vol. 25 no. 18, 6 September 1993, p. 3; and vol. 25 no. 21, 6 October 1993, p. 2.
47 *Sport Intern,* vol. 26 no. 7, 20 April 1994, p. 1.
48 *Sport Intern,* vol. 26 no. 9, 7 May 1994, p. 1.
49 *Sport Intern,* vol. 26 no. 7, 20 April 1994, p. 3.
50 *Sport Intern,* vol. 26 no. 9, 7 May 1994, p. 2.
51 *Sport Intern,* Supplement 9a, 1 May 1993, p. 2; and vol. 26 no. 12, 15 June 1994, p. 2.
52 *Sport Intern,* vol. 26 no. 14, 1 August 1994, p. 3.
53 *Sport Intern,* vol. 26 no. 17, 15 September 1994, p. 5.
54 Radnege described Chung as an 'airways whirlwind' during his campaign for the Asian Federation's vice-presidential seat on FIFA, in between controlling, for his family firm Hyundai, Korea's biggest car plant and the world's largest shipyard. Radnege, 'The Man Who Would Be King', p. 8.
55 *Sport Intern's Inside Soccer* vol. 1 no. 4, 28 March 1994, p. 2.
56 *Japan 2002 and Sir Bobby Charlton in Africa 1994-1995,* 2002 World Cup Japan, 1996, p. 3.
57 Ibid.
58 Interview with authors, Manhattan, New York City, 20 February 1997.
59 Interview with authors, Brechin, Scotland, 9 October 1996.
60 Scott McDonald, Reuter Report, Seoul.
61 Vol. 2, no. 3/96, March 1996, pp. 30–1.
62 As reported by a long-established figure within the Japanese football establishment, during authors' research in Tokyo, March–April 1997.
63 *Asian Football Confederation News,* vol. 2, no. 4/96, pp. 12–13.
64 FIFA Web Site, 30 April 1996.
65 Ibid.
66 *Sharing Our Goal With The World,* Bidding Committee information pack, January 1996.
67 Interview with authors, Tokyo, 21 March 1997.
68 Interview with authors, Manhattan, New York City, 19 February 1997.
69 Reuters, 31 May 1996, Zurich.
70 Interview with authors, Brechin, Scotland, 9 October 1996.
71 Miller, 'Warnings heeded by Havelange', p. 37.
72 Cited in Hughes, 'Compromise Full of Eastern Promise', p. 37.
73 Reuters, Seoul, 30 May 1996.
74 Hughes, 'Compromise Full of Eastern Promise', p. 37.
75 Reuters, 31 May 1996.
76 Interview with authors, Abu Dhabi, United Arab Emirates, 14 December 1996.

77 Authors' interview with Tadao Murata, Tokyo, 21 March 1997.
78 Authors' fieldnotes, UEFA Press Office, 23 and 24 May 1996.
79 Radnege, 'Write and Wrong', p. 15.
80 Sproat was speaking on BBC Radio 4's *Today* programme, 3 February 1997.
81 Cited in Radnege, 'Fax and Fiction', p. 6.
82 Interview with authors, Birmingham, England, 17 January 1997.
83 Robinson and Thorpe, 'England's Football Hopes'.
84 Boggan, 'UEFA Confesses Own Goal', p. 3.
85 *New Labour – because Britain deserves better*, Labour Party Manifesto, London, 1997, p. 30.
86 Moore, G., 'When Football Takes a Back Seat', p. 24.
87 Ibid.
88 Interview with authors, Brussels, Belgium, 3 June 1997.
89 *Independent* (leader page), 'A Game of Two Bureaucracies', 4 February 1997, p. 13.
90 FA pamphlet, 'And Will Their Feet Dance Upon England's Green and Pleasant Grounds?, 1997, p. 2.
91 *Guardian*, 'Germans Want World Cup Talks', 4 February 1997, p. 13.
92 Interview with authors, London, 23 June 1997.

CHAPTER 6 FIFA AND AFRICA

1 Soccer City is otherwise known as FNB (First National Bank) Stadium, in acknowledgement of the funds invested by FNB in the stadium's construction. It serves as the home ground for two of South Africa's most popular teams, Orlando Pirates and Kaiser Chiefs.
2 For a general discussion on soccer and resistance in colonial Africa see Stuart, 'The Lions Stir'.
3 Hitherto this competition had been known as the ANC (the African Nations Cup), but it was decided to change the acronym because of the problems which may have been encountered promoting something with the same initials as the African National Congress.
4 Gleeson, 'Chance of a Lifetime'.
5 Maradas, 'The Long Road to South Africa'.
6 Havelange announced, in December 1996, that he would not stand for re-election in June 1998. Up until this point he had campaigned vigorously in Africa and elsewhere in the face of a likely challenge from Johansson, his arch rival.
7 Murray, *Football*, pp. 229–56.
8 Bediako, *The National Soccer League of Ghana*.
9 Stuart, 'The Lions Stir', p. 34.
10 For a detailed discussion of the politicization of football in pre-independent Algeria see Murray, *Football*, pp. 242–3.
11 Mangan, *The Games Ethic and Imperialism*.
12 Abdel Mohamed, interview with authors, London, 12 June 1997. Dr Halim has been the president of the Sudanese Football Association; a co-founder and former President of CAF; a member of the FIFA Executive; and a member of the IOC.
13 Mahjoub, 'Rendez-vous à Soweto'.
14 Quansah, 'Football is More Than a Game', p. 26.

15 Murray, *Football*.
16 Hughes, 'African Cup Explodes Into Violence'.
17 Milan, 'Stop the Slaughter, Give Africa Back to the Tribes', p. 33.
18 Bayart, *The State in Africa: The Politics of the Belly*. Also, for a general discussion on the socio-political terrain of corruption, see Harris, White and White (eds), *Liberalisation and the New Corruption*.
19 Quansah, 'Football is More Than a Game', p. 26.
20 Yorkshire Television Archive, SCAIR.
21 Interview with authors, London, 12 June 1997.
22 Supplement to the agenda for the executive committee meeting, CAF, 21/22 July, Cairo, 1964, p. 2. Rous papers, SCAIR.
23 Quansah, 'Football Is More Than a Game', p. 26.
24 Rous, *Football Worlds*, p. 159.
25 Interview with authors, Johannesburg, South Africa, 23 January 1996.
26 Rous, *Football Worlds*, p.170.
27 Ibid., p. 171.
28 Interview with authors, London, 22 October 1996.
29 For more detail on the history of South African Soccer, see Archer and Bouillon, *The South African Game*; and Bose, *Sporting Colours*.
30 Bose, *Sporting Colours*, p. 97
31 Ibid., p. 38
32 Interview with authors, Johannesburg, South Africa, 21 January 1996.
33 FASA report to FIFA Commission, Rous papers, SCAIR.
34 Report of Commission to Executive, Rous papers, SCAIR.
35 Rous papers, SCAIR.
36 Confederation Minutes, p. 6, in Rous papers, SCAIR.
37 Rous papers, SCAIR.
38 Rous papers, SCAIR.
39 Interview with authors, Johannesburg, 21 January 1996.
40 Ali, *In the Big League*, p. 10.
41 Interview with authors, Fukuoka, Japan, 5 September 1995.
42 Interview with authors, Johannesburg, South Africa, 23 January 1996.
43 Interview with authors, London, 22 October 1996.
44 Interview with authors, Johannesburg, South Africa, 23 January 1996.
45 Interview with authors, Johannesburg, South Africa, 20 January 1996.
46 Havelange, quoted in Official Souvenir Book, ACN, 1996, p. 7.
47 Cited in editorial in *Africa Confidential*, vol. 31, no. 1, January, 1990, p. 4. For more background on football in Nigeria, see Akpabot, *Football in Nigeria.*
48 Quansah, 'Football is More Than a Game', p. 28.
49 Interview with authors, London, 12 June 1997.
50 Maradas, 'France 1998 World Cup Draw', p. 19.
51 Saro-Wiwa in one of his last public interviews described the plight of his people thus: 'To take away the land of the people who depend on it for their survival and yet refuse to pay them compensation is to subject them to genocide.' See Williams, A., 'Beyond Our Ken'.
52 Cited in ibid.
53 Interview with authors, Johannesburg, South Africa, 23 January 1996.
54 This 'sentence' was reduced to one ACN ban and did not impact upon Nigeria's participation in either the 1996 Olympic Games (at which it won the gold medal), or the qualification series for the 1998 World Cup (for which it

was the first country in the world to qualify).

55 *Bafana Bafana* means 'boys boys' and was the nick-name adopted by South Africa's national football team.

56 Interview with authors, Johannesburg, South Africa, 20 January 1996.

57 *Sport Business*, no. 9, April 1997, p. 31.

58 Haydon, 'Euro Soccer Boss Apologises for "Blackie" Comments'.

59 Interview with authors, Johannesburg, South Africa, 2 January 1996.

60 At the time of writing the Mobutu regime was overthrown by a rebel army led by Laurent Kabila, and the country (re)renamed the Democratic Republic of the Congo. Mobuta himself died in exile in September 1997.

61 Interview with authors, Johannesburg, South Africa, 1 February 1996.

62 Interview with authors, Johannesburg, South Africa, 25 January 1996.

63 For detailed analysis of the financial malpractice which surrounded Cameroon in USA '94 see, Nkwi and Vidacs, 'Football: Politics and Power in Cameroon'.

64 Interview with authors, Johannesburg, South Africa, 31 January 1996. For USA '94 material, see Barnes, feature in *The Times*, 30 June 1994. In 1997, working through FIFA's Legal Department, Bell forced the Cameroon Federation to pay him $40,000 personal compensation.

65 Interview by authors with Carlos Alberto Torres and Yves Yopa (Nike), Johannesburg, South Africa, 23 January 1996.

66 Gleeson, 'Soccer–Corruption Haunts South African Soccer'.

67 Perlman, 'The Price of Success'.

68 Ibid.

69 Interview with authors, Johannesburg, South Africa, 20 January 1996.

70 Interview with authors, Johannesburg, South Africa, 31 January 1996.

CHAPTER 7 FIFA AND ASIA

1 See Mason, 'Some Englishmen and Scotsmen Abroad'.

2 Unpublished account, *A Brief History of the FAS*, from the Football Association of Singapore.

3 'S-League Ball – Gala Dinner & Awards Presentation, 96' dated 15 November 1996, provided by the Football Association of Singapore.

4 This is the first paragraph of the conclusion to Dato' Peter Velappan, *Asian Football in the New Millennium*, presented at the Media Seminar held in conjunction with the XIth Asian Cup, Abu Dhabi, United Arab Emirates, on Saturday, 14 December 1996.

5 Ibid.

6 Ibid.

7 Ibid.

8 Tomlinson, A., 'FIFA and the World Cup', pp. 24–5.

9 The table is from *Asian Football Confederation News*, vol. 3, no. 1/97, January 1997, p. 6. Our thanks to AFC marketing Ltd., Hong Kong, publisher (on behalf of the Asian Football Confederation) of *Asian Football Confederation News* for the use of this table..

10 See Velappan, *Asian Football in the New Millennium*, Section 2.

11 See, too, Stamm and Lamprecht, 'Factors Governing Success'.

12 Interview with authors, Abu Dhabi, 15 December 1996. See too, Sugden and Tomlinson, 'A Gulf in Class?'.

13 See Bernstein, 'Born in China, Made in Brazil'.
14 Velappan, *Asian Football in the New Millennium*.
15 Ibid.
16 Havelange was writing in 'World Focus on the UAE', in *11TH ASIAN CUP – EMIRATES' 96* Official Souvenir Programme, UAE/AFC, p. 6. Velappan was writing and cited in the AFC's *Asian Cup Monthly Review*.
17 This account draws upon Ganguly, 'Lebanon May Play Host'; and the same piece, with no attributed authorship, 'Lebanon favourite as 2000 Cup host', *Gulf Today* (Sport), Sunday, 15 December 1996, p. 36; our own discussions with the AFC official cited as the main, anonymous source of the story; Salem, *Asian Mundial*, an Emirates 96 book; and other official and promotional materials and publications from the event itself.
18 Salem, *Asian Mundial*, p. 17.
19 Ganguly, 'Lebanon May Play Host'.
20 Interview with authors, Kuala Lumpur, Malaysia, 16 March 1997.
21 Ibid.
22 Compiled from *Asian Football Confederation News*, vol. 2 no. 12/96, December 1996.
23 Interview with Mr Yap Nyim Keong, deputy general secretary of the Football Association of Malaysia, Sheraton Hotel, Abu Dhabi, 21 December 1996.
24 'Message from the General Secretary', *Asian Football Confederation News*, vol.3 no. 2/97, February 1997, p. 1.
25 This conference provided the basis for 'Lebanon wins right to host Asian Cup 2000', in *Asian Football Confederation News*, vol. 3 No. 2/97, February 1997, p. 43, from which this account is culled.
26 In interview with authors, Kuala Lumpur, Malaysia, 12 March 1997. This contradicted his immediate announcement on the decision, on 21 December 1996, at the Press Conference Statement in Sheikh Zayed City Media Centre, Abu Dhabi: 'In the interests of the unity of the AFC and to maintain the peace and harmony of football, Malaysia decided not to take part in the bid.'
27 Authors' discussion with General Farouk Bouzo (Syria), Sheraton Hotel, Abu Dhabi, United Arab Emirates, 19 December 1996; and in discussion with Erskine McCullough, of Agence France-Presse, on the same day.
28 Written response to authors' questions, faxed on 4 January 1997.
29 Interview with authors, CONCACAF offices, Trump Tower, Fifth Avenue, New York City, 20 February 1997.
30 Interview with authors, Kuala Lumpur, Malaysia, 16 March 1997.
31 Ibid.
32 Ibid.
33 Platt, 'Cases of Cases', p. 42.
34 Jennifer Platt has reviewed the use of 'cases' in American sociological work, and shows that much case-study theorizing has been conceptually confused. See ibid., and Platt, ' "Case-Study" '. Our own use of case-studies is an intra-methodological, inductive aspect of a wider study of the context of which the cases are a part.
35 The main source of data cited on the UAE is *UAE Yearbook 1996*, Trident Press Ltd., London, 1996. On the growth of soccer in the UAE, we have drawn upon pp. 18–25 of the Official Souvenir Programme of the XIth Asian Cup.
36 For further contextual comment on this elision of the Asian Cup event with

the UAE president's jubilee celebrations, see Tomlinson, A., two features in *Gulf News*.

37 This vignette of the structure of top-level football is based upon an interview with Mr Abbas Mohammad Hassan, at the headquarters of the UAE Football Association, Zayed Sports City, Abu Dhabi, 17 December 1996. Mr Hassan, an expert on football matters in the UAE, was also a FIFA referee of twenty-two years' standing, and acted as a commissioner and instructor with the AFC.

38 'Locals' and 'nationals' in the UAE refers to, respectively, people of Emirate origin, and people who have been granted UAE nationality. Large numbers of people – migrant workers and expatriates – being neither of these, are perceived as outsiders.

39 We follow Winkler's definition of corporatism, which is characterized by unity, order, nationalism, and success. See Winkler, 'The Corporate Economy'.

40 Interview with authors, London, 12 June 1997.

41 The incident is reported in Kemp, 'Iraq v Kazakhstan'.

42 See Horne and Jary, 'Japan and the World Cup'.

43 The following account of the growth of Japanese football and the formation of the J-League is based upon documentation provided by the J-League, the Football Association of Japan and 2002 World Cup Preparatory Committee Secretariat, in March 1997. This material includes: Japan Football Scene monthly newsletters; the 1996 Annual Report of the Football Association of Japan; *Sharing Our Goal With The World*, a dossier of the World Cup Japan Bidding Committee (January 1996); and the J. League profile 1996 (English edition). Interviews with Mr Tadao Murata and Mr Ryo Nishimura at the offices of 2002 World Cup were also most valuable (Tokyo, 21 March 1997). Our thanks go also to Mr Derek Bleakley, for interpreting during parts of the interviews, and for providing – with the historical pedigree of a Preston North End fan! – insights on the specificities of Japan's football history and development.

44 Moore, B., *Social Origins of Democracy and Dictatorship*; Sheldon, *The Rise of the Merchant Class*.

45 This legacy was evident in Japan's victory in the final of the World Student Games football competition in Fukuoka, Japan, in 1995.

46 *J. League Profile*, p. 1.

47 Ibid., p. 1.

48 Interview with authors, Tokyo, Japan, 21 March 1997.

49 This was confirmed in discussion with Chris McDonald, JFA Adviser, at the Yokohama Marinos stadium on 29 March 1997.

50 Sayama writes: 'The word *Mécénat* is originated from the name of the Roman empire politician Maecenes [sic]. Historically, the word indicates the sponsorship of culture by the Medicis. Today *Mécénat* is the term for sponsorship of sports and culture by corporations called the out-manager system.' See Sayama, 'Soccer: the limit of the Japanese society'. Interestingly, the Japanese inflection on *Mécénat* equates the notion of public contribution with the private sponsoring corporation: what it seems really to be is a combination of outreach, philanthropy and public relations.

51 'J. League Enjoys Best Season Ever', Update, *The Japan Football Scene*, January 1996.

52 Commentators suggest that the over-expansion of the J. League has been

followed by a recession (with spiralling wages for foreign stars, declining ticket sales, diminished television revenue, and less sponsorship to go round), but that a far from negligible impact has been sustained. Marketing and image challenges have still to be met – see Fujimoto and Harara, 'A Study on Sports Spectator Market'. But the J. League's impact upon commerce and industry in a locality and community has been demonstrated – see Oga, Kimura and Sato, 'Influence of J. League on Local Community', and Oga, Kimura, Yanagisawa and Nakazawa, 'Influence of J. League on Local Community – Part II. Inoue, 'After the Football Revolution in Japan', points to the continuing aspirations of established community clubs to join the J. League.

53 The case of South Korea also shows the power and effectiveness of such alliances of interest, though football was strongly established within Korean sports culture much earlier than in the Japanese case. British sailors are said to have introduced football into Korea in 1882, when the battleship *Flying Fish* arrived at Inchon. But they played only on the deck of the ship, and were not allowed on land. Korean people nevertheless copied the game, the sailors having left their ball on departure. Firmer institutional roots for the game were established in educational establishments in the early years of the twentieth century, under the influence of European teachers and missionaries. In the 1920s, 'All Korean' games and fixtures expanded, and their rapid growth has been 'attributed to the Japanese colonial rule of Korea. Under the Japanese rule, sport quickly became a way of expressing national sentiment against the Japanese. People felt that although they were controlled politically, they could not be beaten in non-political areas such as sport. This national sentiment is so deeply rooted that Koreans are eager to win in sporting competitions with Japan', Lee, 'World-Cup Co-Hosting', p. 2. Korea's league (dating from 1983) was Asia's first full-time professional football league. The Korean Football Association was clearly a far from autonomous or independent body. In 1997 its president was Dr Chung Mon Joon, heir apparent to the Hyundai Corporation and already a regional and national politician. With highly developed ties between private capital, the state, and civil society in the form of the sports culture, South Korea demonstrated an extreme form of corporatist control and use of the football culture. The general secretary of CONCACAF, Chuck Blazer, also noted this, in relation to the Korean bid for the 2002 World Cup: 'The Korean bid was tremendously well co-ordinated. In all ways, things worked together, with the powers of the government, the private sector and sport combined.' (Interview with authors, Manhattan, New York City, 20 February 1997). Such a powerful congruence of interests fuelled the ferocity of the bidding process for 2002 (see chapter 5 above).

54 Velappan, *Asian Football in the New Millennium..*
55 Interview with authors, Abu Dhabi, UAE, 17 December 1996.
56 Rous, *Football Worlds*, p. 161.
57 Rous papers, SCAIR.
58 Rous papers, SCAIR.
59 Oliver, *The Guinness Book* (2nd Edn), p. 377.
60 Rous, *Football Worlds*, p. 168.
61 Ibid., p. 201.
62 Interview with authors, Abu Dhabi, UAE, 17 December 1996.
63 Interview with authors, Kuala Lumpur, Malaysia, 16 March 1997.

64 Interview with authors, Sheraton Hotel, Abu Dhabi, UAE, 21 December 1996.
65 Written response to authors' questions, received 4 January 1997.
66 Ibid.
67 Murray, *Football*; Saeki, 'Sport in Japan'; Mulling, 'Sport in South Korea'.
68 AFC, *Asian Football Confederation 30th Anniversary*, p. 10.
69 AFC, *Asian Football Confederation 1954–1994*, p. 10.
70 Ibid., p. 11.
71 *Emirates News*, 20 December 1996, p. 16, published a piece by Erskine McCullough, of Agence France-Presse, entitled 'Confidential report slams Asian level'. The following day the same paper – in 'AFC slams "malicious" report', p. 16 – cited the AFC's response, and its confidence that the 2002 World Cup would be the best ever, with Korea and Japan strong contenders, and 'within five to ten years . . . Asia will be a force in world football'. In a piece on the Asian Cup in *FIFA Magazine*, February 1997, pp. 24–9, FIFA's Director of Communications, Keith Cooper, played down this debate, citing the Korean and Japanese rationale as principally targeting their 1998 World Cup qualifiers – see Cooper, 'The Asian Cup'.
72 Interview with Mr. Kim, Sheraton Hotel, Abu Dhabi, UAE, 21 December 1996.
73 This was Argentinian Raoul Blanco, erstwhile coach to the Australian national side: at the time of speaking, assistant to Australia's newly appointed coach Terry Venables. The interview took place in the Sheraton Hotel, Abu Dhabi, UAE, on 18 December 1996.
74 Warawi Makudi, of Thailand, in interview with authors, Sheraton Hotel, Abu Dhabi, UAE, 20 December 1996. In 1997, Makudi was elected as a further AFC delegate onto FIFA's Executive Committee.
75 Authors' interview with German Otto Pfister, Abu Dhabi, UAE, 15 December 1996. At the time Pfister was coach to the Bangladeshi national side.
76 Charlie Charters was interviewed by the authors in Abu Dhabi, UAE, on 16 December 1997.

CHAPTER 8 FIFA AND THE FORMER SOVIET UNION

1 Pipes, *The Formation of the Soviet Union*.
2 Suny, *The Revenge of the Past*.
3 Tomlinson, J., *Cultural Imperialism*.
4 The outstanding examples of this in Western Europe are provided by the club sides, Athletic Bilbao and Barcelona which respectively, for a long time, have served as rallying points for Basque and Catalan separatisms.
5 Sugden, 'As Presently Constituted'; Tomlinson, A., 'Going Global', citing Anderson, *Imagined Communities*, p. 98.
6 Greenfeld, *Nationalism*, p. 3.
7 Anderson, *Imagined Communities*, p. 16.
8 Greenfeld's own term for the process of 'the transformation of the idea of the nation' is intriguingly idiosyncratic. She writes of the final stage in the making of nations as, 'the last transformation in the meaning of the "nation" which may be deduced form the *zigzag pattern* [our italics] of semantic (and by implication social) change', ibid., pp. 5–9. Despite this dogged stance against materialism and, perhaps also anything redolent of Marxism, her conceptual framework could have come straight from

the pages of Hegel and as such we are happy to refer to *zigzag* patterns as broadly dialectical, in the sense that the contradictions apparent in the process come to a form of resolution in a final, and higher phase of development.

9 Ibid., p. 16.
10 Ibid., p. 17.
11 Sennet, *The Fall of Public Man*.
12 Tomlinson, J., *Cultural Imperialism*, p. 82.
13 Tomlinson, ibid.; Anderson, *Imagined Communities*.
14 Our scepticism is shared by J. B. Thompson who, while accepting the notion of the 'imagined community' argues that the evidence of a direct link between it, the print media and nationalism is flimsy. He concludes that, 'the main explanation for the rise of nationalism is likely to be provided by other factors'. See Thompson, *The Media and Modernity*, p. 63.
15 Allison, *The Changing Politics of Sport*.
16 Sugden and Bairner, *Sport, Sectarianism and Society*.
17 Edelman, *Serious Fun*; Edelman and Riordan, 'USSR/Russia and the World Cup'.
18 Perel, *Football in the USSR*.
19 Kochan, *The Making of Modern Russia*.
20 Riordan, 'Sport and Nationalism in the CCCP'.
21 Trotsky, *History of the Russian Revolution*.
22 Gitelman, 'The Nationalists', p. 137.
23 For the authentic position on ethnicity and other, non-class forms of social stratification, see Marx, 'On the Jewish Question'.
24 Gitelman, 'The Nationalists', p. 146.
25 For a detailed discussion of Lenin's strategy concerning the Soviet Union as a multi-national state see Trotsky's essay 'The Problem of the Nationalities', in *History of the Russian Revolution*, pp. 39–62.
26 Gitelman, 'The Nationalists'.
27 Riordan, *Sport in Soviet Society*, p. 4.
28 Edelman, *Serious Fun*.
29 Perel, *Football in the USSR*.
30 Trotsky, *History of the Russian Revolution*.
31 Kochan, *The Making of Modern Russia*.
32 Ibid., p. 296.
33 Gitelman, 'The Nationalists', p. 147.
34 Edelman, *Serious Fun*; Manning and Getty, *The Stalinist Terror*.
35 War communism is the phrase used to cover that period in the 1920s when the Bolsheviks forced through a series of significant and draconian economic reforms in the face of civil war and hostile international relations – see Kochan, *The Making of Modern Russia*, pp. 266–79.
36 Engel, *Between the Fields and the City*.
37 Bailey, *Leisure and Class*; Aronowitz, *False Promises*, esp. chapter 2.
38 Edelman and Riordan, 'USSR/Russia and the World Cup', p. 257.
39 Perel, *Football in the USSR*, pp. 8–21.
40 Riordan, *Soviet Sport*, p. 115; Edelman and Riordan, 'USSR/Russia and the World Cup', p. 256.
41 Russia had been a member of FIFA from 1912 to 1917 during which time they played forty-seven matches with twenty-four wins, eleven draws and

twelve defeats, including drubbings at the hands (feet) of Germany (16–0) and Hungary (12–0).

42 Edelman, *Serious Fun*; Edelman and Riordan, 'USSR/Russia and the World Cup', p. 266.

43 Edelman, *Serious Fun*, p. 129.

44 See Amnesty International, *Annual Report*.

45 Marraquin was talking to Vyv Simson, in Colombia, in 1993. The quote is from Simson's field notes.

46 The report is in the Rous papers, SCAIR. The extracts which follow are from pp. 2, 4 and 5.

47 Rous papers, SCAIR.

48 Chile responded to this suggestion by arguing that the Northern Ireland vs Bulgaria match did not set a precedent because, by shifting the game to England, FIFA had not moved outside of the United Kingdom.

49 Brigade "Einheit" Stahlgusskombinat Karl-Marx-Stadt, 12 November, 1973, Rous papers, SCAIR.

50 H. Reidle, 1973, Rous papers, SCAIR.

51 Rous papers, 1973, SCAIR.

52 Edelman, 'Football and the Rise of Nationalism', p. 2.

53 Interview with authors, Glasgow, Scotland, 27 March 1997.

54 Hoddle is cited in Ridley, feature in the *Independent*.

55 Interview with authors, St Albans, Hertfordshire, UK, 28 April 1997.

56 Interview with authors, Cranleigh, Surrey, UK, 24 November 1996.

57 Edelman, *Serious Fun*, p. 136.

58 See Hargreaves, *Sport, Power and Culture*; Edelman, *Serious Fun*; Sugden and Bairner, *Sport, Sectarianism and Society*; MacClancy, 'Sport, Identity and Ethnicity'.

59 Riordan, *Soviet Sport*, p. 124.

60 Kuper, *Football Against the Enemy*.

61 Riordan, 'The Power of Sport to Save Lives', SCAIR.

62 Ibid.

63 Kuper, *Football Against the Enemy*, pp. 45–46.

64 Edelman, *Serious Fun*, p. 16.

65 Ibid., p. 13.

66 Edelman, 'Football and the Rise of Nationalism', p. 1.

67 Ibid.

68 Kuper, *Football Against the Enemy*, p. 47.

69 Interview with authors, Yerevan, Armenia, 30 April 1997.

70 *Moscow News*, May 1988, p. 15, Yorkshire Television Archive, SCAIR.

71 Edelman, *Serious Fun*, p. 193.

72 Riordan, *Soviet Sport*, p. 126; Edelman, 'Football and the Rise of Nationalism', p. 2.

73 Reported in a 1987 issue of *World Soccer* (p. 30), Yorkshire Television Archive, SCAIR.

74 Edelman, 'Football and the Rise of Nationalism', p. 2.

75 Johansson, in UEFA, *East European Assistance Bureau*, p. 2.

76 Braun, in Aigner, *Report of the General Secretary*, p. 44.

77 Interview with authors, Glasgow, Scotland, 20 December 1996.

78 Johansson, in *UEFA Bulletin*. no. 149, December 1994, p. 19.

79 Riordan, 'Sport and Nationalism in the CCCP', p. 15.

80 Zilberman, 'Break-up of the Soviet state'.
81 Allison, 'Sport in Civil Society'.

CHAPTER 9 FIFA'S FINAL FRONTIER

1 Blatter was cited in *World Soccer*, vol. 35 no. 3, December 1994, p. 10.
2 Oliver, *The Guinness Book* (2nd Edn), p. 824.
3 Letter from B. Jaramillo, CONCACAF assistant secretary general, to Rous, received 7 December 1971, in SCAIR.
4 Letter to Rous, 24 November 1971, in SCAIR.
5 Letter to Rous, 21 December 1971, in SCAIR.
6 Rous summarized the address for the FIFA Executive Committee, paper dated/stamped 8 July 1971.
7 Paper by Lic. I. Juan José Navas C., 'CONCACAF's institutional character – What is CONCACAF?', Guatemala, October 1972, Rous papers, SCAIR.
8 Letter to Rous, stamped 12 March 1973, Rous papers, SCAIR (authors' translation). CONCACAF did not hide its respect for Havelange, though, the previous year, when a CONCACAF selection had lost 5–0 to France and 4–0 to Colombia in the Brazilian Independence Cup, the platform from which Havelange truly launched his campaign for the FIFA presidency. In issue 13 of its information bulletin (July/August/September 1972), the CONCACAF delegation was reported as being truly appreciative of the contribution of their Brazilian hosts, busy as they were in having to 'attend at the same time other participating Delegations' (p. 9). Under a photograph of Havelange, microphone in hand and captioned 'Our recognition to CBD', the CONCACAF general secretariat reported having written personal letters of thanks to the 'highest authorities' in Brazilian sport, and commented on the outcome of the trip: 'The result was an understanding and sincere friendship between Brazil and the family of CONCACAF' (p. 9). Rous, due to visit the CONCACAF secretariat in January 1973, a FIFA president's first ever visit to Central America, would have much ground to make up.
9 Rous, *Football Worlds*, p.162.
10 Ibid.
11 Interview with authors, Cranleigh, Surrey, UK, 24 November 1996.
12 Rous, *Football Worlds*, p. 162.
13 Ibid., p. 195.
14 Interview with authors, Johannesburg, South Africa, 3 February 1996.
15 Interview with authors, Johannesburg, South Africa, 23 January 1996.
16 Miller, 'The Head Boy from Brazil', p. 8a.
17 The decision by FIFA to ban Mexico from the qualifying process, for 'cheating in the World Youth Cup by fielding over-age players' (Oliver, *The Guinness Book*, (2nd Edn) p. 60) raised more than a few eyebrows, apparently easing the USA's passage to Italia' 90. In fact, Costa Rica topped the CONCACAF qualifying group, making it to the second round in the Finals, and then losing 4–1 to Czechoslovakia. The USA qualified from the group in second place, pipping Trinidad after a 1–0 victory over the Caribbean side in Port of Spain, 'much to the relief of FIFA who had just awarded America the staging of the 1994 tournament' (Oliver, ibid). In Italy the USA finished bottom of its group with three defeats in three matches. See also, Gardner, *The Simplest Game*, p. 103.

18 Robertson, 'Mapping the Global Condition', pp. 20, 22, 27. The importance of Robertson's ideas is restated, and applied more generally, in chapter 10.
19 Hobsbawm, *Age of Extremes*, p. 198.
20 Markovits, 'The other "American Exceptionalism"', p. 125.
21 Ibid., p. 125.
22 See Novak, *The Joy of Sports*; and George, *Elevating the Game*.
23 Markovits, 'The other "American Exceptionalism"', p. 135.
24 Ibid., p. 136.
25 See Sugden, 'USA and the World Cup'; Nelson, *Left Foot Forward*; and Watson, *Dancing in the Streets*; these are reviewed more fully in Sugden and Tomlinson, 'What's Left When the Circus Leaves Town'.
26 Palmer, 'A whole new ball game', p. 1.
27 Interview with authors, London, 12 June 1977.
28 Weir, *USA Today*, p. 3C.
29 Lovejoy, 'Pythonesque circus', p. 24.
30 See Lacey, 'Draw poker'; P. Wilson, 'America slow on draw'; and Gardner, 'Lightweight bill'.
31 Palmer, 'A whole new ball game'.
32 Ibid., p. 2.
33 *Media Sports Business*, p. 10.
34 Ibid.
35 *Sports Industry News*.
36 Berlin, 'Where dribbling is child's play'.
37 *Sports Industry News*.
38 *Media Sports Business*, p. 11.
39 Gardner, 'Lightweight Bill',
40 Wilson, 'America slow on draw', p. 39.
41 Glanville, 'No time for this rubbish'.
42 For further discussion concerning the demographics of soccer in the USA post–1994, see Andrews, Pitter, Zwick and Ambrose, 'Soccer's Racial Frontier'.
43 Team Marketing Report, *Sport Sponsor Factbook*, p. 48.
44 Kuper, *Football Against the Enemy*, p. 157.
45 Mason, *Passion of the People?*, p. 152.
46 Lawson, 'Moving the goalposts', p. 25.
47 Reich Collection, transcripts, interview of 22 March 1985.
48 Cart, '$7 Million for World Cup Boss', p. C1.
49 Ibid.
50 Department of the Treasury Internal Revenue Service, *Form 990, 1991*, Part V.
51 Department of the Treasury Internal Revenue Service, *Form 990, 1992*, Statement 11, Part V.
52 Ibid.
53 Cart, '$7 Million for World Cup Boss', p. C1.
54 Palmer, 'A whole new ball game', p. 2.
55 Ibid.
56 Glanville, 'No time for this rubbish', p. 72.
57 Hudson and Boewadt, 'Youth and Collegiate Soccer', p. 266.
58 Fynn and Guest, *Out of Time*, p. 381.
59 Sklair, *Sociology of the Global System*, pp. 5-9.

60 Interview with authors, Manhattan, New York City, 19 February 1997.
61 Interview with authors, Zurich, Switzerland, 21 May 1996.
62 Havelange was writing in FIFA, *Report – FIFA World Cup '94*, p. 5.
63 Ibid., p. 6.
64 Interview with authors, Chicago, USA, 12 November 1996.
65 Interview with authors, Manhattan, New York City, 18 February 1997.
66 Liss, 'Soccer Czar'.
67 Interview with authors, Zurich, Switzerland, 21 May 1996.
68 Interview with authors, Chicago, USA, 12 November 1996.
69 Interview with authors, Manhattan, New York City, 19 February 1997.
70 Interview with authors, Cairo Sheraton, Egypt, 4 September 1997.

CHAPTER 10 CONCLUSION

1 Farah, *Young Havelange*, p. 101.
2 Blatter, 'Keeping Our Eye On The Ball'.
3 Sugden, Tomlinson and Darby, 'FIFA versus UEFA'.
4 Darby, 'Theorising World Football'; and *Sport, Politics and International Relations*.
5 Beckett, 'A better world', p. 6.
6 Tomlinson, J., *Cultural Imperialism*, p. 15.
7 Ibid., p. 17.
8 Ibid., p. 16.
9 Ibid.
10 In 1997 the USA was $1.3 billion 'in debt' to the UN.
11 Tomlinson, J., *Cultural Imperialism*.
12 Stamm and Lamprecht 'Factors Governing Success', pp. 7–10.
13 The confederations are not 'members' of FIFA in any formal sense – the official FIFA line on this is that 'confederations . . . are playing an increasingly important role as an intermediary between FIFA and its affiliated national associations', FIFA, *Activities Report April 1994–March 1996*, p. 8. Strictly speaking, UEFA would have to persuade its constituents to withdraw their individual affiliations to the world governing body.
14 Tomlinson, J., *Cultural Imperialism*.
15 Robertson, 'Mapping the Global Condition', pp. 19, 20 and 22.
16 Ibid., pp. 26 and 27.
17 Golding and Harris, *Beyond Cultural Imperialism*, p. 9.
18 For a detailed discussion and theorization of the dynamics of the local and the global *vis-à-vis* international sport, see Maguire, 'Sport, identity politics and globalisation.'
19 Golding and Harris, *Beyond Cultural Imperialism*, p. 5.
20 Billig, *Banal Nationalism*.
21 Sklair, *Sociology of the Global System*, p. 6.
22 For a full discussion of the economic vulnerability and exploitation of sub-Saharan Africa, see Leys, *The Rise and Fall of Development Theory*, chapter 9, pp. 188–96.
23 Horne, in 'Globalization and Football', p. 59, asks, in the light of the prominence of Japanese companies among FIFA's official sponsors, and the involvement of the world's biggest advertising agency (Japan's Dentsu) with FIFA's long-established marketing partner, ISL (International Sport and Lei-

sure): 'what is the extent of the influence of Japanese corporations on FIFA?' It could be answered, in the wake of the co-hosting decision for the 2002 World Cup, and the knowledge that Dentsu has always had a minority stake, 'not as much as is often implied and perhaps used to be the case in the peak phases of Havelange's personal power.' In fact, in the mid-1990s, Dentsu sold out its ineffective minority stake.

24 Barclay, 'Old Caesar Guards His Empire'; Miller, 'The Head Boy From Brazil'; *Independent*, 'Schemer With the World at His Feet'; *The Times*, 'Mr FIFA Gazes Out on Football's New Horizons'.

AFTERWORD

1 For more than two years while working on this book we sought interviews with FIFA's leading players. An opportunity to speak with Havelange and other senior members of FIFA's executive came two months after the manuscript had been delivered. We are grateful to our publishers for creating the space for this important afterword.

2 Schemo, 'Pele's dispute with FIFA may hurt Brazil', *New York Times*, 10 August, 1997: p. s7.

3 Hayatou quoted in Mahjoub (ed.), *Confederation Africaine de Football, 1957–1997*, p. 120.

4 Hayatou was quoted in Diakité, 'CAF and UEFA', p. 126.

Bibliography

AFC (Asian Football Confederation), *Asian Football Confederation 30th Anniversary 1954–1984*, AFC, Kuala Lumpur, 1984.

AFC (Asian Football Confederation), *Asian Football Confederation 1954–1994*, AFC, Kuala Lumpur, 1994.

Aigner, G., *Report of the General Secretary for 1994 and 1995*, UEFA, Nyon, December 1995.

Akpabot, S.E., *Football in Nigeria*, Macmillan, London, 1984.

Ali, R., *In The Big League: The Rise of African Football*, London, Festac (a division of Afropress Executive Ltd), 1984.

Allison, L. (ed.), *The Changing Politics of Sport*, Manchester University Press, Manchester, 1993.

Allison, L., 'Sport in Civil Society', unpublished paper, Warwick Centre for the Study of Sport in Society, University of Warwick, 1996.

Amnesty International, *Amnesty International Annual Report*, Amnesty International, London, 1993.

Anderson, B., *Imagined Communities – Reflections on the Origins and Spread of Nationalism*, Verso, London, 1983.

Andrews, D., Pitter, R., Zwick, D. and Ambrose, D., 'Soccer's Racial Frontier: Sport and the Suburbanization of Contemporary America', in G. Armstrong and R. Giulianotti (eds), *Entering the Field: New Perspectives on World Football*, Berg, Oxford, 1997, pp. 261–82.

Arbena, Joseph. L., 'International Aspects of Sport in Latin America: Perceptions, Prospects, and Proposals', in E. G. Dunning, J. A. Maguire and R. E. Pearton (eds), *The Sports Process – A Comparative and Developmental Approach*, Human Kinetics Publishers, Champaign, IL., 1993, pp. 151–67.

Archer, R. and Bouillon, A., *The South African Game – Sport and Racism*, Zed Press, London, 1982.

Aronowitz, S., *False Promises: The Shaping of American Working Class Consciousness*, McGraw-Hill Book Company, New York, 1973.

Avignolo, M-L., 'Argentina Bribed Peru in World Cup Scandal', *Sunday Times*, 22 June 1986, pp. 1–3.

Bailey, P., *Leisure and Class in Victorian England – Rational Recreation and the Con-

test for Control 1830–1885, Routledge, London, 1978.

Barclay, P., 'Old Caesar Guards his Empire', *Observer (Sport)*, 3 April 1994, p. 16.

Barnes, S., feature in *The Times*, 30 June 1994, p. 46.

Barnett, S., *Games and Sets – The Changing Face of Sport on Television*, BFI Publishing, London, 1990. ▬

Bayart, J-F., *The State in Africa: The Politics of the Belly*, Addison Wesley, New York, 1996.

Beckett, A., 'A better world, a better life', *Independent on Sunday Review*, 22 October 1995, pp. 6–8.

Bediako, K., *The National Soccer League of Ghana: The Full Story*, Buck Press, Accra, 1995.

Berger, P. and Luckmann, T., *The Social Construction of Reality*, Allen Lane, London, 1968.

Berlin, P., 'Where dribbling is child's play', *Financial Times*, 7 July 1994, p. 4.

Bernstein, K., 'Born in China, Made in Brazil', *Independent on Sunday* magazine, 9 July 1995, pp. 8–11.

Billig, M., *Banal Nationalism*, Sage, London, 1995.

Blatter, J. S., 'Keeping our Eye on the Ball', in FIFA, *Activities Report April 1994– March 1996* [50th FIFA Congress, Zurich 1996], FIFA, Zurich, 1996, p. 3.

Boggan, S., 'UEFA Confesses Own Goal as World Cup Spat Takes New Twist', *Independent*, 4 February 1977, p. 3.

Bose, M., *Sporting Colours – Sport and Politics in South Africa*, Robson Books, London, 1994.

Braverman, H., *Labour and Monopoly Capital – The Degradation of Work in the Twentieth Century*, Monthly Review Press, New York, 1974.

Burke, P., *Popular Culture in Early Modern Europe*, Harper & Row, New York, 1978.

Burns, J., 'Murdoch Quits Race for World Cup TV', *Financial Times*, London Edn 1, 15 May 1996, p. 4.

Burns, J. and Harverson, P., 'Rivals Jostle for FIFA Presidency', *Financial Times*, 6 June 1997, p. 16.

Byrne, P., *Football Association of Ireland – 75 years*, Sportsworld, Dublin, 1996.

Cart, J., '$7 Million for World Cup Boss', *Los Angeles Times*, 19 October 1994, pp. C1/C7.

Chapman, P., 'Don Emilio has some goals of his own', *Guardian*, 27 May 1986, p. 29.

Cooper, K., 'The Asian Cup – When East Meets West', *FIFA Magazine*, February 1997, pp. 24–9.

Darby, P., 'Theorising World Football, FIFA, Dependency and World Systems Theory', in *Scottish Centre Research Papers in Sport, Leisure and Society*, vol. 2, Edinburgh: Moray House Institute, 1997, pp. 100–13.

Darby, P., *Sport Politics and International Relations: Africa's Place in FIFA's Global Order*, unpublished D.Phil. thesis, Faculty of Humanities, University of Ulster, 1997.

Debord, G., *The Society of the Spectacle*, tr. D. Nicholson Smith [1994], Zone Books, New York, 1995.

Department of the Treasury Internal Revenue Service, *Form 990, 1991: Return of Organization Exempt from Income Tax*, "For the Calendar Year 1991", relating to "World Cup USA 1994, Inc., 2049 Century Park East, Suite 4400, Los Angeles, California 90067", 1991–2.

Department of the Treasury Internal Revenue Service, *Form 990, 1992: Return of Organization Exempt from Income Tax*, "For the Calendar Year 1992", relating to "World Cup USA 1994, Inc., 2049 Century Park East, Suite 4400, Los Angeles, CA 90067", 1992–3.

Diakité, A., 'CAF and UEFA: The Convention of Lisbon', in F. Mahjoub (ed.), *Confédération Africaine de Football 1957–1997*, CAF, Cairo, 1997, pp. 124–7.

Douglas, J. D., *Investigative Social Research: Individual and Team Research*, Sage Publications, London, 1976.

Duke, V. and Crolley, L., *Football, Nationality and the State*, Longman, London, 1996. ▬

Edelman, R., *Serious Fun. A History of Spectator Sports in the USSR*, Oxford University Press, Oxford, 1993.

Edelman, R., 'Football and the Rise of Nationalism in the Former Soviet Union', paper presented at *Fanatics! Football and Popular Culture*, conference of Manchester Institute for Popular Culture, Manchester Metropolitan University, 11–13 June 1996.

Edelman, R. and Riordan, J.,' USSR/Russia and the World Cup: Come on you Reds!', in J. Sugden and A. Tomlinson (eds), *Hosts and Champions: Soccer Cultures, National Identities and the USA World Cup*, Arena/ Ashgate Publishing, Aldershot, 1994, pp. 253–78.

Engel, B., *Between the Fields and the City*, Cambridge University Press, Cambridge, 1994.

Farah, E. J. (ed.), *Young Havelange: FIFA in the Third Millennium*, J. S. Propaganda Ltda., São Paulo, Brazil, 1996.

FIFA, *History of FIFA*, Fédération Internationale de Football Association, Official History, Zurich, 1984.

FIFA, *STATUTES – Regulations Governing the Application of the Statutes; Standing Orders of the Congress*, English edn 1994, FIFA, Zurich, 1994.

FIFA, *Report – FIFA World Cup USA '94* (ed. Jurg Nepfer), FIFA, Zurich, 1994.

FIFA, *Activities Report April 1994–March 1996* [50th FIFA Congress, Zurich 1996], editor/author, Keith Cooper, FIFA, Zurich, 1996.

Foulds, S., and Harris, P., *America's Soccer Heritage – A History of the Game*, Soccer for Americans, Manhattan Beach, California, 1979.

Fujimoto, J. and Harada, M., 'A Study on Sports Spectator Market: A Potential Market of Football Spectators in Japan', in Proceedings of Fourth European Congress on Sport Management/First International Sport Management Alliance Conference, Montpellier, France, 1996, pp. 127–37.

Fynn, A. and Guest, L., *Out of Time – Why Football isn't Working*, Simon and Schuster Ltd., London, 1994.

Ganguly, D., 'Lebanon May Play Host to the 2000 Asian Cup', *Emirates News*, 15 December 1996, p. 16.

Gardner, P., 'Lightweight bill in Vegas', *World Soccer*, vol. 34 no. 4, January 1994, p. 4.

Gardner, P., *The Simplest Game: The Intelligent Fan's Guide to the World of Soccer*, Collier Books/Macmillan Publishing Company, New York, 1994.

Gardner, P., 'Pipe dream – Paul Gardner is not convinced by Major League Soccer's plans to lay a pipeline to the stars', *World Soccer*, vol. 35 no. 8, May 1995, pp. 46–7.

George, N., *Elevating the Game: Black Men and Basketball*, Harper Collins, New York, 1992.

Giddens, A., *The Constitution of Society: Outline of the Theory of Structuration*, Polity Press, Cambridge, 1984.

Gitelman, Z., 'The Nationalists', in S. White, A. Pravda and Z. Gitelman (eds), *Developments in Soviet Politics*, Macmillan, London, 1990, pp. 137–58.

Glanville, B., 'FIFA knows how to blow its own trumpet!', *World Soccer*, vol. 25 no. 1, October 1984, pp. 14–15.

Glanville, B., 'World Cup at Risk', *World Soccer*, vol. 26 no. 2, November 1985, pp. 18–19.

Glanville, B., 'No time for this rubbish', *World Soccer*, vol. 35 no. 8, May 1995, p. 72.

Gleeson, M., 'Chance of a Lifetime', *African Soccer Souvenir*, January 1996, p. 12.

Gleeson, M., 'Soccer – Corruption Haunts South African Soccer', Reuters Sports Report, Wire Service, 31 October 1996.

Goffman, E., *Asylums*, Harmondsworth, Penguin, 1966.

Goffman, E., *The Presentation of Self in Everyday Life*, Allen Lane, London, 1968.

Golding, P. and Harris, P., *Beyond Cultural Imperialism: Globalisation, Communication and the New International Order*, Sage, London, 1997.

Greenfeld, L., *Nationalism: Five Roads to Modernity*, Harvard University Press, Cambridge, Massachusetts, 1992.

Gruneau, R., 'Canadian Sport in the Society of the Spectacle', paper presented at *How Sport Can Change the World*, annual conference of the Japan Society of Sport Sociology, Kyoto, Ritsumeikan University, Japan, 27–8 March 1997.

Guardian, 'Germans Want World Cup Talks', 31 May 1997, p. 13.

Guest, L. and Law , P., 'The Revolution Will be Televised', *World Soccer*, vol. 37 no. 4, January 1997, pp. 14–15.

Guldemont, H. and Deps, B., *100 Ans de Football en Belgique 1895–1995*, Union Royale Belge des Sociétés de Football Association, Brussels, 1995.

Guttmann, A., 'The Diffusion of Sports and the Problem of Cultural Imperialism', in E. G. Dunning, J. A. Maguire and R. E. Pearton (eds), *The Sports Process – A Comparative and Developmental Approach*, Human Kinetics Publishers, Champaign, IL., 1993, pp. 125–37.

Hampton, M., 'Treasure Island or Fool's Gold: Can and Should Island Economies Copy Jersey?', *World Development*, vol. 22 no. 2, 1994, pp. 237–45.

Hampton, M., 'Where Currents Meet: The Offshore Interface Between Corruption, Offshore Finance Centres and Economic Development', in B. Harriss-White and G. White (eds), *Liberalisation and the New Corruption, IDS Bulletin*, vol. 27, no. 2, 1996, pp. 78–87.

Hargreaves, J., *Sport, Power and Culture: A Social and Historical Analysis of Popular Sports in Britain*, Polity Press, Cambridge, 1986.

Haydon, S., Reuters Sports Report, Wire Service, 14 November 1996.

Haydon, S., 'Euro Soccer Boss Apologizes for "Blackie" comments', Reuters Sport Report, Wire Service, 15 November 1996.

Henderson, J., 'Clouds Begin to Gather on Sky's Golden Horizon', *Observer*, 4 May 1997, p. 11.

Herren, A. (ed.) , *90 Years of FIFA – 20 Years of FIFA Presidency*, FIFA, Souvenir Edition, Zurich, 1994.

Hobsbawm, E., *Industry and Empire*, Penguin, Harmondsworth, 1968.

Hobsbawm, E., *Age of Extremes – The Short Twentieth Century 1914–1991*, Abacus, London, 1995.

Holt, R., *Sport and Society in Modern France*, Macmillan, London, 1981.

Holt, R., *Sport and the British. A Modern History*, Oxford University Press, Oxford, 1989.

Horne, J., 'Globalization and Football', in Proceedings of *How Sport Can Change the World*, The Japan Society of Sport Sociology, International Conference, Ritsumeikan University, Kyoto, Japan, 26–8 March, 1997, pp. 53–61.

Horne, J. and Jary, D., 'Japan and the World Cup': Asia's First World Cup Final Hosts?', in J. Sugden and A. Tomlinson (eds), *Hosts and Champions – Soccer Cultures, National Identities and the USA World Cup*, Arena/Ashgate Publishing Ltd, Aldershot, UK, 1994, pp. 161–82.

Houlihan, B., *Sport and International Politics*, Harvester Wheatsheaf, Hemel Hempstead, 1994.

Houlihan, B., ' Homogenization, Americanization, and Creolization of Sport: Varieties of Globalization', *Sociology of Sport Journal*, vol. 11 no. 4, December 1994, pp. 356–75.

Howell, D., *Made in Birmingham – the Memoirs of Denis Howell*, Macdonald/Queen Anne Press, London, 1990.

Hudson, D., and Boewadt, R. J., 'Youth and Collegiate Soccer Participation in America – A Foundation for Major League Success?', in S. Fleming, M. Talbot and A. Tomlinson (eds), *Policy and Politics in Physical Education, Sport and Leisure*, Leisure Studies Association, Eastbourne, UK, 1995, pp. 257–74.

Hughes, R., 'African Cup Explodes into Violence', *Sunday Times*, 27 March 1988, p. A32.

Hughes, R., 'Compromise Full of Eastern Promise', *The Times* (Sport), 3 June 1996, p. 37.

Independent, 'Schemer with the World at his Feet – João Havelange, the most powerful man in football', 9 June 1990, p. 18.

Independent, 'A Game of Two Bureaucracies' (article on leader page), *Independent*, 4 February 1997, p. 13.

Inoue, T., 'After the Football Revolution in Japan', in Proceedings of Fourth European Congress on Sport Management/First International Sport Management Alliance Conference, Montpellier, France, 1996, pp. 354–62.

Jennings, A., *The New Lords of the Rings – Olympic Corruption and How to Buy Gold Medals*, Simon and Schuster, London, 1996.

Jones, G. L., ' How wrong can you be?', *Soccer Illustrated 1994 World Cup Review*, 1994, pp. 28–31.

Joy, B., 'The Broken Time Problem', in A. H. Fabian and G. Green (eds), *Association Football*, The Caxton Publishing Company Limited, London, 1960, pp. 453–8.

Kapuscinski, R., 'The Soccer War', in *The Best of Granta Reportage*, Granta Books (in association with Penguin Books), London, 1994, pp. 1–25.

Kemp, A., 'Iraq v Kazakhstan: What Happened Next?', *Observer*, 20 July 1997, p. 1.

King, A., *The Premier League and the New Consumption of Football*, Doctoral Thesis, Institute of Social Research, University of Salford, UK, 1995.

Kochan, L., *The Making of Modern Russia*, Pelican, Harmondsworth, 1962.

Kuper, S., *Football Against the Enemy*. Orion, London, 1994.

Lacey, D., 'Draw poker in the land of stars and hypes', *Guardian*, 18 December 1993, p. 18.

Lawson, M., 'Moving the goalposts', *Independent Magazine*, 29 May 1993, pp. 26–30.

Lee, J-Y., 'World-Cup Co-hosting and the Korean Society', in Proceedings of *How Sport Can Change the World*, The Japan Society of Sport Sociology, International Conference, Ritsumeikan University, Kyoto, Japan, 26–8 March, 1997, pp. 80–104 (Japanese and Korean texts).

Leys, C., *The Rise and Fall of Development Theory*, James Currey, Oxford, 1995.

Lim, B-J., 'Sport and Modernization of the Korean Society', in Proceedings of *How Sport Can Change the World*, The Japan Society of Sport Sociology, International Conference, Ritsumeikan University, Kyoto, Japan, 26–8 March, 1997, pp. 218–21.

Liss, R., 'Soccer Czar to Defend World Cup Success – Former Employee Alleges Rothenberg Sought Personal Gain', *Los Angeles Daily Journal*, 18 May 1997, pp. 1 and 8.

Lovejoy, J., 'Pythonesque circus in a football desert/FIFA keen on world club competition', *Independent*, 18 December 1993, pp. 24 and 26.

Lovejoy, J. 'World Cup 1994', *Independent* (Section II), 20 December 1993, p. 32.

MacAloon, J., 'The Ethnographic Imperative in Comparative Olympic Research', *Sociology of Sport Journal*, vol. 9 no. 2, June 1992, pp. 104–30.

MacClancy, J., 'Sport, Identity and Ethnicity', in J. MacClancy (ed.), *Sport, Identity and Ethnicity*, Berg, Oxford, 1996, pp. 1–20.

Maguire, J., 'Sport, identity politics and globalization: Diminishing contrasts and increasing varieties', *Sociology of Sport Journal*, vol. 11 no. 4, December 1994, pp. 398–427.

Mahjoub, F., 'Rendez-vous à Soweto', *Balafon*, Air Afrique, January/February 1996, pp. 38–50.

Mahjoub, F. (ed.), *Confédération Africaine de Football 1957–1997*, CAF, Cairo, 1997.

Malam, C., 'Mother is alone now children have grown up', *Daily Telegraph*, 13 November 1993, p. 20.

Mangan, J. A., *The Games Ethic and Imperialism – Aspects of the Diffusion of an Ideal*, The Viking Press, London, 1986.

Manning, R. and Getty, J., *The Stalinist Terror: New Perspectives*, Cambridge Univesity Press, Cambridge, 1993.

Maradas, E., 'The Long Road to South Africa', *African Soccer Magazine* (Special Souvenir Edition), January 1996, pp. 16–17.

Maradas, E., 'France 1998 World Cup Draw – And They're Off', *African Soccer Magazine* no. 15, January/February 1996, pp. 18–19.

Markovits, A. S., 'The other "American exceptionalism" – Why is there no Soccer in the United States?', *Praxis International*, vol. 8 no. 2, 1988, pp. 125–50.

Marx, K., 'On the Jewish Question' [1843], in *Early Writings* (introduced by Lucio Colletti, trans. Rodney Livingstone and Gregory Benton), Penguin Books in association with *New Left Review*, Harmondsworth, 1975, pp. 211–41.

Marx, K., 'The Eighteenth Brumaire of Louis Bonaparte' [1852], in K. Marx and F. Engels, *Collected Works Volume II, Marx and Engels 1851–1853*, Lawrence and Wishart, London, 1979, pp. 99–197.

Mason, T., 'Some Englishmen and Scotsmen Abroad: The Spread of World Football', in A. Tomlinson and G. Whannel (eds), *Off the Ball: The Football World Cup*, Pluto, London, 1986, pp. 67–82.

Mason, T., *Passion of the People? Football in South America*, Verso, London, 1995.

McDonald, S., Reuter Report, Seoul, 8 April 1996.

McCullough, E., 'Confidential Report Slams Asian Level', *Emirates News*, 20 December 1996, p. 16.

Media Sports Business, no. 171, Paul Kagan Associates, Inc., Carmel, California, 31 July 1994.

Meisl, W., 'The F.I.F.A.', in A. H. Fabian and G. Green (eds), *Association Football*, The Caxton Publishing Company Limited, London, 1960, pp. 297–305.

Milan, R., 'Stop the Slaughter, Give Africa Back to the Tribes', *Sunday Telegraph*, 8 June 1997, p. 33.

Miller D., 'The Head Boy from Brazil – *The Times* Profile: João Havelange', *The Times*, 29 May 1986, p. 8a.

Miller, D., 'Warnings heeded by Havelange', *The Times* (Sport), 3 June 1996, p. 37.

Moore, B., *Social Origins of Democracy and Dictatorship – Lord and Peasant in the Making of the Modern World*, Penguin, Harmondsworth, 1973.

Moore, G., 'When Football Takes a Back Seat to Politics', *Independent*, 4 February 1977, p. 24.

Moore, K., *Global Sports Marketing, Popular Perception and the Development of Modern Sport*, BA Dissertation, Leisure Policy and Administration, University of Brighton, UK, 1997.

Moorhouse, H. F., 'One State, Several Countries: Soccer and Nationality in a "United Kingdom"', *The International Journal of the History of Sport*, vol. 12 no. 2, 1995, pp. 55–74.

Mulling, C., 'Sport in South Korea: *Ssirum*, the YMCA and the Olympic Games', in E. Wagner (ed.), *Sport in Asia and Africa: A Comparative Handbook*, Greenwood, New York, 1989, pp. 83–100.

Murray, B., *Football: A History of the World Game*, Scolar Press, Aldershot, 1994.

Nelson, G., *Left Foot Forward – A Year in the Life of a Journeyman Footballer*, Headline Book Publishing, London, 1995.

Nkwi, P. and Vidacs, B., 'Football: Politics and Power in Cameroon', in G. Armstrong and R. Giulianotti (eds), *Entering the Field: New Perspectives on World Football*, Berg, Oxford, 1997, pp. 123–40.

Novak, M., *The Joy of Sports – End Zones, Bases, Baskets, Balls, and the Consecration of the American Spirit*, Basic Books Inc., New York, 1976.

Oga, J., Kimura, K. and Sato, M., 'Influence of J-League on Local Community', in Proceedings of the Third European Congress on Sport Management, Budapest, Hungary, 1995, pp. 147–54.

Oga, J., Kimura, K., Yanagisawa, K., and Nakazawa, K., 'Influence of J-League on Local Community – Part II', in Proceedings of the Fourth European Congress on Sport Management/First International Sport Management Alliance Conference, Montpellier, France, 1996, pp. 60–8.

Oliver, G., *The Guinness Book of World Soccer – The History of the Game in Over 150 Countries*, Guinness Publishing Ltd., Enfield/London, 1992.

Oliver, G., *The Guinness Book of World Soccer – The History of the Game in Over 150 Countries* (2nd edn), Guinness Publishing Ltd., Enfield/London, 1995.

Palmer, M., 'A whole new ball game', *Sunday Telegraph Review*, 12 June 1994, pp. 1–2.

Perel, C., *Football in the USSR*, Moscow, Foreign Languages Publishing House, Moscow, 1958.

Perkin, H., 'Teaching the Nations How to Play: Sport and Society in the British Empire and Commonwealth', *The International Journal of the History of Sport*, vol. 6 no. 2, September, 1989, pp. 145–55.

Perlman, J., 'The Price of Success', *When Saturday Comes*, no. 124, June 1997, pp. 38–9.

Philips, D. and Tomlinson, A., 'Homeward Bound: Leisure, Popular Culture and Consumer Capitalism', in D. Strinati and S. Wagg (eds), *Come On Down? Popular Media Culture in Post-War Britain*, Routledge, London, 1992, pp. 9–45.

Pipes, R., *The Formation of the Soviet Union*, Atheneum, New York, 1968.

Platt, J., 'Cases of Cases . . . of Cases', in C. C. Ragin and H. S. Becker (eds), *What is a Case? Exploring the Foundations of Social Enquiry*, Cambridge University Press, Cambridge, 1992, pp. 21–52.

Platt, J., ' "Case-Study" in American Methodological Thought', *Current Sociology*, vol. 40 no. 1, 1992, pp. 17–48.

Quansah, E., 'Football is More Than a Game', *Africa Today*, vol. 2 no. 1, January/February 1996, pp. 26–8.

Radnege, K., 'The Man Who Would Be King', *World Soccer*, vol. 34 no. 8, May 1994, pp. 8–9.

Radnege, K., 'Foreigners Rule Could Go Now', *World Soccer*, vol. 36 no. 5, February 1996, pp. 4–5.

Radnege, K., 'Cashing In', *World Soccer*, vol. 36 no. 12, September 1996, pp. 24–5.

Radnege, K., 'Fax and Fiction – England Force UEFA Climbdown for the Right to Play Host to the World Cup', *World Soccer*, vol. 37 no. 6, March 1997, pp. 4–6.

Radnege, K., 'Write and Wrong', *World Soccer*, vol. 37 no.7, April 1997, p. 15.

Raynor, R., *Los Angeles Without a Map*, Flamingo, London, 1992.

Ridley, I., feature in *Independent*, 9 November, 1996.

Riordan, J., *Sport in Soviet Society*, Cambridge University Press, Cambridge, 1977.

Riordan, J., *Soviet Sport*, Basil Blackwell, Oxford, 1980.

Riordan, J., 'The Power of Sport to Save Lives, Nikolai Starostin: the Footballer who Cheated Death', Yorkshire Televison Archive, in SCAIR (Sports Cultures Archive for Investigative Research), 1990.

Riordan, J., 'Sport in Capitalist and Socialist Countries: A Western Perspective', in E. G. Dunning, J. A. Maguire, and R. E. Pearton (eds), *The Sports Process – A Comparative and Developmental Approach*, Human Kinetics Publishers, Champaign, IL., 1993, pp. 245–64.

Riordan, J., 'Sport and Nationalism in the CCCP, Socialist Internationalism Versus a Strong Russian State', unpublished paper presented at the BSA (British Sociological Association) Annual Conference, University of Reading, 1–4 April, 1996.

Robertson, R., 'Mapping the Global Condition: Globalization as the Central Concept', *Theory, Culture and Society – Explorations in Critical Social Science*, vol. 7 nos. 2–3, 1990, pp. 15–30.

Robinson, N. and Thorpe, M., 'England's football hopes rested with this man', *Guardian*, 4 February 1977, p. 1.

Rothenbühler, U.R. (ed.), *25 Years of UEFA*, tr. and English version by Keith Cooper, UEFA, Berne, 1979.

Rous, S., *Football Worlds – A Lifetime in Sport*, Faber and Faber, London, 1978.

Saeki, T., 'Sport in Japan', in E. Wagner (ed.), *Sport in Asia and Africa: A Comparative Handbook*, Greenwood, New York, 1989, pp. 51–82.

Salem, I., *Asian Mundial*, Emirates 96, United Arab Emirates, 1996.

Sayama, I., 'Soccer – The limit of the Japanese Society and the Bitter Reflection of its Possibility', in Proceedings of *How Sport Can Change the World*, International Conference, The Japan Society of Sport Sociology, Ritsumeikan University, Kyoto, Japan, 26–8 March 1997, pp. 46–52 (Japanese text).

Sennett, R., *The Fall of Public Man*, Cambridge University Press, Cambridge, 1974.

Sheldon, C. D., *The Rise of the Merchant Class in Tokugawa Japan, 1600–1868 – An Introductory Survey*, Augustin, New York, 1958.

Simson, V. and Jennings, A., *The Lords of the Rings – Power, Money and Drugs in the Modern Olympics*, Simon and Schuster, London, 1992.

Sklair, L., *Sociology of the Global System*, Harvester Wheatsheaf, Hemel Hempstead, 1991.

Sports Industry News, February 3, 1995, p. 48 (reported in *The North American Society for the Sociology of Sport Newsletter*, Winter, p. 13).

Stamm, H. P. and Lamprecht, M., 'Factors Governing Success in International Football', *FIFA Magazine*, August 1996, pp. 7–11.

Stuart, O., 'The Lions Stir: Football in African Society', in S. Wagg (ed.), *Giving the Game Away – Football, Politics and Culture on Five Continents*, Leicester, Leicester University Press, 1995, pp. 24–50.

Sugden, J., 'As Presently Constituted, Sport at an International Level Does More Harm Than Good', in G. Cohen (ed.), *Peace and Understanding Through Sport*, Institute for International Sport Monographs, vol. 2 no. 1, 1989, pp. 63–8.

Sugden, J., 'USA and the World Cup: American Nativism and the Rejection of the People's Game', in J. Sugden and A. Tomlinson (eds), *Hosts and Champions: Soccer Cultures, National Identities and the USA World Cup*, Arena, Aldershot, 1994, pp. 219–52.

Sugden, J., 'Fieldworkers Rush In (where theorists fear to tread): The Perils of Ethnography', in A. Tomlinson and S. Fleming (eds), *Ethics, Sport and Leisure: Crises and Critiques*, Meyer and Meyer, Aachen, 1997, pp. 233–44.

Sugden, J. and Bairner, A., *Sport, Sectarianism and Society in a Divided Ireland*, Leicester University Press, Leicester, 1993.

Sugden, J. and Tomlinson, A. (eds), *Hosts and Champions – Soccer Cultures, National Identities and the USA World Cup*, Arena/Ashgate Publishing Ltd, Aldershot, 1994.

Sugden, J., and Tomlinson, A., 'Soccer Culture, National Identity and the World Cup', in J. Sugden and A. Tomlinson (eds), *Hosts and Champions – Soccer Cultures, National Identities and the USA World Cup*, Arena/Ashgate Publishing Ltd, Aldershot, 1994, pp. 3–12.

Sugden, J. and Tomlinson, A., 'The Price of Fame', *When Saturday Comes'*, no. 109, March 1996, p. 39.

Sugden, J. and Tomlinson, A., 'FIFA, UEFA and the Scramble for Africa', paper delivered at the British Sociological Association Annual Conference, *Worlds of the Future – ethnicity, nationalism and globalization*, 2 April 1996.

Sugden, J. and Tomlinson, A., 'What's Left When the Circus Leaves Town? An Evaluation of the 1994 USA World Cup', *Sociology of Sport Journal*, vol. 13 no. 3, September 1996, pp. 236–54.

Sugden, J. and Tomlinson, A., 'A Gulf in Class?', *When Saturday Comes*, no. 120, February 1997, pp. 36–7.

Sugden, J. and Tomlinson, A., 'Global Power Struggles in World Football: FIFA and UEFA 1954–1974, and their Legacy', *The International Journal of the History of Sport*, vol. 14 no. 2, August 1997, pp. 1–25.

Sugden, J., Tomlinson, A. and Darby, P., 'FIFA versus UEFA in the Struggle for the Control of World Football', in A. Brown (ed.), *Power, Identity and Fandom in Football*, Routledge, London, 1998 (forthcoming).

Sugden, J. and Tomlinson, A., 'Theorizing FIFA's Transnational Impact', *Journal of Sport and Social Issues*, 1998 (forthcoming).

Suny, R., *The Revenge of the Past: Nationalism, Revolution and the Collapse of the Soviet Union*, Stanford University Press, Stanford, 1993.

Team Marketing Report, *Sport Sponsor Factbook* (Spring), 1994.

TEAM/UEFA, *UEFA Champions League Season Review 1995/96*, TEAM, Lucerne, 1996.

The Times, 'Mr FIFA Gazes Out on Football's New Horizons'*(Illustrated Profile of Havelange)*, 15 February 1991, p. 36a.

Thompson, J. B., *Ideology and Modern Culture – Towards a Critical Theory of Mass Communication*, Polity Press, Cambridge, 1990.

Thompson, J. B., *The Media and Modernity – A Social Theory of the Media*, Polity Press, Cambridge, 1995.

Tomlinson, A., 'Going Global: the FIFA Story', in A. Tomlinson and G. Whannel (eds), *Off the Ball: the Football World Cup*, Pluto Press, London, 1986, pp. 83–98.

Tomlinson, A., 'Whose Game is it Anyway? The Cultural Analysis of Sport and Media Consumption', *Innovation in Social Science Research*, vol. 5 no. 4, December 1992, pp. 27–42.

Tomlinson, A., 'FIFA and the World Cup – The Expanding Football Family', in J. Sugden and A. Tomlinson (eds), *Hosts and Champions: Soccer Cultures, National Identities and the USA World Cup*, Arena, Aldershot, 1994, pp. 13–33.

Tomlinson, A., 'Olympic Spectacles: Opening Ceremonies and some Paradoxes of Globalization', *Media, Culture and Society*, vol. 18 no. 4, October 1996, pp. 583–602.

Tomlinson, A., from features in *Gulf News*, December 1996, January 1997.

Tomlinson, J., *Cultural Imperialism – A Critical Introduction*, Pinter, London, 1991.

Trotsky, L., *History of the Russian Revolution*, vol. 3, Sphere, London, 1967.

Turner, B., *Orientalism, Postmodernism and Globalism*, Routledge, London, 1994.

UEFA, *Statutes of UEFA – Edition 1993*, UEFA, Berne, August 1993.

UEFA, *East European Assistance Bureau*, UEFA Publications, Nyon, Switzerland, 1994.

United Arab Emirates, *UAE Yearbook 1996*, Trident Press Ltd., London, 1996.

Usborne, D., 'OJ and the Knicks put the world's game in a twist', *Independent*, 20 June 1994, p. 39.

Velappan, P., *Asian Football in the New Millennium*, presentation at Media Seminar, Asian Football Confederation, held in conjunction with the XIth Asian Cup, Abu Dhabi, United Arab Emirates, Saturday 14 December 1996.

Wahl, Alfred (1986), 'Le footballer français: de l'amateurisme aù salariat (1890–1926)', *Le Mouvement social*, no. 135, April–June 1986, pp. 7–30.

Walvin, J., *The People's Game: A Social History of British Football*, Allen and Unwin, London, 1975.

Waters, M., *Globalisation*, Routledge, London, 1995.

Watson, D., *Dancing in the Streets – Tales from World Cup City*, Victor Gollancz, London, 1994.

Watts, J., 'Seoul Survivors?, *When Saturday Comes*, no. 111, May 1996, pp. 24–6.

Weir, T., column in *USA Today*, 17 December 1993, p. 3C.

Whannel, G., 'The Unholy Alliance: Notes on Television and the Remaking of British Sport 1965–1985', *Leisure Studies*, vol. 5 no. 2, May 1986, pp. 22–37.

Whannel, G., *Fields in Vision – Television Sport and Cultural Transformation*,

286

Routledge, London, 1992.

Williams, A., 'Beyond Our Ken', *Africa Today*, vol. 2 no. 1, January/February 1996, pp. 4–9.

Williams, J., 'The Local and the Global in English Soccer and the Rise of Satellite Television', *Sociology of Sport Journal*, vol. 11 no. 4, December 1994, pp. 376–97.

Williams, J. and Giulanotti, R., 'Introduction: Stillborn in the USA?', in R. Giulanotti and J. Williams (eds), *Game Without Frontiers – Football, Identity and Modernity*, Arena/Ashgate Publishing Ltd, Aldershot, 1994, pp. 1–20.

Wilson, J., 'The Big Kickoff'' (The Sporting Scene), *New Yorker*, 1 August 1994, pp. 52–8.

Wilson, N., *The Sports Business*, Mandarin, London, 1988.

Wilson, P., 'America slow on draw for big shoot-out', *Observer* (Sport 2), 8 December 1991, p. 39.

Winkler, J. T., 'The Corporate Economy: Theory and Administration', in R. Scase (ed.), *Industrial Society: Class, Cleavage and Control*, George Allen and Unwin Ltd, London, 1977, pp. 43–58.

Zilberman, V., 'Break-up of the Soviet state and disintegration of the renown sport system', in the official magazine, *International Council for Health, Physical Education, Sport and Dance*, Vol. XXX no. 3, Spring 1994, pp. 36–42.

■ Note on Other Sources

Interviews by authors.

Personal communications to authors.

FIFA, UEFA, CAF, AFC, CONCACAF and CONMEBOL magazines, literature and publications; and those of various national football associations.

Web Sites, such as the FIFA Web Site: http://www.fifa.com

Wire/Press/Agency releases, such as Reuters, Associated Press, Agence France-Presse.

Reich Collection: transcripts of interviews with Los Angeles Olympic Committee personnel, Los Angeles, Amateur Athletic Foundation of Los Angeles, 1985.

SCAIR (Sports Cultures Archive for Investigative Research), Chelsea School Research Centre, University of Brighton: Yorkshire Television Archive; Nally tapes; Rous papers; issues of *Sport Intern*.

Glossary

ABC	American/Associated Broadcasting Association
ACN	African Cup of Nations
AFC	Asian Football Confederation
ANC	African National Congress
APSL	American Professional Soccer League
ASEAN	Association of South-East Asian Nations
ASI	Awesome Sports International
BBC	British Broadcasting Corporation
BCI	Bobby Charlton International
CBD	Brazilian Sports Federation
CAF	Confédération Africaine de Football (African Football Confederation)
CBF	Confederação Brasileira de Futebol (Brazilian Football Federation)
CCCP	see USSR
CIS	Commonwealth of Independent States
CONCACAF	Confederación Norte-/Centroamericana y del Caribe de Fútbol (North and Central American and Caribbean Football Confederation)
CONMEBOL	Confederación Sudamericana de Fútbol (South American Football Confederation)
CWR	Council of World Religions
EEAB	Eastern European Assistance Bureau
EBU	European Broadcasting Union
ESPN	Entertainment and Sports Programming Network
FA	Football Association (English)
FAO	Food and Agricultural Organization
FAS	Football Association of Singapore
FASA	Football Association of South Africa
FAW	Football Association of Wales
FIFA	Fédération Internationale de Football Association
FNB	First National Bank

IAAF	International Amateur Athletic Federation
ICC	International Cricket Conference
IGO	International Government Organization
IMG	International Management Group
INGO	International Non-Government Organization
IOC	International Olympic Committee
ISA	International Sociological Association
ISL	International Sport and Leisure
ITV	Independent Television
JFA	Japan Football Association
KGB	Committee of State Security (Soviet Secret Police)
KOBID	(South) Korean Bidding Committee for the 2002 World Cup
MBM	MBM Multimedia Inc.
MLS	Major League Soccer
NASL	North American Soccer League
NFA	Nigerian Football Association
OAU	Organization of African Unity
OFC	Oceania Football Confederation
OFC	Offshore Financial Centre
PLO	Palestine Liberation Organization
SAFA	Singapore Amateur Football Association
SASF	South African Soccer Federation
SANROC	South African Non-Racial Olympic Committee
SCAIR	Sports Cultures Archive for Investigative Research
SMPI	Société Monaquesque de Promotions Internationale
TEAM	Television Event and Media Marketing AG (formerly The Event Agency and Marketing AG)
TSKA	Central Army Sports Club (Tsentral'ny Sportivny Klub Armii)
TOP	The Olympic Programme
UAE	United Arab Emirates
UCL	UEFA Champions League
UEFA	Union des Associations Européennes de Football (European Football Union/Confederation)
UK	United Kingdom of Great Britain and Northern Ireland
UNESCO	United Nations Educational, Scientific and Cultural Organization
UN	United Nations
USA	United States of America
USSF	United States Soccer Federation
USSR	Union of Soviet Socialist Republics
ZIS	Soviet Motor Works

289

Index

This is a selective, not an exhaustive, index. It indicates recurrent themes and lists some of the most prominent individuals in the football world. It does not include authors or every source of data or evidence, and refers to the main text and not the footnotes. Sources, authors and attributions can be traced via the footnotes and the bibliography.